# Journal of Biblical Literature

Volume 137
2018

GENERAL EDITOR
ADELE REINHARTZ
University of Ottawa
Ottawa, ON K1N 6N5

A Quarterly Published by
SBL Press

# JOURNAL OF BIBLICAL LITERATURE

EDITORS OF THE JOURNAL
*General Editor:* ADELE REINHARTZ, University of Ottawa
*Managing Editor:* JONATHAN M. POTTER, Society of Biblical Literature
*Editorial Assistant:* JONATHAN C. GROCE, Society of Biblical Literature

EDITORIAL BOARD

ELIZABETH BOASE, Flinders University
HELEN BOND, University of Edinburgh
JO-ANN A. BRANT, Goshen College
TONY BURKE, York University
DAVID M. CARR, Union Theological Seminary
RICHARD J. CLIFFORD, Boston College
KELLEY COBLENTZ BAUTCH, St. Edwards University
COLLEEN CONWAY, Seton Hall University
TOAN DO, Australian Catholic University
KATHY EHRENSPERGER, University of Potsdam
GEORG FISCHER, Leopold-Franzens-Universität Innsbruck
PAULA FREDRIKSEN, Hebrew University of Jerusalem
WIL GAFNEY, Brite Divinity School
FRANCES TAYLOR GENCH, Union Presbyterian Seminary
SHIMON GESUNDHEIT, Hebrew University of Jerusalem
MARK GOODACRE, Duke University
MARTIEN A. HALVORSON-TAYLOR, University of Virginia (Charlottesville)
RACHEL HAVRELOCK, University of Illinois at Chicago
ELSE K. HOLT, Aarhus Universitet
DAVID G. HORRELL, University of Exeter
CAROLINE E. JOHNSON HODGE, College of the Holy Cross
JONATHAN KLAWANS, Boston University
JENNIFER KNUST, Boston University
BRUCE W. LONGENECKER, Baylor University
MICHAEL A. LYONS, Simpson University
DANIEL MACHIELA, McMaster University
JOHN W. MARSHALL, University of Toronto
NAPHTALI MESHEL, Hebrew University of Jerusalem
CHRISTINE MITCHELL, St. Andrew's College, University of Saskatchewan
KENNETH NGWA, Drew University
KEN M. PENNER, St. Francis Xavier University
PIERLUIGI PIOVANELLI, University of Ottawa
MARK REASONER, Marian University
THOMAS RÖMER, Collège de France and University of Lausanne
DALIT ROM-SHILONI, Tel Aviv University
JEAN-PIERRE RUIZ, St. John's University (New York)
SETH L. SANDERS, University of California, Davis
KONRAD SCHMID, University of Zurich
WILLIAM M. SCHNIEDEWIND, University of California, Los Angeles
ABRAHAM SMITH, Perkins School of Theology, Southern Methodist University
JOHANNA STIEBERT, University of Leeds
JOHN T. STRONG, Missouri State University
MATTHEW THIESSEN, McMaster University
STEVEN TUELL, Pittsburgh Theological Seminary
CECILIA WASSEN, Uppsala University
EMMA WASSERMAN, Rutgers University
LAWRENCE M. WILLS, Episcopal Divinity School

The Society of Biblical Literature is a constituent member of the American Council of Learned Societies. *President of the Society:* Brian K. Blount, Union Presbyterian Seminary, Richmond, VA 23227; *Vice President:* Gale A. Yee, Episcopal Divinity School, Cambridge, MA 02138; *Chair, Research and Publications Committee:* M. Patrick Graham, Candler School of Theology, Atlanta, GA 30322; *Executive Director:* John F. Kutsko, Society of Biblical Literature, 825 Houston Mill Road, Suite 350, Atlanta, GA 30329.

The *Journal of Biblical Literature* (ISSN 0021–9231) is published quarterly by the Society of Biblical Literature, 825 Houston Mill Road, Suite 350, Atlanta, GA 30329. The annual subscription price is US$55.00 for members and US$220.00 for nonmembers. Institutional and online rates are also available. For information regarding subscriptions and membership, contact: SBL Press, 825 Houston Mill Road, Suite 350, Atlanta, GA 30329. Phone: 866-727-9955 (toll free) or 404-727-9498. E-mail: sblservices@sbl-site.org. For information concerning permission to quote, editorial and business matters, please see the first issue of the year, p. 2. Periodical postage paid at Atlanta, Georgia, and at additional mailing offices. POSTMASTER: Send address changes to SBL Press, 825 Houston Mill Road, Suite 350, Atlanta, GA 30329. Copyright © 2018 by the SBL Press.

*JBL* is indexed in the following resources:

Arts and Humanities Citation Index
Scopus
ATLA Religion Database
Religious and Theological Abstracts
*New Testament Abstracts* (ATLA)
*Old Testament Abstracts* (ATLA)
Periodicals Index online (Proquest)
European Reference Index for the Humanities

PRINTED IN THE UNITED STATES OF AMERICA

# Conceptualizing the Place of Deaf People in Ancient Israel: Suggestions from Deaf Space

**MIKE GULLIVER**
mike.gulliver@bristol.ac.uk
University of Bristol, Bristol BS8 1TH, UK

**WILLIAM JOHN LYONS**
w.j.lyons@bristol.ac.uk
University of Bristol, Bristol BS8 1TH, UK

Building on the recent interest in disability studies within biblical studies, this article considers the place of the deaf in ancient Israel. Positive explorations of disability by Neil Walls, Saul Olyan, and Hector Avalos have moved away from the assumption that a deaf life in the ancient world was necessarily a squalid one. Using the insights into the complexities of deaf experience put forward by the Rev. J. H. Pettingell, a nineteenth-century clergyman who worked with what were then termed the "deaf and dumb," this article explores the different potential scenarios for a male and a female deaf person. It then considers the potential life options for a priestly son deafened early or born deaf. The conclusion notes the possibility of communal Deaf spaces in ancient Israel and calls for an acceptance of one of the central methodological assumptions of deaf studies, that where a group of deaf people come together, a signing community is likely to come into existence.

---

The last twenty years have witnessed an increasing focus on the concept of "disability" and the role of the "disabled" in the ancient Near East.[1] In this essay,

We would like to record our thanks to Jon Morgan, Dai O'Brien, Deane Galbraith, and John Walker; to Laura Zucconi and those attending the Healthcare and Disability in the Ancient World seminar at the Society of Biblical Literature International/European Association of Biblical Studies meeting in Vienna in July 2014; and to the participants in the Bible, Critical Theory and Reception seminar held in Bristol in September 2014, for their constructive comments. Special thanks go to Fiona C. Black for her invaluable late input.

[1] In the introduction to their 2007 edited volume *This Abled Body: Rethinking Disabilities in Biblical Studies*, Hector Avalos, Sarah J. Melcher, and Jeremy Schipper point to two significant

we wish to add to the ongoing impact of those discussions and publications. We ask a fundamental question about how scholarship should best conceptualize deafness and muteness in the ancient world—and in Israel in particular—if we wish to understand fully the sparse references to them in our textual sources and the richer social reality to which these references so fleetingly point. In light of the concept of Deaf space as it has been developed and discussed in disciplines such as anthropology, deaf studies, and geography, an urgent reconsideration is required of the scholarly assumptions that have so far undergirded work on this topic. We begin by briefly outlining three recent scholarly works in biblical studies. We then introduce specific insights about the multiple realities of deafness/muteness and the historical implications of the complexities involved by drawing from an ongoing study on St Saviour's Church for the Deaf and Dumb, Oxford Street, in Victorian London in which we are currently engaged.[2] In the remainder of the essay, we consider what might be inferred about deaf experience both of everyday life and of priestly service and conclude with some thoughts on the significance of our choice of theoretical underpinning for future investigation of the Deaf spaces of ancient Israel.[3]

---

dates in the history of the academic study of the phenomenon of disability: the first was November 1995, with the first meeting of the Religion and Disability Consultation at the AAR/SBL Annual Meeting in Philadelphia, focused on "People with Disabilities and Religious Constructions of Theodicy and Tragedy," and the second was the first session of the Biblical Scholarship and Disabilities Consultation at the same meeting in San Antonio in November 2004, focused on "The Blind, the Deaf, and the Lame: Biblical Representation of Disability"; this consultation met at both the AAR/SBL Annual Meeting and the SBL International meeting. See Avalos, Melcher, and Schipper, "Introduction," in *This Abled Body: Rethinking Disabilities in Biblical Studies*, ed. Hector Avalos, Sarah J. Melcher, and Jeremy Schipper, SemeiaSt 55 (Atlanta: Society of Biblical Literature, 2007), 1–9, here 2–3. In more recent years, we can add seminars on Disability Studies and Healthcare in the Bible and Near East at the Annual Meeting (since 2007) and on Healthcare and Disability in the Ancient World at the International Meeting (since 2011). With an increasing flow of publications from those involved in and encouraged by these various sessions, it appears that disability studies is finally beginning to make its mark on studies of the ancient world.

[2] The study referred to is a three-year project funded by Leverhulme Trust entitled "Scripture, Dissent and Deaf Space: St Saviour's, Oxford Street," running from February 2014 to January 2017. Using the example of St Saviour's Church for the Deaf and Dumb, Oxford Street, London (1873–1923), we hope to challenge simplistic portrayals of the relationship between deaf people and the hearing English churches, interrogating the construction of textual and taught knowledge about deaf persons' place within both established and dissenting churches and the scriptural and traditional origins of this social location and the Deaf spaces that were produced in response. It is the implicit comparison of these Victorian Deaf spaces with those of ancient Israel that has arisen as the study has progressed that has resulted in this essay. We would like to record our thanks to the Leverhulme Trust for their support for the project.

[3] A variety of terms have been used to refer to those who are unable to hear and so, by consequence, are unable to acquire speech; "deaf and dumb" was dominant in the late eighteenth and early nineteenth century and was only imperfectly replaced by a later nineteenth-century use of "deaf mute." More recently, the capitalized term *Deaf* has been adopted by those deaf people

## I. Walls, Olyan, and Avalos on Disability and the Ancient World

Three recent short pieces by Neal H. Walls, Saul Olyan, and Hector Avalos, are of interest.

First, Walls's essay on the disabled body in ancient Mesopotamia uses the myth of Enki and Ninmah to suggest that a widespread "social ideology of inclusion for people of differing abilities" existed in that region. In that story, Ninmah creates a series of men—"weak handed," "blind," "with paralyzed feet" (or, in a variant, an "idiot"), and "incontinent"—and each is assigned a place in life as, respectively, "a servant to the king," as "a court servant," as "a silversmith," with the last one's role being left unclear.[4] Stigma, if it existed, did not preclude such persons from "being assigned jobs as they were able" or being "cared for at home over long periods of time."[5] Walls's positive emphasis on the social reality behind the texts and the existence of "disability" spaces in that culture helps to problematize the assumption of such scholars as William G. Dever that the lives of those considered disabled in earlier periods were brutal and short, an assumption that, we would argue, is an unfortunate legacy of certain attitudes toward historical disability that were common in the eighteenth and nineteenth centuries.[6]

Second, Olyan's chapter on "deafness"/"muteness" terminology in the few biblical texts in which it appears either "literally" (Exod 4:11, Lev 19:14, Ps 38:14-15, Prov 31:8) or "metaphorically" (Isa 6:9-10, 29:18-19, 35:5-6, 42:18-19, 43:8, 56:10, Jer 5:21, 10:5, Pss 115:5-8, 137:5-6) in his book *Disability in the Hebrew Bible* shows that "deafness" and "dumbness" were not categorized as defects (מומים), as blindness and lameness were; the list of defects also included improperly healed or uneven limbs, a hunched back, visible eye damage, some skin conditions, and genital damage (see primarily Lev 21:17-23, 24:19-20, and Deut 23:2

---

who identify as part of a signing, linguistic, and cultural minority. Our use of terms is reflective of the contemporary context, and we return to the discussion of the types and nature of deafness and of d/Deaf people's experience below.

[4] Neal H. Walls, "The Origins of the Disabled Body: Disability in Ancient Mesopotamia," in Avalos, Melcher, and Schipper, *This Abled Body*, 13-30, here 17-18.

[5] Ibid., 30.

[6] Dever posits that, as the result of "the inherent insularity and conservatism of rural folk everywhere" (except in Walls's ancient Mesopotamia perhaps), the "physically handicapped" in Israelite villages were linked with "the village idiot, the leper, the homosexual, even the boy or girl who never married" and regarded "with suspicion or even as outcasts: 'accursed ones'" (*The Lives of Ordinary People in Ancient Israel: Where Archaeology and the Bible Intersect* [Grand Rapids: Eerdmans, 2012], 204). Compare this with the words of John H. Pettingell in 1881: "It was customary, as it is now in less enlightened countries, to regard deaf-mutes as imbeciles, and to treat them with neglect" ("What the Bible Says of the Deaf and Dumb," *American Annals of the Deaf and Dumb* 26 [1881]: 226-38, here 238).

[Eng. 23:1]). This difference between deafness/dumbness and blindness/lameness occurs, Olyan notes, despite all four conditions being physical in nature and characterized by what he calls "somatic dysfunction."[7] (Tempting as it is to assume that visibility of the condition was definitive here, the inclusion of damaged testicles in the category of defects might suggest that things were perhaps not so simple.) Olyan notes that, in contrast to the מומים, the deaf and the dumb were

> subject to no evident restrictions on their access to cultic space and activities in biblical texts. No laws are attested in the biblical anthology that limit the cultic responsibilities of deaf or mute priests (cf. Lev 21:17–23), nor do any biblical texts bear witness to any ban on the entry of deaf or mute persons into the sanctuary (cf. Deut 23:2 [Eng. 1]; 2 Sam 5:8b).[8]

Nevertheless, he cautions against overplaying any advantage that they might have received as a result. Deafness and muteness were often linked with the conditions characterized as defects (Exod 4:11, Lev 19:14, Isa 29:18–19, 35:5–6, 42:18–19, 43:8, Jer 5:21) or were given negative connotations such as failure, inadequacy, or ignorance (Isa 6:9–10, 56:10). Deafness and muteness could also be the negative outcome of a curse (muteness in Ps 137:5–6; deafness in "non-Israelite West Asian sources").[9] Olyan concludes that a "second, unnamed native classification" existed that included all of these conditions and had its "basis in the notion of a shared weakness, vulnerability, and dependence" (see esp. Isa 28:18–19, Ps 38:14–15), the term for which is now lost.[10]

Finally, Avalos's essay on sensory criticism calls for an investigation of the senses in biblical texts. He focuses on the Deuteronomistic History (with Jeremiah) and Job and examines how each values the senses differently, "especially in receiving information about the world and about God's will"; the former is "audiocentric" and the latter is "visiocentric."[11] From the Deuteronomistic History, Avalos offers examples that presume the superiority of hearing over sight. These include the Shema—"Hear, O Israel ..." (Deut 6:4–5)—and the repeated drawing of wrong conclusions based on the "mere use of sight," exemplified by Eli's failure to recognize visually either the "pious worship" of Hannah (1 Sam 1:12–13) or the "impious worship" of his sons, Hophni and Phinehas (1 Sam 2:22). For Avalos, the doomed choice of Saul as king because of his appearance (1 Sam 10:17–24) is a critique of visiocentricity, and Elijah's hearing of the deity in the "still small voice" rather than in the "dramatic audiovisual theophanies" of wind, earthquake, or fire

---

[7] Saul M. Olyan, *Disability in the Hebrew Bible: Interpreting Mental and Physical Differences* (Cambridge: Cambridge University Press, 2008), 47.

[8] Ibid., 48.

[9] Ibid., 48–53.

[10] Ibid., 61; cf. 49–50.

[11] Hector Avalos, "Introducing Sensory Criticism in Biblical Studies: Audiocentricity and Visiocentricity," in Avalos, Melcher, and Schipper, *This Abled Body*, 47–59, here 50.

(1 Kgs 19) is an endorsement of audiocentricity.[12] This sensory bias Avalos attributes to Israelite concerns about the visual nature of idol worship and the "lack of sense" exhibited by these gods made by human hands.[13] In contrast, Avalos's discussion of Job begins with the rather different hierarchy of Job 42:5—"I had heard of you by the hearing of the ear, but now my eye sees you"—and develops from there.[14] The categories of deafness and muteness do not appear in the essay, but the implication of Avalos's argument is that such people would have been disadvantaged in the culture that created the Deuteronomistic History, not least in terms of their knowledge of God.[15]

## II. Looking through a Nineteenth-Century Lens

Interest in deafness and muteness in ancient Israel has been evidenced especially among those who were either deaf and/or mute or those who worked with them. Indeed, from the eighteenth century to the late nineteenth century, it was common for writings pertaining to the educational or moral status of the deaf and mute to situate modern commentary against a more or less detailed account of ancient attitudes toward deaf people and their sign language.[16] Occasionally authors focused more explicitly on the Bible, however, specifically exploring the experiences of those whose lives are reflected in the few biblical texts that mention deafness and muteness. One such study, by the Rev. John H. Pettingell (1815–1887), is entitled "What the Bible Says of the Deaf and Dumb." The study was published in the journal *American Annals of the Deaf and Dumb* in 1881.[17] The

---

[12] Ibid., 51–53.

[13] Ibid., 54–55. Such sensory favoritism meant that Israel's texts could also be rendered problematic. Avalos notes the deity's words in Jer 8:8—"How can you say, 'We are wise, / and the law of the LORD is with us,' / when, in fact, the false pen of the scribes / has made it into a lie?"—and in Jer 31:33, where it is said that the day is coming when the law will be written invisibly upon the heart, rather than visibly upon the scroll (55).

[14] On senses and divine communication in the Psalms and Isaiah, see Rebecca Raphael's literary study *Biblical Corpora: Representations of Disability in Hebrew Biblical Literature*, LHBOTS 445 (London: T&T Clark, 2008), 109–28. Biblical texts are quoted according to the NRSV.

[15] What lies behind Avalos's texts is left largely unspecified. We intend to follow a similar approach. We are well aware that readers will have varied and sophisticated views on the historical settings of and the relationships between texts such as Deuteronomy, the Deuteronomistic History, and Leviticus. We do not wish to make acceptance of any particular reconstruction a precondition for engaging with the central argument we are making. It is our hope that the argument can find a home within any critical reconstruction of ancient Israel.

[16] These studies were relatively standard, containing references to Greek, Hebrew, and often "barbarian" nations and were often designed to show the contrast with the author's more enlightened approach (e.g., Ferdinand Berthier, *Histoire et statistique de l'éducation des sourds-muets* [Paris: Published by the author, 1836]).

[17] See n. 6 above. Pettingell, a Congregationalist minister, worked as a pastor in a number

existence of formal sign languages in the nineteenth century means some parallels are inappropriate, but much remains instructive.

The Old Testament is discussed only in the opening three pages of Pettingell's article, which is devoted primarily to the New Testament. He begins, however, not by discussing texts but by asking who can be considered "deaf and dumb." Those who have aphasia or simple dumbness caused by problems with the organs of speech or with the mind–"speech organ" link are not to be counted as deaf and dumb, Pettingell states. Nor should one who becomes deaf late in life be termed a "deaf-mute." Children who lose their hearing after they have acquired speech but who retain their vocal skills are not deaf-mutes either; these he terms "semi-mutes." The developing complexity of the terminology is well illustrated by the first American deaf-mute minister, Rev. Henry Winter Syle, who was ordained in 1876 and was described that day by Rev. William Bacon Stevens as one who "had the use of the organs of hearing until at 6 years of age, [when] disease deprived him of hearing, and the loss of voice gradually followed."[18] Had Syle retained his speech, as some did, he would not have been a "deaf-mute" and would in consequence have had a radically different experience of the world. Using census data, Pettingell then estimated the numbers of "deaf- and semi-mutes" in his day as ranging from one in 2000 in the United States to one in 150 in the alpine regions of Europe.

When he turns to the Old Testament, Pettingell lists six texts pertinent to the subject (omitting a few that he thinks are "evidently metaphorical"), all of which appear among the larger number included in Olyan's discussion of deafness/muteness. Here are his texts quoted in full:

> Ex. iv, 11 [4:11]. "Who maketh man's mouth? or who maketh the *dumb*, or *deaf* [חרש] or the seeing, or the blind?"
>
> Levit. xix, 14 [19:14]. "Thou shall not curse the *deaf* [חרש], nor put a stumbling-block before the *blind*."
>
> Ps. xxxviii, 13. [38:13]. "But, I, as a *deaf* man [כחרש], heard not, and I was as a *dumb* man that openeth not his mouth."
>
> Is. xxix, 18. [29:18]. "And in that day shall the *deaf* [החרשים] hear the words of the book, and the eyes of the *blind* shall see, out of obscurity and out of darkness."

---

of the eastern states of the United States, before spending five years in Antwerp working for the American Seamen's Friend Society. He eventually became a teacher in the New York Institute for the Deaf and Dumb before resigning and taking a position in the Pennsylvania Institute for the Deaf and Dumb. He published numerous articles in the *American Annals* relating to deaf people and, in 1881, authored a 276-page book entitled *Biblical Terminology Relative to the Future Life* (Philadelphia: Bible Banner Association).

[18] William Bacon Stevens, *A Sermon Preached in St Stephen's Church, Philadelphia, Sunday, October 8, 1876 on Occasion of the Ordination of Henry Winter Syle (A Deaf Mute) as Deacon in the Protestant Episcopal Church* (Philadelphia: McCalla & Stavely, 1876), 24.

Is. xxxv, 5, 6. [35:5–6]. "Then shall the eyes of the *blind* be opened, and the ears of the *deaf* shall be unstopped [ואזני חרשים תפתחנה] then shall the lame man leap as a hart, and the tongue of the *dumb* sing."

Is. xliii, 8. [43:8]. "Bring forth the *blind* people that have eyes, and the *deaf* [החרשים] that have ears." (Evidently figurative.)[19]

Pettingell draws the following conclusion from these texts:

> No mention whatever ... is made of the deaf and dumb, or of deaf-dumbness. Two or three allusions are made to deafness, or to those who are deaf, and about as many to those who are dumb; but nothing is said of the double infirmity of deaf-dumbness, which is so common with us at the present day....
> 
> It may be said that deafness and dumbness may be supposed to belong to the same individual: anything may be *supposed*. All these afflictions may be supposed to belong to one and the same person, as sometimes occurs; but no hint is given in the text that this is the case. Indeed these afflicted persons are spoken of as constituting distinct and separate classes.[20]

That members of the category that Pettingell described as "afflicted" with "deaf-dumbness" are not explicitly described in the biblical texts does not mean that he believed that none such existed in ancient Israel. His numbers for such people in various geographical locations, outlined only a few lines earlier, strongly imply that "deaf-mute" and "semi-mute" Israelites *must* have existed.[21] Moreover, the existence of cousin marriage in Israel, viewed by many in the nineteenth century as the major contributor to pockets of congenital deafness, would also have been suggestive to him of the presence of "deaf-mutes" in Israel.[22] They may even be

---

[19] Pettingell, "What the Bible Says," 228 (his emphasis).

[20] Ibid., 227, 228 (his emphasis).

[21] Not all in this era would have drawn such an implication from the figures. In a discussion in 1877 about the statistical evidence for the significance of consanguineous marriages, Désiré de Haerne offers the following negative opinion on the existence of "deaf-mutism" in ancient Israel: "Now, as to the ancient patriarchs, they certainly belonged to a very robust race, as is proved by the high age they attained; which fact I consider as having been providentially arranged for the propagation and maintenance of the faith among the people of God. This extraordinary strength of the primitive Hebrew race explains sufficiently, I think, the absence of deaf-mutism among them; and it is moreover to be observed that this infirmity is very seldom mentioned in the Old Testament in general, and, consequently, perhaps not in cases of the marriage of near kin" ("Consanguineous Marriages as a Cause of Deaf-Mutism," *American Annals of the Deaf and Dumb* 22 [1877]: 146–57, here 148).

[22] E.g., Alfred Henry Huth, "Consanguineous Marriages," *American Annals of the Deaf and Dumb* 23 [1878]: 144–50. This position was often expressed in contrast to, or in outright opposition to, the belief of such figures as Alexander Graham Bell that a congenitally deaf man marrying a congenitally deaf woman risked breeding a deaf form of humanity (e.g., Alexander Graham Bell, *Memoir upon the Formation of a Deaf Variety of the Human Race* [Washington, DC: National Academy of Sciences, 1878]; Bell, *Marriage: An Address to the Deaf*, 3rd ed. [Washington, DC: Volta Bureau, 1898]). James Hawkins notes that nineteenth-century arguments against cousin

"supposed" by an interpreter—subverting Pettingell's own words—to lie behind one or more of the texts just discussed, but Pettingell is very clear that the texts do not say so explicitly.

Pettingell offers a pertinent point when he employs his experience of the varied concrete realities of deafness, dumbness, and deaf-dumbness of his own day to challenge the assumption that a single condition lies behind our texts. In order to press home that point, we will offer a brief categorization of the multiple experiential realities of deafness that might have existed in a society such as ancient Israel. (Any form of "muteness" that is unrelated to hearing loss will not be considered further.)

### III. Categorizing the Multiple Experienced Realities of Deafness

Pettingell's triad of "deaf-mute" (= deaf from birth, or deaf from infancy, without speech), "semi-mute" (= deaf from infancy, with retained speech), and "deafness" (= postinfancy or late onset) can be significantly enriched by examining these realities under three headings: timing, cause, and experience.

There is a vast gulf in life experience between those born deaf or made deaf as prelingual infants and those who have lost their hearing after having mastered a spoken language, whether language is eventually retained in oral or in written form—or perhaps in both or even neither, in the latter case being available only in internal thought processes. The intellectual development and communication skills of those born deaf would have been affected, perhaps severely, in an ancient setting without a formal sign language, whereas some of those who had mastered a language before losing their hearing might have experienced comparatively little change to their lives and prospects. The role of the social and cultural setting on an individual's experience of deafness should not be underestimated and would have led to a further diversification of life possibilities for the categories of deafness mentioned here. We should note the obvious point that babies born deaf in the ancient world would not have been systematically recognized as such, their deafness becoming clear in many cases only with their failure to acquire language as a two- to three-year-old. A baby with deaf siblings or visible genetic problems might have been recognized as deaf significantly earlier, however.

Both infants and adults could be made deaf at any time through various events; in ancient Israel illness and physical trauma would be the most likely

---

marriage among the congenitally deaf were hindered by appeals to "the Scriptures, and the case of Zelophehad's daughters, who 'were married unto their father's brothers' sons'" (*The Physical, Moral and Intellectual Constitution of the Deaf and Dumb: With Some Practical and General Remarks Concerning Their Education* [London: Longman, Green, Longman, Roberts & Green, 1863], v).

causes. Damaging chemicals and deafening noises—common causes of deafness in industrialized societies—were less prevalent or wholly absent in preindustrial agrarian societies such as ancient Israel. Nevertheless, proximity to extreme natural phenomena like thunder (1 Sam 7:10) or the crash of falling masonry (Isa 30:13) or prolonged exposure to blaring trumpets (Exod 19:16; Lev 25:9; 1 Chr 15:16, 28), to clashing cymbals (Ps 150:5), to a crowd shouting loudly (Ezra 3:13, 2 Chr 32:18, Ezek 8:18), or to both instruments and voices (2 Chr 15:14) might have significantly affected the hearing of those near the noises. The physiological reality behind such occasions of deafness could relate to damage to what Pettingell might call the "organs of hearing" or to the parts of the brain processing aural information, or to both, and might have been accompanied by other physical or psychological symptoms in any given individual.

Nor can one assume consistency and ongoing experience of deafness. Not all deafness is permanent, and some persons experience temporary, intermittent, or worsening effects. Equally, the degree of deafness can vary from the effects of tinnitus through mild hearing loss to profound deafness. Nor is all hearing loss bilateral; significant deafness in only one hemisphere or different degrees of loss on each side can cause specific symptoms. The social impact of any of these conditions would also have depended on factors such as the degree to which one's life was dominated by noisy crowd scenes, quiet one-to-one conversations, interior- or exterior-specific contexts, or, as we shall see shortly, one's gender.

In view of the multiple experiences of deafness possible in ancient Israel, Olyan's suggestion that Hebrew terminology for "deafness" and "muteness" refers to two discrete examples of "somatic disability" must be regarded as deeply problematic. The Hebrew terminology in use—or at least what is available to us—is too unrefined to do justice to the complex and multiple social realities of hearing loss; Israelites affected by hearing loss might have scraped by to survive, might have lived comfortably, or might even have thrived.

## IV. Life Settings

If we are to develop some useful and illuminating information about the experiences of people affected by these forms of deafness, we need to move beyond Olyan's discussion of the terminology and into the realms of what was physically, sociologically, and culturally possible. For reasons of space, we will not consider those who lost hearing late in life but rather will concentrate on those who were born deaf or who lost their hearing before acquiring a spoken language (Pettingell's "deaf-mutes").

Concerning so-called deaf-mutes, we begin with the two individuals described in Harlan Lane's *The Mask of Benevolence* (1999).[23] "Deafie" (female)

---

[23] Harlan Lane, *The Mask of Benevolence: Disabling the Deaf Community*, 2nd ed. (San Diego, CA: DawnSign, 1999), 147–50; the examples in this paragraph are from 147–49.

and "Vincent" (male) were born profoundly deaf to hearing families in rural Burundi, where no formal sign language existed. Their development may offer insight into the experiences of individual deaf-mutes in ancient Israel. Key to the experience of both Deafie and Vincent was their pursuit of visual communication. Both developed informal signs to communicate with hearing parents, siblings, and their extended families, but differences began to emerge. Deafie, regarded by her mother as simple and friendless, helped out with chores like cooking, sweeping, and fetching water. She was unable to marry but had had repeated abortions, being seen by some as an available sex partner. Vincent, in contrast, was regarded by his mother as a much underestimated entrepreneur, happily selling peanuts, fully aware of the value of money and with a reputation as a brawler. Similar gender differences—wholly absent from Olyan's discussion of the Hebrew terminology—may well have marked, and further diversified, deaf experience in ancient Israel.

In describing family life in early Israel, Carol L. Meyers has suggested that each man or woman should be seen as existing within three concentric circles of kinship—the household (based on parents and siblings, plus others), the clan (which could have been of varied size [e.g., Gideon's clan was the "weakest" in Manasseh; Judg 6:15]), and the tribe.[24] Meyers observed that "relatively few people had regular or even any contact with the processes of structures further up the [sociopolitical] pyramid"; for her, the household was, from the earliest period of Israel's history and throughout the period of the monarchy, "the immediate and determinative social context for everyone, sustaining and shaping daily existence for its members. As the basic unit of both production and consumption, it was the single most important economic and social unit; it was also an integral part of Israelite political and religious structures."[25] "The day-to-day dynamics of household life," she points out, "were focused on subsistence activities, not on the policies and practices of the other levels of society."[26] Almost all of the work done by men and women took place in and around the household, with specialized tasks such as metalworking conducted nearby.[27] The possibility of professionalization in areas such as prostitution, "food-processing skills, knowledge of herbal substances, textile work, nursing, and positions in the religious realm" increased as Israelite society developed.[28]

---

[24] Carol L. Meyers, *Rediscovering Eve: Ancient Israelite Women in Context* (Oxford: Oxford University Press, 2012), 115. On the setting of individuals in early Israel, see Meyers, *Discovering Eve: Ancient Israelite Women in Context* (Oxford: Oxford University Press, 1988), 128. On their setting in First Temple Israel, see Joseph Blenkinsopp, "The Family in First Temple Israel," in *Families in Ancient Israel*, by Leo G. Perdue, Joseph Blenkinsopp, John J. Collins, and Carol Meyers, Family, Religion, and Culture (Louisville: Westminster John Knox, 1997), 48–103, here 50. In the preface to her *Rediscovering Eve*, the revision of the 1988 book *Discovering Eve*, Meyers noted the ubiquity of the agrarian household throughout Israelite history (ix).

[25] Meyers, *Rediscovering Eve*, 103.
[26] Ibid.
[27] Ibid., 125, 134.
[28] Ibid., 171–79.

For Meyers, the household had three main components: a material one, a human one, and a performative one.²⁹ On the basis of archaeological evidence she envisages the typical Israelite household as a complex one in which several "conjugal pairs" with assorted others might live in separate physical dwellings (e.g., "four-roomed houses") arranged around a common courtyard, with associated "installations" (e.g., cistern, oven) and "artifacts," "lands" (near and far, level and terraced), and various "animals." A household might have contained not only conjugal pairs and their relations (e.g., grandparents/aunts/uncles, brothers/sisters, sons/daughters/nieces/nephews) but also, in some "well-to-do" households, captives, servants, and sojourners.³⁰ In her earlier volume, Meyers suggested that the household was likely to be twelve to fourteen individuals in total.³¹ A household could be rendered unstable by events such as death, disease, or divorce. In performative terms, sustaining the life of the household was the dominant driver for all work activity, with some tasks allotted to men (e.g., digging cisterns, clearing land, and building terraces), some to women (e.g., food preparation, education), and others shared as technical skill and necessity required (e.g., crafts, animal husbandry, horticulture). Younger members of the household would have contributed from an early age.³² Everyone would have been working hard!

The woman born deaf into such a household would have had a relatively safe place in which to live out her existence, helping with household activities—grinding grain, butchery, baking, cooking, brewing and wine making, spinning yarn, dying and making clothes, creating pots, cleaning—and thereby gaining status within the household.³³ Excursions outside the home would have been either essential—collecting water³⁴ or twigs/dung for cooking, helping with the harvest,³⁵ defecation and urination³⁶—or merely possible—purchasing food perhaps. If such a woman was considered unmarriageable because of her deafness, she could still have had sexual experiences, as was the case with Deafie, and even have borne a

---

²⁹ The discussion of the household in this paragraph is drawn from Meyers, *Rediscovering Eve*, 104–11.

³⁰ Blenkinsopp offers the following list of possible (First Temple) household inhabitants: "grandparents, the families of grown children, an adopted child or adopted children, a divorced adult daughter who had returned to the paternal homestead, male and female servants or slaves, and other dependents" ("Family in First Temple Israel," 52).

³¹ Meyers, *Discovering Eve*, 136.

³² Ibid., 148. On the role of gender in household religion, see Susan Ackerman, "Household Religion, Family Religion, and Women's Religion in Ancient Israel," in *Household and Family Religion in Antiquity: Contextual and Comparative Perspectives*, ed. John Bodel and Saul M. Olyan, Ancient World—Comparative Histories (Oxford: Blackwell, 2008), 127–58.

³³ See, e.g., Jennie R. Ebeling, *Women's Lives in Biblical Times* (London: T&T Clark, 2010), 48–67; see also Meyers, *Rediscovering Eve*, 127–35; and Dever, *Lives of Ordinary People*, 164–65.

³⁴ According to Dever, young girls would have gone back and forth for part of the day, filling large store jars in the house (*Lives of Ordinary People*, 164).

³⁵ Ebeling, *Women's Lives*, 35–36.

³⁶ Dever, *Lives of Ordinary People*, 185; Ebeling, *Women's Lives*, 61.

child, either hearing or deaf. Should the household collapse completely through disease or death, a deaf woman would have arguably been little worse off than any of the other rootless women left to eke out a difficult existence on the margins of Israelite society.[37] Prostitution, as Meyers notes, the professional position for women mentioned most often in the Hebrew Bible, was a possibility.[38]

For an Israelite man born deaf, much would have depended on his context, whether in a household in a rural village or in a walled city, and on his family's social status. In a small village, perhaps situated around a familial connection, a broad back and a willingness to emulate the visual cues given by his relatives would allow him to work as a horticultural laborer, growing and harvesting crops such as wheat, grapes, and olives for subsistence or trade.[39] Caring for sheep, goats, or cattle in the fields might have been more difficult given the need to hear wild animal attacks at night. In a larger village of one to two hundred people[40] formed of several families, however, working with hearing others could have allowed such a role for a deaf man. Emulation would also have allowed the deaf man to work with his hands in cistern digging, building construction, and property maintenance or in skilled crafts such as metallurgy, jewelry making, or bone carving.[41] Israel's emphasis on monumental works and the taxation that such works required in later periods suggests a greater intrusion of the higher levels of the sociopolitical pyramid into household life, creating additional opportunities for activities outside the communal space. Depending on a man's skills, context, and luck, he may even have been able to survive the loss of his family. Dealing with any legal issues that arose without family support, however, would have been nearly impossible.

The legal traditions recorded in the Israelite Scriptures imply the free movement of individuals of both genders outside the household in all periods. In Deut 22:23–29, the woman and man in the cases cited are culpable because of sexual activity; they are not castigated for being out in the city or in the field. Similarly, among the laws collected in Exod 21–23, the need to legislate for injuries caused to the pregnant woman by two men fighting (21:22) or for those caused to a man or woman by an uncontrolled ox (21:28–32) assumes ongoing activities outside the household by both sexes. In Gen 34:1, Dinah goes out to visit the women of the

---

[37] On the place of the widow at the fringe of society, see, e.g., see Paula S. Hiebert, "Whence Shall Help Come to Me? The Biblical Widow," in *Gender and Difference in Ancient Israel*, ed. Peggy L. Day (Minneapolis: Fortress, 1989), 125–41, here 130.

[38] Meyers, *Rediscovering Eve*, 171. This does not seem to be a possibility for the women described by Ebeling, however, although the word *prostitute* does appear in her book (*Women's Lives*, 27, 31, 85, 133, 134).

[39] Dever, *Lives of Ordinary People*, 170–71; cf., e.g., Nathan McDonald, *What Did the Ancient Israelites Eat? Diet in Biblical Times* (Grand Rapids: Eerdmans, 2008).

[40] Dever, *Lives of Ordinary People*, 158.

[41] Ibid., 179–80.

region without censure.[42] There is no reason to assume that deaf men or women would have been more restricted than their hearing counterparts.

Some limitations and the possibility of stigma were undoubtedly the lot of Pettingell's "deaf-mute" in ancient Israel, regardless of gender. Olyan's suggestions of "failure," "inadequacy," and "ignorance" based on notions of "weakness, vulnerability, and dependence"[43] probably had a basis in the life experience of all Israelites who were deaf in some form, but especially perhaps those who were deaf from birth or infancy. We should not assume, however, that deaf persons had no positive route through life. The opposite seems more likely.

## V. Deuteronomistic Audiocentricity and Its Impact

What of those "deaf-mutes" who were born into a different social context? According to Olyan, Lev 21:17–23 suggests that there were no restrictions on the cultic activities of "deaf or mute priests" in at least one Israelite sacrificial system.[44] Given our previous discussion about the multiplicities of deaf experience, however, we should ask whether this rule, were it to be set within a Deuteronomistic setting, could have included boys who were born into priestly families and who were deaf from birth, or deaf from infancy, without speech. According to Avalos, the Deuteronomistic History privileges the auditory over the visual in regard to knowledge of God and of the world.[45] Late-onset deafness would not have affected the knowledge base of an experienced priest, but how might the deaf man envisaged above have coped in the Deuteronomistic context? Could he have acted as a priest? What duties would he have been able to carry out? How would his knowledge of God and the world have been affected by his deafness?

In Deuteronomy, the priests, the sons of Levi (21:5), are described as having care of the law (17:18) and as being charged with carrying the ark of the covenant (10:8–9; cf. 18:1–8). Their role often involved verbal communications to nonpriests: they rendered judgments (17:8–9, 21:5), addressed troops (20:2), pronounced blessings (21:5), instructed (24:8), heard declarations when receiving tithes (26:3), and recited liturgical prayers to all Israel (27:14). In addition, in Joshua–2 Kings, they played musical instruments (Josh 6:6–16) and anointed and acclaimed individuals (1 Kgs 1:39). In contrast to the active involvement of priests in such activities, the sacrificial system described in both Deuteronomy and the Deuteronomistic History involved laypeople slaughtering their own animals at the

---

[42] See, e.g., Duane L. Christensen, *Deuteronomy 21:10–34:12*, WBC 6B (Nashville: Nelson, 2002), 518; Christensen never states that the woman is guilty for being outside the household (521–22).

[43] Olyan, *Disability in the Hebrew Bible*, 48–53.

[44] Ibid., 48; on priestly bodily norms in Leviticus, see Raphael, *Biblical Corpora*, 31–39.

[45] Avalos, *Introducing Sensory Criticism*, 47–55.

altar tended by the priests.⁴⁶ The priests' role in *sacrifice* in the Deuteronomistic cult was thus largely a peripheral one.⁴⁷

While there is no explicit prohibition in Deuteronomy against a deaf man approaching the altar, the verbal skills required might have put the priestly role beyond the capabilities of a man born deaf or deaf from infancy, without speech. This position, however, assumes that the deaf son operated on his own, and it ignores the relational setting in which he may have existed. One cultic role for a deaf son within a priestly family may perhaps be seen in the story of Eli and his two sons, Hophni and Phinehas (1 Sam 1–2, a text discussed by Avalos). Although the text does not state that the two sons are deaf, it says that they would not listen to Eli's voice (2:23–25). Their supporting role in the Shiloh cult suggests that a son born deaf or deaf from infancy, without speech, could have taken a role within the cult—one allowed/encouraged by the apparent lack of a prohibition against entering the sanctuary—so long as someone within the priestly family was able to hear and to speak. The prohibition against sacrificing animals away from "the place that the LORD your God will choose out of all your tribes as his habitation to put his name there" (Deut 12:5; cf. 12:6, 11; 15:22–23) points to the existence of either a single sanctuary or perhaps a small number of sanctuaries. The fewer the sanctuaries, the greater the concentration of priests and the greater the likelihood that a deaf priest could have found a useful role. Deuteronomy 26:3–4 describes the priest who "hears" the words of the supplicant and then "takes the basket from your hand and sets it down before the altar of the LORD your God." How difficult would it have been for a deaf priest to perform such a ritual act?

What of the knowledge of God and of the world of a priest born deaf or one deafened in infancy and without speech? Avalos's argument that hearing is essential for acquiring such knowledge in the society behind the Deuteronomistic History neglects the symbolic knowledge about the deity and the world that is embodied in the numerous rites and acts that made up Israel's communal life. His emphasis on the Shema (Deut 6:4–5) as a recited and heard set of words, for example, does not take into account the complex multisensory rendering of Israel's act of remembrance of the nature of its God as it is described in Deut 6:6–8:

> Keep these words that I am commanding you today in your heart. Recite them to your children and talk about them when you are at home and when you are away, when you lie down and when you rise. Bind them as a sign on your hand,

---

⁴⁶ See, e.g., Deut 12:7, 12, 18, 27; 15:19–21; 16:2–7; 17:1; 18:3; Josh 8:31; Judg 20:26; 21:4; 1 Sam 1:3, 25; 11:15; 16:2–5; 2 Sam 15:12; 1 Kgs 1:9, 19; 3:3; 8:62–64; 2 Kgs 17:35–36.

⁴⁷ On nonsacrificing priests, see, e.g., Richard D. Nelson, *Raising up a Faithful Priest: Community and Priesthood in Biblical Theology* (Louisville: Westminster John Knox, 1993), 9, 59; see also Nelson, "The Role of the Priesthood in the Deuteronomistic History," in *Congress Volume: Leuven 1989*, ed. John A. Emerton, VTSup 43 (Leiden: Brill, 1991), 132–47; and J. Gordon McConville, "Priesthood in Joshua to Kings," *VT* 49 (1999): 73–87.

fix them as an emblem on your forehead, and write them on the doorposts of your house and on your gates.

That the visual symbolic elements of such acts would have conveyed meaning about the deity to the deaf Israelite onlooker or participant can hardly be doubted. Viewing or participating in the acts of sacrifice in the Deuteronomistic cult would have provided priests and supplicants with a complex appreciation for the event, made up of the sensorial experience of the offering—the smell, taste, and touch of the blood and the flesh—and, if heard, of the verbal instructions and/or explanations involved. Explicit explanations of sacrificial systems are notably sparse in the ancient Near East, and it is at least arguable that sight—and perhaps also smell, taste, and touch[48]—would have been of greater significance to participants in the Deuteronomistic cult than the words spoken. Thus, *pace* Avalos, a deaf priest might have been able to gain a significant degree of knowledge about Israel's deity in the Deuteronomistic cult.[49]

## VI. Deaf Spaces in Ancient Israel?

Thus far we have focused on individual experiences of hearing loss. In this section we propose that some of those born deaf in ancient Israel may have experienced deafness as part of a signing "Deaf community." The key to such

---

[48] The importance of the sense of smell for sacrificial efficacy in emphasized in Gen 8:21: "And when the LORD smelled the pleasing odor, the LORD said in his heart, 'I will never again curse the ground because of humankind, for the inclination of the human heart is evil from youth; nor will I ever again destroy every living creature as I have done.'" That the rejection of the aroma is indicative of the rejection of the sacrifice can be seen in the deity's words about punishment for disobedience in Lev 26:31: "I will lay your cities waste, will make your sanctuaries desolate, and I will not smell your pleasing odors." In discussing Egyptian sacrifices, David Frankfurter also notes the importance of the sense of smell: "A third context, somewhat closer to the popular conception of sacrifice, is the ritual incineration of certain animals. These rites were meant in one capacity to please the gods with the aroma of barbecue, but also, more importantly, to ward off chaos through the ritual destruction of cosmic enemies. The animal carcasses are presented as images or incarnations ... of divine enemies, and the grilling process is declared to be the vanquishing of those enemies.... The rite ... revolves around burning and aroma, not killing or blood" ("Egyptian Religion and the Problem of the Category 'Sacrifice,'" in *Ancient Mediterranean Sacrifice*, ed. Jennifer Wright Knust and Zsuzsanna Várhelyi [Oxford: Oxford University Press, 2011], 75–94, here 78–80).

[49] In considering such a situation, the 1881 account by M. Ballard of his deaf life pre-education and its relation to the sacred is worth reading ("Reflections of a Deaf-Mute before Education," *American Annals of the Deaf and Dumb*, 26 [1881]: 31–39; reprinted in *American Annals of the Deaf* 142 [1997]: 24–26). Interest in the thought processes of the "deaf-mute" without a formal sign language was common in the period (see, e.g., W. Wilkinson, "Conscience in the Uneducated Deaf-Mute," *American Annals of the Deaf* 25 [1880]: 45–49; P. Denys, "Primitive Conscience among Deaf-Mutes," *American Annals of the Deaf* 25 [1880]: 50–53).

communities is, as Lane's Deafie and Vincent suggest, the readiness of deaf people to develop visual communication through gesture. The opportunity to develop that system from gesture into one of the world's multitude of natural sign languages depends only on a combination of numbers and proximity.[50]

Although we have no knowledge of the incidence of deafness in ancient Israel, in the modern West approximately one person in a thousand is either born deaf or develops profound deafness before acquiring spoken language. Pettingell concluded his nineteenth-century study with the claim that the number of those who became deaf in infancy—his "semi-mutes"—would have been fewer in the ancient world because some of the relevant diseases are of comparatively recent origin, thus lowering the number of those in this category of deafness.[51] At such a low rate of occurrence, contact between deaf persons could be expected to occur spontaneously only in the very largest cities or to develop only in situations where deaf people were purposefully gathered (a type of action for which no evidence exists in the case of ancient Israel).[52] At other times in the modern era, and in other places around the globe, however, rates of congenital or early-onset deafness have been much higher. For example, among the Al-Sayed bedouin of the present-day Negev, one in twenty is born deaf (150 persons of a total of 3,000, or 5 percent). In Martha's Vineyard, Massachusetts, at one point in the eighteenth century, one in four was being born deaf (25 percent).[53] In individual families, the rate could be higher still. In a letter to the *Times* in 1875, the Rev. Samuel Smith, (hearing) chaplain at St Saviour's, Oxford Street, referred to a family of two married cousins with which he was familiar, eight of whose nine children were born deaf (89 percent).[54] Such

---

[50] Natural sign languages are full human language systems in which movement harnesses light (and sometimes touch), rather than sound, for communication. Emerging locally, their development as linguistic systems is attested as far back as ancient Greece and can, in some situations, like the spontaneous recent emergence of a unique Nicaraguan sign language, be extremely rapid (see Ann Senghas, "The Development of Nicaraguan Sign Language via the Language Acquisition Process," in *Proceedings of the 19th Annual Boston University Conference on Language Development*, ed. Dawn MacLaughlin and Susan McEwen, 2 vols. [Somerville: Cascadilla, 1995], 2:543–52). Their development from gesture to language usually coincides temporally with the emergence of a stable Deaf community providing opportunities for consistent and ongoing use of the language (Mike Gulliver, "DEAF Space, A History: Emergent, Autonomous, Collocated, Disabled" [PhD thesis, University of Bristol, 2009], 61–88).

[51] Pettingell, "What the Bible Says," 238.

[52] In 1800, Paris had a population of between 500,000 and 700,000 and a long-standing Deaf community of over 200 adults (Gulliver, "DEAF Space," 82–83). The most common settings for deaf collocation are residential schools. Other situations, however, do exist, for example, the long-standing deaf community created in the Ottoman court of the sixteenth century (see M. Miles, "Signing at the Seraglio: Mutes, Dwarfs and Jesters at the Ottoman Court, 1500–1700," *Disability and Society* 15 [2000]: 115–34).

[53] Norah Ellen Groce, *Everyone Here Spoke Sign Language: A Hereditary Deafness on Martha's Vineyard* (Cambridge: Harvard University Press, 1984).

[54] Rev. Samuel Smith, "Marriage of Cousins," letter, *Times*, 19 February 1875, 7.

families can extend for many generations, transmitting sign language and, through that language, other cultural knowledge sometimes across hundreds of years.[55] One of the authors of this article knows of one such family that has now reached its tenth generation and can trace its history back over two centuries!

These examples of deaf communication and community suggest that isolation or exclusion need not have been the inevitable result of early-life deafness in ancient Israel. Given the right conditions, what would have prevented deaf people in that society from being a part of a vibrant, active, communicating, signing community? In deaf studies, a foundational critical assumption is that where numbers of deaf people come together with the time and freedom to develop sign languages, then Deaf spaces will inevitably come into being. It is this insight that we wish to introduce into biblical scholarship.[56] In the case of ancient Israel, our textual evidence is entirely lacking for what such Deaf spaces would have looked like. Such (an argument from) silence would normally be seen by biblical scholars as providing evidence only for the absence of such groups. Instead, we want to suggest that, if the conditions were right, Deaf spaces would occasionally have come into existence, even in an ancient culture that, in its literature, seems barely to have noticed deaf people at all.

---

[55] See also Harlan Lane, Richard C. Pillard, and Ulf Hedberg, *The People of the Eye, Deaf Ethnicity and Ancestry* (Oxford: Oxford University Press, 2011); Mary Beth Kitzel, "Chasing Ancestors: Searching for the Roots of American Sign Language in the Kentish Weald, 1620–1851" (PhD thesis, University of Sussex, 2014; available at http://sro.sussex.ac.uk/48877); and Paddy Ladd, *Understanding Deaf Culture: In Search of Deafhood* (Clevedon: Multilingual Matters, 2003).

[56] The nature of Deaf space(s) is still under discussion in anthropology, deaf studies, and geography, and various proposals have been developed. Marion Heap, Gill Valentine, and Tracey Skelton point to visual communication "bubbles" within a dominant hearing world (Marion Heap, "Sign-Deaf Spaces: The Deaf in Cape Town Creating Community, Crossing Boundaries, Constructing Identity," *Anthropology of Southern Africa* 29 [2006]: 35–44; Gill Valentine and Tracey Skelton, "Living on the Edge: The Marginalisation and 'Resistance' of D/deaf Youth," *Environment and Planning A: Economy and Space* 35 [2003]: 301–21). Annelies Kusters removes the inherent imbalance of these descriptions, focusing instead on the parity of hearing and Deaf communication, describing Deaf spaces simply as "how Deaf sociality is produced in space" (*Deaf Space in Adamorobe: An Ethnographic Study in a Village in Ghana* [Washington, DC: Gallaudet University Press, 2015] 22). Mike Gulliver goes further, arguing that if Deaf spaces share parity with hearing spaces, then Deaf spaces are effectively snapshots of "other worlds," alternative realities authored by Deaf people on a visual plane (Gulliver, "DEAF Space," 200). Constructions of Deaf spaces and their relationship to hearing world spaces and geographies are explored by a growing number of scholars, notably Gill Harold ("Reconsidering Sound and the City: Asserting the Right to the Deaf-Friendly City," *Environment and Planning D: Society and Space* 31 [2013]: 846–62), Mary Beth Kitzel ("Chasing Ancestors"), and Claire Shaw ("'We Have No Need to Lock Ourselves Away': Space, Marginality, and the Negotiation of Deaf Identity in Late Soviet Moscow," *Slavic Review* 74 [2015]: 57–78). Their work, and that of others, is available through the resources page of the Deaf Geographies Sandbox (http://www.deafgeographies.com).

# Introducing the
# OLD TESTAMENT
Robert L. Hubbard Jr. and J. Andrew Dearman

"This well-written and beautifully produced volume will be of enormous help to serious Bible readers who desire to dive deeper into their most ancient Scriptures. I commend it warmly."
— Iain Provan

ISBN 9780802867902 • 560 pages • hardcover • $40.00

eerdmans.com

WM. B. EERDMANS
PUBLISHING CO.

# Biblical Myths and the Inversion Principle: A Neostructuralist Approach

ARYEH AMIHAY
aryeh.amihay@gmail.com
University of California, Santa Barbara, CA 93106

The postmodern turn in the humanities is now at a point that requires response and revision to some deconstructionist trends. As a case study, this article examines the inversion principle formulated by Claude Lévi-Strauss against Yair Zakovitch's analysis of mirror narratives through three examples. In the first example, the mirror narratives of two destructions in Genesis are shown to be better explained by the inversion principle. The second example considers aspects of the Mesopotamian flood hero Utnapishtim that have been divided in subsequent Jewish traditions between Enoch and Noah. The third example considers the transformation of the myth of the sacrificial son in Judaism, Christianity, and Islam. These three examples lead to the following conclusions: (1) that other myths, particularly in Genesis, should be reconsidered in light of the inversion principle; (2) that this principle is crucial for the reception history of biblical narratives, as seen in the development of the figure of the flood hero in Second Temple Judaism; and (3) that intentional adaptations are equally susceptible to the subconscious structural changes that occur in the intercultural journeys of myth, as described by Lévi-Strauss.

---

As a powerful story that holds some seemingly true statement about human nature or the meaning of life, myth raises questions of origin, whether it is to be found in a literary dependence or in shared elements of the human psyche.[1] When

---

An earlier version of this paper was presented in the Myth section of the Society of Biblical Literature Annual Meeting in San Antonio, Texas, in November 2016. I am grateful to Debra Ballentine and Austin Busch for including me in their panel and for the comments I received there, especially from Laura Feldt and Tod Linafelt. I further benefitted from comments on various versions or sections of this study from Buzzy Teiser, Martha Himmelfarb, Larry Schiffman, Ariel Feldman, Shani Tzoref, and Arthur Versluis. The anonymous reviewers for this journal offered detailed and perceptive critiques that vastly improved my article. I deeply appreciate each of these contributions and am humbly thankful to all.

[1] For a history of the term *myth* and the problem of its applicability to biblical studies, see

similarities are found in myths from cultures that share a point of contact, the historical context may suggest a literary dependence. Mythic symbols, however, have shown resemblance in disparate cultures[2] in a manner that allows one to postulate an inherent psychological structure that sustains these elements independent of cultural exchange and influence. This article will explore the applicability of Claude Lévi-Strauss's formula of mythic structure to the interpretation of biblical myth as well as to the reception of myth in postbiblical literature. It will seek further to identify a neostructuralist trend in scholarship that embraces the contributions of structuralism to the study of religion while neither fully rejecting the poststructuralists nor ignoring their tenacious criticisms of the former.[3] Finally, in discussing the narratives of the flood, the Akedah, and Moses's infancy, it will propose nuances to Yair Zakovitch's identification of the "mirror narrative" as a literary device and demonstrate the contribution of critical theory to the literary analysis of the Hebrew Bible.

## I. Neostructuralism and Biblical Studies

In his quintessentially neostructuralist book, Naphtali Meshel proposes a grammar of sacrifice.[4] He recognizes his debt to Lévi-Strauss, whose application of linguistic concepts to nonlinguistic phenomena became the hallmark of

---

Debra Scoggins Ballentine, *The Conflict Myth and the Biblical Tradition* (Oxford: Oxford University Press, 2015), 1–21.

[2] Admittedly, some reported resemblances can be in the eye of the beholder and raise questions of scope as well as depth of analysis and literacy in a given culture. See, e.g., Jonathan Z. Smith's critique (*To Take Place: Toward Theory in Ritual*, CSHJ [Chicago: University of Chicago Press, 1987], 1–23) of a specific example by Mircea Eliade (*The Sacred and the Profane: The Nature of Religion*, trans. Willard R. Trask [New York: Harcourt, Brace, 1959], 32–33).

[3] This approach accepts that critiques of power and hegemony have been validated and thus are a postmodern critique that will endure, unlike deconstructionist approaches to meaning. The recognition of forms and intentionalism, which can and should be explained and interpreted through hermeneutical tools, is a moral imperative of the humanities. This is why the poststructuralists, unlike other postmodern critiques, never fully rejected the founding fathers of structuralism, Ferdinand de Saussure and Lévi-Strauss. I maintain that this dualism contributed to the development of a neostructuralist critique. See David Walton, *Doing Cultural Theory* (London: Sage, 2012); Johann Michel, *Ricoeur and the Post-Structuralists: Bourdieu, Derrida, Deleuze, Foucault, Castoriadis*, trans. Scott Davidson (London: Rowman & Littlefield, 2014); and Stephen D. Moore, *The Bible in Theory: Critical and Postcritical Essays*, RBS 57 (Atlanta: Society of Biblical Literature, 2010).

[4] Naphtali S. Meshel, *The "Grammar" of Sacrifice: A Generativist Study of the Israelite Sacrificial System in the Priestly Writings, with a Grammar of Σ* (Oxford: Oxford University Press, 2014).

structuralism.⁵ Meshel faults him, however, along with other structuralists, for applying his method with more vigor than rigor.

> In structural linguistics, clear criteria have been developed to identify elementary units of sound and meaning. By contrast, Lévi-Strauss's conception of "elementary units" and their combinations within non-linguistic semiotic systems, so central to his writings, is at times too vague to be verifiable or conducive to further investigation.⁶

In defense of Lévi-Strauss, Seth Kunin maintains the analogical character of anthropological structuralism in contrast to structural linguistics. Kunin, of course, is not responding to Meshel, since his book was published two decades prior, but to a similar critique.

> It should be emphasized that this is an analogy. It is not the direct application of structural linguistic methodologies to cultural structure. This mistake is made by Turner (1977) when he criticizes Lévi-Strauss for not sticking to the structural linguistic line.⁷

The function of the word *analogy* is of interest in this context. While in any field "analogy" does not denote identity (i.e., exact similarity),⁸ it is more likely to be used in a loose idiomatic meaning of affinity in the humanities than in mathematics, for example. Lévi-Strauss's own thought flowed between his attraction to mathematical formulae and his equal fascination with more fluid systems of symbolism.⁹ This ebb and flow can be seen as a flaw, but it is also a striking feature of his methodology, which tends toward binary paradigms.¹⁰ His scientific "quest for the

---

⁵ Ibid, 11.

⁶ Ibid, 12.

⁷ Seth Daniel Kunin, *The Logic of Incest: A Structuralist Analysis of Hebrew Mythology*, JSOTSup 185 (Sheffield: Sheffield Academic, 1995), 19. The critique Kunin is referring to is an article by Terence S. Turner, "Narrative Structure and Mythopoesis: A Critique and Reformulation of Structuralist Concepts of Myth, Narrative and Poetics," *Arethusa* 10 (1977): 103–63.

⁸ See likewise on the topic of comparison the helpful comments by Smith, *To Take Place*, 13–14.

⁹ See his introductory comments on the relation of myth and science in Lévi-Strauss, *Myth and Meaning*, Massey Lectures 1977 (London: Routledge & Kegan Paul, 1978; repr., New York: Schocken, 1995), 5–14.

¹⁰ For the significance of binary models in Lévi-Strauss's work, see the following of his works: *The Savage Mind*, Nature of Human Society (Chicago: University of Chicago Press, 1966), 135–48, 217–22; *The Raw and the Cooked*, trans. John Weightman and Doreen Weightman (New York: Harper & Row, 1969), 147–83; *Anthropology and Myth: Lectures, 1951–1982*, trans. Roy Willis (Oxford: Blackwell, 1987), 39–49, 197–99, 211–16; as well as his special attention to twins, in *Savage Mind*, 189–90; *Raw and the Cooked*, 171–73, 332–33; *Anthropology and Myth*, 59–63; and *Myth and Meaning*, 28–32. This binary paradigm has its roots in Hegelian dialectics, whose influence is most evident in Lévi-Strauss, *Structural Anthropology*, trans. Claire Jacobson and Brooke Grundfest Schoepf (New York: Basic Books, 1963), 159–63.

invariant," as he summarized his view of structuralism,[11] anticipates its erratic counterpart. But it is precisely the conflicted manner in which Lévi-Strauss adheres to the mathematical element of his methodology that makes it all the more important to note his legacy.[12] His insistence on binary paradigms is crucial for Meshel's grammar of sacrifice, in which the zoological classification of the Priestly author in the Pentateuch "consistently follows a multi-level binary pattern."[13] In this way, Meshel not only successfully applies a major Lévi-Straussian theme to the study of sacrifice but, more importantly, draws a clear connection between myth and ritual in ancient Israel.[14] In suggesting a similarity between the two modes of operation, Meshel differs from those who saw in the biblical sacrificial system a fossilized, legalist religion devoid of the enchantment of the primordial myths but also rejects those who seek to find in the Priestly writings an elevated abstract religion that transcends the primordial myths.[15] A more accurate appraisal should seek the hidden connections and the shared culture between narrative and performance, or myth and ritual.[16]

This tension between Lévi-Strauss's aspirations of mathematical precision and his tendency toward a poetic analysis will resound throughout this study.[17] As

[11] Lévi-Strauss, *Myth and Meaning*, 8.

[12] Clifford Geertz similarly observes, concerning Lévi-Strauss, that "no anthropologist has been more insistent on the fact that the practice of his profession has consisted of a personal quest, driven by a personal vision, and directed toward a personal salvation.... On the other hand, no anthropologist has made greater claims for ethnology as a positive science." See Geertz, *The Interpretation of Cultures: Selected Essays* (New York: Basic Books, 1973), 346.

[13] Meshel, *"Grammar" of Sacrifice*, 33.

[14] The connection between stories civilizations transmit and their lived practices has long been recognized. See helpful remarks in *The Essential Edmund Leach*, ed. Stephen Hugh-Jones and James Laidlaw, 2 vols. (New Haven: Yale University Press, 2000), 1:149–73; Walter Burkert, *Savage Energies: Lessons of Myth and Ritual in Ancient Greece*, trans. Peter Bing (Chicago: University of Chicago Press, 2001; German original, 1990), 64–84. For a critique of the Myth and Ritual school, see Robert Ackerman, *The Myth and Ritual School: J. G. Frazer and the Cambridge Ritualists*, Theorists of Myth (New York: Garland, 1991).

[15] For the critique of the legalist view, see Joseph Blenkinsopp's astute observations on Wellhausen and his legacy: Blenkinsopp, *Sage, Priest, Prophet: Religious and Intellectual Leadership in Ancient Israel*, LAI (Louisville: Westminster John Knox, 1995), 66–68. For the transcendental construction of Priestly law, see Israel Knohl, most emphatically in his *Many Faces of the Monotheistic Religion* [Hebrew] (Tel Aviv: Ministry of Defense, 1995), 9–21, but also in *The Sanctuary of Silence: The Priestly Torah and the Holiness School*, trans. Jackie Feldman and Peretz Rodman (Minneapolis: Fortress, 1995), 124–64.

[16] See, however, Christophe Lemardelé, "Note Concerning the Problem of Samson the Nazirite in the Biblical Studies," *SJOT* 30 (2016): 65–68. Lemardelé points out the danger of assuming such a connection and provides a helpful example from the case of Samson. His caution is good advice, so long as it does not deter scholars from grappling with the true connections that exist.

[17] It could therefore be said that Meshel, who is aware of Kunin and is responding to him in many ways, is reawakening the *Methodenstreit* as they apply to the humanities. On the original *Methodenstreit*, see Geoffrey M. Hodgson, *How Economics Forgot History: The Problem of*

demonstrated by what follows, any attempt to explain the mathematical structure of a narrative is ultimately aided by a literary analysis, which is more intuitive in character.

## II. Different Reflections: The Inversion Principle and the Mirror Narrative

In his study *Structural Anthropology*, Lévi-Strauss qualifies his mathematical analysis of myth by arguing that there is a clear distinction between the study of myth and language. "There is very good reason," he writes, "why myth cannot simply be treated as language if its specific problems are to be solved." Yet he still strives to do so, when he argues that "to invite the mythologist to compare his precarious situation with that of the linguist in the prescientific stage is not enough."[18] Although he goes on to elaborate on the pitfalls of such comparisons, he opens by stating its insufficiency. His desire is to equate and eventually elevate the status of myth studies so that it is even more precise than linguistics, comparable with natural sciences.

What follows is an ardent call for the scientific study of myth accompanied by specific examples and tools. The highlight of Lévi-Strauss's appeal may be found in his insistence that the meaning of myth is relational rather than symbolic. For that reason, the study of myth should focus not on isolated elements but on combinations of elements.[19] This approach contrasts with Mircea Eliade's methodology. Although Eliade is never mentioned by name, it would not be surprising to find that Lévi-Strauss reckons him among the "amateurs" who have infiltrated the study of religion as it had been abandoned by anthropologists.[20]

Lévi-Strauss presents the relation between the various elements of myth as a mathematical equation which, he acknowledges, will still need "to be refined in the future":[21]

---

*Historical Specificity in Social Science*, Economics as Social Theory 17 (London: Routledge, 2002), 75–134. For its implication for religious studies, see Luigi Berzano, "Research Methodology between Descriptive and Hermeneutic Interests," *Annual Review of the Sociology of Religion* 3 (2012): 69–89; and Anthony J. Blasi, *Sociology of Religion in America: A History of a Secular Fascination with Religion*, SHR 145 (Leiden: Brill, 2014), 20–26.

[18] Lévi-Strauss, *Structural Anthropology*, 209 (this chapter in the book was previously published as an article: "The Structural Study of Myth," *Journal of American Folklore* 68 [1955]: 428–44).

[19] Lévi-Strauss, *Structural Anthropology*, 210–11.

[20] Ibid, 206. Their diverging methodology is especially apparent in Eliade's works *The Myth of the Eternal Return*, trans. Willard R. Trask (New York: Pantheon, 1954); *Patterns in Comparative Religion*, trans. Rosemary Sheed (Lincoln: University of Nebraska Press, 1958); and *Images and Symbols: Studies in Religious Symbolism*, trans. Philip Mairet (London: Harvill, 1961).

[21] Lévi-Strauss, *Structural Anthropology*, 228. As Alan Dundes notes, this is not the only attempt to formulate patterns of folklore in mathematical terms, although it is distinct for being

$$F_x(a) : F_y(b) \simeq F_x(b) : F_{a-1}(y)$$

This formula is intended to represent not only the structure of any given myth but also the transposition of paradigms as myths travel from one culture to another. The *a* in the formula signifies a term; the *a-1* is not a lesser degree of that term but rather its opposite; *x* and *y* are functions. This formula is what I call Lévi-Strauss's "inversion principle." It claims that if a certain element is omitted in one version of a myth, its counterpart will resurface in an inverted function. Thus, function *x* relates to term *a* in the original form. Its omission will lead *a-1* to function with *y*, the relation between functions *x* and *y* being equivalent to term *b* in both versions of the myth. Pierre Maranda and Elli-Kaija Köngäs Maranda note that the cause for the change "is always the sociological context."[22] Yet, in their own attempt to verify the formula empirically, they asserted that, while there is indeed a distinction between content, structure, and style, a structural study can never describe a folkloristic item exhaustively.[23]

The opacity of this description has confounded many, leading some to dismiss it entirely and others to fault Lévi-Strauss for neither explaining it more clearly nor adhering to it strictly.[24] The problems might be elucidated by the simple chart that Lévi-Strauss provides in the book, comparing the North American Zuni emergence tale with the European Cinderella:[25]

|  | EUROPE | AMERICA |
|---|---|---|
| *Sex* | female | male |
| *Family Status* | double family (remarried father) | no family (orphan) |
| *Appearance* | pretty girl | ugly boy |
| *Sentimental Status* | nobody likes her | unrequited love for girl |
| *Transformation* | luxuriously clothed with supernatural help | stripped of ugliness with supernatural help |

---

"totally algebraic" ("Binary Opposition in Myth: The Propp/Lévi-Strauss Debate in Retrospect," *Western Folklore* 56 [1997]: 39–50, here 40). See also *Structural Analysis of Oral Tradition*, ed. Pierre Maranda and Elli Köngäs Maranda, Universitiy of Pennsylvania Publications in Folklore and Folklife 3 (Philadelphia: University of Pennsylvania Press, 1971), ix–xxxiv.

[22] Pierre Maranda and Elli Köngäs Maranda, "Introduction" in Maranda and Maranda, *Structural Analysis of Oral Tradition*, ix–xxiv, here xiii; and see another illustrative table there.

[23] Elli-Kaija Köngäs [Maranda] and Pierre Maranda, "Structural Models in Folklore," *Midwest Folklore* 12 (1962): 133–92, here 183. See also 137–39 for further mathematical analysis of the formula.

[24] See the survey of views and criticism in Mark S. Mosko, "The Canonic Formula of Myth and Nonmyth," *American Ethnologist* 18 (1991): 126–51; Maranda and Maranda, *Structural Analysis of Oral Tradition*, esp. 81–121.

[25] Lévi-Strauss, *Structural Anthropology*, 226.

The chart illuminates the meaning of the formula: the inversions are apparent between the two tales, as are the parallels between them. Yet the difficulty of the formula's interpretation, and hence its application, will continue to be a stumbling block that prevents a perfect implementation.

Similar to Lévi-Strauss's delineation of his inversion principle, Yair Zakovitch proposed the term "mirror narrative" in the 1980s to describe a deliberate connection between two biblical stories.[26] The mirror narrative is dependent on an earlier narrative and is intended to draw parallels between two protagonists. Zakovitch argues that in each of these pairs, a variant between the two narratives discloses the purpose of the parallelism. For instance, by fashioning a protagonist along the lines of a familiar story, the author seeks to highlight a positive or negative assessment of the protagonist's actions.[27]

The decisive difference between Lévi-Strauss's inversion principle and Zakovitch's mirror narrative is the issue of intentionalism. Lévi-Strauss unequivocally stresses the lack of authorial intent in the creation of myth in general, and all the more so in the transposition of elements through the inversion principle. The self-driven nature of the process suggested to Levi-Strauss that "myths get thought in man unbeknownst to him."[28] Zakovitch, on the contrary, argues that each mirror narrative reflects a conscious authorial intent to fashion a story according to a model familiar to an author and its anticipated audience. The similarities and the differences between the two stories result from a carefully calculated and crafted creative process.

With these distinctions and two types of inversions in mind, I proceed to examine some biblical myths, demonstrating the various ways the inversion principle operates in their creation and reception.

---

[26] The term in Hebrew is סיפור בבואה. Zakovitch seems to prefer "reflection story" as the English rendition of his term, but the manifold meanings of "reflection" may lead to an ambiguity that does not exist in the Hebrew term. To avoid confusion, I consistently translate it according to my preference.

[27] Perhaps the earliest example of this in Zakovitch's work is his comparison of Moses and Elijah in his article "A Still Small Voice: Form and Content in 1 Ki 19" [Hebrew], *Tarbiz* 51 (1982): 329–46. In this article Zakovitch had not yet coined the term *mirror narrative,* nor in a following study on the binding of Isaac and the death of Absalom, "More on the Ram Caught in the Thicket" [Hebrew], *Tarbiz* 52 (1982): 143–44. He first presented the term in "Mirror Narrative: Another Dimension for the Valuation of Characters in Biblical Narrative" [Hebrew], *Tarbiz* 54 (1985): 165–76, and further explored it in his book *Through the Looking Glass: Mirror Narratives in the Bible* [Hebrew] (Tel Aviv: Hakibbutz Hameuchad, 1995). See also Zakovitch, *An Introduction to Inner-Biblical Interpretation* [Hebrew] (Even Yehuda: Reches, 1992), 42–49. For an English introduction, see his chapter "Inner-Biblical Interpretation," in *Reading Genesis: Ten Methods,* ed. Ronald S. Hendel (Cambridge: Cambridge University Press, 2010), 92–118.

[28] Lévi-Strauss, *Myth and Meaning,* 3; cf. *Raw and the Cooked,* 10–26.

## III. Some Examples

### A. Sexual Transgressions and Cataclysms

It might be helpful to begin with a case Zakovitch describes as a mirror narrative, although the markers of the Lévi-Straussian inversion principle are powerfully present. The two components of the mirror narrative are the story of the flood (Gen 6–9) and the destruction of Sodom and Gomorrah (Gen 19). As Zakovitch notes, each of these stories involves sexual transgressions such as homosexuality and incest, and each involves massive destruction by water (Gen 6–9) or fire (Gen 19).[29] Like sexual intercourse, water and fire are essential for human existence. In addition to their element of necessity, all three can serve as sources of sensual pleasure beyond mere survival (e.g., fire might be crucial for survival on especially cold nights, but its use for cooking is not imperative for subsistence). The two stories then imply that, like water and fire, sex has a dangerous and destructive aspect to it, for all its indispensable qualities. The parallels between the structure of the two narratives are quite striking: preceding the destruction there is an initiation of sexual relations between humans and angels (or other heavenly beings, according to Gen 6:1–4), presumably illicit.[30] Following the flood there is an

---

[29] Zakovitch, *Through the Looking Glass*, 48–49. For an English version, see Avigdor Shinan and Yair Zakovitch, *From Gods to God: How the Bible Debunked, Suppressed, or Changed Ancient Myths and Legends*, trans. Valerie Zakovitch (Lincoln: University of Nebraska Press, 2012), 131–34. While the English book's subtitle may have been chosen to generate curiosity and an aura of secrecy, in the context of this study, it is significant that the authors consider the biblical text as distinct from myth, a point I challenge specifically in relation to these two destruction narratives. Contrast Michael Fishbane's title, *Biblical Myth and Rabbinic Mythmaking* (Oxford: Oxford University Press, 2003). On the problem of defining biblical narratives as myth, see Ballentine, *Conflict Myth*, 8–13; and Hans J. L. Jensen, "The Bible Is (Also) a Myth: Lévi-Strauss, Girard, and the Story of Joseph," *Contagion* 14 (2007): 39–57.

[30] For the identification of "sons of God" as angels and the problems with this identification, see Ronald S. Hendel, "The Nephilim Were on the Earth: Genesis 6:1–4 and Its Ancient Near Eastern Context," in *The Fall of the Angels*, ed. Christoph Auffarth and Loren T. Stuckenbruck, TBN 6 (Leiden: Brill, 2004), 11–34; and Annette Yoshiko Reed, *Fallen Angels and the History of Judaism and Christianity: The Reception of Enochic Literature* (Cambridge: Cambridge University Press, 2005), 116–18.

The idea that sexual intercourse between humans and angels would be illicit is derived mainly from the consequential flood, rendering this argument slightly tautological, but there are other reasons to suggest that this would be the case, such as the taboo against mixing species (Lev 19:19, Deut 22:9–11) and further Second Temple traditions. For instance, the tradition that Cain was conceived by intraspecies intercourse supports the idea that mixing species results in evil. See further in Aryeh Amihay and Daniel A. Machiela, "Traditions of the Birth of Noah," in *Noah and His Book(s)*, ed. Michael E. Stone, Aryeh Amihay, and Vered Hillel, EJL 28 (Atlanta: Society of Biblical Literature, 2010), 53–69, here 55–57.

incestuous scene involving wine. The inversion between the two narratives is spotlighted by a classic pair of opposites for the form of destruction: water and fire. This inversion is marked by a second inversion of locality. The flood is described as universal, destroying the whole world, whereas Sodom and Gomorrah is a local destruction. This spatial aspect corresponds remarkably to the natural elements: through lakes, streams, wells, rain, and the Mediterranean, water is experienced as ubiquitous. Indeed, it is thought to encompass the whole world.[31] Fire, on the other hand, is local and temporary, often sparked and maintained by humans, rarely coming from the sky, never surrounding the earth. For the inversion principle to be complete according to Lévi-Strauss's formula, an element missing in one place of the narrative needs to appear in a corresponding section. This happens in two, or possibly three elements of the scenes of sexual intercourse. In the preceding narrative of the flood the intraspecies intercourse is heterosexual, consummated, and leads to conception and birth. The intercourse that precedes the destruction in Sodom is homosexual and not consummated—on both counts it cannot lead to conception and birth. In both narratives, the destruction is followed by an incestuous scene with a drunken father,[32] in which these elements are correspondingly inverted: the heterosexual intraspecies encounter that preceded the flood is followed by an incestuous homosexual scene. The question of its consummation remains ambiguous, but in any case, it cannot and does not lead to conception and birth. The nonconsummated homosexual intraspecies sex scene in Sodom, on the other hand, is followed by a heterosexual incestuous consummation, resulting in conception and birth.

The following chart summarizes the parallels and the inversion:

---

[31] For a helpful visual portrayal of this worldview, see Alan P. Dickin, *On a Faraway Day: A New View of Genesis in Ancient Mesopotamia* (Columbus, GA: Brentwood Christian Press, 2002), 122. For discussion and analysis, see Wayne Horowitz, *Mesopotamian Cosmic Geography*, MC 8 (Winona Lake, IN: Eisenbrauns, 1998); William P. Brown, *The Seven Pillars of Creation: The Bible, Science, and the Ecology of Wonder* (Oxford: Oxford University Press, 2010).

[32] I am using the ambiguous term *incestuous scene* rather than describing it as intercourse in order to reflect the ambiguity of what was done to Noah. See David M. Goldenberg, "What Did Ham Do to Noah?," in *"The Words of a Wise Man's Mouth Are Gracious" (Qoh 10,12): Festschrift for Günter Stemberger on the Occasion of His 65th Birthday*, ed. Mauro Perani, SJ 32 (Berlin: de Gruyter, 2005), 257–65; John Sietze Bergsma and Scott Walker Hahn, "Noah's Nakedness and the Curse on Canaan (Genesis 9:20–27)," *JBL* 124 (2005): 25–40, https://doi.org/10.2307/30040989; Albert I. Baumgarten, "Myth and Midrash: Genesis 9:20–29," in *Christianity, Judaism and Other Greco-Roman Cults: Studies for Morton Smith at Sixty*, ed. Jacob Neusner, 4 vols., SJLA 12 (Leiden: Brill, 1975), 3:55–71; Brad Embry, "The 'Naked Narrative' from Noah to Leviticus: Reassessing Voyeurism in the Account of Noah's Nakedness in Genesis 9.22–24," *JSOT* 35 (2011): 417–33; Aryeh Amihay, "Noah in Rabbinic Literature," in Stone, Amihay, and Hillel, *Noah and His Book(s)*, 193–214, here 212–14.

|  | Genesis 6–9 | Genesis 19 |
|---|---|---|
|  | *Prior to Destruction* | |
| Illicit (?) relations between humans and angels | Initiated by the sons of God, heterosexual, consummated, leads to birth (Gen 6:1–4) | Initiated by the Sodomites, homosexual, not consummated (Gen 19:4–9) |
|  | *Destruction* | |
| Type of destruction | By water, universal (Gen 7:18–23) | By fire and sulfur, local (Gen 19:24–25) |
|  | *After the Destruction* | |
| Incest perpetrated on the surviving drunken father | Initiated by the son, homosexual, consummated (?), does not lead to birth (Gen 9:20–24) | Initiated by the daughters, heterosexual, consummated, leads to birth (Gen 19:30–38) |

The function of Lévi-Strauss's inversion principle between these two stories accords with their characterization as myth in their employment of supernatural elements; their multiple etiological purposes; and their primeval amalgamation of sex, violence, and family. Furthermore, each of these myths constitutes the foundation for a religious and social practice in ancient Israel. The story of Lot's daughters, which results in the birth of Ammon and Moab, accounts for the Israelite enmity toward these nations and the explicit prohibition against their admission to the Lord's assembly (Deut 23:4).[33] The scene of Noah's drunkenness results in the curse of Canaan, echoing numerous injunctions against mingling and following the ways of the Canaanites (Gen 28:1, 6, 8; Lev 18:3;[34] Deut 7:1–6; Ezek 16:2–5; Ezra 9:1–2). In short, Canaan's curse has the parallel implication in regard to the Ammonites and the Moabites that these nations are somehow defiled at their core.

Thus, these myths convey a tacit meaning made explicit in law, proving once more a direct connection between myth and practice in ancient Israel. They evoke the dangers of intermarriage by associating interspecies intercourse with ensuing

---

[33] This despite the rationale provided in the following verses (Deut 23:5–6). Note the proximity of this prohibition to various sexual transgressions (preceded by the ban on mixed species in Deut 22:9–11!) and especially the taboo of the father in Deut 23:1. On the inner logic of the order of laws in Deuteronomy, see Jack R. Lundbom, *Deuteronomy: A Commentary* (Grand Rapids: Eerdmans, 2013), 416–22, 621–25.

[34] On the comparison of Egypt and Canaan in this verse, see Marc Vervenne's claim that Egypt also is implicated in Noah's curse because Egypt was believed to have descended from Ham (Gen 10:6; cf. Pss 78:51; 105:23) ("What Shall We Do with a Drunken Sailor? A Critical Re-Examination of Genesis 9.20–27," *JSOT* 68 [1995]: 33–55, here 53).

destruction, and the neighboring foreigners with the sexual transgressions of incest and homosexuality.[35] The specific function of each of these elements is inverted, attesting to the significance of the connections between them in each of the narratives. Finally, this analysis demonstrates once more that the primordial myths are not mere entertaining stories of pagans that predated the solidification of theology in ancient Israel. Rather, they preserve in multiple ways direct connections between law and narrative that demonstrate their centrality in the belief and customs recorded in the Hebrew Bible.

## B. Enoch, Noah, Utnapishtim

In addition to exploring the inversion principle in myths within the Hebrew Bible, one can examine the development of myth across distinct cultures separated by place or time. The myth of Noah and the flood (Gen 5:28–9:29) is a unique instance, in that it has parallels in Mesopotamian and Greco-Roman literature, as well as two discernible versions in the Pentateuch and references in the other two major sections of the Hebrew Bible. In addition, it is mentioned in the New Testament and in postbiblical literature, including the Judean Desert Scrolls, the Apocrypha and Pseudepigrapha, the church fathers, the Nag Hammadi library, and midrashic writings by the early rabbis.[36]

The origin of the biblical flood myth is found in Mesopotamia, and the closest parallel is the Gilgamesh epic, in which the flood hero, Utnapishtim, gains eternal life through his ordeal. In the context of Mesopotamian literature, the motif of eternal life is a development of the initial function of the myth. This myth served as an etiology for human mortality, which is evidenced also in the earlier version of the Atrahasis myth.[37] In Genesis, mortality is explained through the creation narrative and the story of the garden of Eden rather than through the flood story, which may serve as an account of the development of humanity and its division into different races.[38] Another similarity between flood and creation myths is found

---

[35] Kunin employs the structuralist method to trace the legacy of this aversion in rabbinic Judaism ("Israel and the Nations: A Structuralist Survey," *JSOT* 82 [1999]: 19–43; cf. Kunin, *Logic of Incest*, 192–95). My argument differs from Kunin, since he stresses the existence of positive views toward incest and endogamy; see, e.g., his critique of Michael P. Carroll ("Genesis Restructured," in *Anthropological Approaches to the Old Testament*, ed. Bernhard Lang [Philadelphia: Fortress, 1985], 127–35) in *Logic of Incest*, 167, which equally applies to me.

[36] See the essays in the following collections: Alan Dundes, ed., *The Flood Myth* (Berkeley: University of California Press, 1988); Florentino García Martínez and Gerard P. Luttikhuizen, eds., *Interpretations of the Flood*, TBN 1 (Leiden: Brill, 1998); and Stone, Amihay, and Hillel, *Noah and His Book(s)*. Another narrative that has a number of parallels is the creation narrative, but its similarities to Mesopotamian literature are not as striking as those of the flood myth.

[37] See Ellen van Wolde, *Words Become Worlds: Semantic Studies of Genesis 1–11*, BibInt 6 (Leiden: Brill, 1994), 190–96.

[38] For Noah as the beginning of humanity, see James C. VanderKam, "The Righteousness of

in the Sumerian version, where the flood concludes with vegetation sprouting up from the earth below, and Ziusudra, similar to Adam as the epitome of humanity, is described as the guardian of vegetation (see Gen 1:28–29; 2:15).[39]

Unlike Utnapishtim, Noah is not graced with immortality, but, curiously, his great-grandfather, Enoch, is. In the biblical text, Enoch and Noah are associated in several ways: through the phonic resemblance of their names; through their genealogy; and, perhaps most decisively, through the similar application of the phrase "to walk with God," its unusual form appearing only in relation to these two figures (Gen 5:22, 24; 6:9; cf. Gen 17:1). The argument for the similarity of their names merits some caution: both names in Hebrew share the two consonants of Noah's name (*nun* and *ḥet*). But the question of whether contemporaneous listeners would sense the homophony would depend on the pronunciation of these names in biblical times. The pun on Noah's name described in Gen 6:8 ("Noah [נח] found favor [חן] in the sight of the Lord"), however, inverts the consonants to the order of Enoch's name, which might plausibly suggest that an ancient audience would have been expected to recognize the homophony.

The argument based on genealogy might seem weak since most major biblical figures belong to a shared lineage, as demonstrated in the primordial history of Genesis. The significance lies not in the mere ancestry but in the order of the generations: Enoch is the seventh generation after Adam, and Noah is the tenth. Thus, both of them are situated in significant positions from the perspective of biblical numerology.[40] This affords them a sense of completion, providing a clue to Enoch's enigmatic ascent. In view of the similar phrase "to walk with God," an audience familiar with the Mesopotamian flood myth may have expected Noah to gain eternal life too.

Thus, the parallelism between Enoch and Noah seems to preserve a primordial memory of their being one and the same person. The omission of the reward

---

Noah," in *Ideal Figures in Ancient Judaism*, ed. John J. Collins and George W. E. Nickelsburg, SCS 12 (Chico, CA: Scholars Press, 1980), 13–32, here 16–21; Amihay and Machiela, "Traditions of the Birth of Noah," 64–66.

[39] See "The Deluge," *ANET*, 42–44, here 44. A new creation following the flood occurs also in the Greek and Latin sources, particularly in Ovid's account of Deucalion (*Metam.* 1.313–437). See Leonard Wooley, "Stories of the Creation and the Flood," in Dundes, *Flood Myth*, 89–99; Ed Noort, "The Stories of the Great Flood: Notes on Gen 6:5–9:17 in Its Context of the Ancient Near East," in García Martínez and Luttikhuizen, *Interpretations of the Flood*, 1–38.

[40] On typological numbers in the Bible, see G. R. Driver, "Sacred Numbers and Round Figures," in *Promise and Fulfilment: Essays Presented to Professor S. H. Hooke in Celebration of His Ninetieth Birthday, 21st January, 1964*, ed. F. F. Bruce (Edinburgh: T&T Clark, 1963), 62–90; Arvin S. Kapelrud, "The Number Seven in Ugaritic Texts," *VT* 18 (1968): 494–99; Gotthard G. G. Reinhold, ed., *Die Zahl Sieben im Alten Orient: Studien zur Zahlensymbolik in der Bibel und ihrer altorientalischen Umwelt / The Number Seven in the Ancient Near East: Studies on the Numerical Symbolism in the Bible and Its Ancient Near Eastern Environment* (Frankfurt am Main: Lang, 2008); Israel Knohl, *The Holy Name* [Hebrew] (Or Yehuda: Devir, 2012).

of eternal life from the flood hero resurfaced in another figure, that is, Enoch, of whom little was known apart from his immortality, now floating in isolation, devoid of context. The motif of eternal life was further replaced by a fall of Noah: rather than gain eternal life, he is debased in his drunkenness. The episode of drunkenness is independent of the flood myth, a point that led Samuel E. Lowenstamm to hypothesize a lost Canaanite myth concerning the first viticulturist conflated with the flood hero in the figure of Noah.[41] In the words of Albert Baumgarten, "Noah the drunken planter cannot come from a Mesopotamian source."[42] The lack of evidence for such a mythic viticulturist has not diminished the tenacity of this theory, propagated by the disjuncture of the two elements of Gen 6–9.

But Lévi-Strauss's inversion principle provides a more sensible explanation than the hypothesis that an unknown hero was attached to the flood hero for no apparent reason: the omission of the element of eternal life results in its inversion. Noah does not gain eternal life but suffers a deep sleep, like Gilgamesh.[43] The reward becomes a punishment, as he is further debased in his sleep, unlike the exalted Utnapishtim of the Gilgamesh epic. Whereas Utnapishtim dwells for the remainder of eternity in a distant and unreachable place, Noah is disrobed in his tent, easily accessible to his sons outside. The wise Utnapishtim to whom Gilgamesh travels to discover the mystery of eternal life is replaced by the unknowledgeable Noah, who gains knowledge only after the fact, when he awakens from his wine (Gen 9:24).

Moreover, the inversion principle has further implications for the flood hero: Noah's mortality remains and results in further debasement, while the element of eternal life that was split between Noah's figure and Enoch's results in a growing similarity between Enoch and Utnapishtim.[44] Second Temple literature shows an increased interest in Enoch and his enigmatic ascent, producing a multitude of

---

[41] Samuel E. Lowenstamm, "Flood," in *Enẓiklopedyah Mikra'it*, ed. Benjamin Mazar (Jerusalem: Bialik, 1970), 4:609–10.

[42] Baumgarten, "Myth and Midrash: Genesis 9:20–29," 58.

[43] I am indebted to Laura Feldt for this observation: Gilgamesh falls into a deep sleep after hearing Utnapishtim's story of the flood. This highlights the contrast between mortal humans and the immortal Utnapishtim, who ironically tells his wife, "behold this hero who seeks life! Sleep fans him like a mist" (lines 201–203). Jeffrey H. Tigay also notes the connections of Gilgamesh's sleep to death (*The Evolution of the Gilgamesh Epic* [Philadelphia: University of Pennsylvania Press, 1982], 5). When Gilgamesh awakes, he is unaware that he has slept for seven days, and the ignorance that comes with sleep is a further echo of the drunken Noah. For a mythical context of this sleep, see an illuminating comparison of Gilgamesh and Odysseus by Gerald K. Gresseth, "The Gilgamesh Epic and Homer," *CJ* 70 (1975): 1–18, here 9–10.

[44] Andrei A. Orlov, *The Enoch-Metatron Tradition*, TSAJ 107 (Tübingen: Mohr Siebeck, 2005), 23–85; see also James L. Kugel, who draws a parallel between the journeys of Enoch and Gilgamesh, in contrast to the two pairs I suggest here (*Traditions of the Bible: A Guide to the Bible as It Was at the Start of the Common Era* [Cambridge: Harvard University Press, 1998], 140).

texts, five of them compiled into a work that is now known as 1 Enoch, preserved fully only in Ethiopic, and further traditions preserved in Slavonic in 2 Enoch.[45] It appears from these texts that, by the third century BCE, Enoch was a well-established figure, while Noah's significance was still developing. First Enoch, however, preserves several important Noachic traditions.[46] In 1 En. 65:4–67:3, for example, there is a shift in the narrating voice, and Noah speaks in the first person. Noah is the one who realizes that destruction is near and seeks to save himself and humankind (65:3). Thus, he is elevated to equality with Enoch.[47] First Enoch 106–107 relates the story of Noah's miraculous birth, which leads his father, Lamech, to suspect that his son was conceived by an angel.[48] Lamech consults with his father, Methuselah, who seeks advice from his own father, Enoch, who dwells "at the ends of the earth" (1 En. 106:8). Enoch then reassures his son concerning Noah, foresees the flood and Noah's salvation, and tells him how to name the son. His dwelling and his knowledge liken him to the Mesopotamian flood hero, while the context of the narrative draws a further connection between Enoch and his great-grandson Noah. Both are deified in this text, Noah through his angelic appearance and Enoch through his immortality. The attribution of Noah's naming to Enoch (rather than his father, as reported in Gen 5:29) brings them even closer.

The inversion principle was effective for the tradition of Noah's drunkenness and also promoted the characterization of Enoch along the lines of Utnapishtim as the elliptical Enochic traditions of Genesis were elaborated. But since Enoch and Noah are the split tradition of the mythic Utnapishtim, the development of Enoch as an immortal sage reunited the two aspects of the myth by drawing greater

---

[45] See Gabriele Boccaccini and John J. Collins, eds., *The Early Enoch Literature*, JSJSup 121 (Leiden: Brill, 2007); George W. E. Nickelsburg, *1 Enoch 1: A Commentary on the Book of 1 Enoch, Chapters 1–36, 81–108*, Hermeneia (Minneapolis: Fortress, 2001); Nickelsburg and James C. VanderKam, *1 Enoch 2: A Commentary on the Book of 1 Enoch, Chapters 37–82*, Hermeneia (Minneapolis: Fortress, 2011); Andrei A. Orlov, *From Apocalypticism to Merkabah Mysticism: Studies in the Slavonic Pseudepigrapha*, JSJSup 114 (Leiden: Brill, 2007); Loren T. Stuckenbruck, *The Myth of Rebellious Angels: Studies in Second Temple Judaism and New Testament Texts*, WUNT 335 (Tübingen: Mohr Siebeck, 2014); see also the essays in Loren T. Stuckenbruck and Gabriele Boccaccini, eds., *Enoch and the Synoptic Gospels: Reminiscences, Allusions, Intertextuality*, EJL 44 (Atlanta: SBL Press, 2016).

[46] See Vered Hillel, "A Reconsideration of Charles's Designated 'Noah Interpolations' in 1 Enoch: 54:1–55:1; 60; 65:1–69:25," in Stone, Amihay, and Hillel, *Noah and His Book(s)*, 27–45; Siam Bhayro, "Noah's Library: Sources for 1 Enoch 6–11," *JSP* 15 (2006): 163–77; and Ralph Lee, "The Ethiopic 'Andəmta' Commentary on Ethiopic Enoch 2 (1 Enoch 6–9)," *JSP* 23 (2014): 179–200.

[47] On Noah's elevation of status in the Second Temple era, see further VanderKam, "Righteousness of Noah," 13–32. See also Devorah Dimant, "Noah in Early Jewish Literature," in *Biblical Figures outside the Bible*, ed. Michael E. Stone and Theodore A. Bergren (Harrisburg, PA: Trinity Press International, 1998), 123–50.

[48] See Amihay and Machiela, "Traditions of the Birth of Noah," 54–63

parallels between the two figures in an attempt to illuminate history through myth.[49] The omitted element of eternal life resurfaces with each retelling. The biblical Noah, who seemed closer to Gilgamesh toward the end of his narrative in Genesis, develops in Second Temple times into a messianic figure, sharing many features with Enoch.[50]

### C. Fiery Prophecy: Moses, Elijah, and Isaiah

The following example is solely within the realm of canonical Judaism, but its life span indicates its significance. A popular Jewish medieval legend about the youth of Moses, found in Exodus Rabbah, recounts a test that Moses had to undergo as an infant on account of his tendency to remove the crown from Pharaoh's head. To determine whether this was mere child's play or a portent of his will to power, Moses was presented with a bowl of gold and a bowl of burning coal; should he send the hand to the gold, his removal of the crown would be deemed meaningful and a threat to the throne.

> So they did so immediately, and he was about to send his hand to take the gold, but the angel Gabriel came and pushed away his hand, and took the coal and put his hand with the coal in his mouth, and his tongue was burned, and this is how he became heavy of speech. (Exod. Rab. 1:26; my translation)

The element of the removal of Pharaoh's crown appears already in Josephus's *Jewish Antiquities*, where Pharaoh places his crown on Moses's head playfully, only for Moses to reject it and cast it to the ground and trample on it. Josephus explicitly describes this action as an omen against the kingdom (οἰωνὸν ἐπὶ τῇ βασιλείᾳ φέρειν, *A.J.* 2.234). This comment alludes to a portent concerning the danger posed by a child to a ruling monarch. A similar motif is present in Matt 2:2, in which King Herod feels threatened after receiving a prophecy about the birth of Jesus.[51] Louis Feldman deemed it "unlikely that Josephus would have added messianic allusions

---

[49] For the role of the mythological traditions of Enoch and Noah in the construction of history in Second Temple literature, see Michael E. Stone, "The Axis of History at Qumran," in *Pseudepigraphic Perspectives: The Apocrypha and Pseudepigrapha in Light of the Dead Sea Scrolls*, ed. Michael E. Stone and Esther G. Chazon, STDJ 31 (Leiden: Brill, 1999), 133–49.

[50] Florentino García Martínez, *Qumran and Apocalyptic: Studies on the Aramaic Texts from Qumran*, STDJ 9 (Leiden: Brill, 1992), 1–44; Juhana Markus Saukkonen, "Selection, Election, and Rejection: Interpretation of Genesis in 4Q252," in *Northern Lights on the Dead Sea Scrolls: Proceedings of the Nordic Qumran Network 2003–2006*, ed. Anders Klostergaard Petersen et al., STDJ 80 (Leiden: Brill, 2009), 63–81; Jeremy S. Penner, "Is 4Q534–536 Really about Noah?," in Stone, Amihay, and Hillel, *Noah and His Book(s)*, 97–112.

[51] The Gospel of Matthew itself mimics the story of Moses's birth with the trope of a persecution of infants by a king (2:16). See Raymond E. Brown, *The Birth of the Messiah: A Commentary on the Infancy Narratives in Matthew and Luke*, new updated ed., AYBRL (New Haven: Yale University Press, 1999), 225–29.

to his narrative."[52] Yet the scene need not be messianic in a Christian sense. Moses's rejection of the crown placed on him could reflect an opposition to human monarchs, recognizing only the kingship of YHWH.[53] But whatever the explanation, the shared motifs between Josephus's narrative of Moses's infancy and Matthew's account of Jesus's infancy cannot be so readily dismissed.

In Josephus's account, Moses's denigration of the crown stirs a sacred scribe (ἱερογραμματεύς) to seek to kill Moses. Josephus, however, does not refer to the test involving coal and gold, which is not found prior to medieval times. In addition to its appearance in Exodus Rabbah, it is recounted in Sefer Hayashar and in a medieval biography of Moses.[54] The latter two versions place Balaam at the scene, who proposes to kill the child, seeing him as a fulfillment of a prior dream.[55] Balaam's proposal is countered by an angel disguised as an advisor to the king. In Exodus Rabbah, however, Balaam is absent and the test is proposed by Jethro.[56]

The image of a burning coal in the mouth evokes Isaiah's call scene (Isa 6:5–7). To YHWH's somewhat flippant question "Whom shall I send?"[57] Isaiah promptly replies, "Here I am [הנני], send me." The Mosaic elements of Isaiah's call are notable: fire appears only twice in prophetic call narratives, here and with Moses, in the

---

[52] Louis H. Feldman, *Josephus's Interpretation of the Bible*, HCS 27 (Berkeley: University of California Press, 1998), 282.

[53] Martin Buber, *Kingship of God* (New York: Harper & Row, 1967); Shawn W. Flynn, *YHWH Is King: The Development of Divine Kingship in Ancient Israel*, VTSup 159 (Leiden: Brill, 2013), esp. 1–32 and further bibliography there. The rabbis refer to the Torah as Moses's crown (ʾAbot R. Nat. B 48), thus emphasizing the supremacy of God's word over material goods and providing further explanation for why Moses would have no use for a crown.

[54] In the Venice print edition of Sefer Hayashar (1625), it appears on pp. 131b–132b. In the Paris print edition of Sefer Divrey Hayamim shel Moshe Rabenu (1628), it appears on pp. 4a–b. Tanḥuma Shemot 8 offers an account similar to Josephus's legend, although there Moses actively removes the crown from the Pharaoh, documenting the initial stage of the evolution of this legend. Feldman (*Josephus's Interpretation of the Bible*, 382) cites also Deut. Rab. 11:10, but the legend is found only in the print edition and is not included in Lieberman's edition, which suggests once more a later date. See Saul Lieberman, *Midrash Debarim Rabbah*, 3rd ed. (Jerusalem: Wahrmann, 1974), xxi–xxiii. In any case, even in the Vilna edition the story includes only the mention of the removal of the crown, not the test.

[55] Balaam's mention of a prior prophecy concerning a usurper is reminiscent of Josephus's account. For traditions concerning Balaam in Pharaoh's court, see Judith R. Baskin, *Pharaoh's Counsellors: Job, Jethro, and Balaam in Rabbinic and Patristic Tradition*, BJS 47 (Chico, CA: Scholars Press, 1983), 88; see also George H. van Kooten and Jacques van Ruiten, eds., *The Prestige of the Pagan Prophet Balaam in Judaism, Early Christianity and Islam*, TBN 11 (Leiden: Brill, 2008), 128, 149, 307.

[56] On Jethro as courtier to Pharaoh, see Baskin, *Pharaoh's Counsellors*, 54–55.

[57] On the formulation of this question, see Moshe Weinfeld, "Ancient Near Eastern Patterns in Prophetic Literature," *VT* 27 (1977): 178–95, here 179; and Mordecai M. Kaplan, "Isaiah 6:1–11," *JBL* 45 (1926): 251–59, https://doi.org/10.2307/3260080. Kaplan's admittedly more theological article nevertheless succeeds in elucidating the multiple layers of the question.

famous burning bush in Exod 3.[58] The seraphs' act of covering their eyes is reminiscent of Moses's covering his eyes as he approaches the burning bush, and their covered legs may be suggestive of YHWH's command to Moses to take off his shoes as a sign of the site's sanctity. In Isaiah's call, his mouth is purged by a burning coal (6:6–7) brought to him by a seraph, or fiery angel. But whereas in Exodus Moses shies away from the call until YHWH is incensed (Exod 4:14), in Isaiah YHWH requests a volunteer and Isaiah dutifully complies. The contrast is marked by the word הנני ("Here I am").[59] Whereas Moses uses it in response to YHWH calling out his name, merely affirming his presence (Exod 3:4), Isaiah uses it to denote his willingness to accept the mission, appending it with the request "send me" (Isa 6:8), as opposed to Moses's request "send someone else" (Exod 4:13).[60]

The connection between the scenes prompted the incorporation of the burning coal into Moses's legendary biography. This exegetical maneuver almost betrays a desire to have Moses respond in the burning bush scene in the manner Isaiah responded in the heavenly court. If Isaiah was given a coal in his mouth as an adult as part of his call, Moses receives one as a child, long before his encounter with YHWH. The differences continue: Isaiah receives the coal from an angel in order to be cleansed,[61] while in the legend of Moses's infancy, he is compelled by an angel

---

[58] On the call narratives, see the classic study by Norman C. Habel, "The Form and Significance of the Call Narratives," *ZAW* 77 (1965): 297–323; and critique by Hava Shalom-Guy, "The Call Narratives of Gideon and Moses: Literary Convention or More?," *JHebS* 11 (2011): http://www.jhsonline.org/Articles/article_158.pdf, as well as Elizabeth R. Hayes, "The Role of Visionary Experiences for Establishing Prophetic Authority in Isaiah, Jeremiah, and Ezekiel: Same, Similar, or Different?," in *"I Lifted My Eyes and Saw": Reading Dream and Vision Reports in the Hebrew Bible*, ed. Elizabeth R. Hayes and Lena-Sofia Tiemeyer, LHBOTS 584 (London: Bloomsbury T&T Clark, 2014), 59–70; Jeffrey Stackert, *A Prophet Like Moses: Prophecy, Law, and Israelite Religion* (Oxford: Oxford University Press, 2014), 55–56. See also Johannes Lindblom, *Prophecy in Ancient Israel* (Oxford: Blackwell, 1962), 47–65.

[59] It is perhaps a telling sign that midrashic literature associates Moses's הנני not with Isaiah's utterance of the word but rather with Abraham's in Gen 22:1 (Gen. Rab. 55:1; Exod. Rab. 2:6; Tanḥ. Shemot 16). Even the thirteenth-century midrash Yalkut Shimoni, which tends to be exhaustive and indeed expounds not only on Abraham's and Moses's utterances (§96) but also on Samuel's (§750; 1 Samuel §111) and Jeremiah (Psalms §831), fails to mention Isaiah's הנני.

[60] On the difficulties of this phrase, see William H. C. Propp, *Exodus 1–18: A New Translation with Introduction and Commentary*, AB 2 (New York: Doubleday, 1999), 212–13; Robert Alter, *The Five Books of Moses: A Translation with Commentary* (New York: Norton, 2004), 327. The rabbis go so far as to cite Moses's hesitation in Exod 4:13 as one of the reasons he did not enter the land of Israel (Mek. Shimon bar Yohai 3:8, 6:2; Lev. Rab. 11:6).

[61] This is a curious detail in the context of biblical literature, where purification is usually performed by water or blood, depending on the type of impurity. See Jonathan Klawans, *Impurity and Sin in Ancient Judaism* (Oxford: Oxford University Press, 2000), 1–42. Neither moral nor ritual impurity, however, applies to the lips in the way Isaiah seems to fear. Victor Hurowitz outlined the Mesopotamian background for the idiom of the pure lips and the divine, rather than human, context for its interpretation ("Isaiah's Impure Lips and Their Purification in Light of Akkadian Sources," *HUCA* 60 [1989]: 39–89).

to take the coal by himself in order to save his life. The coal does not benefit Moses as it did Isaiah but instead inflicts him with a speech impediment. The inversion parallels the contrast of their response in their respective call narratives and serves as an excellent reflection of Levi-Strauss's inversion principle. First, it is never made explicit. Indeed, the silence of midrashic literature on this glaring similarity suggests that any impression of it was suppressed. Second, the operation of the inversion principle in the development of this legend is patently schematic. The similarity between the burning bush scene and Isaiah's visit to the heavenly court is what activated the principle, as if the burning coal placed on Isaiah's mouth was a remnant of the burning bush. The coal motif then resurfaces in an inverted function in a later embellishment of Moses's biography to compensate for the disturbing contrast between the biblical responses of Moses and Isaiah to the call, captured in Isaiah's formula: "Here I am, send me." YHWH's response can likewise be seen as another inversion: in Exod 3–4 YHWH sends Moses who is heavy of speech to speak in YHWH's name to the Israelites and to Pharaoh; in Isaiah, YHWH commands the prophet to make the people's ears heavy lest they understand the prophecy.[62]

Further connections could be drawn from this parallel, because the associations between Moses and Isaiah drawn from the motif of fire also evoke Elijah. Elijah's contrast with Moses at Horeb has been well noted, and Zakovitch rightfully cites it as an example of a mirror narrative.[63] In addition, Elijah's life ends when he ascends in a fiery chariot to the heavens (2 Kgs 2:11–12), connecting him with Isaiah's ascent and vision. Moses, Elijah, and Isaiah thus serve as a triad of fiery prophets suggesting perhaps three prototypes: Moses, who is injured by fire; Elijah, whose intense ferociousness costs him his position as a prophet (1 Kgs 19:16), although he remains unchanged; and Isaiah, who is purified through fire and whose prophetic career is initiated by it. This triad merits further consideration, but that would go beyond the scope of the inversion principle, which is the focus of this study.

### D. *The Sacrificial Son: Isaac, Jesus, Ishmael*

For the sake of a comprehensive consideration of the inversion principle, the mirror narrative, and the relationship between the two, I introduce here the final example of the sacrificial son.[64] The adaptation of this myth cannot be said to be developed "unbeknownst to man" (Lévi-Strauss's formulation). The story is not a

---

[62] Hurowitz concludes his essay by poignantly commenting, "woe to the prophet whose mission is thus, and woe to the people that such is their prophet!" ("Isaiah's Impure Lips," 80).

[63] See Zakovitch, "Still Small Voice," 329–46; Zakovitch, *Through the Looking Glass*, 42–44. For a discussion in English, see Shinan and Zakovitch, *From Gods to God*, 40–42, 183–88.

[64] I realized the relevance of this example for the study during a correspondence with my former student at Lawrence University Michelle E. Johnson. I am grateful for her insights.

"pure" myth in all of its stages, and at least in the ultimate stage that will be considered here—the Islamic tradition—its adaptation is quite likely an intentional choice, that is, the precise difference that distinguishes the approaches of Lévi-Strauss and Zakovitch. I introduce it here in order to consider the possibility that the inversion principle can play a role in the development of a narrative even when the inverted element is intentionally displaced.

Two methodological caveats are noted regarding this example. First, Qur'anic versions of biblical narratives cannot be considered to be exegesis since they do not refer directly to the written texts of those narratives. Biblical retellings are often provided in the Qur'an with later traditions such as midrash already incorporated into them, and it is likely that they were received orally in this manner.[65] For example, the same *sūrah* that relates the myth of the sacrificial son includes also Abraham's iconoclastic actions against his father's idols (Q 37:83–98; cf. 21:51–69, 29:16–35), a tale that is nowhere to be found in Genesis but occurs rather in postbiblical literature (Jub. 12:12–14; Gen. Rab. 38:29). This issue of chronology is not a problem for the present inquiry, since the inverted details are not dependent on awareness of the older text.

Second, the Qur'anic version of the myth of the sacrificial son responds to two separate traditions. The decision whether to consider the inverted elements as they relate to the Hebrew Bible or to the New Testament is an interpretive maneuver of its own. I will consider both options, presenting the complex journey of this myth into Islamic tradition.

The identity of the son Abraham is commanded to sacrifice shifts in the Islamic tradition from Isaac, as in Gen 22, to Ishmael. This shift does not occur in the Qur'an itself, which presents the story with an anonymous son. Since Ishmael is mentioned in various other instances in the Qur'an (e.g., Q 2:136, 140; 4:163; 14:39; 19:54), the silence about the identity of the son in the story of Abraham offers the opportunity to identify the son with Ishmael and to challenge a received tradition. This later shift in identity is not consequential for the consideration of the transposition of mythic elements. The Qur'anic account is as follows (Q aṣ-Ṣāffāt 37:99–111):[66]

---

[65] See David Joel Halperin, "The Hidden Made Manifest: Muslim Traditions and the 'Latent Content' of Biblical and Rabbinic Stories," in *Pomegranates and Golden Bells: Studies in Biblical, Jewish, and Near Eastern Ritual, Law, and Literature in Honor of Jacob Milgrom*, ed. David P. Wright, David Noel Freedman, and Avi Hurvitz (Winona Lake, IN: Eisenbrauns, 1995), 581–94; Bat-Sheva Garsiel, "Influence of Midrashic Bible Interpretations on the Quran" [Hebrew], *Beit Mikra* 50 (2005): 251–60; Carol Bakhos, "Abraham Visits Ishmael: A Revisit," *JSJ* 38 (2007): 553–80, here 555; Bakhos, *The Family of Abraham: Jewish, Christian, and Muslim Interpretations* (Cambridge: Harvard University Press, 2014); Gabriel Said Reynolds, *The Qur'ān and Its Biblical Subtext*, Routledge Studies in the Qur'an (London: Routledge, 2010), 37–38.

[66] Translation quoted from M. A. S. Abdel Haleem, *The Quran: A New Translation*, Oxford World Classics (Oxford: Oxford University Press, 2005), 287.

He [Abraham] said, "I will go to my Lord: He is sure to guide me. Lord, grant me a righteous son," so We gave him the good news that he would have a patient[67] son. When the boy was old enough to work with his father, Abraham said, "My son, I have seen myself sacrificing you in a dream. What do you think?" He said, "Father, do as you are commanded and, God willing, you will find me steadfast." When they had both submitted to God, and he had laid his son down on the side of his face, We called out to him, "Abraham, you have fulfilled the dream." This is how We reward those who do good—it was a test to prove [their true characters]—We ransomed his son with a momentous sacrifice, and We let him be praised by succeeding generations: "Peace be upon Abraham!" This is how We reward those who do good: truly he was one of Our faithful servants.

The differences from the Genesis narrative of the binding of Isaac are easily noted:[68] God does not command the sacrifice; rather, Abraham sees it in his dream. Abraham does not conceal his intent from his son, as he does in Gen 22:7–8. Instead, he discloses it and consults his son, allowing him willingly to be sacrificed. The theological benefits of these variations have also been widely recognized: unlike the Genesis account, the Qur'an's narrative does not explicitly attribute to God an immoral commandment, nor does it have God deceive Abraham or change his mind.[69] The Qur'anic version therefore avoids some of the theological difficulties present in the Genesis story. For this reason, it is possible that the

---

[67] The word is *ḥalīm*. This adjective usually appears in the Qur'an as an attribute of Allāh (e.g., 2:225, 235, 263; 3:155); it is twice said of Abraham (9:114; 11:75) and once of Shu'ayb, a Midianite prophet (11:87). In the two instances of Abraham, Abdel Haleem translates the word as "forbearing," although there is no direct context to suggest an ordeal there. It is conspicuous that he does not choose the same word here, which would better serve to foreshadow the voluntary sacrifice that follows.

[68] See Reuven Firestone, *Journeys in Holy Lands: The Evolution of the Abraham–Ishmael Legends in Islamic Exegesis* (Albany: State University of New York Press, 1990), 107–28; Firestone, "Comparative Studies in Bible and Qur'ān: A Fresh Look at Genesis 22 in Light of Sura 37," in *Judaism and Islam: Boundaries, Communications, and Interaction*, ed. Benjamin H. Hary, John L. Hayes, and Fred Astren, BSJS 27 (Leiden: Brill, 2000), 169–84; Shari A. Lowin, "Abraham in Islamic and Jewish Exegesis," *RC* 5.6 (2011): 224–35; Lutz Richter-Bernburg, "Göttliche gegen menschliche Gerechtigkeit: Abrahams Opferwilligkeit in der islamischen Tradition," in *Opfere deinen Sohn! Das 'Isaak-Opfer' in Judentum, Christentum und Islam*, ed. Bernhard Greiner, Bernd Janowski, and Hermann Lichtenberger (Tübingen: Francke, 2007), 243–55.

[69] I acknowledge that these claims are problematic for the Genesis account: God does not exactly lie to Abraham in the Genesis narrative. It is possible to claim that the command is truthful, although God does not intend Isaac to be sacrificed (either in the case that Abraham fails the test or in a successful case, in which God could have planned to stop Abraham in time, as described). This would also mean that God never intended to command something as abhorrent as human sacrifice. But the problem of the initial command and the deception inherent in the test remain. Evidently, this did not trouble the theological worldview of biblical authors; see J. J. M. Roberts, "Does God Lie? Divine Deceit as a Theological Problem in Israelite Prophetic Literature," in *Congress Volume: Jerusalem 1986*, ed. J. A. Emerton, VTSup 40 (Leiden: Brill, 1988), 211–20; R. W. L. Moberly, "Does God Lie to His Prophets? The Story of Micaiah Ben Imlah as a Test Case," *HTR* 96 (2003): 1–23.

Qurʾanic version was a direct adaptation of the biblical version. Some narrative difficulties remain, however. The Qurʾanic narrative does not explain why Abraham and his son would so readily deduce that the dream is a commandment to be obeyed. Furthermore, since at the conclusion the text is in agreement with Genesis that this was a test from God, the theological problem of God's involvement remains. While God did not explicitly command the sacrifice, his wish was shown in the dream. In short, the myth of the sacrificial son is inverted completely, thereby breaking with the inversion principle, which requires the transposition of a single element: the commandment does not come from God, and the son is not ignorant, but willing.

In this context it seems fruitful to compare this Qurʾanic narrative with the crucifixion narrative, the story where the son's death is not averted. The use of the biblical Akedah as a christological typology has been the center of a rich debate,[70] but the reception of the Akedah in Islamic tradition through a Christian lens is much more obfuscated. The similarity of the birth narrative of Jesus and that of the sacrificial son in the Qurʾan is quite striking. Following the Gospel of Luke, the Qurʾan intertwines the birth narratives of John the Baptist and Jesus. John and Isaac are both the result of a direct supplication to God (Luke 3:38; Q aṣ-Ṣāffāt 37:100). Zechariah, who is not only John's father but the custodian of Mary, prays for offspring, but notes that he is too old to father a child and his wife is barren (Luke 1:7, 18; Q al-Imran 3:40), recalling Abraham's and Sarah's doubts (Gen 17:17, 18:12) and anticipating Mary's own doubts about the virgin birth (Q al-Imran 3:47). The birth of Abraham's son is recounted using the root bšr (Q aṣ-Ṣāffāt 37:101), "bearing good news,"[71] the same root employed in relation to both the birth of Jesus (Q al-Imran 3:45) and that of Isaac (Q 11:71; 37:112).

The analogy drawn between Abraham's son and Jesus highlights the difference between them. Abraham's son faces the danger of sacrifice, but the Qurʾan is emphatic in rejecting two major Christian claims: it denies that Jesus was God's son,[72] while accepting the virgin birth (Q 3:49, 58–62; 4:171; 5:116–117), and it denies that Jesus was crucified (3:55; 4:157). In other words, unlike the unnamed

---

[70] See Jon D. Levenson, *The Death and Resurrection of the Beloved Son: The Transformation of Child Sacrifice in Judaism and Christianity* (New Haven: Yale University Press, 1993); Edward Kessler, *Bound by the Bible: Jews, Christians and the Sacrifice of Isaac* (Cambridge: Cambridge University Press, 2004); David W. Chapman, *Ancient Jewish and Christian Perceptions of Crucifixion*, WUNT 2/244 (Tübingen: Mohr Siebeck, 2008); Martha Himmelfarb, "The Ordeals of Abraham: Circumcision and the Aqedah in Origen, the Mekhilta, and Genesis Rabbah," *Hen* 30 (2008): 289–310.

[71] That this is the literal meaning of εὐαγγέλιον is of little consequence here, since this association would not be made in Arabic. The Qurʾan's reference to the gospel (ʾinjīl) is always as a proper noun, rather than to its etymology or meaning (e.g., Q 3:3, 48, 65; 5:46; 7:157; 9:111; 48:29; 57:27). Abdel Haleem's translation is inconsistent in its rendering of the root bšr as "good news" or any "news," even in the similar context of reports of forthcoming sons.

[72] Hence also the repeated reference to him as "Jesus, son of Mary" (Q 2:253; 3:45; 4:171; 5:110; 19:34).

Ishmael of *sūrah* 37, Jesus is neither a son (in a mythic sense) nor a sacrifice in the Qur'an's rendition of his life. It is precisely this denial that activates the Lévi-Straussian inversion principle. The element that was omitted in Islam's adaptation of a Christian myth, resurfaces in an inverted function in the retelling of Abraham's ordeal. The rejection of Jesus's crucifixion thus resulted in an intensified version of the Aqedah, in which the son voluntarily agrees to die, evocative of Jesus's volition for the sake of God, or the Father (John 18:11, 32).[73] The similar elements in their stories[74] prompted the reemergence of the omitted element of voluntary sacrifice specifically in this narrative of Abraham's son.

The case of the sacrificial son presents a composite process in which the inversion principle operated. The direct references in the Qur'an to the binding of Isaac and to Jesus are intentional—and even polemical—adaptations of inherited traditions. The differences between the Qur'anic versions and the biblical narratives serve theological and propagandistic purposes, in an attempt to unify a community around Muhammad and to present it with a coherent view of God.[75] Some differences, however, are also a result of oral transmission, and even confusion, as seen in the conflation of Miriam and Mary (Q Maryam 19:28). At the same time that these adaptations are being fashioned, myth continues to be generated "unbeknownst to man." The intentional omission results in its subconscious transposition in a way that also bears benefits for Muslim identity: as Christianity champions a selfless sacrifice in its myth, Islam can respond with a comparable myth of submission and sacrifice.

While Lévi-Strauss presented the principle as a structural necessity, making this development an inevitable result of the myth creation process, a neostructuralist

---

[73] The tradition of Jesus's final words (Matt 27:46, Mark 15:34; cf. Luke 23:46) suggests a different interpretation, but here I refer to the common Christian reception of the meaning of the crucifixion.

[74] In addition to the major similarities mentioned, of the birth and the sacrifice, two further elements associate Ishmael and Jesus: Ishmael's description as *ḥalīm*, or forbearing (Q aṣ-Ṣāffāt 37:101; see n. 67) casts him as one willing to suffer, similar to Jesus's image as a suffering servant. Second, the unfulfilled sacrifice is described as a test (Q aṣ-Ṣāffāt 37:106), an inversion of Jesus's claim against testing God (Matt 4:7, Luke 4:12; cf. Deut 6:16), which appears in the Qur'an (al Ma'idah 5:112–115), although interestingly in a context similar to Deuteronomy. Thus, the parallelism of Ishmael and Jesus jointly conveys a similar message: God can test humans, but they are forbidden to test God. See also the claim that "God is the best of schemers" (Q al-Imran 3:54).

[75] On the ecumenical nature of early Islam, see Guy G. Stroumsa, who considers the rise of Islam to constitute "the first real challenge to the belief in the ecumenical destiny of Christianity" (*The Making of the Abrahamic Religions in Late Antiquity*, Oxford Studies in the Abrahamic Religions [Oxford: Oxford University Press, 2015], esp. 139–58; quotation from 1); Fred M. Donner, *Muhammad and the Believers: At the Origins of Islam* (Cambridge: Belknap Press of Harvard University Press, 2010), 56–119. For a different view that stresses supersessionism rather than ecumenism, see Aaron W. Hughes, *Abrahamic Religions: On the Uses and Abuses of History* (Oxford: Oxford University Press, 2012), esp. 57–76.

approach should not ignore the Freudian aspects of this analysis.[76] The conflation of Isaac and Jesus in the unnamed sacrificial son is not only the structural reemergence of the omitted element but also a return of the repressed, as the denied sacrifice of the son demands to be heard. Sigmund Freud considered the myth of Jesus's sacrifice to be an essential response to the guilt for the original sin of killing the father,[77] describing the Christian grievance against the Jews quite vividly: "You will not *admit* that you murdered God.... We did the same thing, to be sure, but we have *admitted* it and since then we have been absolved."[78] The Muslim response to the Christians, then, would be: "By deifying the compensatory sacrifice for the murder of God, you have rendered yourselves guilty of deicide once more; we are willing to submit and offer a human sacrifice to God upon request, and thus he spares us."[79]

## IV. Conclusion

I considered four cases of the inversion principle. The first two concerned two elements of the flood narrative, one formerly identified by Zakovitch as an instance of mirror narratives. As I showed, however, there is little cause to maintain that the

---

[76] While his major writings are almost silent on Freud and the many points of contact between their methodologies, Lévi-Strauss does pay him homage in *Structural Anthropology*, but at the same time expresses hope that his methodology indicates the path that will allow the study of Shamanism "to elucidate obscure points of Freudian theory" (202). This sense of rivalry is evident also in Lévi-Strauss's discussion of Oedipus, where he argues that "not only Sophocles, but Freud himself, should be included among the recorded versions of the Oedipus myth" (217), thus casting Freud as primary literature rather than a fellow scholar. See also his critique of Freud in *The Elementary Structures of Kinship*, trans. James Harle Bell, John Richard von Sturmer, and Rodney Needham (Boston: Beacon, 1969), 490–92. For astute observations on the similar "fascination and weaknesses" of Freud and Lévi-Strauss and the parallels of myth and dream in their work, see Edmund Leach, *Claude Lévi-Strauss* (New York: Viking, 1974; repr., Chicago: University of Chicago Press, 1989), 57–62.

[77] Sigmund Freud, *Totem and Taboo: Some Points of Agreement between the Mental Lives of Savages and Neurotics,* with a biographical introduction by Peter Gay, trans. James Strachey (New York: Norton, 1989; orig., 1900), 125–200; Freud, *Moses and Monotheism: Three Essays*, corr. ed., trans. James Strachey, International Psycho-analytical Library 33 (London: Hogarth, 1974), 85–92.

[78] Freud, *Moses and Monotheism*, 90. In the original German, Freud distinguishes between the refusal to admit and the concession after the fact in a way that is not reflected in the translation (italics in the original): "Ihr wollt nicht *zugeben*, dass ihr Gott ... gemordet haben.... Wir haben freilich dasselbe getan, aber wir haben es *zugestanden* und wir sind seither entsühnt." See Sigmund Freud, *Der Mann Moses und die monotheistische Religion*, ed. Jan Assmann (1939; repr., Stuttgart: Reclam, 2010), 113.

[79] On the significance of the willingness to be sacrificed, see Bakhos, *Family of Abraham*, 190–213. For the Akedah as an exemplar of religious zeal, see Jane L. Kanarek, *Biblical Narrative and the Formation of Rabbinic Law* (Cambridge: Cambridge University Press, 2014), 31–66.

similarities between the flood and the destruction of Sodom and Gomorrah are deliberate, with the intent of casting one in light of the other. I argue that this is not a mirror narrative and does not accord with the excellent examples Zakovitch has provided in the cases of Absalom and the Aqedah, David and Jacob, and so forth. Furthermore, it does not follow the historical rationale of the mirror-narrative analysis, which necessitates an author who can assume readers familiar with the original stories.[80] This has been more successfully demonstrated in narratives from 1 and 2 Samuel echoing JE narratives from the Pentateuch.

I then proceeded to examine the transposition of the flood hero in three contexts: Mesopotamian mythology, the Hebrew Bible, and Second Temple literature. While the latter two are a continuum of the same civilization, ancient Israel and Hellenistic Judea are still distinct cultures separated by time. The omission of the flood hero's immortality in the transposition from Mesopotamian mythology to the Hebrew Bible resulted in the reemergence of the idea in two ways: first, through the association of Enoch with immortality (initially in the Hebrew Bible), and then in the parallelism of the figures of Enoch and Noah in Second Temple literature.

The third example traced the development of a legend about Moses that bears elements of Isaiah's call narrative. The development of this legend, from its early version in Josephus to its medieval retelling, discloses an uneasiness about Moses's initial response to his calling and seeks to correct this through Isaiah. But the introduction of the element of the burning coal from the Isaiah narrative becomes inverted and does not function in the same manner. This inversion does not serve the compensatory purpose of the legend and thus demonstrates the mechanism of the inversion principle.

Finally, I suggested that the myth of the sacrificial son in the Qur'an is the result of two factors: it is a cognizant adaptation of the Akedah narrative (although in no way a mirror narrative) and, at the same time, a subconscious evocation of the death of Jesus, prompted by the emphatic denial of his crucifixion, and a tradition that already associated Isaac with Jesus. This example illustrates how the inversion principle can play a role even in intentional adaptations.

These examples and the arguments that arise from them offer three possible avenues for further research. First, other pairs of mirror narratives should be

---

[80] Tod Linafelt has rightly corrected me on this, claiming that an author writing a sequence can assume that his audience will be familiar with its earlier elements and may even choose to draw such parallels for aesthetic value. This is true, but it is not the import of the mirror-narrative principle, which works best when an author of a completely new story relies on familiarity with an often-told tale. Furthermore, if the myths of Genesis initially developed as oral folklore, as Hermann Gunkel would have it, the similarities are better explained as the modus operandi of myth, rather than the stylization of a later author who compiled them (see Gunkel, *The Legends of Genesis*, trans. W. H. Carruth [Chicago: Open Court, 1901], 4–7, 88–133). It is crucial, then, that a case for a mirror narrative include a conspicuous use of language, which is an argument for stylization, while the inversion principle operates with symbols and elements rather than specific wording.

reconsidered in case they are better explained by the inversion principle, carefully distinguishing stylization and language from symbols and structures. This is especially the case in pairs of narratives that are more likely to have been composed around the same time. In Lévi-Strauss's own words, "the problem is: where does mythology end and where does history start?"[81] Second, and arising from the first, further myths should be considered for this principle. This is particularly true of the primordial history in Genesis 1–11. Devora Steinmetz has brilliantly demonstrated how the myths of Adam, Cain, and Noah are a repetition of the same narrative, citing no fewer than fifteen motifs shared by all three myths.[82] To these three one may add, though with a diminished number of similarities, the myth of the tower of Babel, which all include a construction, a fall, and a further development of human civilization. The parallel discussed above between the flood and Sodom shows that even outside the primordial pericope there are instances of myth duplication and repetition.[83]

In addition to exploring further the inversion principle in the mythic literature of the Hebrew Bible and distinguishing it from mirror narratives, I suggest that this principle should be sought even in cognizant adaptations. The implication of the final example is that these adaptations are not immune to subconscious operations of structural or psychoanalytic processes that interfere in the production of an adaptation. Thus, even clear cases of mirror narratives, like those mentioned above, may prove fruitful for this inquiry, as indicated through the connections of Moses, Elijah, and Isaiah.[84] This will certainly be the case for the reception and adaptation of myths across cultures.

---

[81] Lévi-Strauss, *Myth and Meaning*, 38.

[82] Devora Steinmetz, "Vineyard, Farm, and Garden: The Drunkenness of Noah in the Context of Primeval History," *JBL* 113 (1994): 193–207, here 197–98, https://doi.org/10.2307/3266510. Cf. Embry, "'Naked Narrative,'" 421–27.

[83] In her previous work, Steinmetz traced family patterns in the patriarchal narratives of Genesis, drawing crucial connections between them and the primordial myths; see *From Father to Son: Kinship, Conflict, and Continuity in Genesis*, Literary Currents in Biblical Interpretation (Louisville: Westminster John Knox, 1991). Despite the prominence of kinship in her study, her engagement with Lévi-Strauss is regrettably minimal. See Lévi-Strauss, *Elementary Structures of Kinship*; and Kunin, *Logic of Incest*, 19–48.

[84] Although the prophets are situated in the history of ancient Israel, and for the most part their narratives do not resemble the genre of the primordial myths in Genesis, some mythical elements do exist. See, for example, the structural analysis of prophetic call narratives in Diane M. Sharon, *Patterns of Destiny: Narrative Structures of Foundation and Doom in the Hebrew Bible* (Winona Lake, IN: Eisenbrauns, 2002), 200–202. I have also begun to consider whether the various retellings of Jeremiah's death (4 Bar. 9:21–31; Liv. Pro. 2:1; Apoc. Paul 49) are a further example of the inversion principle, with the figures of Moses and Jesus contributing to the legends about Jeremiah. See my forthcoming article, "The Stones and the Rock: Jewish and Christian Elements in *Vita Jeremiah*."

# SBL PRESS

## New and Recent Titles

### HASMONEAN REALITIES BEHIND EZRA, NEHEMIAH, AND CHRONICLES
Archaeological and Historical Perspectives
*Israel Finkelstein*
Paperback $32.95, 978-0-88414-307-9  Forthcoming, 2018  Code: 062637
Hardcover $47.95, 978-0-88414-308-6  E-book $32.95, 978-0-88414-309-3
Ancient Israel and Its Literature 34

### POVERTY, LAW, AND DIVINE JUSTICE IN PERSIAN AND HELLENISTIC JUDAH
*Johannes Unsok Ro*
Paperback $38.95, 978-1-62837-206-9   318 pages, 2018   Code 062635
Hardcover $53.95, 978-0-88414-286-7  E-book $38.95, 978-0-88414-285-0
Ancient Israel and Its Literature 32

### PERCHANCE TO DREAM
Dream Divination in the Bible and the Ancient Near East
*Esther J. Hamori and Jonathan Stökl, editors*
Digital open-access, 978-0-88414-287-4
https://www.sbl-site.org/publications/Books_ANEmonographs.aspx
Paperback $34.95, 978-1-62837-207-6   232 pages, 2018   Code 062824
Hardcover $49.95, 978-0-88414-288-1   Ancient Near East Monographs 21

### SUPPLEMENTATION AND THE STUDY OF THE HEBREW BIBLE
*Saul M. Olyan and Jacob L. Wright, editors*
Paperback $30.95, 978-1-946527-05-9   240 pages, 2018   Code 140361
Hardcover $45.95, 978-1-946527-07-3  E-book $30.95, 978-1-946527-06-6
Brown Judaic Studies 361

### INTERMEDIATE BIBLICAL HEBREW GRAMMAR
A Student's Guide to Phonology and Morphology
*Eric D. Reymond*
Paperback $44.95, 978-1-62837-189-5   354 pages, 2018   Code 060395
Hardcover $59.95, 978-0-88414-250-8  E-book $44.95, 978-0-88414-249-2
Resources for Biblical Study 89

SBL Press • P.O. Box 2243 • Williston, VT 05495-2243
Phone: 877-725-3334 (toll-free) or 802-864-6185 • Fax: 802-864-7626
Order online at www.sbl-site.org/publications

# Once Again: The *Yam Sûp* of the Exodus

PHILIP Y. YOO
philip.yoo@austin.utexas.edu
The University of Texas at Austin, Austin, TX 78712

The multiple descriptions of a body of water called *yam sûp* (ים סוף) in the Pentateuch present a confusing portrait of when the Israelites reach this body of water and what exactly happens there. In this article, I argue that the *yam sûp* in the Pentateuch is the literary product of multiple hands informed by different, and at times irreconcilable, notions of geography and historiography. In identifying the multiple depictions of the *yam sûp* of the exodus, I consider also the extent to which the redactor intervenes in the text.

## I. LOCATING THE *YAM SÛP*

After the Israelites depart from Egypt, they reach a body of water where they are threatened by the rapidly approaching Egyptian cavalry. YHWH intervenes by turning the waters of the sea against the Egyptian cavalry, and the Israelites escape. Upon closer inspection, however, the biblical texts contain irreconcilable tensions, among which is confusion about the precise geographical location of a sea that is called the *yam sûp* (ים סוף).[1] The *yam sûp* lies certainly somewhere between Egypt and Canaan, yet, depending on the biblical text under consideration, the Israelites crossed this sea *before* they entered the wilderness or *after* they crossed the wilderness.

What emerges from the biblical record is the placement of the *yam sûp* in two strikingly different locations, which has led to a variety of proposals for the precise location of the *yam sûp*.[2] Three biblical descriptions (Judg 11:16, 1 Kgs 9:26, MT

---

I would like to thank Jonathan Kaplan and the anonymous *JBL* reviewer for their insightful comments and suggestions toward improving this article.

[1] The Hebrew ים סוף is often translated into English as either "Sea of Reeds" (NJPS) or "Red Sea" (NRSV). As its meaning and origins are unclear, ים סוף will be retained in transliteration as *yam sûp* throughout this article. Unless otherwise stated, all biblical translations are mine.

[2] For comprehensive reviews of the scholarly literature on the *yam sûp*, see Hedwig Lamberty-Zielinski, *Das "Schilfmeer": Herkunft, Bedeutung und Funktion eines alttestamentlichen Exodusbegriffs*, BBB 78 (Frankfurt am Main: Hain, 1993), 1–31; Marc Vervenne, "The Lexeme סוף

581

Jer 49:21) that place the *yam sûp* nowhere near Egypt but rather on the other side of the wilderness and in close proximity to Edom have suggested an identification of the *yam sûp* with the present-day Gulf of Aqaba/Eilat.[3] This solution, however, does not cohere with other biblical texts. Graham I. Davies observes that, if the *yam sûp* is identified as the Gulf of Aqaba/Eilat, "it fails to give a plausible account of certain passages which imply that Yam Suf was near to Egypt."[4] Another suggestion is that the *yam sûp* of the exodus lies close to—if not within—Egypt proper and before the wilderness.[5] Although some critics maintain that the *yam sûp* is a marshy body of water attested in Egyptian sources,[6] the presumed relationship between *yam sûp* and *pɜ twfy* in Egyptian sources is not certain.[7]

---

(*sûph*) and the Phrase סוּף יָם (*yam sûph*)," in *Immigration and Emigration within the Ancient Near East: Festschrift E. Lipiński*, ed. Karel van Lerberghe and Antoon Schoors, OLA 65 (Leuven: Peeters, 1995), 403–29.

[3] See Jan Jozef Simons, *The Geographical and Topographical Texts of the Old Testament: A Concise Commentary in XXXII Chapters*, SFSMD 2 (Leiden: Brill, 1959), 255; Martin Noth, *Das vierte Buch Mose: Numeri*, ATD 7 (Göttingen: Vandenhoeck & Ruprecht, 1966), 97; Eng. trans., *Numbers: A Commentary*, OTL (Philadelphia: Westminster, 1968), 110; Nili Wazana, *All the Boundaries of the Land: The Promised Land in Biblical Thought in Light of the Ancient Near East* [Hebrew] (Jerusalem: Bialik Institute, 2007) 101, 104; Eng. trans. (Winona Lake, IN: Eisenbrauns, 2013), 103–4, 106.

[4] Graham I. Davies, *The Way of the Wilderness: A Geographical Study of the Wilderness Itineraries in the Old Testament*, SOTSMS 5 (Cambridge: Cambridge University Press, 1979), 71. For instance, YHWH drives locusts out of Egypt and into the *yam sûp* (Exod 10:19), but it is unlikely that the locusts were driven into a sea that lies approximately three hundred miles away from Egypt, that is, the Gulf of Aqaba/Eilat.

[5] See Exod 12:37; 13:18; 15:22; see also Josh 2:10; 24:6–7; Pss 106:7, 9; 136:13, 15–16; Neh 9:9, 19.

[6] In Exod 2:3, סוּף is a marsh on which reeds grow. See also Rashi on Exod 13:18. Suggested locations include a gulf along the northern delta of the Sinai Peninsula (Yohanan Aharoni, *Eretz Israel in Biblical Times: A Geographical History* [Hebrew], 2nd ed. [Jerusalem: Yad Yitshak Ben-Tsevi, 1987], 157; Eng., *The Land of the Bible: A Historical Geography*, 2nd ed. [London: Burns & Oates, 1979], 196); the easternmost border of Egypt proper (Zecharia Kallai, "The Patriarchal Boundaries, Canaan and the Land of Israel: Patterns and Application in Biblical Historiography," *IEJ* 47 [1997]: 69–82, here 74); an "end sea" from the noun *\*sôp* ("end, limit"), which is derived from Semitic root *\*sp* ("reach, arrive") (Maurice Capisarow, "The Ancient Egyptian, Greek, and Hebrew Concept of the Red Sea," *VT* 12 [1963]: 6–13; William A. Ward, "The Semitic Biconsonantal Root SP and the Common Origin of Egyptian ČWF and the Hebrew SÛP: 'Marsh[-Plant]',"  *VT* 24 [1974]: 339–49, esp. 343–46); the present-day Gulf of Suez (Ludwig Schmidt, *Das vierte Buch Mose: Numeri 10,11–36,13*, ATD 7.2 [Göttingen: Vandenhoeck & Ruprecht, 2004], 206; also in 1QapGen ar XXI, 18; see Joseph A. Fitzmyer, *The Genesis Apocryphon of Qumran Cave I [1Q20]: A Commentary*, 3rd ed., BibOr 18B [Rome: Pontifical Biblical Institute, 2004], 226); one of the Bitter Lakes (Umberto Cassuto, *A Commentary on the Book of Exodus*, trans. Israel Abrahams [Jerusalem: Magnes, 1967], 159; but note his comment on Exod 23:31, in which he understands "from the Sea of Reeds" [מִיַּם־סוּף] to mean "from Elath, which is by the Red Sea" [308]); or el-Ballah Lake (James K. Hoffmeier, *Ancient Israel in Sinai: The Evidence for the Authenticity of the Wilderness Tradition* [New York: Oxford University Press, 2011], 75–109).

[7] As expounded in Alan Gardiner, "The Geography of the Exodus," in *Recueil d'études*

Recognizing the contradictions in the biblical record—in which the *yam sûp* lies either before or after the wilderness—some critics argue that the *yam sûp* is an all-encompassing geographical term for waters that abut the entire southern shore of Sinai.[8] To some degree, this suggestion is a revival of classical Greek geography. Herodotus and Strabo identify the "Erythraean" as an expansive sea located between Africa and Asia, one that reaches into both the present-day Gulf of Suez and the Gulf of Aqaba/Eilat and as far as the Indian Ocean.[9] Although this view accounts for the descriptions of the *yam sûp* as adjacent to both Edom and Egypt, it is not entirely convincing. According to John Van Seters, "A solution that proposes the same geographic term for two entirely different things does not seem to me to be acceptable."[10] A renewed examination of the descriptions of the *yam sûp* in the Pentateuchal corpus, I believe, confirms this suspicion.

Departing from historical geography, another suggestion views the *yam sûp* as a symbolic location that contains mythical undertones, similar to the Egyptian

---

*égyptologiques dédiées à la mémoire de Jean-François Champollion à l'occasion du centenaire de la lettre à M. Dacier relative à l'alphabet des hiéroglyphes phonétiques, lue à l'Académie des inscriptions et belles-lettres le 27 septembre 1822* (Paris: E. Champion, 1922), 203–15; Gardiner, *Ancient Egyptian Onomastica*, 3 vols. (London: Oxford University Press, 1947), 2:201–2. Phonetically, a difficulty lies in Egyptian *ṯ* and Hebrew ס [s], a correspondence not realized until Late Egyptian; see Yoshiyuki Muchiki, *Egyptian Proper Names and Loanwords in North-West Semitic*, SBLDS 173 (Atlanta: Society of Biblical Literature, 1999), 251–52. For further critique of the association between *p3 ṯwfy* and *yam sûp*, see Vervenne, "Lexeme סוף," 427–29; *pace* Hoffmeier, *Ancient Israel in Sinai*, 81–83.

[8] Baruch A. Levine, *Numbers 21–36: A New Translation with Introduction and Commentary*, AB 4A (New York: Doubleday, 1964), 518; Menahem Haran, "The Exodus Routes in the Pentateuchal Sources" [Hebrew], *Tarbiz* 40 (1971): 113–43, here 129–30; Haran, *Ages and Institutions in the Bible* [Hebrew] (Tel Aviv: Am Oved, 1972), 58–59; Davies, *Way of the Wilderness*, 70–74; Moshe Weinfeld, "The Extent of the Promised Land—The Status of the Transjordan," in *Das Land Israel in biblischer Zeit: Jerusalem-Symposium 1981 der Hebräischen Universität und der Georg-August-Universität*, GTA 25 (Göttingen: Vandenhoeck & Ruprecht, 1983), 59–75, here 66; Weinfeld, *The Promise of the Land: The Inheritance of the Land of Canaan by the Israelites*, Taubman Lectures in Jewish Studies (Berkeley: University of California Press, 1993), 67; Michael D. Oblath, *The Exodus Itinerary Sites: Their Locations from the Perspective of the Biblical Sources*, StBibLit 55 (New York: Lang, 2004), 116; William H. C. Propp, *Exodus 19–40: A New Translation with Introduction and Commentary*, AB 2A (New York: Doubleday, 2006), 752–53; Angela R. Roskop, *The Wilderness Itineraries: Genre, Geography, and the Growth of Torah*, HACL 3 (Winona Lake, IN: Eisenbrauns, 2011), 151–52.

[9] Herodotus, *Hist.* 2.11; Strabo, *Geogr.* 16.3.1–2. Likewise, the LXX translators generally identify ים סוף as the "Erythraean" sea; see Exod 10:19; 13:18; 15:4, 22; 23:31; Num 14:25; 21:4; 33:10–11; Deut 1:40; 2:1; 11:4. Some of the translators, however, found difficulty with localizing the *yam sûp* as the Eyruthean Sea. For MT Judg 11:16 עד־ים־סוף, LXX^A reads ἕως θαλάσσης ἐρυθρᾶς, but LXX^B reads ἕως θαλάσσης Σείφ; see also Vervenne, "Lexeme סוף," 409–10.

[10] John Van Seters, "Geography of the Exodus," in *The Land That I Will Show You: Essays on the History and Archaeology of the Ancient Near East in Honor of J. Maxwell Miller*, ed. J. Andrew Dearman and M. Patrick Graham, JSOTSup 343 (Sheffield: Sheffield Academic, 2001), 255–76, here 272.

underworld.¹¹ Turning to the Song of the Sea in Exod 15:1b–18—in particular *yam* (v. 4a), *yam sûp* (v. 4b), and *təhōmōt* (v. 5a)—Norman Snaith argues that *yam sûp* was never identified as the Sea of Reeds and simply meant "end sea," which is a deep sea in an unknown distant land to the south.¹² From the threatening descriptions of the sea in Jonah 2:2–9 with its use of סוּף in v. 6, Bernard F. Batto concludes that *yam sûp* is a "Sea of End/Extinction," one fraught with primeval chaos.¹³ Carola Kloos suggests that the myth of the *yam sûp* emerges out of an early portrayal of YHWH's combat with the mythical sea, Yam.¹⁴

Finally, there are explanations of the *yam sûp* that combine geography, cosmic mythology, and diachronic readings of the biblical text. Helmut Utzschneider and Wolfgang Oswald present the *yam sûp* as a border sea (*Grenzmeer*) that stretches from Egypt to the eastern wilderness (including the Gulf of Aqaba/Eilat) and absorbs mythological associations.¹⁵ According to Hedwig Lamberty-Zielinski, the oldest texts (*jahwistische Grundschicht*) conceived of the unnamed *yam* as somewhere along the Mediterranean Sea, and a later hand (*jehowistische Fortschreibung*) relocated the sea inland and reconceived it as a cosmological medium for the destruction of the Egyptians by YHWH's hand. In the Priestly texts (*priesterschriftliche Grundschicht*), the term *yam* is timeless and lacking in geography, yet the *Endredaktor* of the Pentateuch—with JE and P in hand—reverted to a geographical location for the *yam sûp*.¹⁶ Noting the similarities between the Israelite crossing of the *yam sûp* and the Jordan River, Thomas B. Dozeman argues that Deuteronomistic editors reshaped the *yam sûp* from its mythological quality in the Song of the Sea (Exod 15:4) to a geographical location (Exod 13:18; cf. Josh 4:21–24).¹⁷

Some of the critics mentioned above explain the divergent portrayals of the *yam sûp* through insights gleaned from literary criticism. Upholding the *yam sûp* as an important marker, Menahem Haran attributes the difficulties in the wilderness route to the preservation of the pentateuchal traditions and the geographical

---

¹¹ John R. Towers, "The Red Sea," *JNES* 18 (1959): 150–53; Walter Wifall, "The Sea of Reeds as Sheol," *ZAW* 92 (1980): 325–32.

¹² Norman Snaith, "יַם סוּף: The Sea of Reeds; The Red Sea," *VT* 15 (1965): 395–98.

¹³ Bernard F. Batto, "The Reed Sea: Requiescat in Pace," *JBL* 102 (1983): 27–35, here 34, https://doi.org/10.2307/3260744.

¹⁴ Carola Kloos, *Yhwh's Combat with the Sea: A Canaanite Tradition in the Religion of Ancient Israel* (Amsterdam: G. A. van Oorschot, 1986), 152–57.

¹⁵ Helmut Utzschneider and Wolfgang Oswald, *Exodus 1–15*, Internationaler exegetischer Kommentar zum Alten Testament 2.1 (Stuttgart: Kohlhammer, 2013), 301–3.

¹⁶ Lamberty-Zielinski, *Das "Schilfmeer,"* 120–33. For her framework of sources and *Fortschreibungen*, see 50–52.

¹⁷ Thomas B. Dozeman, "The *yam-sûp* in the Exodus and the Crossing of the Jordan River," *CBQ* 58 (1996): 407–16. Questions concerning the possible influence of the Jordan River (in Joshua 4–5) on the exodus will be set aside; for a refutation, see Jan Wagenaar, "Crossing the Sea of Reeds (Exod 13–14) and the Jordan (Josh 3–4)," in *Studies in the Book of Exodus: Redaction—Reception—Interpretation*, ed. Marc Vervenne, BETL 126 (Leuven: Peeters, 1996), 461–70.

realities contained within each tradition.[18] In this article, I argue that the *yam sûp* of the exodus as presented in the pentateuchal corpus is the product of a single hand working with multiple and varied traditions of the wilderness, each with its own view of when the Israelites reached this sea after their departure from Egypt and what precisely occurred at this body of water.[19]

## II. After Egypt: The Events at the Sea in Exodus 14

Exodus 14 contains the report of the Israelites' escape from the Egyptian cavalry at a sea. As is often argued with regard to the pentateuchal corpus, critics are of the opinion that this chapter is the product of multiple hands. I acknowledge that the identification of the constituent parts of biblical texts is a contentious issue with multiple and competing explanations. For the purposes of this article I identify the literary strands of the pentateuchal corpus as P (Priestly), non-P, and D (Deuteronomic).[20] Concerning Exodus 14, most critics are of the opinion that this chapter consists of P and non-P materials, defined variously as sources, fragments, or redactions.[21] The composite nature of Exod 14 can be demonstrated in verse 21:

---

[18] Haran, "Exodus Routes," 113–43; Haran, *Ages and Institutions*, 37–76; Eng. summary in "Exodus, The," *IDBSup*, 304–10, here 307–10. Haran unravels three depictions of the Israelite wilderness as envisioned in J (Yahwist), P (Priestly), and combined E (Elohist) and D (Deuteronomy). In his view, all of these traditions place the Israelites at the *yam sûp* at some point in their journey.

[19] For the argument that the biblical representations of the exodus and Egypt not only were well established in the preexilic period but also experienced significant regional variety, see Stephen C. Russell, *Images of Egypt in Early Biblical Literature: Cisjordan-Israelite, Transjordan-Israelite, and Judahite Portrayals*, BZAW 403 (Berlin: de Gruyter, 2009).

[20] On recent developments in pentateuchal criticism, see the contributions in *The Formation of the Pentateuch: Bridging the Academic Cultures of Europe, Israel, and North America*, ed. Jan Gertz et al., FAT 111 (Tübingen: Mohr Siebeck, 2016). It is my view that the non-P materials can be further identified as E (Elohist) or J (Yahwist); I will restrict my source-critical observations to the following notes. Recognizing that there are many models that explain the formation of the Pentateuch, I propose here, in the context of the interwoven quality of the Pentateuch, that the biblical text preserves at least two coherent, yet competing, views of the location of the *yam sûp*.

[21] For J, E, and P, see Richard Elliott Friedman, *The Bible with Sources Revealed: A New View into the Five Books of Moses* (San Francisco: HarperSanFrancisco, 2003), 142–44. For J and P, see Joel S. Baden, *The Composition of the Pentateuch: Renewing the Documentary Hypothesis*, AYBRL (New Haven: Yale University Press, 2013), 193–213. For P materials, non-P materials (however labeled), and substantial redactional activity, see Peter Weimar, *Die Meerwundererzählung: Eine redaktionskritische Analyse von Ex 13,17–14,31*, ÄAT 9 (Wiesbaden: Harrassowitz, 1985), 29–42; Erhard Blum, *Studien zur Komposition des Pentateuch*, BZAW 189 (Berlin: de Gruyter, 1990), 256–62; Thomas Krüger, "Erwägungen zur Redaktion der Meerwundererzählung (Exodus 13,17–14,31)," *ZAW* 108 (1996): 519–33; and Jan Christian Gertz, *Tradition und Redaktion in der Exoduserzählung: Untersuchungen zur Endredaktion des Pentateuch*, FRLANT 186 (Göttingen:

ויט משה את־ידו על־הים ויולך יהוה את־הים ברוח קדים עזה כל־הלילה וישם
את־הים לחרבה ויבקעו המים

> Moses stretched his hand over the sea. YHWH drove the sea with a strong easterly wind all night and he set the sea as dry land. The waters were divided. (Exod 14:21)

This single verse contains literary tensions that lead to several questions. Who causes the sea to move? Is it Moses by stretching his hand over the sea (vv. 21aα)? Or is it YHWH by causing a strong easterly wind (vv. 21aβ)? What exactly happens to the sea? Is the sea driven back (vv. 21aβ)? Or is the sea divided into two parts (v. 21b)?

Biblical narratives often utilize a sequence in which a command is issued in the imperative and, after the remainder of the speech is completed, that command is fulfilled in the *vav*-consecutive and in the same *binyan*.[22] P utilizes this pattern to emphasize that, when one receives a divine command, this recipient swiftly and properly executes YHWH's command.[23] The command–fulfillment pattern offers a solution to the literary tensions in Exod 14:21. This verse contains Moses's fulfillment of a command issued by YHWH in verse 16:[24]

ואתה הרם את־מטך ונטה את־ידך על־הים ובקעהו ויבאו בני־ישראל בתוך הים
ביבשה

> [YHWH:] And you [Moses] lift your staff, stretch your hand over the sea and divide it, so that the Israelites will go through the middle of the sea on dry ground. (Exod 14:16 [P])

---

Vandenhoeck & Ruprecht, 2000), 189–231; Gertz, "The Miracle at the Sea: Remarks on the Recent Discussion about Origin and Composition of the Exodus Narrative," in *The Book of Exodus: Composition, Reception, and Interpretation*, ed. Thomas B. Dozeman, Craig A. Evans, and Joel N. Lohr, VTSup 164 (Leiden: Brill, 2014), 91–120. For P and non-P, see Thomas B. Dozeman, *Commentary on Exodus*, ECC (Grand Rapids: Eerdmans, 2009), 298–318. For *ältere Exodus-Erzählung*, *P-Komposition*, and *Tora-Komposition*, see Utzschneider and Oswald, *Exodus 1–15*, 307–27. Among critics who deny any pre-Priestly material in Exod 14, see recent arguments for significant post-Priestly Deuteronomistic editorial activity in Christoph Berner, "Gab es einen vorpriesterlichen Meerwunderbericht?," *Bib* 85 (2014): 1–25, and the view that the non-P materials are a combination of post-Priestly redactions and preexilic traditions in Hans-Christoph Schmitt, "Wie deuteronomistisch ist der nichtpriesterliche Meerwunderbericht von Exodus 13,17–14,31?," *Bib* 85 (2014): 26–48. For a departure from the classical source-critical paradigm that advocates for a "sea" tradition without a crossing and (Deuteronomistic-era) *yam sûp* tradition, see Robert D. Miller II, "Crossing the Sea: A Re-Assessment of the Source Criticism of the Exodus," *ZABR* 13 (2007): 187–93.

[22] Joel S. Baden, "A Narrative Pattern and Its Role in Source Criticism," *HS* 49 (2008): 41–54.

[23] In one example, YHWH tells Moses to instruct Aaron to "stretch your hand" (נטה את־ידך) in Exod 8:5. After YHWH finishes his speech, this is precisely what happens in verse 6: "Aaron stretched his hand" (ויט אהרן את־ידו).

[24] YHWH ends his instructions in Exod 14:18. The delay in Moses's fulfillment of the divine command until verse 21aα is a source-critical issue, as the intervening material in verses 19–20 is not from P; see Baden, "Narrative Pattern," 47–48.

The *qal* imperative נטה in verse 16a is followed by the expected *vav*-consecutive in the same *binyan* ויט in verse 21aα. In the Priestly report of the sea, Moses stretches his hand over the sea (v. 21aα), the waters are divided (v. 21b), and the desired result of the Israelites traveling through the sea is achieved (v. 22). What remains in verse 21aβ, ויולך יהוה את־הים ברוח קדים עזה כל־הלילה וישם את־הים לחרבה ("YHWH drove the sea with a strong easterly wind all night and he set the sea as dry land"), lacks any connection to verse 16 and is not from P. It is also not redactional, for at least two reasons. First, in light of the near-perfect congruency between the command in Exod 14:16 and its fulfillment in (the P portions of) verses 21–22, there is little reason for a later hand to insert material into what is otherwise a perfectly readable text. Second, Exod 14:21aβ follows the description of YHWH moving the waters without Moses's assistance and the Israelites remaining stationary (vv. 13–14), which belongs to another account of the sea, one that is part of the non-P narrative.

What may seem in Exod 14:21 to be an apparent digression from the command–fulfillment pattern is rather the product of a redactional hand. In verse 16, following the imperative נטה is another imperative that is pointed as *qal*: וּבְקָעֵהוּ. The fulfillment of the imperative ובקעהו should be a *qal vav*-consecutive, yet ויבקעו in verse 21b not only lacks an object suffix but also is a *niphal vav*-consecutive and is pointed as such: וַיִּבָּקְעוּ. P could have used the grammatically acceptable passive construction ויבקעו המים in Exod 14:21b for emphasis. Yet, given the strength of the command–fulfillment pattern, it is most plausible that P contained Moses's exact fulfillment of YHWH's command ובקעהו in Exod 14:16 and that the Priestly portions of Exod 14:21 originally read (reconstruction underlined):

ויט משה את־ידו על־המים ויבקעהו

Moses stretched his hand over the sea, <u>and he divided it</u>.

In further support of this reconstruction, P continues to employ the command–fulfillment pattern after the Israelites cross the sea. Once the Israelites are safely on the other side, in P YHWH again commands Moses to stretch out his hand over the sea, נטה את־ידך על־הים, so that the waters will return over the Egyptians (v. 26), which is what Moses does: ויט משה את־ידו על־הים (v. 27aα). Whereas *ויבקעהו ("and he [Moses] divided it") in verse 21b makes good sense in the Priestly report, it would be nonsensical in the combined account. The placement of *ויבקעהו immediately after the description of YHWH driving the sea with a strong easterly wind would result in a blatant contradiction; the redactional solution, therefore, was to rework *ויבקעהו (*qal*) to ויבקעו המים (בקע, *niphal*).[25]

---

[25] The harmonization of two separate—and in different *binyanim*—command–fulfillment pairs can be observed elsewhere in Deut 34:1bα (ראה *qal* [P]–ראה *hiphil* [non-P]); see Philip Y. Yoo, "The Four Moses Death Accounts," *JBL* 131 (2012): 423–41, here 429, https://doi.org/10.2307/23488247.

Exodus 14 preserves originally independent accounts of what happened between the Israelites and the Egyptian cavalry at the sea, with each account containing its own specific claims. In one account from P, YHWH—through Moses's agency—splits the sea and the Israelites escape the Egyptian cavalry by crossing the sea through dry land. In the other account, which is non-P, YHWH pushes aside the waters of the sea and both Moses and the Israelites are more or less spectators. These accounts were combined into a single narrative by a redactor (R) who makes the occasional yet necessary intervention into the collated text, as was the case in Exod 14:21b. Although Exod 14 lacks any mention of the *yam sûp*, the events at an unnamed sea in this chapter are crucial to understanding how two different literary tradents, what I have assigned to P and non-P, understood the event of the exodus. A complete picture of the sea of the exodus requires placing the *yam* mentioned throughout Exod 14 with the *yam sûp* in its surrounding materials.

### III. The *Yam Sûp* in Exodus and Numbers

The events at the sea in Exod 14 are part of a wider narrative that describes the Israelites' departure from Egypt and their travels through the wilderness. In what precedes the events at the sea, in Exod 13:17–18, YHWH considers the likelihood that the Israelites would prefer a return to slavery over engaging in hostilities against the Philistines. YHWH then takes the Israelites on an inland detour—that is, away from the more direct route from Egypt to Canaan along the seacoast. This report contains a mention of the *yam sûp*, but what precisely is meant by דרך המדבר ים סוף (v. 18a)?

A couple of grammatical possibilities may be considered. As a construct chain, דרך המדבר ים סוף can be read as a double genitive ("way/road of the wilderness of the *yam sûp*") with the understanding that the *yam sûp* is—from the perspective of Egypt—on the other side of the wilderness. With the conflicting biblical reports of the *yam sûp* in mind, some critics attribute verse 18a, particularly ים סוף, to a late redactional insertion.[26] However, ים סוף does not necessarily need to be a secondary addition to Exod 13:18. The LXX translator made sense of this detail by reading this phrase in apposition (εἰς τὴν ἔρημον εἰς τὴν ἐρυθρὰν θάλασσαν). Another grammatical explanation is that, when followed by a geographical point of interest, דרך can convey the sense of "toward" that named place.[27] Accordingly, in Exod 13:18,

---

[26] Roland de Vaux, *The Early History of Israel*, trans. David Smith (Philadelphia: Westminster, 1978), 378; Gertz, *Tradition und Redaktion in der Exoduserzählung*, 207–9; Gertz, "Miracle at the Sea," 109; Lamberty-Zielinski, *Das "Schilfmeer,"* 131–32; Roskop, *Wilderness Itineraries*, 252; Utzschneider and Oswald, *Exodus 1–15*, 305.

[27] Haran notes that the biblical record reflects the convention in which a road is named by its final destination; accordingly, the same road could have two names, one for each end point. See "Exodus Routes," 122; Haran, *Ages and Institutions*, 49.

דרך המדבר means "toward the wilderness" and what follows immediately, ים סוף, reads as an adverbial accusative: "at the *yam sûp*." The claim in Exod 13:18 is that the *yam sûp* lies close to Egypt with the impression that the *yam sûp* is the first place the Israelites reach after their departure from Egypt, and it is at this place where YHWH takes the Israelites along an inland detour toward the wilderness.

Although the *yam sûp* in Exod 13:18 can been established as a sea close to Egypt, is it the same location where the events described in Exod 14 take place? Following Exod 14, the Song of the Sea (Exod 15:1b–18) commemorates the *yam sûp* as the location where YHWH rescued the Israelites from Pharaoh and the Egyptian cavalry:

מרכבת פרעה וחילו ירה בים
ומבחר שלשיו טבעו בים־סוף

> Pharaoh's chariots and his army he cast into the sea
> His chosen officers were sunk in the *yam sûp*. (Exod 15:4)

While the sea is unnamed in Exod 14, the connection between the *yam* and the *yam sûp* is strong, as the Song recalls some of the details in chapter 14.[28] For instance, YHWH throws "horse and rider" (סוס ורכבו) into the sea (Exod 15:1b; cf. 14:27b). After the defeat of the Egyptian cavalry, the biblical record continues with the Israelites' departure from the *yam sûp* and their journey into the wilderness:

ויסע משה את־ישראל מים־סוף ויצאו אל־מדבר־שור וילכו שלשת־ימים במדבר
ולא־מצאו מים

> Moses ordered Israel to depart the *yam sûp*. They went into the wilderness of Shur. They stayed in the wilderness for three days but did not find water. (Exod 15:22)

In Exod 13–15, the *yam sûp* is close to Egypt, lies before the wilderness, and may be equated with the unnamed *yam* where YHWH rescued the Israelites from the Egyptian cavalry.

The biblical record again mentions the *yam sûp* after the Israelites have gone through the wilderness and reached the other side. In Num 14:25 and 21:4, which refer to the Israelites' movements along the peripheries of Canaan, both mentions of the *yam sûp* apparently designate a sea closer to Canaan than to Egypt (that is,

---

[28] The origin of the Song of the Sea is contested; for its antiquity, see Mark Leuchter, "Eisodus as Exodus: The Song of the Sea (Exod 15) Reconsidered," *Bib* 92 (2011): 321–46; Ronald Hendel, "The Exodus as Cultural Memory: Egyptian Bondage and the Song of the Sea," in *Israel's Exodus in Transdisciplinary Perspective: Text, Archaeology, Culture, and Geoscience*, ed. Thomas E. Levy, Thomas Schneider, and William H. C. Propp, Quantitative Methods in the Humanities and Social Sciences (Cham: Springer, 2015), 70–76. For arguments against the Song's preexilic composition and the dating of its final stages to the Persian period, see Anja Klein, "Hymn and History in Ex 15: Observations on the Relationship between Temple Theology and Exodus Narrative in the Song of the Sea," *ZAW* 124 (2012): 516–27.

on the other side of the wilderness). There remains, however, another possibility. In response to the Israelites' acceptance of the spies' false report of the land of Canaan and its inhabitants, YHWH expresses his displeasure at the Israelites and commands:

> פנו וסעו לכם המדבר דרך ים־סוף

Turn and depart to the wilderness *derek yam sûp*. (Num 14:25b)

Like דרך המדבר in Exod 13:18, דרך ים־סוף in Num 14:25b conveys the sense of "in the direction" or "toward" the *yam sûp*.[29] Rather than turn toward the *yam sûp*, the Israelites do the exact opposite: they infiltrate Canaan, go up to the hill country, and are instantly routed by the Amalekites and the Canaanites (Num 14:39–45). Although the Israelites do not initially obey YHWH's command, they eventually do:

> ויסעו מהר ההר דרך ים־סוף

They departed Mount Hor *derek yam sûp*. (Num 21:4aα)[30]

Following the command in Num 14:25b, דרך ים־סוף means "in the direction of" or "toward" the *yam sûp*. In both Num 14:25b and 21:4aα, the mention of the *yam sûp* has in mind a body of water near Egypt and—from the perspective of Egypt— before the wilderness.[31] This observation aligns with the location of the *yam sûp* envisioned in Exod 13:18; 15:4, 22. Against this view and upholding the position that the *yam sûp* lies alongside the southern shore of Sinai, Angela E. Roskop remarks, "If we try to read Yam Suf in Num 14:25 and 21:4 as though it refers to a place in the Egyptian Delta, the ensuing trip around Edom and into Transjordan makes no sense, and the Israelites appear to be heading back to Egypt."[32] This is, I contend, exactly the claim of the biblical text.

---

[29] Simons, *Geographical and Topographical Texts*, 255.

[30] Numbers 21:4aα, ויסעו מהר ההר דרך ים־סוף, contains two major difficulties: (1) Following the imperative פנו in Num 14:25, we should expect ויפנו in Num 21:4aα (cf. the near-parallel command–fulfillment sequence in Deut 1:40; 2:1a, below). The absence of a corresponding vav-consecutive is, in my view, exceptional. (2) The mention of the departure from Mount Hor in Num 21:4aα is somewhat unexpected, as it is not mentioned in YHWH's command in 14:25b. One explanation for this is that Num 21:4aα is a conflation of multiple sources, including the continuation of the Priestly report of Aaron's death and Eleazer's investiture on Mount Hor (Num 20:25-29). See Haran, "Exodus Routes," 126 n. 18; Haran, *Ages and Institutions*, 54 n. 17; Baden, *Composition of the Pentateuch*, 80, 119. Reinhard Achenbach includes all of Num 21:4-9 as redactional (*Hexateuchredaktor*) (*Die Vollendung der Tora: Studien zur Redaktionsgeschichte des Numeribuches im Kontext von Hexateuch und Pentateuch*, BZABR 3 [Wiesbaden: Harrassowitz, 2003], 347–52). Following the commandment in Num 14:25b, the non-P portion of Num 21:4aα likely read ויסעו דרך ים־סוף.

[31] Contra Haran, who not only attributes Num 14:25b to a different source than 21:4 (ED and J, respectively) but also envisions both occurrences of דרך ים־סוף to refer to a road to the Gulf of Aqaba/Eilat; see "Exodus Routes," 125–26; Haran, *Ages and Institutions*, 54.

[32] Roskop, *Wilderness Itineraries*, 249.

Some of the depictions of the return of the exiles as a second exodus hint at the possibility of a return to Egypt. For instance, the connection of שוב with מצרים in Hos 8:13, 9:3, and 11:5 suggests a reversal of the exodus as a form of divine punishment for a rebellious Israel. The same sense underlies דרך ים־סוף in Num 14:25 and 21:4. After they hear the false report of the spies, the Israelites themselves entertain the possibility of a mutiny against Moses's leadership and their own return to Egypt: נתנה ראש ונשובה מצרימה (Num 14:4; cf. Neh 9:17).[33] After the Israelites' acceptance of the false report, YHWH has had enough of their bickering and commands them to set out toward (דרך) the *yam sûp*—that is, back to Egypt. The Israelites eventually depart in the direction of the *yam sûp*, but, after a brief stay in the wilderness (Num 21:18), it appears that YHWH changes his mind and the Israelites arrive in the Transjordan.

I return now to the following texts: Exod 13:18; 15:4, 22; Num 14:25b; 21:4aα. There is little reason to view any of the mentions of *yam sûp* in these verses as the product of a redactional hand. Furthermore, very little, if anything, in these verses indicates Priestly authorship.[34] The location of the *yam sûp* in these verses also aligns with two non-P verses that mention the *yam sûp*: Exod 10:19, in which YHWH drives locusts into the *yam sûp*, and Exod 23:31, in which YHWH establishes the land of Canaan "from the *yam sûp* to the sea of the Philistines and from the wilderness to the Euphrates." The mention of the Israelites' departure from the *yam sûp* and the phrase *derek* [toward] *yam sûp* are from the non-P materials, in which the *yam sûp* is envisioned as a body of water in close proximity to Egypt.[35]

---

[33] For this understanding of נתנה ראש in Num 14:4, see George Buchanan Gray, *A Critical and Exegetical Commentary on Numbers*, ICC (Edinburgh: T&T Clark, 1903), 152; Noth, *Das vierte Buch Mose*, 95; Eng., 107; Philip Y. Yoo, *Ezra and the Second Wilderness*, Oxford Theology and Religion Monographs (Oxford: Oxford University Press, 2017), 58.

[34] Remarking on חמשים ("armed for battle"), Dozeman assigns Exod 13:18b to P (*Commentary on Exodus*, 303–4). There is little in P, however, before or after this verse that connects well to this word in v. 18b; see Philip Y. Yoo, "Armed for Battle? On the Meaning of חמשים in Exodus 13,18," *ZAW* 128 (2016): 42–48.

[35] Although the non-P materials label the sea of the exodus as *yam sûp* and locate it near Egypt, I believe that Exod 10:19; 13:18; 15:4, 22; 23:31; Num 14:25b; 21:4aα do not belong to a single hand and may be further assigned to either J or E. Both Exod 13:18 and 15:22 describe the Israelites' departure from the *yam sûp*. In Exod 13:18, however, YHWH leads the Israelites into the wilderness at the *yam sûp* while Moses (absent a divine command) orders the Israelites to leave the *yam sûp* in 15:22. Exodus 13:18 belongs to E. In E, although the Israelites are close to Canaan when they reach the *yam sûp* (cf. Exod 23:31), the presence of the Philistines, along with YHWH's actions, however understood, takes the Israelites away from the more direct route to Canaan. If indeed the Song of Miriam (Exod 15:20–21) belongs to E (see Alan W. Jenks, *The Elohist and North Israelite Traditions*, SBLMS 22 [Missoula, MT: Scholars Press, 1977], 43; Friedman, *Bible with Sources Revealed*, 146), then E provides a concise report of YHWH's deliverance at the sea it calls the *yam sûp*. Exodus 15:22, along with v. 4, Num 14:25b, and 21:4aα* (reconstructed in n. 30), is from J. In J, the *yam sûp* is close to Egypt (cf. Exod 10:19) and is one of multiple seas in its report of the wilderness (the unnamed *yam* in either Num 11:31 or 13:29 should not be equated with the *yam sûp*).

## IV. The Yam Sûp in Deuteronomy

In addition to Exodus and Numbers, Deuteronomy contains multiple references to the *yam sûp*, and although the Deuteronomic (D) version of the events at the *yam sûp* closely aligns with some of the materials discussed above, it demonstrates a different understanding of the geography of the wilderness.[36] Framed as Moses's last discourse to the Israelites over a short period of time and before they cross the Jordan River, D recalls past events in the wilderness, including their acceptance of the false report of Canaan at Kadesh Barnea (Deut 1:19–46). D's own recollection of the failed mission is adapted from the non-P version of the spies episode contained in Num 13–14.[37] In the Deuteronomic report, YHWH's command to the Israelites to reverse course reframes the command in Num 14:25:[38]

ואתם פנו לכם וסעו המדברה דרך ים־סוף

Turn and depart for the wilderness, *derek* [toward] *yam sûp*. (Deut 1:40)

---

[36] In Deut 1:1, *sûp* (בערבה מול סוף) may refer to a place near the *yam sûp* but is not to be confused with the sea itself; see Moshe Weinfeld, *Deuteronomy 1–11: A New Translation with Introduction and Commentary*, AB 5 (New York: Doubleday, 1991), 126. Weinfeld discounts the identification of *sûp* (Deut 1:1), which is somewhere in between Horeb and Kadesh (v. 2), to Supah, a place in southern Moab (Num 21:14). The distinction between *sûp* and *yam sûp* is lost to the LXX translator (πλησίον τῆς ἐρυθρᾶς, LXX Deut 1:1).

[37] D addresses the problem of the failed mission having been initiated by YHWH (Num 13:2) by insisting that the Israelites, and not YHWH, conceived of the plan (Deut 1:22); see Weinfeld, *Deuteronomy 1–11*, 141–53; Jeffrey H. Tigay, *Deuteronomy* דברים: *The Traditional Hebrew Text with the New JPS Translation*, JPSTC (Philadelphia: Jewish Publication Society, 1996), 424–25; Baden, *Composition of the Pentateuch*, 142–43. John Van Seters holds the opposite direction of dependency—that Deut 1:19–46 precedes non-P Num 13–14; see *The Life of Moses: The Yahwist as Historian in Exodus–Numbers* (Louisville: Westminster John Knox, 1994), 363–82. For the mediating view that Num 13–14 is the product of a tradition (which influences the *Grunderzählung* in Deut 1:19–46) and successive redactions (which are dependent on Deut 1:19–46), see Eckart Otto, *Das Deuteronomium im Pentateuch und Hexateuch: Studien zur Literaturgeschichte von Pentateuch und Hexateuch im Lichte des Deuteronomiumrahmens*, FAT 30 (Tübingen: Mohr Siebeck, 2000), 26–75 (*pace* Ludwig Schmidt, "Die Kundschaftererzählung in Num 13–14 und Dtn 1,19–46: Eine Kritik neuerer Pentateuchkritik," ZAW 114 [2002]: 40–58); and Reinhard Achenbach, "Die Erzählung von der gescheiterten Landnahme von Kadesch Barnea (Numeri 13–14) als Schlüsseltext der Redaktionsgeschichte des Pentateuchs," ZABR 9 (2003): 56–123.

[38] Weinfeld, *Deuteronomy 1–11*, 151. With YHWH's address to Moses at Horeb in Deut 1:7 (פנו וסעו לכם ובאו הר האמרי), "Depart, and go to the hill country of the Amorites") in mind, D's choice of words accentuates the reversal of the Israelite journey; see Tigay, *Deuteronomy*, 8.

As was the case in the non-P episode of the spies, in D the Israelites are routed after their ill-conceived attempt to overtake the Amorites (Deut 1:41–46), and they eventually fulfill YHWH's command (cf. Num 21:4aα):[39]

ונפן ונסע המדברה דרך ים־סוף כאשר דבר יהוה אלי

> We turned and departed into the wilderness, *derek* [toward] *yam sûp*, as YHWH instructed me. (Deut 2:1a)

The literary connections between the non-P portions of Num 13–14 and D are strong. In both reports, YHWH commands the Israelites to depart toward the *yam sûp*. Using language that yet again recalls the non-P portions of Exod 14–15, D describes the event in which YHWH overthrew the Egyptian cavalry at the *yam sûp*:[40]

ואשר עשה לחיל מצרים לסוסיו ולרכבו אשר הציף את־מי ים־סוף על־פניהם
ברדפם אחריכם ויאבדם יהוה עד היום הזה

> ... what he did to the army of Egypt, to its horses and its chariots, how he caused the waters of the *yam sûp* to flow over them when they pursued you. YHWH destroyed them to this day. (Deut 11:4)

D does not envision that the Israelites crossed the *yam sûp*. On this point, D agrees with its source material but departs on the location of the *yam sûp*, placing it nowhere near Egypt.[41] According to D, after the Israelites depart from Kadesh Barnea in the direction of the *yam sûp* (Deut 2:1a); they skirt the hill country of Seir (v. 2) and receive an order to enter Seir (vv. 3–4). In D, the *yam sûp* lies south of Canaan, is close to Edom, and reflects a geographical reality that bears a closer resemblance to the biblical descriptions of the *yam sûp* in Judg 11:16, 1 Kgs 9:26, and MT Jer 49:21.

---

[39] Weinfeld, *Deuteronomy 1–11*, 158. Specifically, Deut 2:1a is adapted from the non-P portion of Num 21:4aα (see n. 30).

[40] Weinfeld, *Deuteronomy 1–11*, 443.

[41] The divergence in D's geographical understanding of the *yam sûp* from its source materials does not reduce the argument that D, in Deut 1–11, is dependent on its source materials (source critically, E in Menahem Haran, *The Biblical Collection: Its Consolidation to the End of the Second Temple Times and Changes of Form to the End of the Middle Ages* [Hebrew], 4 vols. [Jerusalem: Bialik Institute and Magnes, 1996–2014], 2:197–200; E and less so J in Joel S. Baden, *J, E, and the Redaction of the Pentateuch*, FAT 68 [Tübingen: Mohr Siebeck, 2009], 99–195). D generally accepts the historical claims of its source materials yet also occasionally modifies some of the received details to suit its own interests (for example, the omission of Jethro as advisor in Deut 1:9–18; cf. Exod 18:13–27). As demonstrated by Deut 2:1–4, D's placement of the *yam sûp* south of Edom reflects its own geographical understanding of the Israelite wilderness period.

## V. The Unnamed Sea in the Priestly Materials

In the separate reports of the sea in Exod 14, P lacks any mention of *yam sûp* in its own recollection of the exodus; instead, the *yam* in P's report is unnamed. In P, YHWH commands the Israelites to encamp at Pi-hahirot, which lies before the sea (Exod 14:2), and to cross through the sea (בתוך הים: vv. 22, 29).[42] The Israelites then arrive in Elim (15:27) and move on to the wilderness of Sin (16:1).[43]

There remains, however, a suspected reference to the *yam sûp* in P, specifically in the travel itinerary in Num 33:5–37.[44] In verses 10–11 (see next page), *yam sûp* is listed as an encampment between Elim and the wilderness of Sin, but this site is absent in the corresponding P narrative (Exod 16:1a). Complicating the matter is what precedes Num 33:10–11. The notice in the itinerary that "they [the Israelites] passed through the sea into the wilderness" (ויעברו בתוך־הים המדברה, Num 33:8aβ) is a detail that corresponds to the P narrative (cf. Exod 14:22). In explaining the discrepancy between the P narrative and travel itinerary, it has been suggested that, in P's understanding of the wilderness, the *yam sûp* is another location entirely separate from "the sea."[45] Still, the disagreement between the P narrative and travel itinerary is stark. There is little reason to think that the P narrative (in Exod 16:1a) originally had in mind an encampment at the *yam sûp* between Elim and the wilderness of Sin.[46]

---

[42] The phrase בתוך הים occurs also in Exod 15:19, but this verse is redactional; see Blum, *Studien zur Composition*, 230; Friedman, *Bible with Sources Revealed*, 146; William H. C. Propp, *Exodus 1–18: A New Translation with Introduction and Commentary*, AB 2 (New York: Doubleday, 2006). On the location of Pi-hahirot on an Egyptian military road, see Aren Wilson-Wright, "Camping along the Ways of Horus: A Central Semitic Etymology for *pî ha-ḥîrōt*," *ZAW* 129 (2017): 261–64.

[43] Regardless of whether the P sections of Exod 16 were transposed into their current location (reviving the classical view and in support of its transposition; see Joel S. Baden, "The Structure and Substance of Numbers 15," *VT* 63 [2013]: 351–67, here 354–58; against this view, see Ludwig Schmidt, "Die Priesterschrift in Exodus 16," *ZAW* 119 [2007]: 483–98), verse 1 (P) is considered to be in its rightful place.

[44] Numbers 33:5–37 is, classically, a P text; see Levine, *Numbers 21–36*, 511; Israel Knohl, *The Sanctuary of Silence: The Priestly Torah and the Holiness School* (Minneapolis: Fortress, 1995), 100–101; contra significant (post-P) redactional activity according to Noth, *Das vierte Buch Mose*, 238; Eng., 220–21; and Achenbach, *Die Vollendung der Tora*, 622–28. Following the view that P (or, the Priestly *Grundschrift*, $P_G$) originally ends at Sinai (among the suggestions, Lev 16:34 in Christoph Nihan, *From Priestly Torah to Pentateuch: A Study in the Composition of the Book of Leviticus*, FAT 2/25 [Tübingen: Mohr Siebeck, 2007], 20–68), some scholars see significant (post-P) redactional activity throughout Numbers. For a discussion of the continuation of P into Numbers—although without mention of Num 33—see Jean-Louis Ska, "Old and New in the Book of Numbers," *Bib* 95 (2014): 102–16.

[45] See, e.g., Haran, "Exodus Routes," 129; Haran, *Ages and Institutions*, 58.

[46] Contra William Johnstone, "The Use of Reminiscences in Deuteronomy in Recovering

| Exodus 16:1a | Numbers 33:10-11 |
|---|---|
| ויסעו מאילם | ויסעו מאילם |
|  | ויחנו על־ים־סוף |
|  | ויסעו מים־סוף |
| ויבאו כל־עדת בני־ישראל אל־ | ויחנו במדבר־סין |
| מדבר־סין |  |
| אשר בין־אילם ובין סיני |  |
| They departed Elim. | They departed Elim and encamped by the *yam sûp*. |
|  | They departed the *yam sûp* and encamped in the wilderness of Sin. |
| All the congregation of the Israelites came to the wilderness of Sin which is between Elim and Sinai. |  |

The mention of the *yam sûp* in a P text is somewhat extraordinary. Elsewhere in the P materials, the *yam sûp* does not register in P's geography. P's boundary list of Canaan in Num 34:3-12 contains no mention of a sea called *yam sûp*; instead, P lists the southern border of Canaan as "from Azmon to the wadi of Egypt and its end at the *yam*" (v. 5). In P, the *yam* lies at the frontier of the land of Canaan, and it follows that, according to P, the events at the unnamed sea occurred soon after the Israelites left Egypt. The appearance of the *yam sûp* as an encampment site in Num 33:10b-11a is then explained by the observation that this notice is an insertion into an originally P itinerary.[47] After combining the *yam sûp* (from the non-P materials) and an unnamed sea (from P) into a single location in Exod 13-15, where YHWH rescues the Israelites from the Egyptian cavalry, R accounts for the absence of the *yam sûp* in the P travel itinerary with the insertion of ויחנו על־ים־סוף ויסעו מים־סוף (Num 33:10b-11a).

Numbers 33:10b-11a can be construed as R's factual correction. This

---

the Two Main Literary Phases in the Production of the Pentateuch," in *Abschied vom Jahwisten: Die Komposition des Hexateuch in der jüngsten Diskussion*, ed. Jan Christian Gertz, Konrad Schmid, and Markus Witte, BZAW 315 (Berlin: de Gruyter, 2002), 247–73, esp. 261–62; see also Batto, "Reed Sea," 29. Johnstone argues that a Priestly editor responsible for the insertion of Exod 15:22bβ–19:2a harmonizes the conflicting P and D itineraries (he assigns Exod 13:18 and 15:4, 22 to D), which leads to the suppression of ים סוף in Exod 16:1. The existence of contradictions throughout the Pentateuch suggests that the redactor(s) opted to preserve, as much as possible, the source materials, regardless of their representative ideological unorthodoxies or historiographical inconsistencies.

[47] Noth, *Das vierte Buch Mose*, 211; Eng., 244; Frank Moore Cross, *Canaanite Myth and Hebrew Epic: Essays in the History of the Religion of Israel* (Cambridge: Harvard University Press, 1973), 309; Roskop, *Wilderness Itineraries*, 139–40.

correction is necessary because of the conflicting portrayals of the *yam sûp* near Egypt in the non-P materials, an unnamed sea near Egypt in P, and the *yam sûp* near Canaan in D. Although R's intervention in Num 33:10b–11a blurs the geographical precision of his source materials and results in a more expansive *yam sûp* that lies along the entire southern shore of the Sinai Peninsula, it does not create significant problems in R's presentation of the wilderness.

## VI. Reshaping Geography

The presentation of the *yam sûp* in the Pentateuch reflects R's efforts to preserve his source materials to the extent possible and also his effort to intervene as little as possible. Rather than attribute substantial materials to R, I suggest that R's contributions, confined here to harmonizing his source materials, are limited but necessary "for clarity, to correct mistakes, or to overcome difficulties in the text."[48] In collating his source materials, R's task was to present the different episodes at the sea as a single event with minimal interpolations, and the success of this enterprise rests on the seamless collation of the source materials. As evidenced in Exod 14:21b, this enterprise required R's occasional and subtle, yet essential, change of a word when originally independent reports were arranged into a single narrative.

Whereas R could correct the (originally P) travel itinerary, logic prevented him from returning to the corresponding narrative and inserting ים סוף after ויסעו מאילם in Exod 16:1a (P), which would have resulted in the Israelites' departure from the *yam sûp* (Exod 15:22) followed shortly thereafter by a return to the body of water with the same name. It would make little sense for R to place these events consecutively for the reason that the Egyptian cavalry could not be vanquished twice in rapid succession. Returning to the P travel itinerary, R could have inserted סוף into ויעברו בתוך־הים המדברה in Num 33:8a (P). What would amount to a simple insertion would align more closely with R's finished product in Exod 13–15, in which the *yam sûp* could be equated with the unnamed sea. Such an insertion, however, would not be an improvement; nowhere in Exod 13–15 do the Israelites cross (עבר) the *yam sûp*.[49] Instead, R subtly addresses the absence of the *yam sûp* in the P materials by adding *yam sûp* to the list of encampment sites in Num 33.

R, in turn, preserved the divergent—yet at times contradictory—presentations of the *yam sûp* and the events leading to YHWH's intervention at this sea that were originally envisaged by his source materials. In the non-P materials, the *yam*

---

[48] John Van Seters, *The Edited Bible: The Curious History of the "Editor" in Biblical Criticism* (Winona Lake, IN: Eisenbrauns, 2006), 22. Van Seters offers a critique and call for methodological clarity on the role of a redactor, with a focus on the pentateuchal corpus.

[49] Cf. Exod 15:16b: עד־יעבר עמך יהוה עד־יעבר עם־זו קנית, "until your people, YHWH, passed by, / until the people whom you acquired passed by." It is unlikely that the Song itself referred to the crossing of the *yam sûp*; see Russell, *Images of Egypt*, 150–51.

*sûp* is among the first stages of the Israelite sojourn through the wilderness. In P, the Israelites pass through an unnamed sea near Egypt. In D, the *yam sûp* lies along the southern shore of Edom. Informed by their own ideological, geographical, and historiographical understandings of the Israelite wilderness, each of the constituent strands of the Pentateuch held a different view of the location of the sea of the exodus. Each literary construction of the *yam sûp* and/or the unnamed sea is grounded on the envisioned route and the events that occurred on this route, which the Israelites undertook from Egypt to Canaan. After each of the constituent strands is identified throughout the pentateuchal corpus, the sea of the exodus— the *yam sûp* or an unnamed *yam*—is well placed within the literary imagination and historiographical claims of the source materials.

In his finished product, R's treatment of his received traditions of the sea removes the geographical precision of each of his sources and ultimately results in a more expansive *yam sûp*. The *yam sûp* is not the only example of conflated geography in the Pentateuch. In another example, Sinai (Exod 19:1 [P]) and Horeb (Deut 1:6 [D]) become one location, as in the redactor's mind the theophany occurred at a single time at a single wilderness mountain.[50] R's presentation of the Israelites' journey through the wilderness, along with his treatment of geographical points of interest, is successful. Some of the earliest interpreters of the Pentateuch who reimagine the exodus and the wilderness periods present the *yam sûp* and the unnamed sea as a single body of water (Neh 9:9–11,[51] Wis 10:18–19). As is the case with all—if not most—of the geographical points of interest between Egypt and Canaan that are recorded in the Israelite wilderness accounts, the *yam sûp* in the Pentateuch cannot be identified with a known body of water, ancient or modern. It is the product of multiple, and at times irreconcilable, understandings of a body of water that stimulated the imaginations of the Israelite historiographers who celebrated the events at the sea of the exodus.

---

[50] Other examples of a later reader conflating originally different geographical points of interest were noted above in nn. 30, 36. The eventual acceptance of Sinai and Horeb as a single location is evident in Ben Sira's praise of Elijah. In 1 Kgs 19:18, Elijah fasts at Horeb (with no mention of Sinai throughout 1 and 2 Kings), yet in Sir 48:7, Horeb and Sinai are identified as the same; see Patrick W. Skehan and Alexander A. Di Lella, *The Wisdom of Ben Sira: A New Translation with Notes*, AB 39 (New York: Doubleday, 1987), 533.

[51] See Sara Japhet, "What May Be Learned from Ezra-Nehemiah about the Composition of the Pentateuch?," in Gertz et al., *Formation of the Pentateuch*, 543–60, here 551; Yoo, *Ezra and the Second Wilderness*, 44–47.

# Womanist Midrash

## A Reintroduction to the Women of the Torah and the Throne

### Wilda C. Gafney

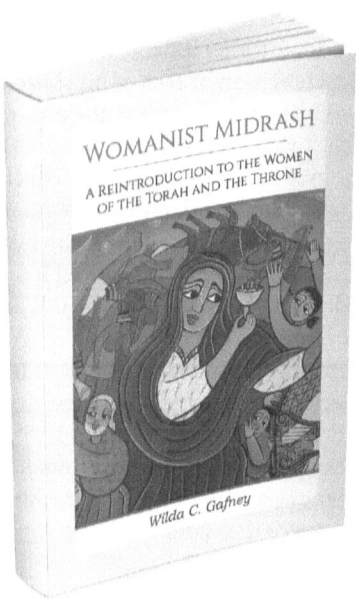

Paperback • 340 Pages • 6 x 9 • 9780664239039 • $35.00

*Womanist Midrash* is an in-depth and creative exploration of the well- and lesser-known women of the Hebrew Scriptures. Using her own translations, Gafney offers a midrashic interpretation of the biblical text that is rooted in the African American preaching tradition to tell the stories of a variety of female characters, many of whom are often overlooked and nameless.

**WJK** WESTMINSTER JOHN KNOX PRESS
www.wjkbooks.com | 1.800.523.1631

# The Gēr (Stranger) in Deuteronomy: Family for the Displaced

**MARK GLANVILLE**
markrglanville@gmail.com
Vancouver, BC V5N 1H7, Canada

This study investigates an ethic of inclusivism for the *gēr* (גֵר, "stranger") in Deuteronomy. The trend in recent scholarship identifies the *gēr* in Deuteronomy as a foreigner. A fresh examination of the relevant texts suggests that the term *gēr* in Deuteronomy simply identifies a vulnerable person who is from outside the core family. Further, recent scholarship discerns in Deuteronomy efforts to include the *gēr* within the community as well as limitations upon the inclusion of such people. I explore the social-scientific dynamics of inclusion, showing how Deuteronomy's ethical vision for the *gēr* has to do with kinship: displaced persons needed to be incorporated into the clans. Deuteronomy not only stipulates a system of protection for the *gēr*, but the central impulse of Deuteronomy's vision, expressed in a multiplicity of ways, is to foster the incorporation of the *gēr* as kindred, specifically within the household, within the clan, and within the nation. This vision is achieved through the interplay of the various subgroups of laws—social law, law of judicial procedure, and feasting texts. In addition, in Deuteronomy's framework (chs. 1–11, 27–34), as Israel was reconstituted, the incorporation into the "nation" of those who had been separated from patrimony and from kindred was a primary goal.

An ethic of inclusivism for the *gēr* (גֵר, "stranger") in Deuteronomy is the focus of this investigation. Put simply, in Deuteronomy, I argue, the term *gēr* identifies a vulnerable person who is from outside the core family. The noun *gēr* occurs twenty-two times in Deuteronomy.[1] The high number of occurrences of *gēr*, the appearance of this figure within the very first instruction in Deuteronomy

---

I am indebted to comments by M. Daniel Carroll R., Reinhard Achenbach, and Markus Zehnder on an earlier version of this article. This article summarizes some of the content and conclusions of my forthcoming monograph, *Adopting the Stranger as Kindred in Deuteronomy*, AIL (Atlanta: SBL Press, forthcoming).

[1] See Deut 1:16; 5:14; 10:18, 19 (2x); 14:21, 29; 16:11, 14; 23:8; 24:14, 17, 19, 20, 21; 26:11, 12, 13; 27:19; 28:43; 29:10; 31:12. References to texts in the Hebrew Bible are from Deuteronomy unless it is indicated otherwise.

(1:16–17), and especially the presence of the *gēr* in the covenant ceremonies of 29:9–14 and 31:9–13 suggest that displacement was a most pressing social issue in the societies that Deuteronomy was addressing, especially in the periods of the Dtr and post-Dtr redactions.[2]

Numerous monographs and articles examine the *gēr* in the Hebrew Bible.[3] In 2014, Mark A. Awabdy and Ruth Ebach each produced a book-length study of the stranger in Deuteronomy.[4] Like the present study, Awabdy's monograph is focused on the *gēr*, contributing a close study of each occurrence of the term. Awabdy concludes that Deuteronomy offers a vision that integrates the *gēr*, both socially and religiously, and he further asserts that religious inclusion is limited to the framing chapters (chs. 1–11, 27–34).[5] Ebach explores how Deuteronomy is concerned with collective Israelite identity formation and the ways in which Deuteronomy establishes Israel's identity precisely in relation to the stranger. Certain issues emerge in these studies and in others that call for further research: for example, the question of the identity of the *gēr* in Deuteronomy, the need for analysis of the dynamics of inclusivism in Deuteronomy, and Israelite identity formation in relation to the inclusion of the *gēr*.

In this analysis, I will pursue these issues by adopting an integrative methodology, bringing together legal, sociological, literary, theological, social-historical, and literary-historical approaches. I will proceed by addressing the following

---

[2] Dtr = Deuteronomistic. It is generally thought that Deuteronomistic scribes added a framework (chs. 1–11, 27–34) around the law corpus (chs. 12–26). Dtn = Deuteronomic. The Deuteronomic redaction is the earliest version of Deuteronomy, generally thought to be a core version of the law corpus.

[3] E.g., Christoph Bultmann, *Der Fremde im antiken Juda: Eine Untersuchung zum sozialen Typenbegriff "ger" und seinem Bedeutungswandel in der alttestamentlichen Gesetzgebung*, FRLANT 153 (Göttingen: Vandenhoeck & Ruprecht, 1992); José E. Ramírez Kidd, *Alterity and Identity in Israel: The גר in the Old Testament*, BZAW 283 (Berlin: de Gruyter, 1999); Markus Zehnder, *Umgang mit Fremden in Israel und Assyrien: Ein Beitrag zur Anthropologie des "Fremden" im Licht antiker Quellen*, BWANT 168 (Stuttgart: Kohlhammer, 2005); Reinhard Achenbach, "Der Eintritt der Schutzbürger in den Bund (Dtn 29, 10–12): Distinktion und Integration von Fremden im Deuteronomium," in "*Gerechtigkeit und Recht zu üben*" (*Gen 18,19*): *Studien zur altorientalischen und biblischen Rechtsgeschichte, zur Religionsgeschichte Israels und zur Religionssoziologie; Festschrift für Eckart Otto zum 65. Geburtstag*, ed. Reinhard Achenbach and Martin Arneth, BZABR 13 (Wiesbaden: Harrassowitz, 2009), 240–55; Nadav Na'aman, "Sojourners and Levites in the Kingdom of Judah in the Seventh Century BCE," *ZABR* 14 (2008): 237–79; Christiana van Houten, *The Alien in Israelite Law: A Study of the Changing Legal Status of Strangers in Ancient Israel*, JSOTSup 107 (Sheffield: JSOT Press, 1991).

[4] Mark Awabdy, *Immigrants and Innovative Law: Deuteronomy's Theological and Social Vision for the גר*, FAT 2/67 (Tübingen: Mohr Siebeck, 2014); Ruth Ebach, *Das Fremde und das Eigene: Die Fremdendarstellungen des Deuteronomiums im Kontext israelitischer Identitätskonstruktionen*, BZAW 471 (Berlin: de Gruyter, 2014).

[5] E.g., Awabdy, *Immigrants and Innovative Law*, 253. Awabdy's conclusions concerning the limitations upon such inclusion are discussed below.

questions: (1) What are the identity and origins of the *gēr* in Deuteronomy? (2) To what extent could outsiders be integrated into kinship groupings? (3) How is Deuteronomy's system of protection and inclusion of the *gēr* expressed through the various subgroups of laws—social law, law of judicial procedure, feasting texts, and the frame of Deuteronomy? (4) How does the displacement that is evident in these texts relate to the social history of ancient Israel-Judah? (5) How may the apparent tension between elements of inclusivism and elements of exclusivism in Deuteronomy be reconciled? Three central conclusions will emerge from this investigation. First, the *gēr* in Deuteronomy is simply a vulnerable person or family who is from outside the kinship grouping within which the *gēr* resides. Second, and most important, Deuteronomy's response to displacement was to foster the incorporation of the *gēr* within the kinship groupings, namely, within a household, within a clan, and within the nation. Third, Deuteronomy achieved this inclusion through the specific functions of various subgroups of laws.

## I. The Identity of the *Gēr*

### *The Identity of the* Gēr *in the Covenant Code and in the Holiness Code*

The term *gēr* occurs four times in the Covenant Code (Exod 22:20; 23:9 [2x], 12). Here, the *gēr* is a person who is both displaced and also dependent in this new context, as in Deuteronomy.

The Holiness Code and the so-called holiness redaction use the term *gēr* with two different meanings.[6] Less commonly it refers to people who are both displaced and also dependent, reflecting the usage in the Covenant Code and in Deuteronomy (Lev 19:9–10, 18, 33–34; 23:22). The second and dominant use of the term is to designate a stranger who is not dependent and may even be of some means.

### *The Identity of the* Gēr *in Deuteronomy*

Regarding translating the term *gēr*, Frank Anthony Spina has suggested the gloss "immigrant," stating that "*gēr* should be translated by a word that underscores not simply the outsider status in the adopted social setting, but in addition those factors and conditions related to the emigration in the first place."[7] This suggestion

---

[6] See Rainer Albertz, "From Aliens to Proselytes: Non-Priestly and Priestly Legislation concerning Strangers," in *The Foreigner and the Law: Perspectives from the Hebrew Bible and the Ancient Near East*, ed. Reinhard Achenbach, Rainer Albertz, and Jakob Wöhrle, BZABR 16 (Wiesbaden: Harrassowitz, 2011), 53–70, esp. 57–58.

[7] Frank Anthony Spina, "Israelites as *gērîm*, 'Sojourners,' in Social and Historical Context," in *The Word of the Lord Shall Go Forth: Essays in Honor of David Noel Freedman in Celebration of*

is challenged, however, on the grounds that *gēr* is a term from legislative texts in particular that reference the present dislocation of an individual or family and does not distinguish regarding the circumstances behind the displacement. Christiana van Houten and many others suggest the translation "resident alien."[8] While this translation may be appropriate for the *gēr* in the Holiness Code, it is not suitable for Deuteronomy, where, in every reference to the *gēr* across the redactional layers, the *gēr* is not only resident in a new context but also dependent in that context. The dependency of the *gēr* is visible in the *gēr*'s labor within the household and the settlement (5:14, 24:14); in the *gēr*'s inclusion within the triad of the vulnerable, "the fatherless, the widow, and the *gēr*" (e.g., Deut 16:11a, 14); in the reference to "your *gēr*" (5:14, 29:10) in the phrase "in your midst,"; and in the local provision for their sustenance (14:28–29, 26:12–15).[9] Nadav Na'aman accurately recognizes three characteristics of the *gēr* in Deuteronomy. The *gēr* is dependent, landless, and on the lowest rung of the social ladder.[10] A helpful translation is "dependent stranger." The strangers have left kinship ties, settlement, and land and now dwell in a context in which they have no blood relations. They are therefore without the security and privileges that family ties and place of birth afford. The strangers are in social limbo: on the one hand, they are free and not enslaved; yet, on the other hand, they are without land and meaningful connection. The strangers may be easily oppressed, as they have no family members to come to their defense.

Much of scholarship has assumed a correspondence between the noun *gēr* and the verb גור, such that both words refer to displaced persons seeking a new home. José E. Ramírez Kidd has brought greater precision to a definition of the noun *gēr* by investigating its relation to the verb גור: the verb tends to be used in narrative texts and to refer to "specific events in the lives of concrete characters,"[11] while the noun *gēr* tends to be used in legal texts. This is significant for the scholarly discussion, for while texts such as 2 Sam 4:3, Ruth 1:1, and Isa 16:4, in which the verb גור occurs, are examples of displacement that would fit the common understanding of the noun *gēr*, the noun is altogether missing from these texts![12]

Three contending views for the referent of *gēr* in Deuteronomy obtain in the scholarship: a refugee displaced by the Assyrian invasion of the northern kingdom,[13]

---

*His Sixtieth Birthday*, ed. Carol L. Meyers and M. O'Connor, ASOR Special Volume Series 1 (Winona Lake, IN: Eisenbrauns, 1983), 321–36, here 323.

[8] Van Houten, *Alien in Israelite Law*, 16; Nathan MacDonald, *Not Bread Alone: The Uses of Food in the Old Testament* (Oxford: Oxford University Press, 2008), 99.

[9] It is likely that displacement was prevalent in the communities that these texts addressed (especially in the Dtr and post-Dtr redactions; see below); and that every displaced person was referred to as *gēr* regardless of gender.

[10] Na'aman, "Sojourners and Levites," 258.

[11] Ramírez Kidd, *Alterity and Identity*, 15.

[12] In fact, *HALOT* cites these texts under the entry for the noun.

[13] See, e.g., Moshe Weinfeld, *Deuteronomy and the Deuteronomic School* (Oxford: Clarendon, 1972), 90–91; Alfred Bertholet, *Die Stellung der Israeliten und der Juden zu den Fremden* (Freiburg

a foreigner from a kingdom other than either Judah or the northern kingdom,[14] or an internally displaced Judahite.[15] The second view represents the current scholarly trend. I contend, however, that the *gēr* in Deuteronomy is simply one who is a dependent "outsider" in relation to the kinship grouping within which that person resides.[16] This would certainly include internally displaced persons. During the seventh century, it would also likely include displaced northerners. It would also include people who were non-Judahite/non-Israelite.

Scholarship on the *gēr* has often proceeded following a binary linear narrative of Israel and the foreigner, ignoring how in an ancient culture someone who is from a different clan may also be considered an outsider. It is overly simplistic, however, to consider ethnicity in exclusively "national" categories, whereby "Israel" is a clearly defined group in the eyes of all actors and whereby the primary identification of the members of the community before the text is as "Israel," yielding a simple binary distinction—Israel/not-Israel. Rather, as Ronald S. Hendel has argued, "The individual is a point of intersection among many genealogical relationships, both to living relatives and dead ancestors.... An individual is the child of X, of the clan of Y, of the tribe of Z, of the people of Israel."[17] Correspondingly, an *outsider* may simply be a person from another clan. So Walter Houston asserts, "In a lineage-based agrarian society the immigrant from another tribe or even the next village is just as much of an outsider."[18] Indeed, Deuteronomy most often refers to the *gēr* in relation to the household and the clan (note the household list and the integration formula, בשעריך, "within your gate," e.g., in 16:11, 14, discussed below). Otherness is conceived of at this local level. To be sure, in Deuteronomy and especially in Deuteronomy's frame (chs. 1–11, 27–34), "all-Israel" is a dominant group

---

im Breisgau: Mohr Siebeck, 1896), 123–78; Roland de Vaux, *Ancient Israel: Its Life and Institutions* (London: Darton, Longman & Todd, 1961), 74–76; Kellermann, *TDOT* 2:445; Mark G. Brett, *Political Trauma and Healing: Biblical Ethics for a Postcolonial World* (Grand Rapids: Eerdmans, 2016), 173–74.

[14] See, e.g., Awabdy, *Immigrants and Innovative Law*, 110–16; Ebach, *Das Fremde und das Eigene*, 41, 316; Reinhard Achenbach, "gēr – nåkhrî – tôshav –zār," in Achenbach, Albertz, and Wöhrle, *Foreigner and the Law*, 29–52, here 32; van Houten, *Alien in Israelite Law*, 89–90; Albertz, "From Aliens to Proselytes," 61; Ramírez Kidd, *Alterity and Identity*, 46.

[15] Recently, Na'aman, "Sojourners and Levites." See also Bultmann, *Der Fremde im antiken Juda*, 213; Georg Braulik, "Deuteronomy and Human Rights," in *Theology of Deuteronomy: Collected Essays of Georg Braulik, O.S.B.*, trans. Ulrika Lindblad, BIBAL Collected Essays 2 (Richland Hills, TX: BIBAL, 1994), 131–50, here 138.

[16] Bultmann defines the term *gēr*: "Der ger ist von daher 'fremd' in der jeweiligen Relation zu seinem Aufenthaltsort" (*Der Fremde im antiken Juda*, 17). On the basis of social-historical reconstruction, Bultmann makes the further supposition that the *gēr* in Deuteronomy is a displaced Judahite.

[17] Ronald S. Hendel, *Remembering Abraham: Culture, Memory, and History in the Hebrew Bible* (Oxford: Oxford University Press, 2005), 34.

[18] Walter J. Houston, *Contending for Justice: Ideologies and Theologies of Social Justice in the Old Testament*, LHBOTS 428 (London: T&T Clark, 2006), 108.

identity. Yet I will demonstrate that, even when the *gēr* appears in the context of all Israel, the otherness of the *gēr* is located in the *gēr*'s relation to the household and to the clan (29:10, 31:12). Significant too is that foreignness is not germane to the noun *gēr* in Northwest Semitic texts. In these texts the term *gēr* in and of itself simply refers to the quality of a person as an outsider, one who is operating in a sphere outside of one's circle of affiliation.[19] Finally, I will show that the contexts that Deuteronomy originally addressed, according to the bulk of critical opinion, were contexts of massive internal displacement in Judah. As Na'aman points out, given the reality of internally displaced people in Israel, it would be odd if Deuteronomy made provisions for displaced people from other nations but none for internally displaced people.[20]

Thus, the term *gēr* in Deuteronomy simply identifies a vulnerable person who is from outside the core family. Separated from land and from kindred, this person no longer receives the protection that kinship and patrimony afford and is therefore vulnerable to exploitation and abuse. Clarifying the origins of these displaced persons whom Deuteronomy is concerned to protect is important, but it does not significantly impact our analysis of Deuteronomy's intervention on behalf of such people.

## II. Malleable Kinship

Eckart Otto accurately perceives the fundamental need of the *gēr*: "The landless and their families needed to be integrated into the clans."[21] Deuteronomy reacts to this basic need, for, as I will argue, the central impulse of Deuteronomy's vision for the *gēr*, expressed in a multiplicity of ways, is to foster the *gēr*'s incorporation as kindred. In order to explore this possibility, it will be helpful to explain some of the key features of kinship as it is understood by social anthropologists.

The cultures of ancient Israel and its neighbors were communal, whereby people shared a collective identity in a way that is quite different from the more individualistically oriented West today. Marshall Sahlins describes collective identity as a "mutuality of being," an "intersubjective solidarity."[22] This "mutuality of being" is visible in the Hebrew Bible, for example, in pronouncements of generational benediction and malediction (e.g., Exod 34:7). The promise that the sins of

---

[19] See, e.g., *KAI* I.181.16; 37 A 16, B 10; *KTU* 1.19 III 47 = *RS* 3:366. Note also the Ethiopic verb *gwr* and noun *gōr* (e.g., Wolf Leslau, *Comparative Dictionary of Ge'ez (Classical Ethiopic)* [Wiesbaden: Harrassowitz, 1991], 207).

[20] Na'aman, "Sojourners and Levites," 256. Na'aman confines his analysis to the Dtn redaction.

[21] Eckart Otto, "שער," *TDOT* 15:359–405, here 380.

[22] Marshall Sahlins, *What Kinship Is—and Is Not* (Chicago: University of Chicago Press, 2013), 2, 43.

the fathers will fall upon the children until the third and fourth generation has parallels in communal cultures today.²³ In West Semitic tribal groups, "kinship relations defined the rights and obligations, the duties, status, and privileges of tribal members, and kinship terminology provided the only language for expressing legal, political, and religious institutions."²⁴

Westerners today, at least among white majority communities, tend to conceive of kinship in terms of blood ties. Related to this is the immutability of the category of who is one's kin: families are *given*, for better or for worse! In communal cultures, however, kinship is thought of as adaptive and mutable. For example, Mac Marshall describes how a Trukese man may speak of another as "my sibling from the same canoe," referring to a man with whom he survived a life-threatening experience on the ocean.²⁵

Numerous examples of grafting into kinship are visible in the Hebrew Bible and in the ancient Near East. Frank Moore Cross asserts, "In West Semitic tribal societies we know best, such individuals or groups were grafted onto the genealogies and fictive kinship became kinship of the flesh or blood. In a word, kinship-in-law became kinship-in-flesh."²⁶ For example, marriage is a kind of adoptive kinship, demonstrated in the words "bone of my bone, flesh of my flesh" (Gen 2:23). The possibility of becoming kin-in-law is at the root of political covenants (e.g., 2 Sam 5:2, 1 Chr 11:1). As for individuals, Tikva Frymer-Kensky observes, "In the Near Eastern milieu the term 'firstborn,' like the terms 'son,' 'father,' 'brother,' and 'sister,' is essentially a description of a juridical relationship which may be entered into by contract as well as by birth."²⁷ Thus, in narrative texts of the Hebrew Bible, the grafting of individuals into kinship groupings is common (e.g., Joseph's entry into Pharaoh's household; Gen 41:40). In addition, where clan structures were disrupted in ancient Israel (in particular through the devastation of the Babylonian conquest and its aftermath), "adoptive" clan groupings that were based on vocation or geography became important.²⁸

Kinship is forged in seemingly endless ways, apart from blood descent; in

---

²³ Ibid., 49.

²⁴ Frank Moore Cross, *From Epic to Canon: History and Literature in Ancient Israel* (Baltimore: John Hopkins University Press, 1998), 4.

²⁵ Sahlins, *What Kinship Is*, 29, citing Mac Marshall, "The Nature of Nurture," *American Ethnologist* 4 (1977): 643–62.

²⁶ Cross, *From Epic to Canon*, 7.

²⁷ Tikva Frymer-Kensky, "Patriarchal Family Relations in Ancient Near Eastern Law," *BA* 44 (1981): 209–14, here 214.

²⁸ See further Hugh G. M. Williamson, "The Family in Persian Period Judah: Some Textual Reflections," in *Symbiosis, Symbolism, and the Power of the Past: Canaan, Ancient Israel and Their Neighbors from the Late Bronze Age through Roman Palaestina; Proceedings of the Centennial Symposium, W. F. Albright Institute of Archaeological Research and American Schools of Oriental Research, Jerusalem, May 29/31, 2000*, ed. William G. Dever and Seymour Gitin (Winona Lake, IN: Eisenbrauns, 2003), 469–85.

some cultures genetics plays a very minimal role in determining kinship.[29] Kinship may be forged by sharing land; cohabiting in the same house and eating from the same hearth; nurturing; giving and sharing food; name sharing; working together; mutual assistance; sharing in migration; and especially the hard work, effort, and commitment of living together for the long haul.[30] In light of these endless possibilities, the incorporation of outsiders into kinship groups in any given culture should be understood in terms of the broader matrix of meanings and symbols within that culture.[31]

My purpose here is to demonstrate that grafting into kinship was natural in the relations that structured Israel and the ancient Near East. This is a clarifying frame for interpreting Deuteronomy's vision for the *gēr*: Deuteronomy is fostering the inclusion of the *gēr* into a household, into a clan, and into all Israel. Indeed, the mere fact of Deuteronomy's expectation that the household and clan care for the *gēr* is a signal to us that Deuteronomy is moving in the domain of kinship. "Kinsfolk are expected to be loving, just and generous to one another and not to demand strictly equivalent return of one another."[32] Such behavior would be mere charity, or even foolishness, when directed toward those outside of one's kinship grouping. For the *gēr*, kinship-in-law would eventually become kinship-in-flesh.

## III. Gēr in Legislative Subgroups

The Deuteronomic law corpus is composed of a number of legislative subgroups, and the laws within each subgroup are related to one another conceptually and lexically.[33] I examine in turn the *gēr* in social laws, laws of judicial procedure, and feasting texts. I then examine the treatment of the stranger in Deuteronomy's framework (chs. 1–11, 27–34).

### The Gēr in Social Law: Protection and Participation

Deuteronomy's social law is aimed at protecting vulnerable populations against exploitation, essentially restraining a creditor's ability to accumulate indentured workers and slaves. The subgroup of social laws is characterized by motivation clauses concerning YHWH's blessing upon agricultural production (e.g., 15:4, 6, 10; 24:13, 19) and the Egypt-exodus motif (e.g., 15:15, 23:5, 24:22).

---

[29] Sahlins, *What Kinship Is*, 74–86.

[30] Ibid., 29, 71; Janet Carsten, *After Kinship*, New Departures in Anthropology (Cambridge: Cambridge University Press, 2004), 149.

[31] E.g., ibid., 41.

[32] Meyer Fortes, *Kinship and the Social Order: The Legacy of Lewis Henry Morgan* (Chicago: Aldine, 1969), cited in Cross, *From Epic to Canon*, 5.

[33] In addition to social law, judicial law, and feasting texts, there are family laws, laws regarding warfare, laws regarding public office, and laws of divine privilege.

## Hireling Law (24:14–15)

> Do not oppress a needy and destitute hired laborer, whether one of your brothers[34] or the stranger who is in your land and within your gates.
>
> You shall give him his wage in his day, before night comes upon him, for he is poor, he is always in dire need of it, so he will not call out against you to YHWH and you will incur guilt.[35]

We learn from the hireling law (24:14–15) that a *gēr* often found employment as a temporary laborer.[36] A hireling was among the poorest in ancient Near Eastern society.[37] The two stipulations in this law consist of a provision against oppressing a day laborer and instructions for prompt payment.[38] In addition, with the phrase "whether one of your brothers or sisters or the stranger" (24:14), this law implicitly incorporates the *gēr* within Deuteronomy's brother–sister ethic. The law is also grounded theologically, for the mistreatment of a hireling may prompt that person to call down imprecations upon the employer. YHWH's ear is attentive to the needy and is responsive to their cries, cries both of blessing (24:13aβ, b) and of curse (24:15b).

## Gleaning Stipulations (24:19–22)

The noun *gēr* occurs three times in three parallel stipulations that concern leaving the residue of the harvest for the vulnerable (24:19–21).[39] The liturgical and highly paraenetic style of this law attempts to motivate more than mere compliance with the letter of the law; it aims to arouse deep compassion and create a shift in the reader's conscience by repeating with lyrical cadence that the harvest belongs

---

[34] Elsewhere I argue that many of those referenced as "*gēr*" were women (*Adopting the Stranger*, chapter 3).

[35] Translations from the Hebrew Bible are my own.

[36] An original version of the hireling law is generally ascribed to the Dtn redaction. See, e.g., A. D. H. Mayes, *Deuteronomy*, NCB (Grand Rapids: Eerdmans, 1979), 325.

[37] See further Karen Radner, "Hired Labor in the Neo-Assyrian Empire," in *Labor in the Ancient World: A Colloquium Held at Hirschbach (Saxony), April 2005*, ed. Piotr Steinkeller and Michael Hudson, International Scholars Conference on Ancient Near Eastern Economies 5 (Dresden: ISLET, 2015), 329–43.

[38] The LXX and 1QDeut[b] have "wages" (μισθός, שכר) in the place of שכיר ("hireling"), rendering "do not withhold the wages of the poor and needy." The verb עשק ("oppress"), however, always has a personal collective as its object in the Hebrew Bible, and the MT therefore is likely correct.

[39] All three stipulations within the gleaning law appear to belong to the Dtn redaction, for the passage is structured according to the Mediterranean triad of foodstuffs, which also appears in a pre-Dtr text within the Covenant Code (Exod 23:10–11; cf. Deut 12:17, 14:23, 18:4, 24:19–22; contra Rosario Pius Merendino, *Das deuteronomische Gesetz: Eine literarkritische, gattungs- und überlieferungsgeschichtliche Untersuchung zu Dt 12–26*, BBB 31 (Bonn: Hanstein, 1969), 307–8.

to all: לגר ליתום ולאלמנה יהיה, "it shall be for the stranger, for the fatherless, and for the widow" (19aβ, 20b, 21b).

*Sabbath Command (5:12–15)*

> ... but the seventh day is a Sabbath to YHWH your God. Do not do any work, you, your son or daughter, your male or female servant, your ox or your ass or any of your cattle, or your stranger who is within your gates. (5:14)

The command that the *gēr* is also to participate in Sabbath observance disrupts class distinctions between the stranger and the landed household. The *gēr* was explicitly associated with a seventh-day rest in the Covenant Code (Exod 23:12), and this is the primary source text for 5:12–15.[40] Deuteronomy's Decalogue institutes a "Sabbath," framing this day as "before YHWH" by adapting the Dtn cultic ritual formula: שבת ליהוה אלהיך, "a Sabbath before YHWH your God" (5:14a; cf. 16:10, 15).[41] The Sabbath command includes the גר as a participant in the community by identifying that person as a coheir of the gifts of land and of its bounty and as a partner in the "rest" that is the result of this gift.

*Provision of the נבלה, "Meat Not Properly Slaughtered" (14:21)*

Deuteronomy 14:21a provides that kinfolk may give to the *gēr* for food the carcass of a clean animal that has not been properly slaughtered (נבלה).[42] The majority opinion is that 14:21 demonstrates that "the Deuteronomic legislators did not regard the *gērīm* as members of Israel."[43] To be sure, the *gēr* in this text may be a foreigner, in contradistinction to the general, ambivalent use of *gēr* in Deuteronomy. Alternatively, dislocation from a lineage group may sever one from the worshiping community and so render the matter of consuming the נבלה an open question.[44]

One other social law that concerns the stranger is the law concerning a fleeing slave (23:16–17).[45] In sum, Deuteronomy's social law for the stranger operates in three related spheres: economic, social, and religious.

---

[40] Deuteronomy inserts three units of text into the source text (Exod 23:12), at the beginning, at the *sof-passuq*, and at the *athnaḥ* of Exod 23:12.

[41] Thus, we agree with the majority of critical scholars who ascribe the Decalogue to the Dtr redaction (see Dominik Markl, "The Ten Words Revealed and Revised: The Origins of Law and Legal Hermeneutics in the Pentateuch," in *The Decalogue and Its Cultural Influence*, ed. Dominik Markl; HBM 58 [Sheffield: Sheffield Phoenix, 2013], 13–27, here 13).

[42] See Kent Sparks, "A Comparative Study of the Biblical נבלה Laws," *ZAW* 110 (1998): 594–600, here 596.

[43] E.g., Albertz, "From Aliens to Proselytes," 55.

[44] Compare the importance of tracing lineage in Ezra-Nehemiah (Ezra 2; 8:3–14; Neh 7; 11:4–20).

[45] The escaped slave is displaced within his or her new context, without kindred and without means, so the fleeing slave becomes, in effect, a *gēr*. The lexical and conceptual field of Deut 23:16–17 associates with laws concerning the *gēr* rather than with slave law.

*Economic*: the social law provides that the *gēr* is a corecipient of the gift of land and of its abundance (24:19–22).

*Social*: The Deuteronomic law corpus disrupts class distinctions (5:12–15), and it includes the *gēr* within Deuteronomy's sister–brother ethic (24:14–15).

*Before YHWH*: Deuteronomy's social ethic is performed before the face of YHWH (5:14a, 13b, 15b).

### Gēr *in Law of Judicial Procedure: Protection and the Possibility of Subsistence*

The law of judicial procedure is a second subgroup of laws in Deuteronomy's system of protection and inclusion. These stipulations require that the *gēr* receive a hearing and a judgment without bias due to landlessness and lack of kinship connection. In ancient Israel and in the ancient Near East, displaced persons lacked influential advocates and could be ignored in their lawsuits.[46]

The protection of the stranger in law of judicial procedure has largely gone untreated in biblical scholarship.[47] Yet the great significance of the laws of judicial procedure concerning the *gēr* is demonstrated by their location at key points in Deuteronomy: 1:16–17 is the primary stipulation, and 10:17–19 and 27:19 are located in sections that together frame the law corpus.[48]

The Covenant Code, specifically Exod 23:1–8, is the primary source for Deuteronomy's law of judicial procedure. This block of law is concerned with ensuring that advantages of wealth, power, and connections do not impede a fair hearing and just judgment. The *gēr* is included within the scope of judicial protection via Exod 23:9. Exodus 23:1–8 is revised in Deuteronomy within a set of core laws of judicial procedure (16:18–20, 17:2–7, 17:8–13, 19:15–21). These core judicial laws

---

[46] See, e.g., Gen 12:10–20, 19:9, 26:6–11; Raymond Westbrook, "Slave and Master in Ancient Near Eastern Law," in *Law from the Tigris to the Tiber: The Writings of Raymond Westbrook*, ed. Bruce Wells and Rachel Magdalene, 2 vols. (Winona Lake, IN: Eisenbrauns, 2009), 1:161–216, here 171.

[47] On law of judicial procedure more broadly, see Frank Crüsemann, *The Torah: Theology and Social History of Old Testament Law*, trans. Allan. W. Mahnke (Minneapolis: Fortress, 1996), 238–40; Bernard M. Levinson, *Deuteronomy and the Hermeneutics of Legal Innovation* (New York: Oxford University Press, 1997), 325–404; see also Hans Jochen Boecker, *Law and the Administration of Justice in the Old Testament and Ancient Near East* (Minneapolis: Augsburg, 1980); Herbert Niehr, *Rechtsprechung in Israel: Untersuchungen zur Geschichte der Gerichtsorganisation im Alten Testament*, SBS 130 (Stuttgart: Katholisches Bibelwerk, 1987).

[48] Deuteronomy 27:19, regarding judicial procedure, is the sole reference to social law in the Shechem curse list, which gives this stipulation emphasis. The importance of judicial law in Deuteronomy is evident also in its association with the centralization formula of Deut 12 (e.g., 1:17; 17:8, 10) and with the exclusive worship of YHWH via the phrase ובערת הרע מקרבך (13:6; cf. 17:7, 12; 19:19).

are distinct in Deuteronomy by virtue of their location within a group of stipulations concerning public offices (16:18–18:22), by their motivation clauses (17:7; cf. 19:19, 20; 17:13; cf. 19:20), and by their common concern for impartiality. The core laws of judicial procedure are concerned with fairness—what has been called "blind justice." Yet the explicit concern for the poor and the displaced exhibited in the Covenant Code (see especially Exod 23:3-9) is omitted in these core texts.[49] This omission is highly unusual, for Deuteronomy characteristically enriches the social impetus of the Covenant Code. The procedural law that concerns the *gēr* supplements the concern for impartiality exhibited in the core texts with Deuteronomy's particular concern for the stranger.

*The First Stipulation (1:16–17)*

1:16b

שמע בין־אחיכם ושפטתם צדק בין־איש ובין־אחיו ובין גרו

Hear cases between your brothers and sisters,[50] and judge justly between a person and his or her brother or sister and his or her *gēr*.

Deuteronomy 1:16–17 is a socially oriented redaction of 16:18–20 that insists that the *gēr* is on an equal legal footing with the kinsperson in lawsuits.[51] In 1:16, שפט ("judge") is augmented by שמע ("hear"), highlighting the right of the stranger to a hearing at the gate. The stipulation against judicial corruption in the core text, 16:18–20, assumes that both parties will receive a hearing—in 16:18–20 corruption threatened at the point of judgment. Deuteronomy 1:16, however, considers the plight of the stranger explicitly; in 16:18–20 it is not assumed that the stranger's case will even receive a hearing. So, in 1:16 the verb שמע is used, the infinitive absolute functioning as a command (cf. 5:12, 6:17).

*YHWH the Righteous Judge (10:17–19)*

For YHWH your God, he is God of gods …, who is impartial in judgment, who does not accept a bribe, the one who secures justice for the fatherless and the widow, and who loves the stranger, giving him/her food and clothing. So you are to love the stranger, for you were strangers in the land of Egypt.

---

[49] Observe, for example, how reference to the poor in Exod 23:6 is deleted in the revision in Deut 16:19.

[50] Both men and women had the right to give testimony at the gate (e.g., 21:18–20).

[51] Only a few scholars have observed that 1:16–17 is a redaction of 16:18–20; however, this point is crucial within the dynamic of this law. In searching for a literary-historical context for 1:16–18, one can see that the verses must be dated in relation to 16:18–20. Deuteronomy 1:9–18 functions within chapters 1–3, suggesting that it follows 16:18–20. With Timo Veijola, I find no evidence that 1:16–17 is a secondary addition to 1:9–18 (*Das fünfte Buch Mose, Deuteronomium: Kapitel 1,1–16,17*, ATD 8 [Göttingen: Vandenhoeck & Ruprecht, 2004], 22).

Deuteronomy 10:17–19 is primarily judicial law, a point that is generally unrecognized in both scholarly and popular studies.[52] "Loving the *gēr*" (v. 18) must include ensuring that that person's rights are protected at the gates. The text depicts the ongoing activity of YHWH as a just judge "who is impartial in judgment." YHWH models for Israel's officials a refusal to be swayed by persons of means and association.[53]

*The Judicial Rights of the Stranger Protected in a Curse Ceremony (27:19)*

> Cursed be anyone who perverts the justice due to the stranger, fatherless, or widow. And all the people shall say, "Amen."

Injustice in legal procedure may be hidden from the eyes of the community, and the significance of the curse of 27:19 is that YHWH, the divine judge, sees this evil and intervenes.[54]

A further procedural law concerning the stranger is 24:17a, "You shall not deprive a stranger or an orphan of justice." In sum, given the vulnerability of displaced persons at the gates, Deuteronomy insisted as a matter of the highest priority that such persons should receive a hearing and just judgment in their lawsuits. These laws would have at times required elders and judges to decide a case against their own kinsfolk. Such judicial inclusivism had implications for the social structure of ancient Israel. For, while law codes generally had the function of stabilizing interclass relationships,[55] the judicial rights given here create the possibility of the *gēr* acquiring self-sufficient subsistence.

## Gēr *in Feasting Texts: Incorporation*

The feasting stipulations (14:22–29, 16:1–17, 26:1–15) are a third subgroup of laws that concern the *gēr*. These laws relate in particular to social law and to law of

---

[52] Veijola assigns 10:12–11:32 to the Dtr redaction, taking 10:14–11:1 and 11:29–30 as secondary (*Das fünfte Buch Mose*, 244–45). Otto, however, observes the many parallels between 10:12–11:30 and postexilic texts, assigning most of the unit to a postexilic redaction ("The Books of Deuteronomy and Numbers in One Torah: The Book of Numbers Read in the Horizon of the Postexilic Fortschreibung in the Book of Deuteronomy; New Horizons in the Interpretation of the Pentateuch," in *Torah and the Book of Numbers*, ed. Christian Frevel, Thomas Pola, and Aaron Schart, FAT 2/62 [Tübingen: Mohr Siebeck, 2013], 383–98, here 391).

[53] The two participles in verse 18, (משפט) עשה ("securing" [justice]) and ואהב ("loving"), are active-fientive, depicting the ongoing activity of YHWH the just judge.

[54] The interweaving of Dtr and Priestly concerns signals that 27:15–26 postdates these strata. See further, Achenbach, "gêr – nåkhrî – tôshav –zâr," 35.

[55] Moshe Weinfeld, *Deuteronomy 1–11: A New Translation with Introduction and Commentary*, AB 5 (New York: Doubleday, 1991), 64.

divine privilege.⁵⁶ The potential of Deuteronomy's feasts to affect the incorporation of the *gēr* within the community is clarified by the study of food and of pilgrimage feasts in cultural anthropology. Victor Turner has explored the power of pilgrimage feasts to break down social structure and stratification.⁵⁷ During a pilgrimage, social norms and status are suspended, producing what Turner calls *"communitas,"* a concept that is "antistructural," "in that [it is] undifferentiated, equalitarian, direct, non-rational."⁵⁸ Within this antistructure of *communitas*, kinship is experienced and friendships are forged, all of which erode status lines to some degree. Significantly, Turner asserts the potential of pilgrimages to form lasting friendships and to recast social structures and dynamics permanently.⁵⁹ Turner's research is a clarifying frame for Deuteronomy's harvest festivals, wherein the whole community shares a pilgrimage feast, establishing a communal identity as the people of God and becoming kindred as they feast before YHWH.

*Festival Calendar (16:1–17)*

The Festivals of Weeks (16:9–12) and of Booths (16:13–15) are harvest festivals to which the whole community gathers for joyful feasting to celebrate YHWH's abundant yield.⁶⁰ Georg Braulik rightly observes, "The deuteronomic cult order, which is otherwise very reticent about stipulations, never tires of enumerating the participants in sacrifices or feasts."⁶¹ A list of participants appears in the texts concerning both Weeks and also Booths.

> Feast before YHWH your God! You, your son, your daughter, your male slave, your female slave, the Levite who is in your gates, the stranger, the fatherless, and the widow who is in your midst. (16:11a; cf. 16:14)

The key verb in the festival calendar is שמח ( "feast!" Deut 16:11a, 14). The contextual meaning of שמח in Deuteronomy is to proclaim a joyful household

---

⁵⁶ For an extensive study of Deuteronomy's feasts in light of ancient Near Eastern feasting and anthropology, see Peter Altmann, *Festive Meals in Ancient Israel: Deuteronomy's Identity Politics in Their Ancient Near Eastern Context*, BZAW 424 (Berlin: de Gruyter, 2011).

⁵⁷ Victor Turner, *Dramas, Fields, and Metaphors: Symbolic Action in Human Society*, Symbol, Myth, and Ritual (Ithaca, NY: Cornell University Press, 1974). John Eade and Michael J. Sallnow's volume (*Contesting the Sacred: The Anthropology of Christian Pilgrimage* [New York: Routledge, 1991]) contests Turner's thesis, arguing that pilgrimage feasts may reinforce social divisions and privilege. However, it is evidents from what follows that Deuteronomy's feasts aim to unite rather than to divide.

⁵⁸ Ibid., 47.

⁵⁹ Ibid., 200–201, 205–6.

⁶⁰ Deuteronomy 16:1–17 revises Exod 23:14–17, and as such it is identified as Dtn by most critical scholars, e.g., Mayes, *Deuteronomy*, 257. Reinhard Kratz argues that only 16:16–17 is Dtn (*The Composition of the Narrative Books of the Old Testament*, trans. J. Bowden [London: T&T Clark, 2005], 122). However, see Altmann's rebuttal, *Festive Meals*, 193.

⁶¹ Braulik, "The Joy of the Feast," in *Theology of Deuteronomy*, 27–66, here 52.

pilgrimage feast.[62] The participant lists are highlighted in the text by their length, repetition, and motivation clauses. Through this list, the stranger, too, is caught up in the joy of the festival. Together with the core family, the stranger shares in the fellowship, the ritualized time, the smell of boiling meat, the warmth of wine, the tastes of festal recipes, the long pilgrimage with winding conversations, the waiting, the fulfillment, the liturgical life—all before YHWH, who supplies the harvest! Turner's study of the potential of pilgrimage feasting to nourish *communitas* suggests that a goal of Deuteronomy's pilgrimage festivals was to incorporate the stranger within the community.

*Incorporation within a Household*

The list of participants is structured, as it were, in concentric circles of natural affiliation within the household, progressing from the paterfamilias at the center, outwards to בן ("son") and בת ("daughter"), then to household slaves, then to Levites, and outward again to vulnerable people who also participated in the life of the household. Within a settlement each extended family had an independent dwelling that was sometimes attached to other dwellings by shared walls. The size of rural dwellings indicates that an extended family along with some vulnerable people probably lived under one roof.[63] Anthropologist Janet Carsten refers to the kinship-making function of households: "The house brings together spatial representations, everyday living, meals, cooking, and the sharing of resources with the often intimate relations of those who inhabit this shared space." This is a "dense overlay of different experiential dimensions of living together." Carsten reflects that "the very qualitative density of experiences in the houses we inhabit leads many people around the world ... to assert that kinship is made in houses through the intimate sharing of space, food, and nurturance that goes on within domestic space."[64] Of course, not every household functions in this way. Deuteronomy's inclusivist ethic for the stranger, however, and especially the mutuality that characterizes the feasts (see below), strongly suggest that Deuteronomy's household lists are deliberately evocative for forging kinship within a household. Deuteronomy's ultimate aim was for the stranger to come under the protection of the paterfamilias and to share in the commonwealth of the extended family.

*Incorporation within a Clan*

If the list of participants associates the stranger with the household, the phrase "within your gates" (16:11a, 14; cf. 5:14; 14:21, 29; 16:14; 24:14; 26:12; 31:12)

---

[62] See further Gary A. Anderson, *A Time to Mourn, a Time to Dance: The Expression of Grief and Joy in Israelite Religion* (University Park: Pennsylvania State University Press, 1991), 1, 14–18.

[63] See further Avraham Faust, *The Archaeology of Israelite Society in Iron Age II*, trans. Ruth Ludlum (Winona Lake, IN: Eisenbrauns, 2012), 12.

[64] Carsten, *After Kinship*, 35.

associates the stranger with the clan grouping of a settlement, or within a town or city. In Israel and in the ancient Near East, the city gate was the place where the poor gathered to receive charity, to find work, or to seek justice (e.g., Amos 5:12).[65] Similarly, in a village context the gate had a social and a symbolic function. The village gate symbolized shelter and succor for the vulnerable (e.g., Deut 16:14): the third-year tithe is stored "within your gates" (14:29); the fleeing slave may reside "within your gates" (23:16–17); and the laboring stranger resides "within your gates" (24:14). The phrase "within your gates" in Deuteronomy operates by synecdoche as a reference to a whole village, town, or city and to the protective shelter that this sociopolitical space offers for the stranger.[66] In Deuteronomy's feasts and social laws, the gate is not an exclusionary boundary but a demarcation of responsibility. The gate is the social perimeter within which the stranger finds economic support, association, and identity.[67]

*Does the* Gēr *Participate in Passover-Maṣṣot?*

Scholars often observe that the *gēr* is omitted from the description of Passover-Maṣṣot (16:1–8), concluding that the stranger is not welcome to this festival. Passover-Maṣṣot is a remembrance of the exodus, it is argued, and this renders the festival ethnically exclusive—for ethnic Israelites only.[68] In Deuteronomy, however, the exodus is a symbol not of ethnic particularity but of redemption, justice, and inclusion.[69] Furthermore, if ethnic identity were the explanation for why the *gēr* is not mentioned in Passover-Maṣṣot, then 16:1–8 would go too far, as it also fails to mention the Levite, the fatherless, and the widow. Stranger still, ובנך ובתך ("and your son and your daughter") are not mentioned. Indeed, this list has no participants at all. This observation signals that the omission of the list of participants does not indicate exclusion of the *gēr* due to ethnicity. Rather, absence of a list of participants for Passover-Maṣṣot, in contrast to its presence for Weeks and Booths, is explained by the fact that Weeks and Booths are harvest pilgrim festivals and the

---

[65] See further Faust, *Archaeology of Israelite Society*, 100, 105–6; Otto, *TDOT* 15:395.

[66] Similarly Otto, *TDOT* 15:367–68. The protective sense of the phrase בשעריך ("Within your gates") explains the fact that the נכרי ("foreigner") is never said to be בשעריך. This does not mean that the נכרי does not dwell within the community; rather the נכרי is not dependent on the protection and generosity of the community.

[67] Otto states, "Like the suffixes in the list of members of the nuclear family and their slaves in 12:18; 16:11, 14, the suffix added to *šaʿar* in the integration formula shows clearly that this lexeme … has not only a local connotation but also a genealogical connotation, in the sense of 'clan' or 'extended family' (cf. Ruth 3:11; 4:10)" (*TDOT* 15:380).

[68] E.g., van Houten, *Alien in Israelite Law*, 89–90; C. L. Crouch, *The Making of Israel*, VTSup 162 (Leiden: Brill, 2014), 291; Ebach, *Das Fremde und das Eigene*, 54; Achenbach, "gêr – nåkhrî – tôshav –zâr," 32; Albertz, "From Aliens to Proselytes," 61; Ramírez Kidd, *Alterity and Identity*, 46.

[69] Note the use of the exodus motive clause in the relation to the *gēr*: 5:14–15; 16:11–12; 24:19–22; 29:11, 16, and also the *gēr*-in-Egypt motive clause: 10:18–19, 23:8, 26:5.

list of participants occurs in the context of an exhortation to "feast" (שמח) at the harvest. Passover-Maṣṣot is not a harvest festival; remembrance of affliction characterizes this ritual.

*Festival of the Firstfruits (26:1–11)*

In the festival of the firstfruits, the theme of the gift of land and its abundance is the theological basis for a grateful pilgrimage feast before YHWH, in which the Levite and the *gēr* are explicitly included. This inclusivism for the *gēr* is also embedded in Israel's own formative narrative, which is recited in the declaration (26:5b–10). Israel's own vulnerability as *gēr* in Egypt is connected with the vulnerable *gēr* in its midst, prompting Israel to offer to the *ger* the kind of hospitality that Israel itself would have liked to receive (26:5b–6, 11).[70]

*Third-Year Tithe (16:28–29, 26:12–15)*

In the third-year tithe, the provision of the sacred portion for the *gēr* dignifies the stranger with the offering that is customarily reserved for the sacred places and for sacred people, communicating that the *gēr* too belongs to the people of YHWH (14:28–29, 26:12–15).[71] The concern with cultic purity (26:14a) signals that the third-year provision for the vulnerable is a religious duty, an aspect of Israel's covenant relationship with YHWH.[72]

*Exploitation or Communitas?*

It could be argued that these feasting texts co-opt the stranger into a highly hierarchical or exploitative arrangement. To be sure, as a stranger is incorporated into the kinship structure of a household, that person also comes under the authority of the household paterfamilias and the elders. Yet comparison with ancient Near Eastern feasting texts shows that these relationships are inclusive rather than exploitative. Both the absence of certain common ancient Near Eastern feasting motifs and the presence of others suggest a diminishing of the distinction between the paterfamilias and the stranger, tending toward mutuality. First, the host's contributions for the feast are not enumerated as they are in many ancient Near Eastern feasting texts. Rather, generosity is ascribed to YHWH. Second, signifiers of

---

[70] Deuteronomy 26:1–11 appears to be of a later stratum than the other feasting texts, probably the Dtr or post-Dtr redactions. Texts in Deuteronomy containing P material are generally thought to be of the post-Dtr redaction (see, e.g., Thomas Römer, *Israel's Väter: Untersuchungen zur Väterthematik im Deuteronomium und in der deuteronomistischen Tradition*, OBO 99 [Göttingen: Vandenhoeck & Ruprecht, 1990], 155–57).

[71] In Deut 26:12aα, כי תכלה לעשר ("when you have finished tithing") links 26:12–15 with 14:28–29.

[72] Deuteronomy 26:12–15 appears to be a Dtr development of 14:28–29, which is likely Dtn. See further, Mayes, *Deuteronomy*, 335.

status are missing such as seating arrangements and the host's cup.[73] Third, common motifs for hosting a banquet are missing, such as food preparation, invitations, the meat/wine consumption sequence, and the expression "to give to eat/drink."[74] All this may be explained by the central idea that, according to the Deuteronomic law corpus, the feasts are localized kinship festivals that are relatively egalitarian in character, with YHWH as host.

That these texts seek to transform relationships between the vulnerable and the household is critical. In the ancient Near East, the *gēr*, the fatherless, and the widow commonly offered cheap labor in order to survive. Turner's research on *communitas* helps to clarify that, through pilgrimage feasting, Deuteronomy was transforming these relationships in the direction of kinship. YHWH himself is the divine kinsperson, and as the *gēr* feasts לפני יהוה אלהיך ("before YHWH your God," 16:11a, 16) and as the *gēr* consumes the sacred tithe, the *gēr* is incorporated into the family of YHWH. Deuteronomy's vision for the *gēr* is that that person ultimately would become grafted into the household, the clan, and the nation as kinsfolk.

*The* Gēr *before YHWH: Religious Inclusion in the Feasting Texts*

The conclusion that the feasting is inclusive of the *gēr*, however, challenges most of the recent scholarship on the *gēr*. C. L. Crouch, for example, insists that the feasting texts do nothing to promote the inclusion of the *gēr* within the Israelite community: "he remains clearly distinguished from Israelites and is excluded from activities relating to Israelite self-definition."[75] Alternatively, Awabdy has recently argued that, while in the Deuteronomic law corpus (chs. 12–26) the *gēr* was integrated socially, in the frame of Deuteronomy (chs. 1–11, 27–34) the *gēr* was integrated both socially and religiously.[76] Awabdy contends that the laws of admission (23:2–9) are an interpretive key explaining this distinction. On the basis of this text Awabdy suggests that those immigrants[77] who have shown commitment to YHWH and to his people for three generations are admitted into the assembly. Deuteronomy 23:2–9, therefore, provides a "religious and social transition from the DC [Deuteronomic law corpus] to the P-E [prologue–epilogue]."[78] But it is unlikely that immigrants who dwelled in Judah for three generations would fit the social profile for a *gēr*—a stranger who is dependent on a household and on a clan for sustenance, akin to the fatherless and the widow. Furthermore, Awabdy's

---

[73] See Irene Winter, "The King and the Cup: Iconography of the Royal Presentation Scene on the Ur III Seals," in *Insight through Images: Studies in Honor of Edith Porada*, ed. Marilyn Kelly-Buccellati in collaboration with Paolo Matthiae and Maurits Van Loon, BMes 21 (Malibu, CA: Undena, 1986), 253–68, here 265.

[74] On the practice of sending invitations and the consumption sequence, see Murray Lichtenstein, "The Banquet Motifs in Keret and in Proverbs 9," *JANESCU* 1 (1968): 19–31.

[75] Crouch, *Making of Israel*, 219.

[76] Awabdy, *Immigrants and Innovative Law*, 122–23.

[77] Awabdy asserts that the *gēr* is a foreigner.

[78] Ibid., 66–83, 123–25, 242 (bracketed words added).

assumption that sociality and religion can be so easily separated within a communal Mediterranean society is simplistic.[79] Most importantly, both Awabdy and Crouch underestimate the religious significance of the *gēr* appearing in Dtn feasting texts "before YHWH your God" (לפני יהוה אלהיך, 16:11, 16; 26:10–11; etc.). This so-called cultic formula is the primary expression for worship at the chosen place in the Dtn redaction. So, if the *gēr* is not included in the religious life of the nation in the Dtn redaction through the cultic formula, how this redaction includes anyone in the religious life of the nation is difficult to see. The view that the framework creates a new religious inclusivism overlooks the religious inclusivism of the (earlier) feasting texts, which aim, over time, to incorporate the *gēr* within the family of YHWH.

In her recent study, Ebach contends that the Dtn redaction includes the *gēr* only in a limited way, and that the Dtr and post-Dtr redactions enhance this inclusion.[80] Ebach's analysis lacks precision, however, for rather than displaying unprecedented religious inclusivism, Deuteronomy's (later) framework prescribes *a further set of cultic practices in which the* gēr *is included*, this time with an all-Israel focus. To be sure, displacement becomes the central social concern of the framework. Nonetheless, the apparent intensification of inclusion is, in reality, a shift of text type, away from legislation and toward covenant renewal ceremonies, as we shall see in the following section.

### The Gēr *within the Framework:* "National" *Kinship (chs. 1–11, 27–34)*

Deuteronomy 1–11 and 27–34 comprise the theological and narrative framework of the law corpus. In these chapters Israel is poised to enter the land. This geographical turning point is also a place of decision: to be faithful or not, to worship the one true God or to worship other gods and thereby abandon the life of gratitude and justice that YHWH has set out in torah.[81] The *gēr* plays a dual role in this theater, appearing both as one who is incorporated into the covenant (29:9–14) and as one to whom justice and inclusion are due as a matter of covenant fidelity (27:19). While we observed in the Deuteronomic law corpus a particular emphasis on the clan and the household, in the framing texts the *gēr* is incorporated also into the kinship grouping of all Israel and of Israel's divine kinsperson. The critical consensus is that chapters 1–11 and 27–34 postdate the original law corpus.[82]

---

[79] See, e.g., Bruce J. Malina, *The Social Gospel of Jesus: The Kingdom of God in Mediterranean Perspective* (Minneapolis: Fortress, 2001), 16–18, 101–2 (Malina is discussing first-century CE Mediterranean culture).

[80] Ebach, *Das Fremde und das Eigene*, 200, 312. The composition history of the feasting texts is discussed in the preceding footnotes.

[81] See J. Gordon McConville and J. G. Millar, *Time and Place in Deuteronomy*, JSOTSup 179 (Sheffield: Sheffield Academic, 1994), 44.

[82] For an analytical demarcation between the Dtn and Dtr redactions, see Eckart Otto, *Das*

*Kinship and Covenant, 10:12–11:1*

Deuteronomy 10:17–19 has already been discussed in relation to judicial law.[83] The verb אהב ("to love") appears three times in related statements: YHWH loves Israel; YHWH loves the *gēr*; and Israel is to love the *gēr* (10:15, 18, 19).[84] Three related senses of the term אהב are relevant here. First, William L. Moran has shown that אהב in Deuteronomy belongs to the ancient Near Eastern terminology of international relations.[85] The verb אהב is a covenant term, expressing a covenant commitment to the stranger. Second, Frank Moore Cross, among others, has demonstrated that the language of ancient Near Eastern covenant treaties is taken from the language of kinship: "love," "brotherhood," "fatherhood," "fealty," and so on.[86] Through this motif the *gēr* is enfolded into the web of kin and covenant relations between Israel and Israel's divine kinsperson.[87] Third, Jacqueline E. Lapsley has shown that אהב in this context even entails an emotional connection between the *gēr* and the kinsperson.[88]

DIAGRAM. A TRIANGLE OF KINSHIP RELATIONS IN DEUTERONOMY 10:17–19

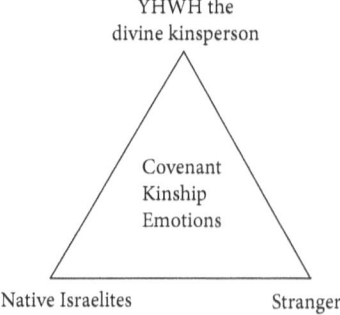

---

*Deuteronomium: Politische Theologie und Rechtsreform in Juda und Assyrien*, BZAW 284 (Berlin: de Gruyter, 1999), 238–351.

[83] On the literary history of 10:12–11:1, see the previous discussion of this text.

[84] The larger text block, 10:12–11:1, is unified by five occurrences of the verb אהב (10:12, 15, 18, 19; 11:1).

[85] William L. Moran, "The Ancient Near Eastern Background for the Love of God in Deuteronomy," *CBQ* 25 (1963): 77–87.

[86] Cross, *From Epic to Canon*, 6–7. On covenant and kinship, see Erhard S. Gerstenberger, "Covenant and Commandment," *JBL* 84 (1965): 38–51, here 39–40, http://dx.doi.org/10.2307/3264071; Scott W. Hahn, *Kinship by Covenant: A Canonical Approach to the Fulfillment of God's Saving Promises*, AYBRL (New Haven: Yale University Press, 2009), 59–60.

[87] On אהב as covenant and kinship, see Cross, *From Epic to Canon*, 3–21.

[88] Jacqueline E. Lapsley, "Feeling Our Way: Love for God in Deuteronomy," *CBQ* 65 (2003): 350–69, here 362.

*The Gēr in the Covenant Renewal Ceremony (29:9–14)*

The *gēr* is included in the covenant ceremony at Moab in Deut 29:9–14.[89] These verses are occupied with the themes of rootage: consanguinity (vv. 9–10a, 12, 14b) and the absence of kinship affiliation (vv. 10, 13). The group referenced by the phrase "but with the one who is standing here with us this day before YHWH our God" (29:14a) is grammatically linked with those who are referred to as "your stranger."[90] By virtue of the stranger's inclusion in the covenant, the stranger is also drawn into the blessings of the covenant (29:8; 30:1, 9, 16) and into the covenant obligations (28:69; 30:10). Further, the stranger is grafted into the narrative of the twin generations of the Deuteronomic History, the Horeb generation and the Moab generation (29:1–8), and also into the narrative of the ancestors and the covenant that was sworn to them (29:12b). These are the traditional kinship structures of Israel. Thus, the covenant ceremony creates relations of adoptive kinship for the stranger within the community, whereby the *gēr* shares in a "state of fellowship posited among blood brothers,"[91] with YHWH as the divine kinsperson.

*Seventh-Year Reading of Torah (31:9–13)*

The *gēr* is included in the assembly of all Israel for the seventh-year reading of torah (31:9–13), which assumes its importance as the acme of what is arguably the most important event in the Deuteronomic cultic calendar, the seventh-year remission (שמטה) at the Feast of Booths.[92] Chapter 31 establishes a relationship between the *gēr* and the book of law, for three motive clauses concerning *hearing, learning, fearing, and obeying* torah apply to the *gēr* also (31:12–13). The phrase ולמען ילמדו ויראו ("so that you may learn and fear," 31:12b) and related texts (31:13a,

---

[89] Elements of 29:9–14, including the assembly of Israel, the covenant, and the "national" focus of the participant list are characteristic of the Dtr redaction. See further Mayes, *Deuteronomy*, 65. Achenbach reflects the common view that the singular address (29:10aβ–12) is a post-Dtr insertion, while the remainder of the text is the Dtr redaction (Achenbach, "Der Eintritt der Schutzbürger," 249–51). Nowhere, however, is covenant making expressed only in the negative, the result of Achenbach's reconstruction (29:13a). It is likely, then, that 29:10aβ–12a is original. Yet the phrase וכאשר נשבע לאבתיך לאברהם ליצחק וליעקב ("as he swore to your ancestors, to Abraham, to Isaac, and to Jacob," 29:12b [Eng. 29:13b]) may be a postexilic interpolation, as the sworn covenant with the ancestors is characteristic of the final (Pentateuch) redaction, and as the doubling of כאשר is highly unusual (29:12a, b; cf. Gen 26:29).

[90] The singular collective form ישנו ("to exist," 29:14a) corresponds to the singular collective form וגרך ("your stranger," 29:10a).

[91] Gottfried Quell, "διαθήκη," *TDNT* 2:106–24, here 114.

[92] Deuteronomy 31:9–13 appropriates the feasting trope from the Dtn redaction, and the *gēr* appears in both the source texts (14:28–29; 16:11, 14; 26:11) and in 31:12. The reappearance of the chosen place (31:12) is consistent with the presentation of Jerusalem as a location of blessing instead of curse during the postexilic period (see David M. Carr, *The Formation of the Hebrew Bible: A New Reconstruction* [New York: Oxford University Press, 2011], 213).

17:19b) are appropriated from 14:23b (concerning the tithe). Uniquely in the present text, the *lamed* prefix is omitted; ויראו is a *vav*-relative whereby the "fearing" is both future and relative to the "learning."[93] Here, therefore, the emphasis is on learning. The *gēr*, as a member of Israel, will also hear and learn the torah and in so doing will fear and obey YHWH.

Three other texts from Deuteronomy's frame have already been discussed—1:16–17 (judicial law), 5:12–15 (social law), and 27:19 (judicial law; curse ceremony). I have omitted discussing 28:43–44, due to space.

*Observations on the* Gēr *in Deuteronomy's Framework*

Four points may be made in light of the foregoing analysis of the frame of Deuteronomy. First, in Deuteronomy's framework, as Israel was reconstituted, the inclusion of those who had been separated from patrimony and from kindred was a primary goal. In the frame of Deuteronomy other vulnerable categories of people recede into the background, and the inclusion of the stranger becomes the dominant social concern.[94]

Second, in these chapters the *gēr* is included within the kinship grouping of all Israel. While feasting texts nourish the incorporation of the *gēr* into the clan and into the household, the framing texts nourish the incorporation of the *gēr* into the grouping of all Israel and of Israel's divine kinsperson.[95]

Third, the near consensus in the scholarship that the framework (chs. 1–11, 27–34) initiates a new religious inclusivism that is not to be found in the (earlier) law corpus (chs. 12–26) underestimates the religious significance of the *gēr* appearing in Dtn feasting texts פני יהוה אלהיך, "before YHWH your God" (16:16; etc). Rather than an unprecedented religious inclusivism, the frame prescribes a further set of cultic practices in which the *gēr* is to be included, this time with an all-Israel focus. For example, the public reading of torah (31:9–13) is an addition to the already established tradition of Booths (16:12–15) within which the *gēr* was previously included. The seventh-year reading of torah is presented syntactically as an additional practice within an already established cultic tradition.[96] Deuteronomy 31:9–13, then, does not entail a new and unprecedented religious inclusivism for the *gēr* but a new *practice* for all Israel in which the *gēr* is included.

Fourth, the data do not suggest that the *gēr* in Deuteronomy's frame is exclusively a non-Judahite or non-Israelite. The all-Israel focus of the frame does not require that *outsiderism* be identified exclusively at a "national" level. In 29:10, the

---

[93] See further *IBHS*, 519–20.

[94] The framework also references slaves (5:12–15) and the vulnerable triad (10:17–18, 27:19).

[95] Nonetheless, in the Dtn redaction the *gēr* is incorporated into the people of YHWH by means of cultic feasting before YHWH.

[96] The phrase בבוא כל-ישראל ("when all Israel comes") is an infinitive clause that is subordinate to the verbs תקרא and הקהל (31:11–12).

pronominal suffix form וגרך ("your *gēr*") clearly identifies the *gēr* as a household dependent, locating the insider–outsider distinction primarily at the level of the household. In addition, in the seventh-year reading of torah, identification of the *gēr* with a household (וגרך, 31:12a) and within a settlement (בשעריך, "within your gates," 31:12a) locates the insider–outsider distinction primarily at the level of the household and the settlement. Further, the prominence of the figure of the *gēr* in 31:9–13 suggests that there was a large number of displaced persons in the society that the text addresses. The large contingent of scholars who maintain that the *gēr* is non-Israelite or non-Judahite and who also assign 31:9–13 to the postexilic period[97] must explain why a large number of immigrants would have infiltrated Persian Yehud and why these supposed immigrants desired the "harsh realities of life"[98] in Persian Yehud. Such "harsh realities" included widespread socioeconomic stratification and poverty, which has led some scholars to conclude that Persian Judah was "undesirable as a location for immigration."[99] Similarly, those who hold that the *gēr* is exclusively a foreigner and who date 1:16–17 and 29:9–14 to exilic Judah[100] must explain why the primary social concern in Judah, following the devastation of the Neo-Babylonian invasion, was for foreigners. If the Dtr and post-Dtr redactions emerge in sixth-century Judah and Persian Yehud, respectively, then arguably the internally displaced person, especially, must be enfolded into the covenant, the one who has been severed from land and from genealogy. The point of the *gēr* texts throughout Deuteronomy is not the following: *as we renew Israel, let's include lots of non-Israelites*. Rather, the point is this: *in this context of social upheaval, where as many people are displaced as are not, how may those who have been displaced from kindred and patrimony be enfolded into the covenant?* To repeat, the term *gēr* itself does not refer exclusively to an internally displaced person, a non-Israelite or non-Judahite, or a "northerner"; *gēr* probably referred to all of these categories of people at various times, and the causes of the displacement to which Deuteronomy was responding were diverse.

## IV. Social History

We may make some tentative observations relating the foregoing analysis to Israel's social history. Throughout the analysis, in the footnotes, the passages

---

[97] For example, Achenbach ("Der Eintritt der Schutzbürger," 252) and Ebach (*Das Fremde und das Eigene*, 316–17) each assert both that the post-Dtr redaction addresses Persian Yehud and also that the *gēr* is a foreigner.

[98] See John Kessler, "Diaspora and Homeland in the Early Achaemenid Period: Community, Geography and Demography in Zechariah 1–8," in *Approaching Yehud: New Approaches to the Study of the Persian Period*, ed. Jon L. Berquist, SemeiaSt 50 (Atlanta: Society of Biblical Literature, 2007), 137–66, here 165.

[99] Ibid.

[100] E.g., Mayes, *Deuteronomy*, 43–44, 359.

discussed are tentatively connected with redactional layers. The following pattern emerges: the original Dtn layer projects a society before the text that is confronted with pervasive displacement (e.g., 16:1–17; 24:14–15, 17, 19–21). The displacement is only intensified in the Dtr redaction, for the *gēr* is the overriding social issue of Deuteronomy's framing texts, almost exclusively (e.g., 1:16–18, 5:12–15, 29:9–14). Displacement remains an insistent social issue in texts that seem to be authored later, referred to as the post-Dtr redaction (e.g., 10:17–19, 31:9–13). This breakdown suggests that Deuteronomy was written over connected periods of deep and persistent but differentiated displacement.

## V. Inclusion and Exclusion: Antithesis or Contextualization?

Deuteronomy holds a tension, at least on the surface of the text, between the inclusion of the *gēr* and elements of exclusivism. Indeed, Deuteronomy's relentless ethic of inclusion for the *gēr* is, as Rainer Albertz reflects, all the more "amazing" in light of other texts that demand the exclusion of others.[101] This apparent tension calls for discussion. Erhard S. Gerstenberger explains these differing postures by the existence of "varied theological groupings" within the community that was devoted to YHWH.[102] In certain texts, however, "insider" themes coexist with themes of inclusivism in the same redactional layer, challenging this assertion (e.g., 23:1–7; cf. 23:8; 29:9–14; cf. 29:10aβ). Gerstenberger's solution runs the risk of obscuring deeper theological aims within Deuteronomy. A better explanation of the data is that this complex of responses is an authentic attempt, on the one hand, to preserve the religious and social identity of the people of YHWH as a marginalized community and, on the other hand, to express *an inclusivism that is central to this very identity*. By this logic, the *gēr* is, by definition, vulnerable and isolated, so that person is unlikely to threaten the faithfulness of the community. Yet consolidated groups who do not worship YHWH may pose a real threat.

## VI. Concluding remarks

An ethic of inclusivism for the *gēr* as found in the book of Deuteronomy has been the central investigation of this study. The term *gēr* in Deuteronomy simply identifies a vulnerable person who is from outside the core family. This displaced

---

[101] Albertz, "From Aliens to Proselytes," 55.
[102] Erhard S. Gerstenberger, *Israel in the Persian Period: The Fifth and Fourth Centuries B.C.E.*, trans. Siegfried S. Schatzmann, BibEnc 8 (Atlanta: Society of Biblical Literature, 2011), 441.

person no longer receives the protection that kinship and patrimony afford and is therefore vulnerable to exploitation and abuse. Deuteronomy's vision for the *gēr*, expressed in a variety of ways, is to foster the *gēr*'s inclusion as kindred within the household, within the clan, and within all Israel.

This inclusion and protection for the *gēr* in Deuteronomy is achieved through the interplay between various subgroups of laws. First, the social law guards against exploitation, also indicating that the *gēr* is a corecipient of the gift of land and of its abundance. Second, the law of judicial procedure secures justice at the gates for displaced persons, opening the possibility of their full economic and social participation. Third, through cultic feasting Deuteronomy transforms the relationships between the *gēr* and kinsfolk in the direction of kinship, incorporating the *gēr* within the household and the clan. Finally, the framework of Deuteronomy (chs. 1–11, 27–34) is concerned with the renewal of the family of YHWH. In these frame texts, as Israel was reconstituted, the incorporation of those who had been separated from patrimony and from kindred was a primary goal. Deuteronomy's ethic of inclusion for the *gēr* is embedded theologically, within YHWH's own actions and character and also within Israel's own historical narrative.

**BIBLICAL HEBREW**
*An Introductory Grammar*
Second Edition
Page H. Kelley
Revised by Timothy G. Crawford
ISBN 9780802874917
540 pages • paperback • $40.00

**A Handbook to**
**BIBLICAL HEBREW**
*An Introductory Grammar*
Second Edition
Page H. Kelley, Terry L. Burden, and Timothy G. Crawford
ISBN 9780802875013
249 pages • paperback • $28.00

**THIS SECOND EDITION** has updated text throughout while preserving the Page Kelley approach that has made *Biblical Hebrew* so popular over the years.

The accompanying handbook provides a complete answer key to the exercises in the grammar as well as practical guidance, footnotes, word lists, test suggestions, and other supplementary material.

At your bookstore,
or call 800-253-7521
eerdmans.com

**Wm. B. Eerdmans**
**Publishing Co.**

# Separating the Wheat from the Chaff: The Independent Logic of Deuteronomy 22:25–27

SARA J. MILSTEIN
sara.milstein@ubc.ca
University of British Columbia, Vancouver, BC V6T 1Z1, Canada

Although the three laws on illicit sexual intercourse in Deut 22:23–29 are often treated as a set, close examination indicates that the assault of an engaged woman in a field (vv. 25–27) represents the literary core to which verses 23–24 and 28–29 were appended. The isolation of 22:25–27 from its secondary frame enables its independent legal reasoning to emerge. The scribe presents an unusual scenario by ancient Near Eastern legal standards, in that the assault of the victim transpires without witnesses. Curiously, the solution favors the woman by comparing the assault to a homicide and then positing a hypothetical situation whereby the victim is imagined to have shouted for help. I propose that the closest parallel for this display of legal reasoning is found not in another cuneiform law collection but rather in the "Nippur Homicide Trial," a Mesopotamian "model case" that was utilized in second-millennium scribal education. Not only does this model case shed fresh light on the legal reasoning that undergirds Deut 22:25–27, but its genre also provides a new lens through which to reconsider the origins of a wider set of women and family laws in Deuteronomy.

---

Deuteronomy 22:23–29 features three laws regarding illicit sexual intercourse between a man and an engaged/unengaged woman.[1] At first glance, the unit

I am grateful to Daniel Fleming, Shawn Flynn, Reinhard Kratz, Christoph Levin, and Bruce Wells for their helpful feedback at various stages in the development of this article. Research for this article was generously supported by the Social Sciences and Humanities Research Council of Canada (SSHRC) and by the Killam Foundation.

[1] On the unit, see esp. Alexander Rofé, "Family and Sex Laws in Deuteronomy and the Book of Covenant," *Hen* 9 (1987): 131–59; Eckart Otto, *Kontinuum und Proprium: Studien zur Sozial- und Rechtsgeschichte des Alten Orients und des Alten Testaments*, OBC 8 (Wiesbaden: Harrassowitz, 1996), 15–38; Otto, *Das Deuteronomium: Politische Theologie und Rechtsreform in Juda und Assyrien*, BZAW 284 (Berlin: de Gruyter, 1999), 203–21; Cynthia Edenburg, "Ideology and Social Context of the Deuteronomic Women's Sex Laws (Deuteronomy 22:13–29)," *JBL* 128 (2009):

appears to reflect typical Near Eastern legal reasoning, in that a base scenario is followed by two cases that substitute different factors in order to yield alternative outcomes. A man lies with an engaged woman in the town (vv. 23–24); this is followed by a man who forcefully lies with an engaged woman in the field (vv. 25–27); in the third scenario, an unengaged woman is assaulted with location no longer relevant (vv. 28–29).[2] As is widely recognized, several cuneiform collections likewise include series of laws concerning illicit sex that present variations on a core case. Deuteronomy 22:23–29 also displays a set of linguistic and structural ties to 22:13–22. It is thus not surprising that a number of studies emphasize the unity of 22:23–29 or, more broadly, that of 22:13–29 as a whole.[3]

A close examination of Deut 22:23–29 reveals that the unit is rooted in the "field" scenario alone. Once verses 25–27 are isolated from their secondary frame, their singular mode of legal reasoning begins to emerge. Only in this case does the scribe present an analogy to another crime, coupled with a reconstruction of events that inexplicably favors the woman's word over the man's. Surprisingly, we find the closest parallel for this line of reasoning not in another cuneiform law but in the "Nippur Homicide Trial," a Mesopotamian model case that likewise addresses the matter of a woman's potential guilt. Notwithstanding the chronological and geographical distance between these two texts, the particular mode of legal reasoning in the Nippur Homicide Trial helps illuminate the logic of this biblical law. Moreover, I propose that awareness of this pedagogical genre provides a new lens through which to view the origins of Deut 22:25–27, along with a larger set of casuistic laws in Deuteronomy.

---

43–60, https://doi.org/10.2307/25610164; Robert S. Kawashima, "Could a Woman Say 'No' in Biblical Israel? On the Genealogy of Legal Status in Biblical Law and Literature," *AJS Review* 35 (2011): 1–22; and Carolyn Pressler, *The View of Women Found in the Deuteronomic Family Laws*, BZAW 216 (Berlin: de Gruyter, 1993), 21–43.

[2] Questions regarding the applicability of the term *rape* to biblical texts center on the lack of an ancient equivalent to the modern concept of consent. Kawashima argues that the lack of women's rights in "biblical Israel" indicates that the concept of forcible rape did not exist in their legal system ("Could a Woman Say 'No'?," 2).

[3] Gordon J. Wenham and J. Gordon McConville see the larger unit of Deut 22:13–29 as reflecting an "essential unity" and draw attention to the logical order of the cases, the chiastic order of the punishments, and the triadic division of the entire section ("Drafting Techniques in Some Deuteronomic Laws," *VT* 30 [1980]: 248–52, here 248–49). Rofé refers to Deut 22:22–29 and Exod 22:15–16 as reflecting the application of "systematic legal thinking … with both an attention to detail and an awareness of the larger picture" ("Family and Sex Laws," 150). Kawashima identifies a chiastic arrangement in Deut 22:22–29 with regard to "various combinations of two features: +/- virginity and +/- married" ("Could a Woman Say 'No'?," 15). Edenburg deems the larger unit of Deut 22:13–29 "a carefully drafted, self-contained collection of laws," unlike the "haphazard" rulings that precede and follow it ("Ideology and Social Context," 44). She determines that, while 22:13–29 may have derived from multiple sources, this section of laws "was conceived and composed as a whole" (48). Pressler points to the unification of 22:13–29 at "a redactional level" in terms of content, form, and wording (*View of Women*, 21).

## I. The Secondary Nature of Deuteronomy 22:23–24 and 22:28–29

In its present position, Deut 22:25–27 is the second of three interconnected scenarios. In the first case, a man finds and lies with an engaged "virgin" (בתולה) in the town; the two are then stoned to death in order to "remove evil from [the people's] midst" (vv. 23–24).[4] Justification for each party's execution is provided: the young woman is punished "because she did not shout (for help)," while the man is killed for "degrading" (ענה) another man's wife.[5] Grammatically, Deut 22:25–27 is then dependent on the first unit: the clause begins with ואם ־ and not כי, a typical feature of secondary legal paragraphs; and it refers to both culprit and victim with the definite article (האיש את־הנער [הנערה] המארשה).[6] In this case, the man finds and grasps hold of the engaged woman in the *field*, but only the man receives the death penalty. An explanation likens the crime to a homicide and states that the woman shouted for help but she had no savior. The third case then omits the offended fiancé from the equation but retains the violence. As in the second case, only the man is found guilty, but this time he must marry the victim, with no option for divorce.

### The Secondary and Anomalous Nature of Deuteronomy 22:23–24

At first glance, Deut 22:23–24 and 22:25–27 reflect a classic case and counter-case whereby the substitution of one factor for another yields a different outcome.[7]

---

[4] Drawing connections to Akkadian and Ugaritic cognates, Gordon J. Wenham claims that the term בתולה denotes not a "virgin" but rather "a girl of marriageable age" ("*Bᵉtûlāh*: A Girl of Marriageable Age," *VT* 22 [1972]: 326–48). *CAD* defines the Akkadian cognate *batultu* as an "adolescent, nubile girl"; note also the corresponding term *batūlu* ("young man") (2:173–74). While the use of בתולים in Deut 22:13–19 would seem to upend this reading, given that most understand that the girl's parents produced "tokens of her virginity," Wenham argues that the term refers to clothing stained by menstrual blood. In this way, the parents prove that their daughter was not pregnant prior to marriage, a concern that is evidently at the heart of the accusation ("*Bᵉtûlāh*," 334–35).

[5] My translation here follows Ellen van Wolde, who concludes that the term ענה is semantically tied to a downward movement and is thus better translated as "to debase" ("Does *'innâ* Denote Rape? A Semantic Analysis of a Controversial Word," *VT* 52 [2002]: 528–44, here 543–44). The translations of the biblical texts throughout are my own.

[6] For an insightful discussion of the varied use of these terms, see Bernard Levinson and Molly Zahn, "Revelation Regained: The Hermeneutics of כי and אם in the Temple Scroll," *DSD* 9 (2002): 295–346; on the use of these terms in Deut 22:13–29, see Edenburg, "Ideology and Social Context," 45.

[7] In fact, multiple factors distinguish the two protases: in verses 25–27, the location is in the

It is notable, however, that only verses 23–24 are marked by stereotypical language regarding the integrity of the people, what Alexander Rofé terms $D_2$ and what I identify as "post-Deuteronomic."[8] With its second-person exhortation to bring the two offenders to "the gate of that town" and "stone them to death," an act that will enable the people to "remove the evil" from their midst (the "בערת [biʿartā] formula"), the verdict resonates with the punishments outlined for apostates in Deut 13 and 17, as Rofé notes.[9] Deuteronomy 22:23–24 also echoes verses 20–21, an unequivocally secondary unit in which a guilty bride is brought to the entrance of her father's gate and stoned to death, a punishment that likewise "removes the evil" from the people's midst.[10] In this light, it is possible that Deut 22:23–24 was not merely *revised* by a post-Deuteronomic editor but rather that the entire unit was invented by an editor from scratch, like verses 20–21.[11]

Deuteronomy 22:23–24 is also governed by somewhat curious reasoning. The protasis states that a man "finds" and "lies" with an engaged virgin in the town, a scenario that on its own terms seems to imply rape. Both actions are attributed only to the man; no action or mental state is assigned to the woman; and while the root שכב ("to lie") is not exclusively violent, other biblical verses utilize this verb with

---

field, not the town; a violent verb, חזק ("to grasp hold of"), supplements the neutral verb שכב ("to lie"), and the woman's designation as a "virgin" is missing. The apodoses, moreover, introduce another contrast: while the woman did not shout for help in the first case, she did shout out in the second.

[8] Rofé attributes to this editor the integration of what he identifies as an inherited collection of sex and family laws into the book of Deuteronomy ("Family and Sex Laws," 143). Edenburg refers to the author throughout this entire legal section as "the Deuteronomist" ("Ideology and Social Context," 50 and passim); likewise, see Rosario Pius Merendino, *Das deuteronomische Gesetz: Eine literarkritische, gattungs- und überlieferungsgeschichtliche Untersuchung zu Dt 12–26*, BBB 31 (Bonn: Hanstein, 1969), 273.

[9] Rofé, "Family and Sex Laws," 142–43. Given that all of this content is more concerned with the maintenance of integrity than with cult centralization, it apparently reflects a late phase in the development of Deuteronomy, one that postdates those texts that arguably represent the earliest "core" of the book. For discussion of the "core" of Deuteronomy, see esp. Reinhard G. Kratz, *The Composition of the Narrative Books of the Old Testament*, trans. John Bowden (London: T&T Clark, 2005), 117–23.

[10] Not only do Deut 22:13–19 and 20–21 manifest distinct styles and lengths, but the scenario that launches the first case, "If a man marries a woman … and hates her, and lays groundless accusations upon her," does not apply to verses 20–21. As Clemens Locher notes, "Die Spannungen zwischen 22,13–19 und 22,20f. erklären sich ohne weiteres, wenn der erste Teil von einer solchen Vorlage abhängig, der zweite dagegen nachträglicher Zusatz des 'Gesetzgebers' ist, der das Prozessprotokoll zu einem kasuistischen Gesetz umforte" ("Deuteronomium 22,13–21 vom Prozessprotokoll zum kasuistischen Gesetz," in *Das Deuteronomium: Entstehung, Gestalt und Botschaft*, ed. Norbert Lohfink, BETL 68 [Leuven: Leuven University Press, 1985], 298–303, here 303).

[11] Cf. Otto, who isolates verses 23 and 24a as "pre-Dtn" content (*Das Deuteronomium*, 204–5).

reference to nonconsensual sex.[12] The apodosis, however, introduces *new* information, now stating that the woman "did not shout (for help) in the town." Such a detail suggests that the young woman either consented to intercourse or worse yet, conspired with the man in question to commit adultery.[13] There appears, then, to be a logistical tension between implied rape in the protasis and implied consent in the apodosis.

This sequence is indeed unusual in the context of ancient Near Eastern law. While a number of laws concerning illicit sex provide justification for a woman's guilt, none suspends the *reason* for her guilt to the apodosis.[14] Thus, in the Laws of Ur-Nammu (LU) §7, the protasis specifies that the woman initiated intercourse: "If the wife of a young man, *on her own initiative*, approaches a man and initiates sexual relations with him ...."[15] In Middle Assyrian Laws (MAL) A §13, a woman initiates adultery by going to another man's house; unsurprisingly, both fornicators are killed. While the Laws of Eshnunna (LE) §28 implicates a (married) woman, in this case, it is specifically if she is "seized in the lap of another man." Likewise, the protasis of §129 in the Laws of Hammurabi (LH) involves a guilty woman who is "seized lying with another male," and MAL A §15 involves a man who catches another man with his wife in flagrante delicto. These laws thus more closely parallel Deut 22:22, where the couple is "found," presumably by the woman's husband. MAL A §§55 and 56 then distinguish between a man who seizes an unengaged virgin, a crime that leads solely to the man's guilt; and a virgin who *willingly* gives herself to a man. In the latter case, the man must hand over a "triple" portion of the girl's value, while the girl's fate lies in the hands of her father. In addition, MAL A §55 stipulates that this crime may take place in *any* location, so that the man is guilty whether the rape is committed "within the city or in the countryside, or at

---

[12] See, e.g., Gen 34:7 and 39:14. At the same time, the scribe's use of a neutral term in the first case is surely deliberate, in that it supports and anticipates the woman's guilty verdict.

[13] Once the bride-price had been paid, an engaged woman was of the same legal status as a married woman. G. R. Driver and John C. Miles refer to this as "inchoate marriage" (*The Babylonian Laws*, 2 vols., Ancient Codes and Laws of the Near East [Oxford: Clarendon, 1952], 1:248–49). This appears to be the underlying issue in Deut 22:13–21; namely, a man accuses his wife of having had intercourse during the engagement period, an offense that would ostensibly compromise the certain paternity of her child.

[14] For discussion of the parallels between the Deuteronomic laws and other Near Eastern laws, see Raymond Westbrook, "Adultery in Ancient Near Eastern Law," in *Law from the Tigris to the Tiber: The Writings of Raymond Westbrook*, 2 vols., ed. Bruce Wells and F. Rachel Magdalene (Winona Lake, IN: Eisenbrauns, 2009), 1:245–87; and Edenburg, "Ideology and Social Context," 48–56. Edenburg likewise notes that of the closest parallels to Deut 22:23–27, namely, the Laws of Ur-Nammu §6, the Laws of Eshnunna §26, and the Laws of Hammurabi §130, none of them makes a distinction on the basis of location and none holds the girl accountable for her "deflowering" (53).

[15] Translations of Mesopotamian precepts follow Martha T. Roth, *Law Collections from Mesopotamia and Asia Minor*, WAW 6 (Atlanta: Scholars Press, 1995).

night, whether in the main square, a granary, or during the city festival." In all of these cases where the woman is found guilty, then, the *protasis* specifies either her agency or that the couple was caught in the act.[16]

Several other laws require further discussion. Hittite Laws (HL) §197 prescribes different punishments for illicit sex in different locations; it thus appears to parallel the two cases in Deut 22:23–24 and 22:25–27. HL §197, however, distinguishes between a man who seizes a woman in the *mountains* and one who does so in a woman's *house*. In the former case, the man is killed; in the latter, the woman is killed. This law thus constitutes different circumstances, for fornication in a woman's house would appear to indicate her consent in the Near Eastern legal mind-set. Moreover, given that the discovery of the two would likely be by the woman's husband—and indeed, the law goes on to permit the spouse to kill the fornicators if he catches them in the act—HL §197 appears to work more in the vein of LE §28, LH §129, MAL A §15, and Deut 22:22.

MAL A §14 involves two cases of a man fornicating with another man's wife— in an inn or in a city square. While the woman is not definitely punished in either case, both cases allow the husband to exercise the option. In the first, if the offender knew that the woman was married, the law stipulates, "they shall treat the fornicator as the man … wishes his wife to be treated." If the offender was unaware of the woman's status, however, he is innocent. It then states that the husband *shall prove the charges against his wife* and treat her as he wishes. This latter case is thus instructive, in that the husband can punish his wife only *after* he establishes her guilt. Given that the first case does not automatically result in the wife's guilt, it is probable that any penalty would also be based on an assessment of the woman's complicity. Furthermore, as Raymond Westbrook points out, the inn and city square represent "typical haunts of a prostitute," suggesting that both cases involve women who intentionally commit adultery.[17] In any case, MAL A §14 does not provide justification for the woman's guilt in the apodosis.

This leaves MAL A §16. Like MAL A §14, this law covers two cases pertaining to illicit fornication. In the first, a man apparently sleeps with a married woman at her invitation; the woman's penalty is predictably in the hands of her husband.[18] The second case is more problematic. In this instance, the law states that a man slept with a married woman by force (*emūqamma ittiakši*). In this case, "they shall prove the charges against him," and his punishment will match that of the woman (*ḫīṭašu kî ša aššat aʾīlemma*). While this part of the law allows for the (presumably

---

[16] Anthony Phillips notes that it is probable that prosecution for adultery required catching the couple in the act; to his mind, this explains why cases that rest on unsubstantiated accusations of adultery are missing from Deuteronomy ("Another Look at Adultery," *JSOT* 20 [1981]: 3–25, here 7).

[17] For Westbrook, this fact explains the man's potential ignorance of the woman's status in the second case ("Adultery in Ancient Near Eastern Law," 254).

[18] Though the text is broken, the term *pīša* ("her mouth") is legible, suggesting that the woman initiated intercourse.

innocent) woman to be punished, it stands to reason that the required legal procedure would have to assess her role as well, as in MAL A §14. In any case, MAL A §16 is unclear whether the woman is to be executed, and, again, the apodosis provides no justification for her guilt. In this sense, Deut 22:23–24 remains a legal anomaly.

Both the internal and external data thus suggest that Deut 22:23–24 was composed as a countercase to verses 25–27, where the woman *does* shout for help and is treated as an innocent victim.[19] This proposed process of development would parallel the composition of both Deut 22:13–21, where a case involving an innocent woman (vv. 13–19) is supplemented with a post-Deuteronomic countercase that ends with a woman who is stoned to death for her transgression (vv. 20–21); and Deut 21:15–21, where a law preventing a man from favoring his younger son is followed by a post-Deuteronomic countercase that features a son who is stoned to death for his disobedience.[20] Like Deut 22:23–24, the two secondary cases include the biᶜartā formula. The principle guiding these supplementations is evidently the same, whether they were added by the same scribe/editor (thus constituting a "redaction") or by different contributors at different points in time. Each law—Deut 21:18–21, 22:20–21, and 22:23–24—as with chapters 13 and 17, prescribes harsh punishment against those who are disloyal, whether to their parents, their fiancé/husband, or YHWH.[21]

### The Secondary Nature of Deuteronomy 22:28–29

It is well known that the case of Deut 22:28–29 resonates with MT Exod 22:15–16 (LXX 22:16–17) and may reflect a revision of it.[22] This parallel has led some to conclude that Deut 22:28–29 represents the core of the series and that the town and

---

[19] While Phillips holds the Deuteronomic writer responsible for introducing provisions that implicate women alongside their male counterparts, as in Deut 22:22 (cf. Lev 20:10), he attributes verses 23–24 and 25–27 to the same legislator ("Some Aspects of Family Law in Pre-Exilic Israel," *VT* 23 [1973]: 349–61, here 353).

[20] While the cases in Deut 21:15–17 and 18–21 are less closely tied, it is noteworthy that only Deut 22:18–21 exhibits signs of post-Deuteronomic composition, as suggested especially by its ties to chapters 13 and 17. On this link, and on the "moralistic" nature of this unit, see Rofé, "Family and Sex Laws," 151. Yet cf. Timothy M. Willis, who concludes that Deut 21:18–21aα is pre-Deuteronomic, in contrast to 13:7–12, which he identifies as Deuteronom(ist)ic (*The Elders of the City: A Study of the Elder-Laws in Deuteronomy*, SBLMS 55 [Atlanta: Society of Biblical Literature, 2001], 173). As Willis rightly points out, there are parallels between the ordering of Deut 21:15–21 and LH §§167–168: both follow a law pertaining to the division of property among two sons with a law pertaining to a man who wishes to remove his son from his house.

[21] See Edenburg's eloquent discussion of how the theme of marital loyalty parallels fidelity to YHWH, something that would have been crucial in the postexilic period ("Ideology and Social Context," 58–59).

[22] Most conclude that Deut 22:28–29 represents a revision of Exod 22:15–16. See, e.g., Phillips, "Some Aspects of Family Law," 351 n. 1; and Phillips, "Another Look at Adultery," 9–13.

field laws were developed as additions.²³ While Deut 22:28–29 may be rooted in the Exodus law, however, this does not guarantee its priority in the unit.

Deuteronomy 22:28–29 and Exod 22:15–16 both deal with a man who lies with an unengaged virgin, a crime that requires the perpetrator to pay the father and marry the woman. The two differ, however, in multiple ways:

a. In Deut 22:28, the victim is identified as "a young woman, an unengaged virgin" (נער [נערה] בתולה אשר לא־ארשה) while in Exod 22:15, she is simply "an unengaged virgin" (בתולה אשר לא־ארשה).
b. Only Deut 22:29 specifies that the rapist cannot divorce his victim because he "degraded" her (ענה).
c. In Deut 22:28, the man "*seizes*" (ותפשה) the woman, while in Exodus, he "*persuades*" (יפתה) her.
d. Only in Deut 22:28 does the man "find" (ימצא) the woman and are the two "found" (ונמצאו).
e. The attacker pays the father fifty shekels in Deut 22:29, while in Exodus he pays an undisclosed bride-price.
f. Only Exod 22:16 states that the father may refuse his daughter to the rapist.

While one could argue that the two texts represent variations on the same basic law, it is significant that most of the details unique to Deut 22:28–29 share content with the preceding laws in verses 13–27. Moreover, in some cases, this content is better suited to those other contexts than to verses 28–29. I shall proceed in order of the list above:

a. Deuteronomy 22:23 provides a parallel redundant epithet for the victim ("a young woman, a virgin engaged to a man").
b. The man in Deut 22:24 is likewise deemed guilty because he "degraded" the woman.²⁴ In 22:29, however, the reference to this "degradation" interrupts the logical sequence that the woman will become his wife and he

---

²³ See, e.g., Eckart Otto, who sees Deut 22:22a and 28–29 as "scholastically expanded" by Deut 22:23–27 ("Aspects of Legal Reforms and Reformulations in Ancient Cuneiform and Israelite Law," in *Theory and Method in Biblical and Cuneiform Law: Revision, Interpolation, and Development*, ed. Bernard M. Levinson, JSOTSup 181 [Sheffield: Sheffield Academic, 1994], 160–96, here 192). For Otto, Deut 22:23–24 and 25–27 represent subcases that expound upon Deut 22:22a (*Kontinuum und Proprium*, 129). Merendino, who views verses 23–24 and 25–27 as secondary to verse 22 and verses 28–29, outlines a similar theory (*Das deuteronomische Gesetz*, 262). The circumstances of Deut 22:22a ("If a man is *found* lying with a woman who is married to a man …"), however, do not explicitly apply either to verses 23–24 or to verses 25–27.

²⁴ The repetition of the verb in verses 24 and 29 was noted already by Merendino (*Das deuteronomische Gesetz*, 264); see also Bruce Wells, who notes that both statements reflect the "typical Deuteronomic" practice of providing a rationale for the penalties ("The Interpretation of Legal Traditions in Ancient Israel," *HBAI* 4 [2015]: 234–66, here 253–54 n. 67).

cannot divorce her. The same sequence is uninterrupted in 22:19: "She shall be his wife; he cannot [literally] send her out all of his days."

c. The explicitly violent verb in verse 28 ("he seizes her") parallels the violent verb in verse 25 ("he grasps hold of her").

d. In all three cases in the series, the man is said to "find" the woman, yet while this discovery is embedded in a specific location in verses 23–27 (town or field), in verses 28–29, the man simply "finds" the woman, with no coordinates given.

e. Finally, the two men in 22:13–19 and 22:28–29 are each punished with a specific fine and prohibition of divorce (לא־יוכל לשלחה כל־ימיו).[25] Again, this verdict better suits 22:13–19, where the lying plaintiff evidently tries to *divorce* his bride *without* pecuniary damages.[26]

Given that much of the "distinct" terminology in 22:28–29 echoes phrases in 22:13–19, 22, 23–24, and 25–27 *and* displays evidence of borrowing, I propose that verses 28–29 represent a late addition to the wider collection of laws concerning illicit sex in 22:13–27. While it may reflect knowledge of some version of Exod 22:15–16, it is also dependent on the block of laws concerning marriage and illicit sex that precedes it. It is not clear, however, that 22:28–29 derives from the same hand as verses 23–24, given that verses 28–29 lack the stereotypical post-Deuteronomic language and themes that define 22:23–24, 21:8–21, 22:20–21, and chapters 13 and 17.

---

[25] On the overlapping terminology here, see, e.g., Phillips, "Another Look at Adultery," 12. Rofé observes that the unique formulation לא־יוכל occurs only in these two instances, Deut 21:16 and 24:4 ("Family and Sex Laws," 133).

[26] The fine of one hundred shekels is generally taken to be twice the bride-price, an assumption that is based exclusively on the "payment" of fifty shekels in Deut 22:28–29 (Pressler, *View of Women*, 28). It stands to reason, however, that the reverse is the case—that the number in 22:28–29 is based on the larger fine in 22:13–19. Regarding the bridegroom's intention to divorce his wife and to recover the bride-price, see the nuanced argument in Bruce Wells, "Sex, Lies, and Virginal Rape: The Slandered Bride and False Accusation in Deuteronomy," *JBL* 124 (2005): 41–72, https://doi.org/10.2307/30040990. Wells tries to reconcile the seeming discrepancy between 22:13–21 and 19:16–21, given that the latter prescribes that false accusers should receive the same punishment that they intend for their opponents. Considering that the guilty bride is executed in 22:20–21, why is the bridegroom in 22:13–19 given the relatively "light" penalty of flogging, a fine, and no option for divorce? Drawing on Near Eastern evidence of "full" and "partial" measures of punishment, Wells claims that the execution in verses 20–21 represents the severest possible penalty, while the husband in verses 13–19 most likely wanted to humiliate his wife, divorce her, and reclaim his bride-price. In this sense, the man's punishment in verses 13–19 directly mirrors his original intentions; that is, it represents an ingenious employment of *lex talionis* (63–72). There may be a simpler solution, however. The patent secondary nature of 22:20–21 indicates that it was composed subsequent to 22:13–19. It is thus not necessary to assume that the same logic drives the penalties in both cases.

Once we recognize the secondary nature of both Deut 22:23–24 and 22:28–29, the singular logic of *22:25–27 begins to emerge.[27] Faced with an absence of evidence, this text uses an analogous crime—intentional manslaughter—to make a case for the woman's innocence. The analogy is then followed by a statement that supports the woman's "victim" status: the man apparently seized her in the field and she shouted for help, but she had no savior. Curiously, this reconstruction seems to privilege the woman's word over the man's, given that there are no witnesses who could substantiate either party's claim. In order to make sense of this reasoning, it is useful to examine it alongside the Nippur Homicide Trial (NHT), a model case from Babylonia that demonstrates an analogous expression of the Near Eastern legal imagination. Not only does the NHT exhibit parallels to this particular section of Deut 22:25–27, but its genre may also shed light on the origins of this and several other laws in Deuteronomy.

## II. Fact or Fiction? The Nippur Homicide Trial and Deuteronomy 22:25–27

Among the tens of thousands of excavated legal documents from Mesopotamia, a handful of Sumerian school texts from the Old Babylonian period (early second millennium BCE) form a distinct genre. Like the trial records from this period, these texts detail conflicts between two parties, but, unlike the records, they lack dates, witnesses, and seals. This group of texts includes a homicide case (NHT), two cases of adultery, a dispute over inheritance, a case pertaining to a raped slave, and a dispute over office. Most of the texts refer either to the "assembly of Nippur" or simply to the "assembly," suggesting a general association with Nippur, the southern Babylonian town that has yielded over 80 percent of all known Sumerian literary texts.[28] Martha T. Roth identified them as "model court records," and later as "model cases," and proposed that they represent sample cases that were copied by scribes, perhaps as an instructive precursor to the production of actual trial records.[29] In this sense, they would parallel the "literary letters" and model

---

[27] The first half of Deut 22:26 ("But you shall not do a thing to the young woman. The young woman has no offense [deserving] of death") is likely a secondary addition due to its redundancy with 22:25 ("only the man who lay with her shall die") and its second-person address. The phrase "offense of death" (חטא מות) occurs only in Deut 22:26; one would expect "death sentence" (משפט מות), as in Deut 19:6, 21:22 (though note the combination here of all three terms), Jer 26:11, and 26:16.

[28] Over fourteen hundred tablets were excavated at House F in Nippur; on this site, see Eleanor Robson, "The Tablet House: A Scribal School in Old Babylonian Nippur," RA 95 (2001): 39–66.

[29] Martha T. Roth, "The Slave and the Scoundrel: CBS 10467, A Sumerian Morality Tale," JAOS 103 (1983): 275–82, here 279; Roth, "'She Will Die by the Iron Dagger': Adultery and

contracts that were also copied by junior scribes during the Old Babylonian period.[30] Unlike the letters and contracts, however, the model cases are attested in scant numbers, and thus it is not possible to determine the extent of their practical application beyond the school setting.

Two of these texts—NHT and one of the adultery "cases"—are particularly literary and dramatic in nature. The adultery text involves a cuckolded husband who ties the adulterers to a bed and carries it to the assembly; it closes with a threefold punishment in which the man pierces his wife's nose, shaves her pudenda, and parades her around the city.[31] NHT includes a robust debate among the assembly members regarding the woman's innocence, a discussion without parallel in the contemporaneous trial records. While scholars have assumed that these texts are grounded in actual cases, I am inclined to treat at least NHT and the adultery text, if not the entire set, as fictional compositions.[32] Indeed, Alexandra Kleinerman draws a similar conclusion regarding a set of literary letters that was discovered at Nippur, despite its inclusion of actual individuals from Nippur.[33] In order to

---

Neo-Babylonian Marriage," *JESHO* 31 (1988): 186–206, here 196. William W. Hallo first described them as "a literary collection of legal decisions by the kings of Isin" ("The Slandered Bride," in *Studies Presented to A. Leo Oppenheim, June 7, 1964* [Chicago: Oriental Institute of the University of Chicago, 1964], 95–105, here 105), though he later adopted Roth's designation, likening the texts to model contracts ("A Model Court Case concerning Inheritance," in *Riches Hidden in Secret Places: Ancient Near Eastern Studies in Memory of Thorkild Jacobsen*, ed. Tzvi Abusch [Winona Lake, IN: Eisenbrauns, 2002], 141–54, here 142–43).

[30] Regarding the letters, see Alexandra Kleinerman, *Education in Early 2nd Millennium BC Babylonia: The Sumerian Epistolary Miscellany*, CM 42 (Leiden: Brill, 2011). On the contracts, see Walter Bodine, *How Mesopotamian Scribes Learned to Write Legal Documents: A Study of the Sumerian Model Contracts in the Babylonian Collection at Yale University* (Lewiston, NY: Mellen, 2014). Bodine notes that the model contracts were used both to teach scribes Sumerian grammar and to train them in the composition of functional contracts (178).

[31] The definitive edition remains that of Samuel Greengus, "A Textbook Case of Adultery," *HUCA* 40–41 (1969): 33–44.

[32] Thorkild Jacobsen nonetheless observes that the procedure in this text is unlike procedures that are typically followed in civil trials, where fact-finding constitutes the bulk of the record ("Ancient Mesopotamian Trial for Homicide," in *Toward the Image of Tammuz and Other Essays on Mesopotamian History and Culture*, ed. William Moran, HSS 21 [Cambridge: Harvard University Press, 2014], 193–215, here 205). While Greengus acknowledges the fanciful nature of the "bed" detail in the adultery case, he suggests that it "may very well be only a literary embellishment of an actual case, a dramatic infusion of storytelling into a legal report. We need not, however, doubt the essential historicity of the trial and the penalties" ("Textbook Case of Adultery," 44 n. 34). J. J. Finkelstein likewise assumes the reality of the rape of the slave girl case: "the explanation [for the discrepancy in compensation between the model case and the corresponding law in LE 31] would lie in the fact that the Nippur case is one that came to trial" ("Sex Offenses in Sumerian Laws," *JAOS* 86 [1966]: 355–72, here 360).

[33] Kleinerman, *Education in Early 2nd Millennium BC Babylonia*, 55.

emphasize the legal/literary "hybrid" nature of these texts, I will refer to them instead as "Sumerian Legal Fictions," or SLFs.[34]

## Parallel Legal Reasoning in the Nippur Homicide Trial and Deuteronomy 22:25–27

Of the SLFs, only NHT exists in multiple copies, including several compilation tablets that include two other SLFs. Thorkild Jacobsen published an edition of the text in 1959, which was subsequently the subject of a brief study by Roth; Piotr Michalowski is in the midst of preparing a new edition. The "case" pertains to a certain Nin-Dada, a widow whose husband, Lu-Inanna, was murdered by three confirmed assailants. Early on, Nin-Dada is said to have "not open[ed] her mouth; she covered it with a cloth," a detail that both echoes a line in the adultery text and foreshadows her guilty verdict.[35]

The matter of the woman's culpability is brought before the assembly of Nippur, and a debate follows. The first contingent insists that Nin-Dada should be executed alongside the men. The second contingent then protests: "Given that Nin-Dada, daughter of Lu-Ninurta, might have killed her husband—but [as] a woman, what can she do, to warrant that she be killed?" For Roth, this statement indicates that, even if Nin-Dada was involved in the murder, as a woman, she neither could have prevented the act nor brought the perpetrators to justice.[36] The first contingent then defends its claim by stating, "A woman who does not value her husband might surely *know* his enemy; he [i.e., the enemy] might kill her husband; he might then inform her that her husband has been killed. Why should he not make her keep her mouth shut about him? It is she who killed her husband; her guilt exceeds even that of those who kill a man." This contingent thus bases its case on a *hypothetical scenario*, delivered in generic terms: a "woman" who does not value "her husband" (i.e., commits adultery) might know "his enemy" and then keep quiet.

---

[34] The term *legal fiction* was first introduced in the 1930s by Lon L. Fuller as "either (1) a statement propounded with a complete or partial consciousness of its falsity, or (2) a false statement recognized as having utility" (*Legal Fictions* [Stanford, CA: Stanford University Press, 1967], 9). I employ the phrase not in its literal sense but rather for its ability to capture both the legal and literary aspects of these texts. For an excellent discussion of actual legal fictions in the context of rabbinic law, see Christine Hayes, *What's Divine about Divine Law? Early Perspectives* (Princeton: Princeton University Press, 2015), 212–18. For a compelling study of biblical law through the lens of narrative, with attention to its literary features, see Assnat Bartor's *Reading Law as Narrative: A Study in the Casuistic Laws in the Pentateuch*, AIL 5 (Atlanta: Society of Biblical Literature, 2010).

[35] Here and elsewhere I utilize Martha T. Roth's translation of NHT in "Gender and Law: A Case Study from Ancient Mesopotamia," in *Gender and Law in the Hebrew Bible and the Ancient Near East*, ed. Bernard M. Levinson, Tikva Frymer-Kensky, and Victor H. Matthews, JSOTSup 262 (Sheffield: Sheffield Academic, 1998), 173–85, here 176–77.

[36] Ibid., 178.

This "increasingly paranoid fantasy," as Roth puts it, reimagines Nin-Dada as the architect of the murder and in turn determines her guilt.[37] For my purposes, it suffices to stress that this scenario stems from an absence of evidence. Rather than order the woman to undergo an ordeal or take an oath to determine her innocence, two procedures in Old Babylonian trials that typically follow from inadequate evidence, the first contingent presents its version of the most plausible sequence of events based on the available data.

Knowledge of this debate may shed light on the logic that drives Deut 22:25–27. Let us review the hypothetical scenario in NHT alongside the apodosis in Deut 22:25–27:

| Nippur Homicide Trial, lines 44–52 | Deuteronomy 22:25–27 |
| --- | --- |
| A woman who does not value her husband might surely know his enemy; he might kill her husband; he might then inform her that her husband has been killed. Why should he not make her keep her mouth shut about him? It is *she* who killed her husband; her guilt exceeds even that of those who kill a man. | Only the man who lay with her shall die … for this matter is like that of a man who rises up against his neighbor and murders him…. For he found her in the field, the engaged woman (may have) shouted (for help), but she had no savior. |

It is first noteworthy that each of these units is anticipated by details that are given earlier. In NHT, Nin-Dada is already implicated in lines 6–14, where it is stated that, when the men told her what they did, she "covered [her mouth] with a cloth." This detail is then echoed in the above reference to Nin-Dada's "shut" mouth. Likewise, the determination of the biblical woman's innocence is signaled by the explicit use of a violent verb in verse 25: the man "finds the woman … and *grasps hold of her* [והחזיק־בה] and lies with her." These details predispose the reader to expect Nin-Dada's guilt and the biblical victim's acquittal.

In addition, NHT 44–52 is formulated in response to the minority opinion that Nin-Dada is innocent because, as a woman, she is more susceptible to coercion.[38] Although Deut 22:25–27 does not include a "minority opinion," verses 26–27 counter the stance that, without a witness, the woman's complicity remains in question. The scribe thus devises a creative scenario that is independent of any assessment of the woman's consent: (even if) she cried out, there would have been no one to (hear and) save her.[39] While this scenario is delivered in the perfective

---

[37] Ibid., 180. As Roth points out, the assembly's use of the Sumerian verb /zu/ ("to know") serves as a double entendre to implicate the woman as an adulterer.

[38] On this line of reasoning, see ibid., 178.

[39] While the analogy in verse 26 to a murder victim is often viewed as a reference to Deut 19:11–13 (see, e.g., Merendino, *Das deuteronomische Gesetz*, 264), this link need not be assumed. Both texts indeed refer to a man who comes upon his neighbor and kills him, but only Deut 19:11–13 emphasizes the man's deliberate act of *waiting* for his victim, *striking* him, and then

aspect, its position after the analogy confirms its theoretical quality, as is expressed in some translations.⁴⁰

In both cases, then, the "verdict" rests neither on evidence nor on third-party testimony but rather on the power of the hypothetical scenario that the scribe invents. As such, these texts independently display two direct glimpses into the Near Eastern legal imagination: first, in their exposition of legal quandaries outside the norm and, second, in their efforts to "solve the case" through deductive reasoning. In the case of NHT, the scribe demonstrates how *inaction* can be a marker for culpability, anticipating by several millennia our modern notion of "accessory after the fact." Given Nin-Dada's failure to report her husband's murder to the proper authorities, she must be complicit in some way, and so the first contingent reasons backward from this established fact. Further, although a number of biblical and Near Eastern laws address rape, Deut 22:25–27 is unique in that it pairs this crime with the unequivocal absence of witnesses. Rather than conclude that such a case cannot be settled, the scribe reveals that the question of the woman's resistance is a moot point. Whether or not she called for help, there was no one around to hear her, so her resistance may be assumed. In this sense, the lawmaker works "forward" from the fact of the isolated scene of the crime. This extreme case is then accentuated in the Temple Scroll, where the field is situated "in a distant place" (במקום רחוק), far from the town (11Q19 LXVI, 4–5).

## III. Further Implications

If Deut 22:25–27 indeed represents the literary core of the series, in what *context* might such a text have independently circulated? Any answer to such a question must remain speculative, for the Israelites' use of perishable writing materials has resulted in a shortage of evidence for the independent circulation of biblical texts and/or older, alternative collections of biblical content.⁴¹ We also know relatively little about preexilic Israelite scribal education, given that few school texts

---

*fleeing* to one of the cities of refuge, an act that is addressed by turning the criminal over to the victim's blood avenger. The issue in Deut 19:11–13 is thus not murder per se but rather the possibility that intentional murderers would take advantage of the refuge system. In contrast, the scribe in Deut 22:25–27 simply draws a link between the general crimes of murder and rape in order to strengthen his case for the woman's innocence.

⁴⁰ Moreover, it is possible that in this case the perfective conveys an expression of a perpetual truth. On the use of *qaṭal* to express either a permanent truth or "truths of experience," see Joüon, 2:361.

⁴¹ This statement is not meant to minimize the documented evidence of radically different versions of biblical books and texts, such as MT/LXX Daniel, Esther, Jeremiah, and others. Rather, I am referring to earlier versions of texts and/or collections that surely existed but are unattested in the manuscript evidence.

(outside of abecedaries) have been discovered.⁴² While we can assume with some confidence that certain texts (e.g., acrostic Psalms and Proverbs) emerged and were copied in pedagogical contexts, the relationship between most biblical texts and scribal training remains opaque.

Comparative evidence may be illuminating where native Israelite content is lacking. Unlike their Israelite counterparts, Mesopotamian scribes used the more durable medium of clay and thus left behind hundreds of thousands of tablets, including documentary and literary texts of various types. Drawing on evidence from scribal exercises and literary catalogs, scholars have even managed to reconstruct different phases in the Old Babylonian scribal curriculum, at least with respect to Nippur.⁴³ While the SLFs do not appear to have played a major role in the scribal curriculum, awareness of this pedagogical genre allows us to consider the possibility that the Israelites composed their own "legal fictions." Indeed, Clemens Locher's observations of stylistic similarities between Deut 22:13–19 and the "model case" of the raped slave girl prompted him to propose that a text of a similar type lay behind the biblical law.⁴⁴ I propose that a pedagogical context may best account for the early transmission of a text like Deut 22:25–27 (at least in some early form) and perhaps, too, for that of a wider set of laws in Deuteronomy.

Scholars have long posited that the Deuteronomic laws pertaining to women and family may have circulated as an independent collection, something akin to the collection of women's law in MAL Tablet A. This posited "tractate" generally includes Deut 21:15–17, the case of the man with two wives, one loved, the other hated; Deut 22:13–21, the case(s) of the slandered bride; Deut 22:22, the case of adulterers caught in flagrante delicto; Deut 22:23–29, the triad of assault cases; Deut 24:1–4, the case of the two-time divorcée; and Deut 25:5–10, the case of the widow and the reluctant brother-in-law.⁴⁵ The highly detailed nature of Deut

---

⁴² This has not prevented scholars from reconstructing certain aspects of Israelite scribal education in helpful and persuasive ways. See the informed studies of David M. Carr, *Writing on the Tablet of the Heart: Origins of Scripture and Literature* (Oxford: Oxford University Press, 2005); Karel van der Toorn, *Scribal Culture and the Making of the Hebrew Bible* (Cambridge: Harvard University Press, 2007); Seth L. Sanders, *The Invention of Hebrew*, Traditions (Urbana: University of Illinois Press, 2009); and Christopher Rollston, *Writing and Literacy in the World of Ancient Israel: Epigraphic Evidence from the Iron Age*, ABS 11 (Atlanta: Society of Biblical Literature, 2010).

⁴³ See esp. Niek Veldhuis, "Elementary Education at Nippur: The Lists of Trees and Wooden Objects" (PhD diss., Rijksuniversiteit Groningen, 1997); Veldhuis, *History of the Cuneiform Lexical Tradition*, GMTR 6 (Münster: Ugarit-Verlag, 2014); and Steve Tinney, "On the Curricular Setting of Sumerian Literature," *Iraq* 61 (1999): 159–72.

⁴⁴ Locher, "Deuteronomium 22,13–21," 107. For further discussion of the relationship between Deut 22:13–21 and the slave-girl text, see Locher, *Die Ehre einer Frau in Israel: Exegetische und rechtsvergleichende Studien zu Deuteronomium 22,13–21*, OBO 70 (Freiburg, Schweiz: Universitätsverlag; Göttingen: Vandenhoeck & Ruprecht, 1986), 93–101.

⁴⁵ For Rofé, this "reconstructed [biblical] tractate" also includes Exod 22:15–16, the seduction of the unengaged virgin; and Exod 21:22–25, the injury of a pregnant woman during a fight

22:13–21 and 25:5–10 in particular prompted Rofé to state further that these texts "almost read like transcripts of trials later rewritten as laws."[46] This statement resonates with the general theory among Assyriologists that the laws in the cuneiform collections are not *prescriptive* but rather *descriptive*; that is, they are rooted in actual scenarios that were stripped of their specifics and generalized into law.[47] While this notion is persuasive, it is important to note that no trial records from Mesopotamia have been identified as actual *sources* for laws in the collections.[48] Moreover, trial records across all periods and regions in Mesopotamia are marked by a kind of opaque legal shorthand that is distinct from the straightforward nature of texts such as NHT, the aforementioned adultery text, Deut 22:13–19, and Deut 25:5–10. Moreover, this proposed "tractate" includes some laws that feature virtually no post-Deuteronomic language (e.g., Deut 22:13–19) and others that strongly

---

(*Deuteronomy: Issues and Interpretation*, OTS [London: T&T Clark, 2002], 172). The parallel between the overarching Deuteronomic program and Tablet A of MAL has been most strongly drawn by Otto, who sees both as evidence of legal reforms. For Otto, the "Familienrechtsammlung" includes Deut 21:15–21aα; 22:13–21a, 22a, 23, 24a, 25, 27, 28–29; 24:1–4a; and 25:5–10 (*Das Deuteronomium*, 217). Pressler proposes a similar early collection and includes the law regarding the captive bride in Deut 21:10–14 (*View of Women*, 4, 9–10).

[46] Rofé, *Deuteronomy*, 184.

[47] In a seminal essay, Fritz R. Kraus launched a redefinition of the nature of the Laws of Hammurabi ("Ein zentrales Problem des altmesopotamischen Rechtes: Was ist der Codex Hammu-rabi?," *Geneva* 8 [1960]: 283–96). As Kraus points out, the epilogue of LH itself refers to the preceding content as "just decisions" (*dīnāt mīšārim*). He suggests that the recognition of the collection "als Werk der altbabylonischen wissenschaftlichen Literatur" puts it in a new light (284–89). This line of thought was developed further by Jean Bottéro in another important essay: "The 'Code' of Hammurabi," in *Mesopotamia: Writing, Reasoning, and the Gods*, trans. Zainab Bahrani and Marc van de Mieroop (Chicago: University of Chicago Press, 1992), 156–84, esp. 169–77. See also Raymond Westbrook, "Biblical and Cuneiform Codes," in Wells and Magdalene, *Law from the Tigris to the Tiber*, 1:3–20.

[48] Several "verdicts" from the Ur III period (known as "ditilla texts"), however, do reflect legal scenarios that are also featured in LH. Brief descriptions of cases and their verdicts from the Ur III period are preserved in several collections. In his chapter on these verdicts, Bertrand Lafont points to parallels between #5 (in his chapter) and LH §148; #6 and LH §131; #7 and LU §9; and #24 and LH §238, though he does not suggest that such texts served as sources for the laws. Rather, he notes that certain situations appear in the records several centuries before they are represented in parallel form in the law collections ("Les textes judiciaires sumériens," in *Rendre la justice en Mésopotamie: Archives judiciaires du Proche-Orient ancien [III$^e$-I$^{er}$ millénaires avant J.-C]*, ed. Francis Joannès, Temps & espaces [Saint-Denis: Presses universitaires de Vincennes, 2000], 34–67). Regarding the letters, Bottéro mentions one that mirrors LH §32 ("'Code' of Hammurabi," 167), and Dominique Charpin makes reference to another Old Babylonian letter known in two copies that parallels LH §28 (*Writing, Law, and Kingship in Old Babylonian Mesopotamia*, trans. Jane Marie Todd [Chicago: University of Chicago Press, 2010], 79–80). As Charpin notes, however, the direction of dependence is difficult to determine, especially given the fact that the letter exists in two copies and may have been used for pedagogical purposes.

suggest composition by post-Deuteronomic scribes, namely, Deut 22:20–21, 22:22, and 22:23–24.

I propose that a parallel genre of "Israelite Legal Fictions" (ILFs) might better account for the origins of several of these laws in Deuteronomy, specifically, Deut 19:4–6; 21:15–17; 22:13–19, 25–27; 24:1–4; and 25:5–10. To this group we might also add the case of the man who takes another wife in addition to his slave girl (Exod 21:9–11), given that it apparently represents another "native" Israelite legal text.[49] Like NHT and the adultery text, these biblical laws exhibit *literary* features, such as direct speech (Deut 22:13, 16–17; 25:7–8) and theatrical details (e.g., the bloody sheet in Deut 22:15–17; the widow spitting in her brother-in-law's face in Deut 25:9);[50] they thrive on triangular dynamics (Exod 21:7–11; Deut 21:15–17; 22:13–19, 25–27; 24:1–4; and 25:5–10); they include threefold verdicts (Exod 21:7–11; Deut 22:13–19; and Deut 25:5–10); they cover "boundary problems," that is, legal issues that arise outside of the norm (Deut 21:15–17; 22:13–19, 25–27; 24:1–4; and 25:5–10); and, notwithstanding detectable additions, they generally exhibit a stand-alone quality.[51]

The concept of law was clearly learned in the context of Israelite education, as suggested by the numerous proverbs devoted to the perversion of justice and the problems of strife.[52] A logical extension of this early training would be exposure to exercises that could illustrate the proper execution of justice and/or present and solve legal conundrums. If Israelite scribes copied such legal exercises in school, it would be natural for them to end up in some form in the law collections that they later produced, whether deliberately (i.e., a scribe learned the exercises in school and set out to recast them) or by happenstance (i.e., a scribe simply discovered a copy of the exercises and put them to new use). This may have been the case with

---

[49] This law is unique in the context of the casuistic laws in the Covenant Code, the majority of which correlate with and arguably derive from cuneiform laws. It does, however, share a basic principle with LH §148, which stipulates that a man who marries another woman in addition to his ill (possibly infertile) wife must continue to provide for the first wife. For discussion of the relationship between the Covenant Code and the Laws of Hammurabi, see David P. Wright, *Inventing God's Law: How the Covenant Code of the Bible Used and Revised the Laws of Hammurabi* (Oxford: Oxford University Press, 2009).

[50] Tikva Frymer-Kensky points to the ease with which the parents could manufacture such evidence in the slandered bride case ("Law and Philosophy: The Case of Sex in the Bible," in *Women in the Hebrew Bible: A Reader*, ed. Alice Bach [London: Routledge, 1999], 296); this may be another factor that points to its fictitiousness.

[51] On the concept of "boundary problems," see Bruce Wells, "Competing or Complementary? Judges and Elders in Biblical and Neo-Babylonian Law," *ZABR* 16 (2010): 77–104, here 102.

[52] See, e.g., Prov 12:17; 14:5, 25; 16:10, 29; 17:8, 14, 23; 18:5, 17; 19:5, 9, 28; 20:8; 21:6, 28; 23:33; 24:23, 28; 25:2; 26:17, 21; 29:9, 12, 14, 26; and 31:8–9, 23. Proverbs are commonly thought to have formed an early stage of Israelite scribal education due to their pithy and didactic nature; this is supported by the fact that Sumerian proverbs were learned at an early stage of scribal education.

NHT, given that LH §153 likewise deals with a woman whose extramarital relationship prompts her to arrange for her husband's death, the very situation that is floated by the first contingent.[53] While this parallel could be merely coincidental or could reflect scribal play with known code law, it is possible that the generalized hypothetical scenario in NHT spawned the precept in LH.[54] In fact, NHT is not alone in this regard: several of the other SLFs share links to precepts in the collections.[55] However we account for these parallels, they point to some sort of relationship between the model cases and law collections. It is possible that an analogous process took place in the context of ancient Israelite scribal culture.

In taking up these "stand-alone" texts and supplementing them with additional scenarios, the post-Deuteronomic editor put the classic Near Eastern method of generating law by creating variations on a core case to radically new use. For Bottéro, this method, which extends beyond the realm of law to omen and medical collections, embodied the Mesopotamians' systematic effort to attain universality.[56] Rather than use this method to cover as much legal ground as possible, however, the biblical editor deployed it to re-present "private" quandaries between individuals as major threats to cultic order in Israel. This shift in logic is most apparent in Deut 22:13–21 and Deut 22:23–29. The effects of the expansion in each case are different, however, due to the position of the secondary units. Because Deut 22:20–21 is situated after the original case, its derivative nature is more evident. In contrast, in prefacing Deut 22:25–27 with verses 23–24, the editor recast the once-independent exercise as merely one more variation on the theme of assault. In the process, he eclipsed the unique legal reasoning that underlies Deut 22:25–27, a text that uses a reasonable presumption to solve what appears to be an impossible quandary.

It is possible that other series of Near Eastern laws, whether biblical or cuneiform, were likewise built from the ground up, so that their origins are to be found

---

[53] The parallel is noted in Jacobsen, "Ancient Mesopotamian Trial," 212–13; and in Roth, "Gender and Law," 180.

[54] It is noteworthy, however, that most of the actual *copies* of the SLFs are either contemporaneous with the law collections or later than them, save for one copy of NHT that Jacobsen dated to the early years of Rim-Sin of Larsa, or ca. 1800s BCE ("Ancient Mesopotamian Trial," 196). Most of the postulated dates for the SLFs are based on names, not archaeological find-spots, and so the possibility remains that we are dealing with a corpus that is largely contemporaneous with LH rather than prior to it.

[55] As Greengus observes, his adultery text has parallels in LH §§141–143, in that both feature a woman committing three crimes—appropriating goods, squandering household possessions, and being wayward ("Textbook Case of Adultery," 37–38). The other adultery text deals with a husband who catches his wife "in the lap" of her lover; the king then puts both the woman and her lover to the stake, a verdict that bears resemblance to LH §129. Finally, the case detailing the rape of a slave girl corresponds to LE §31, in that both require the rapist to pay a fine to the girl's master (Finkelstein, "Sex Offenses in Sumerian Laws," 360).

[56] See Bottéro, "'Code' of Hammurabi," 169–77.

not in the initial scenario but rather in subsequent laws. Such a proposal would be in line with the Near Eastern scribal method of transforming material by supplementing it at the front and/or back ends. In this case, the process of separating the "wheat" (Deut 22:25–27) from the chaff (22:23–24 and 28–29) both sheds fresh light on 22:25–27 and opens the door to a new way of accounting for the *Sitz im Leben* of a distinct set of storylike laws in Deuteronomy that are independent of the Covenant Code. The notion that Deut 19:4–6, 21:15–17, 22:13–19, 22:25–27, 24:1–4, and 25:5–10 are rooted in a set of pedagogical exercises not only has potential parallels in the wider ancient Near East but also suits the distinct nature of these texts as stand-alone, legal-literary hybrids. While this thesis may represent yet another "hypothetical scenario," it is arguably the most plausible solution given the available data.

# SBL PRESS

## New and Recent Titles

### STUDIES IN THE HISTORY OF THE GREEK TEXT OF THE APOCALYPSE
The Ancient Stems
*Josef Schmid*
*Translated and Edited by Juan Hernández Jr., Garrick V. Allen, and Darius Müller*
Paperback $39.95, 978-1-62837-204-5   338 pages, 2018   Code: 067011
Hardcover $54.95, 978-0-88414-282-9  E-book $39.95, 978-0-88414-281-2
Text-Critical Studies 11

### LUCIFER OF CAGLIARI AND THE TEXT OF 1-2 KINGS
*Tuukka Kauhanen*
Paperback $62.95, 978-1-62837-205-2   444 pages, 2018   Code: 060469
Hardcover $82.95, 978-0-88414-283-6  E-book 62.95, 978-0-88414-284-3
Septuagint and Cognate Studies 68

### THE RHETORIC OF ABRAHAM'S FAITH IN ROMANS 4
*Andrew Kimseng Tan*
Paperback $44.95, 978-1-62837-208-3   348 pages, 2018   Code: 064822
Hardcover $59.95, 978-0-88414-289-8  E-book $44.95, 978-0-88414-290-4
Emory Studies in Early Christianity 20

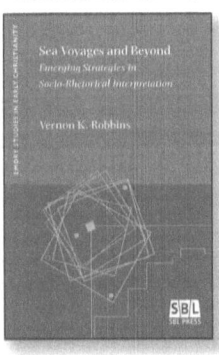

### SEA VOYAGES AND BEYOND
Emerging Strategies in Socio-Rhetorical Interpretation
*Vernon K. Robbins*
Paperback $54.95, 978-1-62837-219-9   338 pages, 2018   Code: 064823
Hardcover $74.95, 978-0-88414-321-5  E-book $54.95, 978-0-88414-322-2
Emory Studies in Early Christianity 14

### TRADITION AND INNOVATION
English and German Studies on the Septuagint
*Martin Rösel*
Paperback $49.95, 978-1-62837-220-5  Forthcoming, 2018  Code: 060468
Hardcover $64.95, 978-0-88414-323-9  E-book $49.95, 978-0-88414-324-6
Septuagint and Cognate Studies 70

SBL Press • P.O. Box 2243 • Williston, VT 05495-2243
Phone: 877-725-3334 (toll-free) or 802-864-6185 • Fax: 802-864-7626
Order online at www.sbl-site.org/publications

# "All That You Have Done ... Has Been Fully Told to Me": The Power of Gossip and the Story of Ruth

**PHILIP F. ESLER**
pesler@glos.ac.uk
University of Gloucestershire, Cheltenham, GL50 2RH United Kingdom

The literary qualities of the book of Ruth are the subject of considerable scholarly attention. The aim of this article is to contribute to this research with particular reference to what Boaz says to Ruth, "All that you have done ... has been fully told to me" (2:11), where what he has learned has clearly been in Ruth's favor. Boaz can have gained such information only through what we call gossip. I will first outline social-scientific research into gossip, which has already been fruitfully applied to various parts of the New Testament. Second, I will discuss informal networks among ancient Israelite women that feature in the way gossip functions in this narrative. Third, I will apply these perspectives to the passages in the text that depend on gossip's occurrence. This exercise will substantiate the dictum of anthropologist Robert Paine that "gossip is a catalyst of social process," by uncovering the remarkable extent to which, in the book of Ruth, character is developed and the plot of the book propelled to its resolution by gossip.

---

In recent decades, the literary qualities of the book of Ruth have attracted much attention.[1] Of particular interest have been the ways in which its characters are portrayed and relate to one another, issues that inevitably impact how the plot is propelled to its resolution.[2] This article aims to extend the investigation of

[1] For recent approaches to Ruth, see Edward Allen Jones III, *Reading Ruth in the Restoration Period: A Call for Inclusion*, LHBOTS 604 (London: Bloomsbury T&T Clark, 2016), 1–9.

[2] As a sample, see Danna Nolan Fewell and David Miller Gunn, *Compromising Redemption: Relating Characters in the Book of Ruth*, Literary Currents in Biblical Interpretation (Louisville: Westminster John Knox, 1990); Athalya Brenner, "Naomi and Ruth," in *A Feminist Companion to Ruth*, ed. Athalya Brenner, FCB 3 (Sheffield: Sheffield Academic, 1993), 70–84; Tod Linafelt and Timothy K. Beal, *Ruth and Esther*, Berit Olam (Collegeville, MN: Liturgical Press, 1999); Kristin Moen Saxegaard, *Character Complexity in the Book of Ruth*, FAT 2/47 (Tübingen: Mohr Siebeck, 2010); and Jennifer L. Koosed, *Gleaning Ruth: A Biblical Heroine and Her Afterlives*, Studies on Personalities of the Old Testament (Columbia: University of South Carolina Press, 2011).

characterization and plot in Ruth by examining how gossip functions in the unfolding narrative. While this theme has attracted occasional mention,[3] it has not been studied in depth. My aim is first to set out social-scientific perspectives on gossip and then apply them to the text in its narrative order. Studies using social-scientific ideas on gossip have already illuminated New Testament texts.[4] This approach will allow me to analyze characterization (especially of Ruth and Boaz) and plot in this Hebrew Bible text within a particular ancient social context, where women were especially prominent, in ways that included but were not limited to their participation in women's networks.

## I. Social-Scientific Approaches to Gossip

Gossip has attracted interest from social scientists and evolutionary biologists.[5] Anthropologist David Gilmore, writing in 1978, observed that "gossip as a general category is not one thing or the other, but a diverse range of behaviors all of which have something in common."[6] He also commented that "no one has made an effort to break down this catch-all term into its components or to evaluate the meaning of the variability of gossip forms in relation to community social dynamics in general."[7] Unfortunately, that remains largely the situation today, in spite of some partial efforts at typologizing. Indeed, it is probably the case that "gossip does not lend itself to simple formulaic definitions or uniform explanations."[8] While everyone has a sense of what gossip is, modeling it is a complex enterprise.[9] Accordingly, I will draw selectively on social-scientific research to create a profile of gossip that will inform the investigation of the book of Ruth that follows. By "inform" I mean both posing new questions to the text and also providing an interpretative framework for making sense of the answers, a process akin to "connecting the dots."

---

[3] E.g., Marjo C. A. Korpel, *The Structure of the Book of Ruth*, Pericope 2 (Assen: Van Gorcum, 2001), 126–28, 132.

[4] See Richard L. Rohrbaugh, "Gossip in the New Testament," in *Social Scientific Models for Interpreting the Bible: Essays by the Context Group in Honor of Bruce J. Malina*, ed. John J. Pilch, BibInt 53 (Leiden: Brill, 2001), 239–59; Marianne Bjelland Kartzow, *Gossip and Gender: Othering of Speech in the Pastoral Epistles*, BZNW 164 (Berlin: de Gruyter, 2009); and John W. Daniels Jr., *The Gossiping Jesus: The Oral Processing of Jesus in John's Gospel* (Eugene, OR: Pickwick, 2013).

[5] For a review, see Eric K. Foster, "Research on Gossip: Taxonomy, Methods, and Future Directions," *Review of General Psychology* 8 (2004): 78–99. Robin Dunbar has related gossip to evolutionary biology in *Grooming, Gossip and the Evolution of Language* (London: Faber & Faber, 1996).

[6] David D. Gilmore, "Varieties of Gossip in a Spanish Rural Community," *Ethnology* 17 (1978): 89–99, here 89.

[7] Ibid.

[8] Foster, "Research on Gossip," 80.

[9] Ibid.

In common parlance and scholarly discourse, the core content of gossip is "the exchange of information about absent third parties," even though on rare occasions the person being discussed may be present.[10] Sometimes such information lacks "valence," that is, positive or negative evaluations of the person being spoken about. This type of gossip simply entails the neutral dissemination of news: who has had a baby, graduated from university, and so on. More commonly, however, the information exchanged about an absent third party is, to some extent at least, evaluative.[11]

Very often the evaluation will be negative. This was overwhelmingly the case among the population of the Spanish town studied by Gilmore, where gossip dominated its social life and required eleven different terms to express its diverse forms.[12] That many, if not most, societies have explicit sanctions against gossip demonstrates a widespread view that gossip has a dark side.[13] Apart from damaging reputations, it can "steal illusions, wreck relationships, and stir up a cauldron of trouble."[14]

Yet gossip is not always negative in character. Often the evaluations of the absent person aired in the exchange of information are positive. Many researchers have made this point,[15] even though in common parlance gossip tends to carry a negative dimension. Machiavelli's *The Prince* accurately expresses the reality of the phenomenon: "all men, when they are talked about ... are remarked upon for various qualities which bring them either praise or blame."[16] The fact that gossip can convey a positive view of someone will figure prominently in my examination of the phenomenon in Ruth.

Gilmore's view that gossip consisted of a diverse range of behaviors with something in common was influenced by two approaches that emerged among anthropologists in the 1960s and are still significant. First, in 1963, Max Gluckman, adopting a functionalist approach, argued that gossip was a type of spontaneous collective sanction by which public opinion enforced conformity to community values and objectives.[17] In a manner clearly disclosing his focus on the negative dimension of gossip, he noted, "The values of the group are clearly asserted in

---

[10] Ibid., 81.

[11] Ibid., 82.

[12] Gilmore, "Varieties of Gossip," 94–97.

[13] Foster, "Research on Gossip," 78–79.

[14] Ralph L. Rosnow, "Rumor and Gossip in Interpersonal Interaction and Beyond: A Social Exchange Perspective," in *Behaving Badly: Aversive Behaviors in Interpersonal Relationships*, ed. Robin M. Kowalski (Washington, DC: American Psychological Association, 2001), 203–32, here 203.

[15] See Daena Goldsmith, "Gossip from the Native's Point of View," *Research on Language and Social Intention* 23 (1989): 163–193; R. F. Baumeister, L. Zhang, and K. D. Vohs, "Gossip as Cultural Learning," *General Review of Psychology* 8 (2004): 111–21; and Foster, "Research on Gossip," 82 (and the works there cited).

[16] Quoted by Foster, "Research on Gossip," 82–83.

[17] Max Gluckman, "Gossip and Scandal," *Current Anthropology* 4 (1963): 307–16, here 312.

gossip and scandal, since a man or woman is always run down for failing to live up to these values."[18] One aspect of the social-conformity dimension of gossip is that, if it is to be influential, those involved must agree on the prevailing norms of acceptable behavior and gossipers frequently articulate those norms.[19] Sally Engle Merry has cited considerable evidence to the effect that

> The role of gossip in achieving social control in stable, bounded, morally homogenous, and close-knit societies where escape and avoidance are difficult differs markedly from its function in large, fluid, open, and morally heterogeneous communities where escape and avoidance are realistic possibilities.[20]

The deterrent and control aspects of gossip are much greater in the former type of society,[21] which corresponds to the Bethlehem of Naomi, Ruth, and Boaz.

The second approach to the subject came in a critique of Gluckman's position from Robert Paine, one of the Newfoundland "transactionalists," from a perspective of methodological individualism.[22] Paine's rejection of Gluckman's approach is encapsulated in the following statement: "It is the individual and not the community that gossips. What he gossips about are his own and others' aspirations, and only indirectly the values of the community."[23] Paine argued that gossip was a form of information management, in particular, a genre of informal communication intended to forward and protect individual interests. He asked whether Gluckman's view that the values of the group were asserted in gossip was true and important only "primarily in the sense that individuals appeal to each other in terms of these values in order to forward their own interests."[24] He reinforced his belief in the instrumental use of gossip with reference to the way the Sarakatsani (transhumant shepherds of northern Greece) used gossip to cast doubts on other families to improve the claims of their own family to moral recognition.[25] This approach allowed Paine to focus on social activity at lower than a community-wide level. He pointed out, for example, that a group often turns out to be "a coterie of rival interest-based quasi-groups,"[26] although in my view a better term would be "subgroups." People in subgroups, which have distinct interests, will often need

---

[18] Ibid., 313.

[19] Foster, "Research on Gossip," 86.

[20] Sally Engle Merry, "Rethinking Gossip and Scandal," in *Reputation: Studies in the Voluntary Elucidation of Good Conduct*, ed. Daniel B. Klein, Economics, Cognition, and Society (Ann Arbor: University of Michigan Press, 1997), 47–74, here 48.

[21] Ibid.

[22] Gilmore, "Varieties of Gossip," 89.

[23] Robert Paine, "What Is Gossip About? An Alternative Hypothesis," *Man* 2 (1967): 278–85, here 280–81.

[24] Ibid., 278, 280; quotation from 280.

[25] Ibid., 281, citing J. K. Campbell, *Honour, Family, and Patronage: A Study of Institutions and Moral Values in a Greek Mountain Community* (New York: Oxford University Press, 1964), 265, 280–81, 286, 315.

[26] Paine, "What Is Gossip About?," 282.

information about people in other subgroups. "Gossip," Paine reasonably suggested, "is a very general, and important, way of obtaining this information: sometimes it is the only way."[27] Much of his conclusion is worth quoting:

> In this view of gossip, there is no *a priori* assumption that gossip of itself either avoids conflict or exacerbates it, that is brings people together or pushes them into opposing factions. It may have implications in either or both of these directions. On the other hand, I think it can be demonstrated that gossip is a catalyst of social process, so that one or another of the effects just mentioned is likely to be produced.[28]

In 1978, Gilmore found truth in both of these positions. Unfortunately, the two approaches "had hardened into competing interpretations instead of being thought of as complementary approaches to a phenomenon which obviously has both communicative and social-control dimensions."[29] He held that Gluckman and Paine were both right, for they were talking about different forms of gossip, not about gossip as a general category. Gilmore argued that Gluckman had focused on "collective gossip," meaning the "moral indictment by the entire community" that had only "a minimal 'communicative' significance." Gilmore's use of "indictment" rather than a more neutral term such as "evaluation" reflected his experience of gossip in the Spanish town, where gossip was always derogatory. According to Gilmore, Paine, on the other hand, had been speaking of "small group gossip," which was "'newsy' communication exchanged informally by individuals within pre-existing social networks." Similarly, in 1997 Merry observed, "Gluckman's and Paine's perspectives are not mutually exclusive but complementary. One looks at the functions gossip performs for social groups, the other at the motivations for actors to engage in gossiping. Neither perspective alone is adequate."[30] When investigating Ruth we will discover that both forms of gossip are found there, but that Paine's approach illuminates more of the data.

Another aspect of gossip relevant to the book of Ruth is its function in promoting friendship or intimacy. This occurs both in dyadic exchanges and also when gossip has the effect of bringing groups together through the sharing of norms that establish "boundaries to distinguish insiders from outsiders."[31] Gossip is probably more common between friends than between casual acquaintances or strangers "because shared social meanings and history are essential to understanding the subtleties of the gossip."[32] This issue of shared social meanings brings us to a consideration of women's social networks in ancient Israel.

---

[27] Ibid.
[28] Ibid., 283.
[29] Quotations from Gilmore in this paragraph come from "Varieties of Gossip," 89, 98.
[30] Merry, "Rethinking Gossip and Scandal," 50.
[31] Foster, "Research on Gossip," 85.
[32] See ibid., and the works cited there.

## II. Informal Networks among Ancient Israelite Women

The importance of women in Ruth necessitates considering a particular social pattern among ancient Israelite women. In 1999, Carol L. Meyers invoked recent research showing that women in non-Western settings and in premodern farming households played a far more significant social role than had previously been believed.[33] This reappraisal entailed problematizing the widely accepted dichotomy between the public realm (of the large social unit, especially villages and towns) and the domestic/private realm (of the family unit), where men and women were respectively dominant.[34] In fact, in most village-based societies, including ancient Israel, the lines between such spheres are blurred: "public and private are thus overlapping and integrated domains in many aspects of family and community life in traditional societies."[35] Meyers also pointed out that decades of ethnographic research had shown that women in peasant societies are invariably connected to each other via a series of informal relationships often designated as "women's networks."[36] She finds evidence for such informal networks among women in ancient Israel, including a compelling example from the book of Ruth, as we will see below. Katherine Southwood has recently agreed with Meyers on this issue and aptly cites the comment of Alicia Suskin Ostriker that "Ruth is the only book of the Bible that gives us a hint of a women's community and social life existing alongside yet distinct from male society."[37] Fokkelien van Dijk-Hemmes even argued that the book of

---

[33] Carol L. Meyers, "'Women of the Neighborhood' (Ruth 4:7): Informal Female Networks in Ancient Israel," in *Ruth and Esther*, ed. Athalya Brenner, FCB 2/3 (Sheffield: Sheffield Academic, 1999), 110–27.

[34] For the old view, see Michelle Zimbalist Rosaldo, "Women, Culture, and Society: A Theoretical Overview," in *Women, Culture, and Society*, ed. Michelle Zimbalist Rosaldo and Louise Lamphere (Stanford, CA: Stanford University Press, 1974), 17–42. For the new view, see Dorothy O. Helly and Susan M. Reverby, eds., *Gendered Domains: Rethinking Public and Private in Women's History; Essays from the Seventh Berkshire Conference on the History of Women* (Ithaca, NY: Cornell University Press, 1992); and Janet Sharistanian, *Beyond the Public/Domestic Dichotomy: Contemporary Perspectives on Women's Public Lives*, Contributions in Women's Studies 78 (Westport, CT: Greenwood, 1987).

[35] Meyers, "Women of the Neighborhood," 115.

[36] Ibid., 116–19. Meyers cites especially V. Maher, "Kin, Clients, and Accomplices: Relationships among Women in Morocco," in *Sexual Divisions and Society: Process and Change*, ed. Diana Leonard Barker and Sheila Allen, Explorations in Sociology 6 (London: Tavistock, 1976), 52–75, here 52–53; and Kathryn S. March and Rachelle L. Taqqu, *Women's Informal Associations in Developing Countries: Catalysts for Change?*, Women in Cross-Cultural Perspective (Boulder, CO: Westview, 1986).

[37] Katherine E. Southwood, "Will Naomi's Nation Be Ruth's Nation? Ethnic Translation as a Metaphor for Ruth's Assimilation within Judah," *Humanities* 3 (2014): 102–31, 131 n. 108, citing Alicia Suskin Ostriker, *For the Love of God: The Bible as an Open Book* (New Brunswick, NJ: Rutgers University Press, 2007), 41.

Ruth was itself the product of collaboration between a tradition of wise women narrators and a predominantly female audience.[38]

In applying these insights to ancient Israel, Meyers noted that married Israelite women had an advantage over men in being connected to both their natal and their marital families/descent groups.[39] The links that women retained with their birth families were often vital to their lives in the families and communities into which they married. While Meyers recognized that the existence of regular female contact across households allowed women's networks to share information, she focused on situations in which women would become aware of acute labor needs in a household caused by the illness or absence of a family member or members.

More recently, Marianne Kartzow has provided examples from the Mishnah of information sharing among ancient Jewish women. First, she mentions an account of how hardworking women who "spin by moonlight" formed (and communicated) a view as to whether another woman had committed adultery. Second, she discusses the account of how women who visit the bathhouse were a useful source of information as to whether a particular woman they saw there had physical flaws that would affect her value as a marriage partner.[40] In both of these examples, women were communicating information interesting to themselves but also useful to men—husbands in the first case, and prospective husbands and their families in the second.

### III. Application to the Book of Ruth

#### Naomi, Ruth, and Orpah (1:1–18)

Chapter 1 of Ruth sets out basic information about Naomi and her immediate family (natal and affinal) and their movements between Bethlehem in Judah and Moab. It also provides critical insights into social dynamics among women in this context and into Ruth's character that will heavily influence the way the plot develops. I make no assumptions here about the historicity of this story; statements concerning events relate to how the story would have been understood by its original audience in their social world.

We must first look at the broad social situation that an ancient Israelite audience would have discerned in the text. Elimelech and Naomi, with their two sons, Mahlon and Chilion, left Bethlehem during a famine, traveled to Moab "and they

---

[38] Fokkelien van Dijk-Hemmes, "Ruth: A Product of Women's Culture?," in Brenner, *Feminist Companion to Ruth*, 134–39.

[39] For the discussion in this paragraph, see Meyers, "Women of the Neighborhood," 117–18, 123.

[40] Kartzow, *Gossip and Gender*, 104–10, citing m. Soṭah 6:1 and m. Ketub. 7:8.

were there" (ויהיו־שם; 1:1–2).[41] Such an audience would probably have interpreted this to mean that they had acquired a house and taken up farming, the dominant economic activity.[42] Then Elimelech died, leaving Naomi and her two sons. Naomi and her sons presumably went on working the land. Then the sons married Moabite women, one called Orpah (her husband probably Mahlon) and the second (probably the younger) called Ruth (her husband probably Chilion).

Ten years elapsed and then Naomi's two sons died. Unstated but implied in the text is that neither Ruth nor Orpah had produced any children, even after ten years of marriage. It is interesting that neither son had married a second wife in the hope of producing children. One might expect this to be a rather tense household. In a social context characterized by patrilineality and patrilocality, a wife suffers the loneliness of having left her natal family and must come under the authority of, and build relationships with, her new relatives.[43] Sometimes the relationship between mother-in-law and daughter-in-law can be difficult, and a daughter-in-law who has not produced a son would be in a worse position. Upon the birth of her first son, a daughter-in-law's status in the house improves greatly. The failure of Ruth and Orpah to produce children negatively impacted the family's capacity to run a farm and support itself. Yet this factor did not sour relations between mother-in-law and daughters-in-law here, as might have been expected. As the story develops, we observe close emotional bonds between these three women related by marriage that set the scene for informal women's networks to appear later in the text.

But what about the birth families of Ruth and Orpah? As already noted, married women could and did keep in touch with their natal families, yet that process presupposes geographical proximity, with both families in the same village or in villages not too far apart (as probably to be understood here). This issue of staying in touch is implied in the text. Initially, with her husband and sons dead, when she heard that famine was over in Judah, "Naomi rose and her daughters-in-law with her and she began to return from the country of Moab" (1:6). But Naomi took no action at this point to send her daughters-in-law back to their families. Only when they had come away from the place (in Moab) where they had been living and "were

---

[41] Hebrew translations are my own unless otherwise specified.

[42] Far less plausibly, the Targum amplifies the elliptic ויהיו־שם of the MT by stating that they had been "lords" (רבנין) in Bethlehem and were "governors" (רופילין; from Latin *rufuli*) in Moab! See D. R. G. Beattie, *The Targum of Ruth*, ArBib 19 (Collegeville, MN: Liturgical Press, 1994), 18.

[43] For a graphic description of the position of daughters-in-law among the patrilineal and patrilocal Sarakatsani, see Campbell, *Honour, Family*, 59–69. "The bride takes most of her orders from her mother-in-law under whose critical and watchful direction she works" (64). Upon the arrival of a bride's first child among the Sarakatsani, the attitude of the whole extended family toward the bride "shifts from tolerance to acceptance and affection for her as the mother of their tiny kinsman" (69).

traveling along the road to return to the land of Judah" (1:7) did it occur to Naomi to send them home.

Accordingly, she suggested that they return to their mothers' houses, so that God might reward their kindness to their late husbands and to her by giving them security and status—naturally in this context identified with marriage or "finding rest [מנוחה] in the house of a husband" (1:8–9). That Naomi refers to their mothers' houses and not their fathers' is noteworthy, since both of Ruth's parents were still alive at this time (2:11). Probably an ancient reader would have understood that Naomi mentioned their mothers because they were the relatives most likely to compensate for their leaving her. Perhaps, however, we should imagine that Naomi knew the mothers personally from attending the weddings of Ruth and Orpah. In any event, the story is being told from the women's point of view, and the narrator suggests Naomi's slowness in coming to terms with the difficult situation of her daughters-in-law in her seeking to send them home only at the last moment.

The close emotional bond between these women is evident when she kisses them goodbye; their tears and protestations that they did not wish to leave her (1:10) accentuate this bond. While this may seem unsurprising to us, it may have been surprising in antiquity, given that these two women had failed to give Naomi any grandsons or granddaughters. Naomi next provided the specific reason for them to go home, namely, that she neither had nor would have other sons for them to marry (1:11–13). She implied that, if they returned home, they could find Moabite husbands. This seemed the main factor in Naomi's mind; the fact that, once back with their families, even if they did not remarry, they would also find help with lodging and subsistence—in a way that may have been difficult for Naomi to provide—passes unnoticed in the text.

The good social sense in Naomi's advice was evident to Orpah, who, having kissed Naomi, returned home (1:14). The fact that she did so only after hearing Naomi's advice and not earlier, for example, upon the death of her husband or before they had started out on the journey to Judah, hints at the depth of her devotion to her mother-in-law.[44]

Although Orpah's behavior was unusual, Ruth's response was remarkably so. She clung to Naomi when Orpah left (1:14) and resisted Naomi's warning that she should follow her sister-in-law and return to "to her people and to her god" (1:15). The words Ruth uttered to Naomi when explaining why she could not follow Orpah are widely familiar (1:16–17). Nevertheless, we tend to miss their full force because we underestimate how unlikely Ruth's response was in its ancient context and how unambiguously not motivated by a sense of personal self-preservation in a setting where women almost invariably sought fulfillment through marriage and giving

---

[44] For a nuanced and sympathetic discussion of Orpah's decision, see Judy Fentress-Williams, *Ruth*, AOTC (Nashville: Abingdon, 2012), 48–50. For a harsher view, see Ruth Nielsen, *Ruth: A Commentary*, OTL (Louisville: Westminster John Knox, 1997), 48.

birth to children. Some modern interpreters find the book disconcerting for this very reason.[45]

Let us look at Ruth's words seriatim:

A. Do not entreat me to leave you and to return from following you,
B. for wherever you go, I will go,
C. wherever you lodge, I will lodge.
D. Your people [עמך] will be my people [עמי],
E. and your God my God.
F. Wherever you die, I will die and there will I be buried.
G. May YHWH do this to me and more as well, if even death should separate us.

Clauses A and B signal Ruth's abandonment of her natal family and the husband it could provide her in favor of her marital family embodied (at this stage) solely in Naomi. But it also conveys her forfeiting of the security to be found where her birth relatives reside for a possible life on the move with her mother-in-law. While it later emerges that Naomi retained some property in Bethlehem, there is no indication that Ruth knew about it at this time. The point is solidified in clause C with its expression of Ruth's willingness to lodge, that is, to make an overnight stay, wherever Naomi does.

In clauses D and E Ruth responds to Naomi's recommendation that she return to "her people and to her god" (1:15) by insisting that (henceforward) Naomi's people and God are her people and her God. How are we to explain this? *Pace* Mark Smith's argument, developing an earlier idea of Tikva Frymer-Kensky,[46] these words have nothing to do with covenant or agreement. Superficial similarity of language should not distract us from the basic difference in the two situations: a covenant needs both parties to agree and to form some new entity. But here Naomi does nothing, while Ruth does everything. It is also wrong to see here a religious "conversion."[47] As long ago as 1988, before the discussion of ethnic identity had become common in biblical scholarship, Adele Berlin providently suggested that Ruth was engaged in a change of identity, from Moabite to Israelite: "Religion was bound up with ethnicity in biblical times; each people had its land and gods (cf.

---

[45] See the discussion by Cheryl B. Anderson, "Ruth and Esther as Models of the Formation of God's People: Engaging Liberationist Critiques," in *Focusing Biblical Studies: The Crucial Nature of the Persian and Hellenistic Periods; Essays in Honor of Douglas A. Knight*, ed. Alice Hunt and Jon L. Berquist, LHBOTS 544 (London: T&T Clark, 2014), 137–57, here 139–40.

[46] Mark S. Smith, "'Your People Shall Be My People': Family and Covenant in Ruth 1:16–17," *CBQ* 69 (2007): 242–58. He cites (246) Tikva Frymer-Kensky's notion that the words of Ruth's speech "resonate with the Bible's cadence of covenant and contract." See her *Reading the Women of the Bible: A New Interpretation of Their Stories* (New York: Schocken, 2002), 241.

[47] This is a common interpretation; see Smith, "'Your People Shall be My People,'" 243–45.

Mic 4:5), so that to change religion meant to change nationality."[48] Biblical research since then often cites the typical indicators of ethnic identity as formulated by John Hutchinson and Anthony Smith: (1) a common proper name for the group; (2) a myth of common ancestry; (3) a shared history; (4) a common culture, embracing customs, language, and religious phenomena; (5) a link with a homeland; and (6) a sense of communal solidarity.[49] Religious phenomena thus form only one part of six possible indicators of the more inclusive ethnic identity. The social pattern in view is a movement from one ethnic identity, Moabite, to another, Israelite—not a religious conversion—even though both ethnic identities have a strong religious dimension. Southwood has astutely described Ruth's movement in the text as one of "ethnic translation" and Naomi's as one of "ethnic re-translation."[50] Some centuries after Ruth was written, Philo described the process of becoming a Judean in unmistakably ethnic terms (*Virt.* 102–103).[51]

It is also a mistake to treat the word עַם as meaning only "family" or "clan," as Mark Smith does.[52] The עַם is predominantly the Judean ethnic group that is implied throughout the narrative and becomes explicit with mention of the "House of Israel" in 4:11–12. The עַם (people or ethnic group) of Israel, with its God, stands in contrast to the עַם (the people or ethnic group) of Moab (1:15), with its gods. Moab is a people living on its homeland (1:2, 6, 22), which is ethnic indicator 5 above. Moreover, Boaz distinguishes the land of Moab from Ruth's "mother and father" in 2:11. Ruth's natal ethnic identity is evoked whenever she is called a Moabite[53] (1:4, 22; 2:6; 4:5, 10).

Clause F carries the affirmation that the commitment expressed in the previous four statements is lifelong. Thus, Ruth gives up the family, people, and god of her birth and deliberately attaches herself instead to the family or clan, people, and God of Naomi. We witness Ruth at the very moment that she eloquently and momentously declares her adoption of new familial, ethnic, and religious identities. In clause G she emphasizes the irrevocability of her choice immediately after this by making operational—in the dramatic form of a curse—the attachment she has just expressed to the God of Israel. Seeing such determination, Naomi, unsurprisingly, says nothing more (1:18).

---

[48] Adele Berlin, "Ruth," *HBC*, 262–67, here 263. Another scholar who has recognized that Judean and Moabite ethnic identities were in play is Victor H. Matthews, in "The Determination of Social identity in the Story of Ruth," *BTB* 36 (2006): 49–54, here 51.

[49] John Hutchinson and Anthony Smith, "Introduction," in *Ethnicity*, ed. John Hutchinson and Anthony Smith, Oxford Readers (Oxford: Oxford University Press, 1996), 3–14, here 6–7.

[50] Southwood, "Will Naomi's Nation Be Ruth's Nation?," passim.

[51] See my discussion in Esler, *God's Court and Courtiers in the Book of the Watchers: Re-interpreting Heaven in 1 Enoch 1–36* (Eugene, OR: Cascade, 2017), 16–17.

[52] Smith, "'Your People Shall be My People,'" 257.

[53] The preferred form in English is the gender-neutral *Moabite*, rather than *Moabitess*, but the form in Hebrew is feminine מואביה.

Ruth 1:16–17 thus contains an extraordinary succession of loyalty statements, not least loyalty to Israel's God. The work provides no explanation for why Ruth adopts this position. It is just a donnée of the text. She was an extraordinary person and this is her story!

### The Return to Bethlehem (1:19–21)

The return of Naomi and Ruth to Bethlehem elicited quite a response: ותהם כל העיר עליהן (1:19, "the whole town was stirred because of them" [NRSV]). Here the Hebrew word תהם requires analysis. The initial question is whether it derives from הום (or the closely related form המם) or המה.[54] If it represents the imperfect *niphal* of הום or המם (either is grammatically possible), the primary reference, according to David J. A. Clines (who treats the verb as a form of הום), is to people being stirred up or in uproar or distraught.[55] Gerhard Lisowsky, similarly, favors הום and offers "*verwirren* / to stir, to discomfit / *perturbare*."[56] BDB translates "be in a stir."[57] H.-P. Müller suggests that the reference is "to the panic brought about by human uproar or by dismaying news."[58] Yet this is a little too negative, since the words can also refer to the excitement or uproar occasioned by a happy event, such as its use in relation to the earth's reaction to Israel's shouting when the ark arrived in the camp (1 Sam 4:5) or the response of Jerusalem to the shouts of Solomon's supporters when he is anointed king (1 Kgs 4:5). So we are talking about a group of people being stirred up or excited but also with noise being produced. It is less likely that תהם represents the *niphal* of המה, since the *niphal* of this verb is not otherwise attested in the Hebrew Bible.[59] If this is the underlying verb, however, the stress would fall more on the acoustic dimension of the event, its noisiness, with associations of tumult and confusion.[60] This meaning is less appropriate than uproar over what was perceived to be a stirring or exciting but yet essentially positive event. Thus, I follow most lexicons in regarding the verb as הום and suggest "was in noisy uproar" as an appropriate translation.

The arrival of Naomi and Ruth, presumably at the town gate (see 4:1), inevitably caused quite a stir and commotion: two unaccompanied women, one of them old and a younger one still of child-bearing age, had unexpectedly appeared.

---

[54] See Paul Joüon, *Ruth: Commentaire philologique et exégétique*, 2nd ed., SubBi 9 (Rome: Biblical Institute Press, 1986), 43; and Jones, *Reading Ruth*, 29.

[55] *DCH*, 2:504.

[56] Gerhard Lisowsky, *Konkordanz zum Hebräischen Alten Testament*, 2nd ed. (Stuttgart: Württembergische Bibelanstalt, 1958), 381.

[57] BDB, s.v. "הום."

[58] See H.-P. Müller, "המם," *TDOT* 3:419–22, here 422.

[59] It is always in the *qal*; see Lisowsky, *Konkordanz*, 426; and A. Baumann, "הָמָה," *TDOT* 3:414–18, here 414.

[60] Baumann, "הָמָה," *TDOT* 3:415.

As a crowd gathered around, people must have been wondering who the women were, where they came from, and why they were here. They were not immediately recognized, and it took at least a moment for some realization to dawn: "And the women asked, 'Is this Naomi?'" (1:19). The Midrash suggests that she looked different because she was sickly from hunger.[61] The women cannot have been expecting her. That Naomi had not been in touch with them during her sojourn in Moab is evident from the fact that she acquired her information about the famine's end by hearing about it in Moab (1:6), not from a report from Bethlehem.

We must imagine men, women, and children gathering to witness their arrival. That it is *the women* who recognize Naomi is a highly significant aspect of her homecoming (1:19): "And they [fem. pl.] asked, 'Is this Naomi?'" Meyers rightly recognizes behind this question an instance of informal networks such as she argues were widespread in ancient Israel.[62] Naomi was someone whom the Bethlehem women once knew well and often talked with, perhaps around a well, at a common bread-oven, while spinning, or while engaged in the other tasks that women shared. Their surprised recognition of Naomi—whom they had not seen in ten years since she had left Bethlehem with her husband and their two sons and who has now returned without the men but with a young woman—must have provoked intense curiosity on their part. André Lacocque remarks, "In their return to Judah, the Judean women welcome Naomi, but Ruth passes unnoticed."[63] This interpretation, however, does not really capture the women's response. The whole town had been stirred up "concerning them" (עליהן, 1:19), that is, by the arrival of *both* of them. Ruth had certainly been noticed. Their question "Is this Naomi?" is not yet a welcome, since it is uttered among themselves and not directed to Naomi (yet which Naomi overheard). But it also reflects the doubt that attended their recognition even of Naomi.

Naomi immediately moved to answer their curiosity as to whether this really was she. Yet she did so in a very negative and, at this point, very general way, talking not to the townsfolk at large but only to the women who alone had recognized her:

> And she said to them [עליהן], "Do not call me Naomi, call me Mara, for the Almighty has dealt very bitterly with me. I went away full, and the Lord has brought me back empty. Why call me Naomi, when the Lord has brought calamity upon me?" (1:20–21)

This statement would have raised as many questions as answers in the minds of the women present. They would certainly have wanted to discover the nature of and

---

[61] James McKeown, *Ruth*, Two Horizons Old Testament Commentary (Grand Rapids: Eerdmans, 2015), 33.

[62] Meyers, "Women of the Neighborhood," 120.

[63] André Lacocque, *Ruth: A Continental Commentary*, trans. K. C. Hanson, CC (Minneapolis: Fortress, 2004), 27.

reason for the bitterness and calamity that Naomi mentioned but also the identity of the young woman accompanying her and the circumstances of her doing so. But, according to the text, this is the extent of Naomi's remarks to them on this occasion, with the next verse simply rehearsing their return from Moab at the beginning of the barley harvest.

Danna Nolan Fewell and David M. Gunn take it amiss of Naomi that she says nothing about Ruth at this point.[64] How can Naomi say she is returning empty when she has an extraordinarily devoted daughter-in-law at her side? But this is probably to take too modern a view of the situation, to condemn Naomi with respect to a view on the position of women not current in her social context. As with other women in her culture, Naomi's life had revolved around the men in her life, her husband and her sons. Without a man in her life the prospects for her and, it must be stressed, for her daughter-in-law, were bleak indeed. That is why she said she came home empty and that YHWH had brought calamity upon her.

At this point the issue of gossip, especially among the women of Bethlehem, comes into its own. Any ancient audience of this text would have assumed that Naomi later communicated to the women, either singly or in a group, the full story of her tragic experience in Moab and the reason for Ruth's arrival with her and that this knowledge then spread throughout Bethlehem. This will be confirmed as the story proceeds.

### The First Two Encounters between Boaz and Ruth (2:1–17)

Although the narrator tells us that Naomi had a wealthy kinsman related to her husband named Boaz (2:1), for some reason Naomi (if she knew) did not tell Ruth about him. She had the opportunity to mention Boaz to Ruth but failed to do so when she agreed to Ruth's going out to glean. This is surprising given that Ruth was interested in catching the attention of some man in the process (2:2). This is confirmed by the fact that it happened by chance, not by her intention, that Ruth gleaned in Boaz's fields (2:3) and by the later mention of Boaz by Naomi (2:20). When Boaz came from Bethlehem (2:4), he asked the overseer in charge of the reapers, with reference to Ruth, "To whom does this young woman belong?" (2:5). The overseer's answer is worth noting: "The young woman is the Moabite who returned with Naomi from the country of Moab" (2:6). He then added that she had sought his permission to glean and she had been doing so since morning (2:7).[65]

How had the overseer learned Ruth's identity? Three possibilities present themselves: (1) from gossip in Bethlehem before she arrived in his master's fields,

---

[64] Fewell and Gunn, *Compromising Redemption*, 75–76.
[65] See McKeown, *Ruth*, 43–44, for a plausible argument (based largely on 2:3) that 2:7 does not mean that Ruth had been standing around all day but not gleaning. Fewell and Gunn, in a less likely interpretation, suggest that the overseer did not permit Ruth to start gleaning (*Compromising Redemption*, 35).

(2) from Ruth when she sought his permission to glean, or (3) from a mixture of both. Since he does not say that he asked Ruth who she was or that she told him, the more likely source of his information was gossip plus his assumption that this woman, perhaps hitherto unknown to him, who asked to glean could only be the Moabite newly arrived in the town. The overseer says nothing negative of Ruth to Boaz; indeed he provides the apparently positive report that she has been gleaning since early morning. Equally, he had heard nothing negative about her that would have led him to refuse her request to glean. It is significant that Boaz does not ask his overseer for any further details. We will soon learn that this is because he is already in possession of them, in their entirety.

Although unmentioned in the text at this stage, it emerges from what follows (2:9) that at this point, before speaking to Ruth, Boaz gave instructions that his servants were not to molest her and should permit her to drink from his pitchers of water. In other words, as soon as he realized who this young woman was, Boaz sprang into purposive action to assist her. Only later will we learn what had motivated this immediate and solicitous concern for the Moabite.

There next occurs a critical interaction, the first in the narrative between Boaz and Ruth (2:8–13). Taking the initiative, Boaz begins rather abruptly. Addressing her as "my daughter," he tells her to glean only in his fields and with his servants, whom he has ordered not to molest her, and to drink from his pitchers of water (2:8–9). Although Boaz has not told Ruth who he is, this message informs her that he is the owner of these fields and that he is a wealthy man who can afford servants to harvest them.

Faced with this sudden and utterly unexpected profusion of good will from someone clearly of wealth and influence, Ruth, not surprisingly, falls on her face, bows herself to the ground, and asks him the very natural question (2:10), "Why have I found favor in your sight that you should have regard for me, me, a foreigner?" Boaz's reply uncovers the motivation behind his attitude and actions toward her:

> All that you have done for your mother-in-law after your husband's death has been fully told to me, and that you left your father and your mother and the land where you were born and you came to a people that you did not know before. May YHWH reward your actions, and may a full recompense be made to you by YHWH, the God of Israel, under whose wings you have come to seek refuge. (2:11–12)

Above all, Boaz knows what Ruth said to Naomi when insisting that she would follow her (1:16–17), that is, he knows everything in clauses A, B, C, D, and E as set out above. That she intended to die and be buried wherever Naomi was (clause F) flows naturally from this. But Boaz knows more about Ruth than this. In referring to everything that she did for Naomi after her husband's death, Boaz evokes the period preceding their departure for Judah. Rather than simply leave Naomi and return home when Chilion died, a natural thing to do in this context, Ruth had stayed with Naomi, no doubt assisting her, *before* their journey to Judah. Boaz relies on this particular fact in forming an opinion of Ruth. It is true that "für Boas ist sie deshalb nicht mehr einfach 'eine Ausländerin.'"[66] Nevertheless, there is no sign he regards Ruth favorably because she is like Abraham (Gen 12) and Rebekah (Gen 24:4, 7), who left their own homeland to go to a foreign country.[67] In addition, it is sometimes suggested that Boaz's interest in Ruth has been prompted by his sexual attraction to her.[68] This, however, goes beyond, and runs against, the evidence.

More needs to be said about Boaz than this, however. The expression "has been fully explained [הֻגֵּד הֻגַּד] to me," with the *hophal* and the infinitive absolute, is striking. The *hophal* of נגד is used of gossip in Gen 38:13, where Tamar was told (probably by another woman) that Judah had gone off to the sheep shearing. The only other instance in the MT of the *hophal* of נגד together with the infinitive absolute is in Josh 9:24, where it refers to reliable knowledge—the Gibeonites' certainty that YHWH would give the whole country to the Israelites following Joshua's capture of Jericho and Ai. Here my translation "fully explained" is meant to convey an explanation that is both detailed and reliable. It suggests that Boaz has gone out of his way to gain all the accurate information about Ruth that he possibly could. She has struck him as someone exceptionally loyal to Naomi and her family, to Israel and to Israel's God. Lurking in the background here is the notion of חסד, a rich concept meaning faithful and devoted loyalty and kindness (in relationships and covenants), a concept Boaz will expressly invoke in relation to Ruth's conduct later.

We are probably meant to understand that, once Boaz had heard the broad facts of the return of Naomi and Ruth, he went out of his way to learn the whole story. It is beyond doubt that he was captivated by what he heard, including the fact that Ruth had chosen YHWH as her God. He regarded her as a person of outstanding inner beauty, whatever she may have looked like. The fact that nothing is said about Ruth's physical appearance in this text now falls into place: that issue was irrelevant to how Boaz regarded her.

Boaz must have known that sooner or later he was going to encounter Ruth. Bethlehem was a village, after all. Moreover, he must have been looking forward to meeting the woman about whom he knew so much and whose character, especially the loyalty that typified it, he so admired. Probably he guessed who this woman was—someone he had never met before in so small a place as Bethlehem—even before his overseer told him her identity.

As soon as we ask how it was that Boaz came by this all-important information about Ruth, we enter the realm of gossip, as profiled above. The foundational dimension of gossip is present: Ruth is an absent third party about whom other people have been exchanging information. Moreover, the information possessed

---

[66] Erich Zenger, *Das Buch Ruth*, ZBK.AT 8 (Zurich: Theologischer Verlag, 1992), 56.
[67] This has been suggested by Korpel, *Structure of the Book*, 126.
[68] See Fewell and Gunn, *Compromising Redemption*, 40–41.

valence. It was not just the neutral dissemination of news about the arrival of the Moabite with her mother-in-law and the specifics of Ruth's behavior, attitudes, and dispositions; it also extended to an evaluation of them. There is no sign that the evaluation of Ruth was anything other than positive. While much gossip is negative in character, the situation of Ruth represents one of those cases when it is positive.

Just as Gilmore and Merry saw virtue in Gluckman's functionalist approach and Paine's transactionalist perspective, both views of the diverse phenomenon of gossip assist in elucidating what happened in Bethlehem in relation to Ruth. Gluckman regarded gossip as a collective sanction by which public opinion enforced conformity to community values and objectives as articulated by the gossipers. This means that the action gossiped about was likely to be regarded as a transgression against those values and objectives. (We will see data comparable to this later in the text.) Ruth's case is different, however. One certainly encounters a strong sense of community values implied, even articulated, in Boaz's attitude to her. In a setting where group belonging was important, Boaz and his informants valorize loyalty to family, people, and God as fundamental values. For this reason, these virtues must be regarded as representative of wider Israelite values. In this respect they conform to Gluckman's approach. Yet, contrary to what Gluckman's view would argue, they do not see Ruth as failing to live up to these values, with gossip about her as a means to bring her into line. Rather, they regard her as embodying their values and as worthy of praise in consequence. They do not exchange information about the absent Ruth negatively because she is a threat to their community's values but laud her because she, a Moabite of all people, exemplifies their own values.

Paine's argument that gossip constituted a form of information management, a genre of informal communication intended to forward and protect individual interests, also resonates with the information exchanged about Ruth. In Paine's view, gossip is not necessarily either conducive to or destructive of community cohesion, bringing people together or pushing them apart. It can and probably does have either effect, but the consequence will depend on individuals using it to their advantage. This is how it serves as a catalyst of social process.

Paine's ideas cohere quite closely with the narrative. As the story advances, it becomes difficult to believe that Boaz has attended so closely to gossip about Ruth in order to engage with her merely as a proponent or enforcer of public opinion and social order. Even at this early stage he is more than someone who is just a mouthpiece for the community in telling her how closely she aligns with its values. Rather, he is captivated by her for the reason set out above, and this motivates his direct personal interest in her. We have confirmation later that he was attracted to Ruth but assumed he was too old for her when he thanked her for showing him kindness (חסד) and for "not going after young men, poor or rich" (3:10). He must have expected she would not be interested in him, wealthy or not, because of his age. His engagement with gossip about Ruth thus becomes the key way in which he learns enough about her to begin a relationship that will result in their marriage.

In other words, he is using gossip to further his own interests, but these interests also concide with those of the subgroup represented by himself, Naomi, and Ruth.

But what was the ultimate source of Boaz's knowledge about Ruth? Marjo C. A. Korpel provides an answer that is correct but only as far as it goes: "The unnamed source of his information is obviously village-gossip."[69] We can dig more deeply by drawing on Meyers's description of the informal Israelite women's networks. We have seen that, at the moment of her return to Bethlehem with Ruth, Naomi spoke to the women of the town whom she knew previously, rather than to the men. While this is Meyers's first evidence in the text for women's networks, she also provides a second example. Near the end of the text, after Ruth had borne a son, the women spoke to Naomi, praising YHWH for the child's birth and its benefits (4:14). Then "the women who were her neighbors [השכנות]," uniquely in the Hebrew Bible, named the child Obed (4:17).[70] These verses suggest that Naomi was very close indeed to the women of Bethlehem, that they formed a network (or even networks) of the type described by Meyers. The information about Ruth was released into the community through Naomi's speaking to the women, either at large or, more plausibly, to those women who were her immediate neighbors. With the latter she was on such intimate terms that it would be they who named Ruth's son.

Yet the information had to move from at least one of these women to Boaz. When he says that everything Ruth had done had been fully told to him, the person doing the telling must have been one of these women. This situation thus becomes intriguingly close to the cases (noted above) that Kartzow has identified in the Mishnah, where women (either those who spin together or visit bathhouses) provide information concerning other women to men who have a direct interest in it. Here the information was positive in nature: the woman must have passed on to Boaz the high praise of Ruth that Naomi had communicated to her. It is essential to observe for the argument of this article that gossip had produced the initially favorable impression that Boaz formed of Ruth and that prompted him to assist her.

One opacity in the text is whether we are meant to assume that Boaz knew he was a kinsman of Naomi by marriage, a member of her husband Elimelech's clan, when he was talking to Ruth, a fact he failed to mention to her. Given that he had so carefully obtained information about her, we should probably assume that Boaz did know this.

Ruth gracefully and humbly thanked Boaz for what he arranged for her, addressing him as אדני ("my lord," 2:13). Although she learned the name of the man

---

[69] Korpel, *Structure of the Book*, 126. Although he does not mention gossip as the mechanism, McKeown reasonably suggests that Boaz could only have heard about Ruth from information that Naomi had shared with others (*Ruth*, 47).

[70] Meyers, "Women of the Neighborhood," 120.

in whose fields she had been gleaning during that day, she did not know at that stage that he had any connection with her.

Later that day, at mealtime, on what was their second encounter, Boaz gave Ruth food, so that she ate till she was satisfied and had some food left over (2:14). He also instructed his servants to let her glean directly among the sheaves, leaving ears of grain specifically for her. She went home with an ephah of barley and showed Naomi the food and the barley (2:17–18). All of this testifies to the partiality Boaz showed Ruth as a result of what he had learned about her via the medium of gossip. Boaz's generosity also pricked Naomi's curiosity; she wanted to know the identity of the man whose eye Ruth had caught, and Ruth told her it was a man called Boaz (2:19). Only at this point (as noted above) did Naomi tell Ruth that Boaz was a relative of theirs with a right of redemption over them (2:20).

### Boaz's Third Encounter with Ruth, on the Threshing Floor (3:6–15)

The third meeting between Boaz and Ruth occurred because Naomi decided it would be appropriate for Ruth and Boaz, her kinsman, to marry. The unorthodox means Naomi chose to initiate this plan was for Ruth to sleep under Boaz's blanket on the threshing floor and to do what he said (3:1–5). Why Naomi simply did not negotiate with Boaz so as to conclude a marital contract is unclear. Her plan really constituted an elaborate device for Ruth to tell Boaz she would marry him. In any event, Ruth carried out the plan and Boaz awoke with a start to find a woman lying at his feet (3:6–8). It has been suggested she was naked,[71] but this is inconsistent with her dressing up for Boaz but keeping out of his sight until she lay at his feet (3:3). He asked who she was, and Ruth told him, while also reminding him (we soon see he already knew) that he was her kin, thus implying that he had a right of redemption over her (3:9). His response illustrates once again the power of gossip in propelling the plot of this narrative:

> And he said, "May you be blessed by YHWH, my daughter; for this latter act of faithful kindness [חסד] you have done is greater than the first, in that you have not gone after young men, whether poor or rich. And now, my daughter, do not fear; I will do for you everything that you ask, for all the people in my town know that you are a woman of good character [אשת חיל]. (3:10–11)

In verse 10 Boaz is aligning Ruth's kindness and loyalty in the past to Naomi—presumably by not abandoning her for another husband in Moab after her first husband died—with how she has now behaved to him, by not forsaking him for a young man. The use of חסד, a quality connected with loyalty and highly valued by Boaz as implied in his conversation with her in the field, is closely connected with the fact that he is a kinsman, to whom loyalty is especially appropriate.

---

[71] See, e.g., Nielsen, *Ruth*, 74.

But the next verse demonstrates the power of gossip in the town and the sway it holds over him. It matters greatly to Boaz that the people of Bethlehem all think highly of her. Although this is an unusual use of חיל, it does convey the meaning proposed above.[72] In Prov 4:5 חיל introduces a eulogy of a wife of noble character.[73] Among the population of Bethlehem are to be numbered the women of the town who, near the end of the text, express to Naomi, another woman, one aspect of Ruth's admirable character: "Your daughter-in-law, who has given him birth, loves you and is better for you than seven sons" (4:15).

In Boaz's reference to Bethlehem's opinion of Ruth we see the merits of Gluckman's understanding of gossip as a form of group sanction by which public opinion enforces conformity to community values. But rather than the inhabitants of Bethlehem having a negative view of Ruth and criticizing her departure from group norms, they think highly of her, and this gives comfort to Boaz that he might marry her without risk to his reputation. He immediately proceeds to tell her that he will redeem her, meaning marry her, so long as another person closer in kin with the right of redemption does not exercise it (3:12–13). That Boaz knows about this other person and that he has a prior claim further substantiates his having already given thought to marrying Ruth.

The relevance of Gluckman's view also surfaces in the thought that came to Boaz when she was leaving:

> So she lay at his feet until the morning, but got up before a man could recognize his neighbor; and he thought [ויאמר], "Let it not be known that the woman came to the threshing floor." (3:14)[74]

Once again the power of community opinion and values is in play. Boaz fears that the reputation, probably of both himself and Ruth, would be damaged if it were known that she had spent the night—and presumably had sex—with him. It is noteworthy that Naomi does not seem to have entertained this concern herself, since her instructions to Ruth (3:1–4) did not include advice to avoid being seen by anyone coming or going. Perhaps she thought that Boaz would have to marry her if he had sex with Ruth on the threshing floor. The scene ends with Boaz sending Ruth off with six measures of barley in her cloak (3:15).

## *Boaz at the Town Gate (4:1–12)*

The final example of how gossip in the text propels the story line occurs when Boaz acts to secure his marriage to Ruth. Seated at the town gate, Boaz explains to the kinsman with the closer claim on Ruth in the presence of ten of the town's elders

---

[72] Note Joüon, *Ruth*, 74: "חיל ici au sens de *force morale*, lat. *virtus, vertu*."

[73] Noted by Nielsen, *Ruth*, 77.

[74] Here ויאמר is translated "and he thought" (not "and he said") because his use of the expression "the woman" indicates that he is not speaking to Ruth but musing to himself.

that Naomi is selling the portion of the land that had belonged to Elimelech, Chilion, and Mahlon (4:1–3, 9). He then adds:

> So I thought that I would tell you [literally, "disclose to your ears"] and say, "Buy it in the presence of those sitting here.... If you will redeem it, redeem it; but if you will not, tell me." (4:4)

The reference to this land comes as a surprise; this is the first mention of it in the text. Equally surprising and new is that Naomi is selling the land. Plainly, the closer kinsman was unaware of Naomi's intention to sell it—that is why Boaz has to tell him. In other words, Boaz possesses valuable information concerning an absent third party, here Naomi, unknown to this other kinsman. Boaz has access to gossip, which he deploys to his advantage, that the other kinsman does not. It matters not whether Boaz has obtained this information from women to whom Naomi revealed it or from Naomi herself—which is not impossible, given her confidence in telling Ruth that Boaz was going to sort out that whole matter on that very day (3:18). However he acquired this information, it is gossip in the sense of "the exchange of information about absent third parties."

Boaz is artful in arranging a flow of information to himself on critical matters, first concerning Ruth's character, then concerning the existence of a closer relative with the right of redemption, and now concerning the fact that Naomi, his kinswoman by marriage, plans to sell her husband's property in Bethlehem. In this regard Boaz resembles Paine's individual gossiper, who carefully engages in informal communication and information management to forward and protect his interests and those of his subgroup, here his affinal kin Naomi and Ruth. The other kinsman was no doubt at the center of another web of kin relations, and we see in Bethlehem a community comparable to the coterie of rival interest-based subgroups described by Paine, in which gossip is used by individuals in one subgroup to secure advantages in relation to the others. The information that Boaz has obtained about Naomi's intended sale of the properties allows him to orchestrate his victory over the other kinsman, in that he is able to plan how he will link the acquisition of the property to marriage with Ruth in a way that the other man would find unpalatable, perhaps because he lacked the means to buy the property.

## IV. Conclusion

In terms of literary genre as viewed by Northrop Frye, the book of Ruth is close to that of a comedy: "The theme of the comic is the integration of society, which usually takes the form of incorporating a central character in it."[75] Many comedies involve an initially difficult situation for the characters that is resolved

---

[75] Northrop Frye, *Anatomy of Criticism: Four Essays* (Princeton: Princeton University Press, 1957), 43.

during the course of the plot so that a happy ending ensues, typically in the form of a marriage; here, very necessary for a successful resolution in this ancient social context, we also have the birth of a child. An important means by which the plot of the book of Ruth is propelled to this conclusion is that of gossip. In the text we observe phenomena closely comparable to that of the dominant theoretical approaches to gossip: first, following Gluckman, as a system of social control and, second, following Paine, as a form of information management, of informal communication intended to forward and protect individual interests that serves as a catalyst for social processes. Paine's approach is the more illuminating, given the extent to which Boaz's attraction toward Ruth from the outset depends on his use of gossip he has derived from women or women's networks in Bethlehem. He has also learned, possibly by gossip, that Naomi is selling her late husband's property. At the same time, however, we witness the force of gossip as an agent of social control in a positive sense, in that the fact that the community in Bethlehem has come to a positive view of Ruth strengthens Boaz's confidence in marrying her, but also in a negative sense, in his fear of the consequences if it is learned that Ruth has visited him on the threshing floor at night. On either approach, however, we are able to discover an important means by which this text works as a narrative. There is more to the unfolding story of Ruth than the role of gossip, but gossip, nevertheless, plays a major role.

# Utterance of David, the Anointed of the God of Jacob (2 Samuel 23:1–7)

**MAHRI LEONARD-FLECKMAN**
mleonard@holycross.edu
College of the Holy Cross, Worcester, MA 01610

Building on earlier studies of 2 Sam 23:1–7, I explore unique features of the poem that set it apart from the conceptual framework of Samuel–Kings and reflect a later development in the Davidic traditions. My primary foci are the concept of David the prophet (vv. 1–2) and the link between David and the God of Jacob (vv. 1 and 3), as well as the description of the just and perhaps unidentified ruler (vv. 3–7) and the panorama of divine names throughout. The poem represents the earliest witness to the development of David's prophetic image in early Judaism and Christianity. Yet the poetry does not merely demonstrate independence and innovation; rather, it draws deeply from earlier traditions, including the Balaam material and imagery from the Prophets and the Psalms. This analysis furthers earlier proposals that, before its inclusion in the appendix of 2 Samuel, the likely context for "David's last words" was the Psalms.

---

At the core of the appendix in 2 Samuel lies 2 Sam 23:1–7, the enigmatic poetry framed as "David's last words."[1] It is curious that the appendix in this book became the most compelling place for David's first "last words,"[2] with no attempt

---

Earlier versions of this article were delivered at the Colloquium for Biblical and Near Eastern Studies and at the Society of Biblical Literature Annual Meeting (both in November 2016 in San Antonio, Texas), and at the Old Testament Colloquium (February 2017 in Collegeville, Minnesota). I wish to thank those colleagues in attendance for their many helpful comments and questions; this article benefited greatly from their feedback.

[1] I borrow the word *enigma* from Antony F. Campbell's description of the entire appendix of materials in "2 Samuel 21–24: The Enigma Factor," in *For and against David: Story and History in the Books of Samuel*, ed. A. Graeme Auld and Erik Eynikel, BETL 232 (Leuven: Peeters, 2010), 347–58; and from K. L. Noll's description of 2 Sam 23:1–7 in *The Faces of David*, JSOTSup 242 (Sheffield: Sheffield Academic, 1997), 154. Second Samuel 23:1–7 is one of two poems at the heart of the collection of materials in 2 Sam 21–24, alongside 2 Sam 22.

[2] Noll asks a similar question from a synchronic rather than diachronic perspective: Why has the (single) narrator of the David story chosen to narrate this utterance out of sequence? See the question and Noll's proposals in *Faces of David*, 154–57.

to incorporate the poem more systematically into 2 Samuel. It should be noted that this poem conveys not the last but the almost-last words of David, before his final words to Solomon in 1 Kgs 2:1–10. First Chronicles 28:9–10 conveys yet another final statement to Solomon, before David hands over the temple plans to his son.[3] Neither 1 Kgs 2 nor 1 Chronicles reflects awareness of 2 Sam 23:1–7, and proposals that the poem circulated independently of Chronicles or reflects a "post-Chronistic addition" to Samuel are compelling.[4]

The poem's language and ideas are unique to Samuel–Kings, strikingly so. The poetry links David with the "God of Jacob," a term that is found overwhelmingly in the Psalms yet never in Samuel–Kings.[5] David is described as a prophet (vv. 1–2), a conception that has no parallel elsewhere in the Bible, and certainly not in Samuel, where the boundaries between king and prophet are clear when it comes to David (e.g., 2 Sam 7, 12).[6] David is unmentioned after verse 2, and the core poem describes the just ruler using imagery and language that recall the Prophets more than Samuel–Kings.[7] Apart from references to the "house" (בית) and the perpetual covenant (ברית עולם) in verse 5, verses 3–7 need not be about David at all.[8] The term ברית עולם is otherwise foreign to Samuel–Kings, which uses the term דבר ("word/promise") to describe the covenant with the Davidic line.[9]

For these reasons, the poem warrants a fresh examination. Building on earlier studies of 2 Sam 23:1–7, I will explore those unique features of the poem that set it

---

[3] Shimon Bar-Efrat describes the increasing idealization of David in biblical and postbiblical literature; in 1 Chronicles, he becomes an exemplary, pious king ("From History to Story: The Development of the Figure of David in Biblical and Post-Biblical Literature," in Auld and Eynikel, *For and against David*, 47–56).

[4] Cynthia Edenburg, "II Sam 21,1–14 and II Sam 23,1–7 as Post-Chr Additions to the Samuel Scroll," in *Rereading the relecture? The Question of (Post)chronistic Influence in the Latest Redactions of the Books of Samuel*, ed. Uwe Becker and Hannes Bezzel, FAT 2/66 (Tübingen: Mohr Siebeck, 2014), 167–82. Edenburg lists a set of criteria by which a text in the books of Samuel could be a post-Chronistic addition: (1) it disrupts the narrative continuity of Samuel; (2) it is not shared with Chronicles; (3) its tendencies do not run against those of Chronicles (in other words, the Chronicler did not omit it on ideological grounds); and (4) it displays characteristics of late composition.

[5] In this article I use the term *Psalms* synonymously with *Psalter* to refer to the texts within the book of Psalms.

[6] Unlike David, Saul demonstrates the permeable boundaries between prophet and leader in the proverb "Is Saul too among the prophets?" (1 Sam 10:11; 19:24).

[7] By *Prophets*, I mean those books included in the prophetic corpus following the Christian canonical groupings, excluding the "Former Prophets" according to the Jewish canon.

[8] Campbell writes that "the poetic texts do not apply particularly well to David; their emphasis sits better with the ideal for kingship in ancient Israel" ("2 Samuel 21–24," 357).

[9] See Steven L. McKenzie for a careful examination of the term ברית עולם in "The Typology of the Davidic Covenant," in *The Land That I Will Show You: Essays on the History and Archaeology of the Ancient Near East in Honor of J. Maxwell Miller*, ed. J. Andrew Dearman and M. Patrick Graham, JSOTSup 343 (Sheffield: Sheffield Academic, 2001), 152–78.

apart from the conceptual framework of Samuel–Kings and reflect a later development in the David traditions. The primary foci of the article will be the concept of David the prophet (vv. 1–2) and the link between David and the God of Jacob (vv. 1 and 3), the description of the just and perhaps unidentified ruler (vv. 3–7), and the panorama of divine names throughout. The poem represents the earliest witness to the development of David's prophetic image in early Judaism and Christianity. Yet I propose that the poetry does not merely demonstrate independence and innovation; rather, it draws deeply from earlier traditions, including the Balaam material and imagery from the Prophets and the Psalms. This analysis furthers earlier proposals that, before its inclusion in the appendix of 2 Samuel, the likely context for "David's last words" was the Psalms.

## I. 2 Samuel 23:1–7: Some Textual Issues

David's last words read as follows:[10]

| | |
|---|---|
| ¹וְאֵלֶּה דִבְרֵי דָוִד הָאַחֲרֹנִים | And these are the last words of David: |
| נְאֻם דָּוִד בֶּן־יִשַׁי | Utterance of David son of Jesse, |
| וּנְאֻם הַגֶּבֶר הֻקַם עָל | Utterance of the man whom El exalted, |
| מְשִׁיחַ אֱלֹהֵי יַעֲקֹב | Anointed of the God of Jacob |
| וּנְעִים זְמִרוֹת יִשְׂרָאֵל | And beloved of the Strong One of Israel. |
| ²רוּחַ יְהוָה דִּבֶּר־בִּי | The spirit of YHWH spoke through me, |
| וּמִלָּתוֹ עַל־לְשׁוֹנִי | His word was on my tongue. |
| ³אָמַר אֱלֹהֵי יַעֲקֹב | The God of Jacob spoke, |
| לִי דִבֶּר צוּר יִשְׂרָאֵל | The Rock of Israel said to me: |
| מוֹשֵׁל בָּאָדָם צַדִּיק | He who rules men justly, |
| מוֹשֵׁל יִרְאַת אֱלֹהִים | He who rules in awe of God, |
| ⁴וּכְאוֹר בֹּקֶר יִזְרַח־שָׁמֶשׁ | Is like the morning light at sunrise, |
| בֹּקֶר לֹא עָבוֹת | A morning without clouds, |
| מִנֹּגַהּ מִמָּטָר | Bright without rain, |
| דֶּשֶׁא מֵאָרֶץ | [Bringing] grass up from the earth. |
| ⁵כִּי־לֹא־כֵן בֵּיתִי עִם־אֵל | For is not thus my House with El? |
| כִּי בְרִית עוֹלָם שָׂם לִי | For an eternal covenant he set before me, |
| עֲרוּכָה בַכֹּל וּשְׁמֻרָה | Ordered in all things and secure. |
| כִּי־כָל־יִשְׁעִי וְכָל־חֵפֶץ | Will he not cause to sprout all my help and |
| כִּי־לֹא יַצְמִיחַ | my desire? |
| ⁶וּבְלִיַּעַל כְּקוֹץ | But the wicked are like thorns |
| מֻנָד כֻּלָּהַם | That are all thrown away, |
| כִּי־לֹא בְיָד יִקָּחוּ | For they cannot be taken in the hand, |
| ⁷וְאִישׁ יִגַּע בָּהֶם | He who touches them, |

---

[10] In the following presentation of the text and translation, I follow the line breaks that best suit the English translation, according to the JPS Hebrew-English Tanakh. I do not follow the Hebrew text of *BHS* exactly; differences will be explained below. The translation is my own.

| | |
|---|---|
| ימלא ברזל | must arm himself with iron |
| ואץ חנית | or the shaft of a spear, |
| ובאש שרוף ישרפו בשבת | And in fire they are utterly consumed on the spot. |

The poem is poorly preserved, yet the Qumran manuscript (4QSam<sup>a</sup>) and the Lucianic recension of the Old Greek (G<sup>L</sup>) help to elucidate some of the MT's textual issues.[11] In terms of the above textual and translation choices, note especially the following:

1. In verse 1, I tentatively follow the reading of 4QSam<sup>a</sup> (הקים אל, "exalted by El") rather than the MT's הקם על, "set on high." Both 4QSam<sup>a</sup> and G<sup>L</sup> preserve אל rather than על. P. Kyle McCarter notes the interchange of the preposition אל in 2 Sam 22:42 (MT and 4QSam<sup>a</sup>) to על in Ps 18:42 and considers it "safer" to read אל here, in accordance with Frank Moore Cross.[12] Elsewhere, we see connections between El and Jacob in MT Ps 146:5; in the Jacob stories, in which the God revealed to Jacob is El (e.g., Gen 35:3, 7); and in the Balaam material of Numbers (e.g., Num 24:5–8). Some regard the *hiphil* as preferable and consider על to represent the divine name "Most High" (עלי), thus reading the expression הקים על.[13] Alternatively, Gregorio del Olmo Lete considers all interpretations "equally valid."[14]

2. Also in verse 1, a traditional translation renders נעים זמרת ישראל as "the favorite/sweet one of the songs/psalmist [MT זמרות] of Israel," which makes sense in the context of the poetry. In light of its parallel with the "God of Jacob," however, a number of commentators view the expression as a divine epithet, which translates something like "Beloved of the Strong One of Israel."[15] In this case, נעים matches

---

[11] For verse-by-verse analyses, see H. Neil Richardson, "The Last Words of David: Some Notes on II Samuel 23:1–7," *JBL* 90 (1971): 257–66, https://doi.org/10.2307/3262715; Frank Moore Cross, *Canaanite Myth and Hebrew Epic: Essays in the History of the Religion of Israel* (Cambridge: Harvard University Press, 1973), 233–34; Tryggve N. D. Mettinger, "'The Last Words of David': A Study of Structure and Meaning in II Samuel 23:1–7," *SEÅ* 41–42 (1977): 147–56; Gregorio del Olmo Lete, "David's Farewell Oracle (2 Samuel XXIII 1–7): A Literary Analysis," *VT* 34 (1984): 414–37; P. Kyle McCarter, *II Samuel: A New Translation with Introduction and Commentary*, AB 9 (Garden City, NY: Doubleday, 1984), 476–79; Gary Rendsburg, "The Northern Origin of 'The Last Words of David' (2 Sam 23,1–7)," *Bib* 69 (1988): 113–21; Rendsburg, "Additional Notes on 'The Last Words of David,'" *Bib* 70 (1989): 403–8; Martin Kleer, *Der liebliche Sänger der Psalmen Israels: Untersuchungen zu David als Dichter und Beter der Psalmen*, BBB 108 (Bodenheim: Philo, 1996), 39–77; Noll, *Faces of David*, 165–69; László T. Simon, *Identity and Identification: An Exegetical and Theological Study of 2Sam 21–24*, TGST 64 (Rome: Gregorian University Press, 2000), 268–83.

[12] McCarter, *II Samuel*, 477; also Cross, *Caananite Myth*, 52 n. 31, 234 n. 66.

[13] See Michael Barré, "'My Strength and My Song' in Exodus 15:2," *CBQ* 54 (1992): 623–37, esp. 627; also McCarter, *II Samuel*, 477; Noll, *Faces of David*, 165 n. 41.

[14] Del Olmo Lete reviews the possibilities and the scholars who subscribe to each in "David's Farewell Oracle," 415.

[15] Cross translates the expression as "Favorite of the Mighty One of Israel" (*Canaanite Myth*, 234–36); McCarter as "the darling of the stronghold of Israel" (*II Samuel*, 476–80); and Richardson

the epithet for heroes and royalty known from Ugaritic texts ("beloved one, darling"),[16] and the root זמר compares to the Ugaritic *ḏmr* ("strengthen, protect") and the Amorite *zimri* ("protection").[17] In Hebrew, the divine epithet occurs only in Exod 15:2, Isa 12:2, and Ps 118:14, all in the standard expression עזי וזמרת י, "My Strength and my Stronghold." Here the translation is open to interpretation, yet, in the context of poetic parallelism, I prefer the divine epithet as the appropriate continuation of "God of Jacob" in the preceding phrase.

3. As commonly accepted, I follow G[L] in verse 3, which reads "Jacob" rather than the MT "Israel."[18] Reading alongside verse 1, Israel in the subsequent phrase requires the parallel Jacob here.

4. In verse 4, the latter part is difficult to interpret. Cross suggested that it was "hopelessly corrupt" and left it untranslated.[19] Tryggve N. D. Mettinger translates, "And as the sun shines forth at daybreak, [as] a morning without clouds after dawn, [as] after rain grass (comes) from the earth."[20] I have translated as simply as possible according to the poetic structure of the verse.

Ultimately, we lack certainty regarding the date of this material. Like many of the psalms, the poem contains a perplexing combination of arguably earlier and later elements.[21] Regardless of how the text evolved over time and how we might date a more "fixed" form, certain features in the text could reflect earlier traditions. For example, the central metaphor of the poem (vv. 3–4) bears similarities to a משל ("proverb") or a wisdom saying of sorts and shares affinities with Mal 3:19–20 in

---

as "the Guardian of Israel" ("Last Words of David," 261). Kleer holds open both translation possibilities (*Der liebliche Sänger*, 40–42, 47), while McKenzie prefers the traditional translation ("Typology of the Davidic Covenant," 164). Jon D. Levenson has drawn attention to the connection between the root נעם and revelations or positive omens in a number of biblical texts; in the case of 2 Sam 23:1, he proposes that David is God's "favorite" because he communicates divine revelation ("A Technical Meaning for NʿM in the Hebrew Bible," *VT* 35 [1985]: 61–67).

[16] See, e.g., *KTU* 1.17 VI 45 and 1.18 IV 14, in which first Anat and then YTPN refer to Aqhat as *nʿmn*. According to Mark S. Smith, when applied to warrior contexts, the word reflects the "magnetism of successful warriors or military leaders" (*Poetic Heroes: Literary Commemorations of Warriors and Warrior Culture in the Early Biblical World* [Grand Rapids: Eerdmans, 2014], 134).

[17] Barré discusses the meaning of *zmrt* as derived from the proto-Semitic *ḏmr* ("'My Strength and My Song,'" 623–37).

[18] See Cross, *Canaanite Myth*, 234 n. 69; Leer, *Der liebliche Sänger*, 42; McCarter, *II Samuel*, 477.

[19] Cross, *Caananite Myth*, 235 n. 73.

[20] Mettinger, "'Last Words of David,'" 151–52, 155. Note also Noll's translation, "Like morning light [when] the sun rises, a cloudless morning intensely shining, and after rain, greenery springs from the earth" (*Faces of David*, 166).

[21] Edenburg notes that arguments for dating the composition of 2 Sam 23:1–7 range from the tenth-century northern kingdom to the second half of the Persian period ("II Sam 21,1–14 and II Sam 23,1–7," 178 n. 64).

its hopes for a restored ruler. The parallels with Malachi could suggest a late dating, yet the proverb is timeless. McCarter has argued that the sun imagery has a particularly "Egyptian flavor" that contrasts with Malachi in its perception of the ruler as a present reality.[22] Depending on one's opinion of the date of the material, other unique elements of the poem under discussion here (including the terminology "God of Jacob" and the relation between the Balaam material and 2 Sam 23:1–2) could also be viewed as representing earlier conceptual understandings of David based on their independence from other biblical traditions about David.

Yet certain imagery and terminology point toward a later dating.[23] The most obvious is the possibly Aramaized term מלה as a synonym of דבר ("word," v. 2), as well as other phrases and nouns that occur almost exclusively in later texts, including משל ב- ("rule over," v. 3), חפץ ("desire," v. 5), and שמר ("secure") as related to covenant (v. 5).[24] The rich imagery of the just ruler as connected to the prosperity of the earth (v. 4) and the term צמח ("to sprout, spring up," v. 5) are unique to Samuel–Kings and recall prophecies of the renewal of Israel and the Davidic line in Isaiah and Jeremiah. Isaiah prophesies that YHWH's spirit will pour out over the offspring of Jacob, who will "sprout" (צמח) like grass (44:4) (חציר), while Jeremiah states that YHWH will "raise up" (צמח) a true branch (צמח) from David's line who shall do what is just (משפט) and right (צדקה) in the land (33:15).[25]

Finally, ברית עולם (v. 5) appears elsewhere in texts that arguably date to the exile at the earliest: these include Judg 2:1, part of the framing material from the last stages of the book's formation; Priestly material (Gen 9:16; 17:7, 13, 19; Exod 31:16; Lev 24:8; Num 18:19; 25:14); later portions of Isaiah (24:5; 55:3; 61:8); other exilic/postexilic prophetic texts (Jer 32:40, 50:5, Ezek 16:60, 37:26); and late psalms (Ps 105:8, 10 [= 1 Chr 16:17]; Ps 111:5, 9).[26] Nowhere else does the expression relate to the Davidic line. Samuel–Kings uses the term דבר exclusively as the "promise" made to David and his descendants, while outside of Samuel–Kings, the word ברית in relation to the Davidic line is attested in Isa 55:3; Jer 33:20–21, 25–26; Ps 89:4, 29, 35, 40; and 2 Chr 13:5; 21:7. Unlike 2 Sam 23:1–7, each of these cases is preoccupied explicitly with the Davidic line as his "house" and, apart from Isa 55, refers to David's offspring (see the discussion below). Besides Ps 89 and 2 Sam 23, the texts are easy to date as late exilic or postexilic.[27] While the uniqueness of the ברית

---

[22] McCarter, *II Samuel*, 484. For arguments that the central metaphor exposes a later perspective, see McKenzie, "Typology of the Davidic Covenant," 162; and McCarter, *II Samuel*, 485.

[23] For a list of the evidence, see McKenzie, "Typology of the Davidic Covenant," 162–64.

[24] See Edenburg, "II Sam 21,1–14 and II Sam 23,1–7," 178.

[25] See also Isa 42:9, 43:19, 45:8, 55:10, 58:8, 61:11.

[26] This information is found in McKenzie's careful study of the language of the Davidic covenant in "Typology of the Davidic Covenant."

[27] See McKenzie, who examines each of these attestations ("Typology of the Davidic Covenant," 156–77).

עולם in 2 Sam 23 gives pause, the language itself points to a later, post-Deuteronomistic framework.[28]

## II. David as Prophet (2 Samuel 23:1-2)

The prophetic description of David in verses 1-2 begins with the "utterance" (נאם) of David in verse 1.[29] This is one of only three biblical examples in which humans give "utterance," including Balaam the prophet in Num 23:3b-4, 15b-16, and Agur in Prov 30:1. Otherwise, YHWH is the subject of the remaining 366 "utterances" that are found overwhelmingly (356 times) in the prophetic books.[30] Steven McKenzie proposes that the word נאם is so common in prophetic literature that a later writer could easily transfer the term to David in 2 Sam 23 to portray David as a prophet.[31] When compared to YHWH as the common source of oracles, however, the sparseness of human "utterances" in the Bible gives pause for thought. These few examples represent an unusual collapsing of boundaries between the human and the divine, considering that the formula "'oracle' of YHWH" helps to distinguish the divine "voice" from the secondary "voice" (or narrative voice) of the prophet.[32] In the case of the Agur material in Prov 30:1-9, the נאם claims divine origin, yet the subsequent statements are not necessarily prophetic. Such statements are generally formulated in Agur's own words, and they communicate neither insights about the future nor any new information beyond already-known truths.[33]

---

[28] Simon, *Identity and Identification*, 304.
[29] Contra McCarter, who isolates the prophetic description of David to verse 2 alone and views it as a late addition to an otherwise early text (*II Samuel*, 480-81).
[30] This number includes the unusual occurrence of נאם linked with פשע ("transgression"), as if in construct, in MT Ps 36:2 (נאם־פשע לרשע, "transgression speaks to the wicked"). On the text-critical problems there, see Hans-Joachim Kraus, *Psalms 1-59: A Commentary*, trans. Hilton C. Oswald (Minneapolis: Augsburg, 1988), 396-97; and Peter C. Craigie and Marvin E. Tate, *Psalms 1-50*, 2nd ed., WBC 19 (Nashville: Nelson, 2004), 289-90. Kraus reads נעם and translates as "pleasing" ("Pleasing is transgression to the ungodly"); while Craigie and Tate take נאם as a word that stands independently to describe the first part of the psalm (vv. 2-5). On the term נאם associated with prophetic utterances, see Noll, *Faces of David*, 154 n. 6.
[31] McKenzie, "Typology of the Davidic Covenant," 163. Reading synchronically, Noll proposes that David himself, as the author of the text, invokes a formula that he knows to come from the oracles of Balaam (*Faces of David*, 162).
[32] On the question of the relationship between biblical prophecy and writing, see the discussion in Sara J. Milstein, "'Who Would Not Write?' The Prophet as Yhwh's Prey in Amos 3:3-8," *CBQ* 75 (2013): 429-45. Milstein distinguishes between a "writing prophet" like Ezekiel and scribes who took on the label of "prophet."
[33] Michael V. Fox, *Proverbs 10-31: A New Translation with Introduction and Commentary*, AYB 18B (New Haven: Yale University Press, 2009), 853. The Agur material is of uncertain date

In the case of Balaam (Num 23–24), the third and core poem (24:3–9, with repetition in the fourth, perhaps expanded material) bears remarkable resemblance to the opening two verses of "David's last words."[34] The poem begins, "Utterance [נאם] of Balaam son of Beor / utterance of the man [נאם הגבר] whose eye is opened [שתם העין] / utterance of him who hears the words of El / who sees visions of Shaddai / prostrate, with eyes uncovered" (Num 24:3–4). Balaam is viewed as an ecstatic, a visionary, who proceeds to prophesy about Israel's future glory over its enemies. While some regard the Balaam material as postexilic, it contains thematic and religious similarities with the late ninth- to early eighth-century Deir ʿAlla plaster texts (ca. 800 BCE) and exposes Transjordanian traditions that run contrary to later perspectives.[35] Such traditions include the portrayal of Balaam positively as a seer (contra Deut 23:4–5, Neh 13:2, Num 31:16); the vision of a collection of acting deities (El in 24:4 and 8; YHWH in 24:6; Elyon in 24:16; Shaddai in 24:4, 16); the identification of El and YHWH as two separate deities; the notion that El brought the people out of Egypt (23:22, 24:8); a lack of awareness of a journey through the Transjordan on the way from Egypt to Canaan; and a focus on a settled Israelite presence east of the Jordan, with little regard for Israel in the west.[36]

Similarly, 2 Sam 23:1 opens with the "utterance" of the "man" or, perhaps, "warrior" (גבר) David, who is also described both in relation to his father's line and

---

and origin. Though an addition to the core Proverbs material (Prov 10–29), the Agur poem (30:1–9) and the collection of appendixes in chapters 30–31 may have been written earlier than the core material and later added to it. The Agur material could also have been written as a reaction to the core material and may exhibit awareness of Deuteronomy (see Prov 30:6). Fox dates the material to the late fifth to the end of the third centuries BCE, based on the tension between human and divine wisdom (ibid., 862, 956–57).

[34] Richardson writes that the parallels between the Balaam poetry and David's last words "cannot be overlooked in any consideration of the date of the poem [David's last words] under discussion" ("Last Words of David," 260).

[35] For arguments concerning dating and a genealogy of scholarship, see Stephen C. Russell, *Images of Egypt in Early Biblical Literature: Cisjordan-Israelite, Transjordan-Israelite, and Judahite Portrayals*, BZAW 403 (Berlin: de Gruyter, 2009), 81–88. Some possible features that could be interpreted as "late" (postexilic) include the Israel/Jacob poetic parallelism (Num 23:21, 23; 24:5); the use of נאם in connection with a human being as a late development in prophetic speech; the names שדי (Num 24:4, 16) and עליון (24:16) as exilic and postexilic expressions of the deity; and the religious perspectives in the oracles, which demonstrate a date of origin subsequent to the Deir ʿAlla plaster inscriptions.

[36] Russell, *Images of Egypt*, 78–119. Russell further notes that the arguments for a postexilic provenance are unconvincing, due in large part to the paucity of data available to make such claims. The corpus of biblical material that might date to the eighth century or earlier is relatively small; the interpretation that all Israel/Jacob poetic parallelism is late is subjective; and the divine names for God appear in many periods. See also Baruch A. Levine, *Numbers 21–36: A New Translation with Introduction and Commentary*, AB 4A (New York: Doubleday, 2000), 241–75; Daniel E. Fleming, *The Legacy of Israel in Judah's Bible: History, Politics, and the Reinscribing of Tradition* (Cambridge: Cambridge University Press, 2012), 128–32.

to the God of many names.[37] In verses 1–2, David is the one "exalted" by El (or perhaps the Most High), the "anointed of the God of Jacob," the beloved of the "Strong One of Israel," and the recipient of the "spirit of YHWH." Like the Balaam poetry, 2 Sam 23 recollects an assembly of deities. The single reference to YHWH is tied to the "spirit" as the source of David's prophetic impulse (v. 2), while the reference(s) to "El" (vv. 1[?], 5) describe a basic bond between David and "(the) God." The references to the God of Jacob (vv. 1, 3) are paired with epithets that use nouns for divine protection by fortification in relation to "Israel." Elohim then appears in verse 3. While the Balaam poetry betrays a perspective in which El and YHWH are not yet fully synthesized (it is El alone who brings the people out of Egypt), it is difficult to identify distinct functions of one divine title over the other in 2 Sam 23:1–7, and the divine names are more likely a poetic device.

Arguments for an early dating of the core Balaam poetry are convincing, and the language of David as prophet in 2 Sam 23:1–2 likely reflects dependence on this poetry. Still, the conception of David as prophet is distinct and innovative; it has no parallel elsewhere in the Hebrew Bible and appears only in early Judaism and Christianity (e.g., Acts 2:30; Josephus, *Ant.* 6.166; 8.109; 11QPs[a] XXVII, 11; the targum; b. Soṭah 48b). McCarter seeks to excise verse 2 as a late addition based on these much later, extrabiblical references, and verse 2 (with its Aramaized term מללה) may indeed reflect a later expansion. Further evidence for the secondary nature of verse 2 is the expression דבר־בי, "has spoken through me," a phrase that is attested elsewhere in relation to divine communication to the prophet (Hab 2:1; 11x in Zechariah). In the case of 2 Sam 23:1–7, the expression דבר־בי may draw out secondarily from לי דבר ("said to me") in verse 3. Yet one cannot excise the prophetic description of David in verse 2 without also excising verse 1, which clearly sets up David as the recipient of a divine oracle.

Without these opening two verses, verses 3–7 recall God's generalized words of instruction to a righteous ruler, with a possible interruption of commentary regarding the Davidic line in verse 5.[38] The core wisdom in verses 3–4 and 6–7 does not mention David and need not be about David at all.[39] The general description in verse 4 recalls Ps 72 (later inscribed "For Solomon"), which proclaims the just king's actions as rain (מטר) upon the earth (v. 6), while the combined terminology of מטר ("rain") and דשא ("grass") is attested elsewhere only in the extended poem

---

[37] Noll describes David's self-perception as both a prophet and warrior (*Faces of David*, 162).

[38] Fox states that God's words of praise to the righteous ruler in this poetry "recalls a sapiential generalization" rather than prophecy (*Proverbs 10–31*, 853). Noll proposes that the oracle is limited to verses 3b–4, followed by David's commentary on the oracle (*Faces of David*, 161). See Simon's overview of various scholarly opinions on the structure of the poem in *Identity and Identification*, 286–87.

[39] For example, Campbell writes that the poem is "perplexing" if applied to David and proposes that the emphasis of the poetic texts works better for a general ideal of kingship than for David himself ("2 Samuel 21–24," 353, 357; see also n. 8 above).

attributed to Moses in Deut 32. Together, verses 3–4 and 6–7 contrast the just and the wicked using natural imagery; in verse 5, the extended line length and conceptual shift toward the perpetual covenant give pause. One might even argue that verses 3–4 are about Moses the prophet, repurposed at the end of 2 Samuel.[40]

The ברית עולם in verse 5, however, reorients the poem toward the Davidic line. Here the reference to the covenant is brief, and the broader perspective behind the terminology is elusive. The poetic line begins with the speaker's "house," which is described only as "with El," and then extends to the ברית עולם, which is "set before" the ruler alone. Whether the ברית is unconditional depends on how one understands the description of the covenant as "ordered" (ערך) and "secure" or "guarded" (שמר). In the early twentieth century, S. R. Driver described the terminology as legal and containing certain stipulations,[41] a notion that could be further strengthened by the inclusion of the word חפץ ("delight/desire") as connected with ancient Near Eastern treaties.[42]

Though some would argue that the covenantal language here is dependent on the promise to David in 2 Sam 7, the language and imagery in the poem are quite distinct from 2 Sam 7.[43] Compare verse 5 with 2 Sam 7:11–16, in which YHWH makes a דבר to David that *after* David dies, YHWH will raise up his seed (זרע), and David's "house," kingship, and throne will be "secure" or "established" (כון) "forever" (עד־עולם). In 2 Sam 7, the preoccupation of the writers is quite clear in describing the establishment and security of the Judahite monarchy (i.e., David's line or house). In the case of 2 Sam 23, the connection to progeny is implicit in the notion of future continuity, but the emphasis is on the ruler himself, and in such a way that puts the covenant of 2 Sam 7 to shame.[44] The distinctiveness of the ברית עולם, which is otherwise unattested in Samuel–Kings and appears in texts that

---

[40] On the relationship between "double prophetic summary speeches" in 2 Sam 22/23:1–7, Deut 32–33 and Josh 23–24, see Noll, *Faces of David*, 154–65. He notes that the use of מטר in Genesis–Kings often carries with it the connotation of divine intervention in human affairs (171 n. 57).

[41] S. R. Driver, *Notes on the Hebrew Text and the Topography of the Books of Samuel* (Oxford: Clarendon, 1913), 360; also Cross, *Canaanite Myth*, 236–37.

[42] See Erin Fleming, "Political Favoritism in Saul's Court: חפץ, נעם, and the Relationship between David and Jonathan," *JBL* 135 (2016): 19–34, esp. 24–28, https://doi.org/10.15699/jbl.1344.2016.2929. Fleming argues that certain biblical and Near Eastern examples of חפץ and its cognates are clearly political in nature, including חפץ in 1 Sam 18:22, 19:1, and 2 Sam 20:11; the term חפץ in the eighth-century Aramaic Sefire Inscriptions; and the Akkadian verb ḫašāḫu in two royal inscriptions that date to the Middle Assyrian and Neo-Assyrian periods.

[43] Those who argue that the covenant in 2 Sam 23 is dependent on 2 Sam 7 include McKenzie, "Typology of the Davidic Covenant," 164; Tryggve N. D. Mettinger, *King and Messiah: The Civil and Sacral Legitimation of the Israelite Kings*, ConBOT 8 (Lund: Gleerup, 1976), 257–58; Levenson, "Technical Meaning for NᶜM"; Noll, *Faces of David*, 161; and Jacques Vermeylen, *La loi du plus fort: Histoire de la rédaction des récits davidiques de 1 Samuel 8 à 1 Rois 2*, BETL 154 (Leuven: Leuven University Press, 2000), 418.

[44] As Campbell writes, "Despite 2 Samuel 7 in its most exalted form, the claim 'Is not my

arguably date to the exilic or postexilic period, and the "house" as connected explicitly with the ruler suggest a distinct conceptual perspective from other traditions of YHWH's covenant with the Davidic line.

With verses 1–2 and 5, the glory of the unidentified just ruler in verses 3–7 comes to rest on David. The distinctiveness of the prophetic vision in verses 1–2 represents a later depiction of David, a depiction that became "more glorious as time passed" in biblical and extrabiblical references.[45] Aside from its resonances with the Balaam material, the image of David as prophet in the Hebrew Bible is singular. The idea might have developed in relation to David as psalmist, as demonstrated by the inclusion of David's last words at the end of the Qumran Psalter 11QPs$^a$. According to the order of 11QPs$^a$, David's last words precede a description of the Davidic authorship of the Psalms (11QPs$^a$ XXVII, 2–11), which states that David uttered the songs through prophecy from the Most High (line 11). Two pseudo-autobiographical psalms about David (Pss 151A and 151B) then follow this description. Cynthia Edenburg proposes that the book of Psalms as represented by 11QPs$^a$ represents the original context of David's last words. According to Edenburg, the fragmentary Samuel scroll (1Q7) lacks space for 2 Sam 23:1–7, and at some point, a later scribe copying the Samuel scroll transferred the poem to the end of 2 Samuel.[46]

Later Jewish and Christian perspectives were likely inspired by the poetry here. According to Josephus, the divine spirit departed from Saul and rested on David, who instantly began to prophesy (*Ant.* 6.166); then, when Solomon transferred the ark to the temple, he declared that God had shown David everything that would come to pass in the future (*Ant.* 8.109). Alluding to Ps 132:11 and 2 Sam 7, the writer of Acts 2:30 declares that David was a prophet who knew that God had sworn to put one of his descendants on the throne. The targum then embellishes the opening of 2 Sam 23 in the following way: "These are the words of the prophecy of David which he prophesied about the end of the world.... David said, 'In a spirit of prophecy before YHWH I am speaking these things, and I am arranging his holy

---

house like this with God?' (v. 5) would rightly bring a blush to the Davidic cheek" ("2 Samuel 21–24," 354).

[45] Mark S. Smith, *The Memoirs of God: History, Memory, and the Experience of the Divine in Ancient Israel* (Minneapolis: Fortress, 2004), 134. Bar-Efrat discusses the slow development of ideas about David in biblical and postbiblical literature, in which David transitions from a realistic figure (Samuel), to an ideal, pious, wise figure (Chronicles, Qumran, Josephus, Matthew, Babylonian Talmud), and finally to a "mere idea" (Kabbalah) ("From History to Story," esp. 55–56). In Kabbalah, Bar-Efrat notes that the Zohar describes a heavenly counterpart to the earthly David in accordance with the idea of Platonic forms. Bar-Efrat does not discuss the development of David as a prophet in biblical and postbiblical literature.

[46] See Edenburg, "II Sam 21,1–14 and II Sam 23,1–7," 179. See also James A. Sanders, *The Psalm Scroll of Qumran Cave 11 (11QPs$^a$)*, DJD IV (Oxford: Clarendon, 1965), 92–93; Simon, *Identity and Identification*, 307; Yuzuru Miura, *David in Luke-Acts: His Portrayal in Light of Early Judaism*, WUNT 232 (Tübingen: Mohr Siebeck), 81–82.

words in my mouth'" (Tg. Neb. 2 Sam 23:1–2; my translation). With no other biblical comparisons, the poetry in 2 Sam 23:1–7 preserves a prophetic vision of David that is thoroughly unique to biblical writing and provides the fodder for later interpretations. Yet it does not emerge out of nothing; rather, the poetry borrows from the language and vision of the Balaam poetry, the Prophets, and the Psalms and applies it innovatively to David.

## III. God of Jacob

The only attestations of the "God of Jacob" in Joshua–Kings are found in 2 Sam 23:1–7. This divine title is attested with greatest frequency in the Zion psalms and is therefore linked with Judah and the Jerusalem temple. Certain biblical attestations of the "God of Jacob," however, may reflect northern origins, and the Jacob tradition itself is associated with the northern kingdom. In the case of 2 Sam 23:1–7, the "God of Jacob" is linked with David and Israel, yet without mention of Judah or Jerusalem. Psalm 132 similarly links the "God of Jacob" (or "Holy One of Jacob," אביר יעקב) to David, yet there the psalm's explicit focus is Jerusalem and the ark tradition. While a study of the "God of Jacob" warrants careful investigation outside the confines of this article, 2 Sam 23:1–7 is the sole witness to this divine title in relation to David and Israel, rather than Judah, and therefore compels some discussion here. In this section I will raise initial questions of the relationship between the "God of Jacob" and Judah that I hope to develop in a further study of the divine title in the Psalms.

The Jacob tradition in the book of Genesis has long been associated with the northern kingdom of Israel, based on its geography and political understanding.[47] Scholars have argued that the first written Jacob story likely dates to the mid-eighth century BCE, and that the story may preserve an old tradition that reflects the realities of the end of the second millennium BCE.[48] In the Bible, especially the

---

[47] See Albert de Pury, *Promesse divine et légende cultuelle dans le cycle de Jacob: Genèse 28 et les traditions patriarcales*, EBib (Paris: Gabalda, 1975); Erhard Blum, *Die Komposition der Vätergeschichte*, WMANT 57 (Neukirchen-Vluyn: Neukirchener Verlag, 1984); David M. Carr, *The Formation of the Hebrew Bible: A New Reconstruction* (Oxford: Oxford University Press, 2011), esp. 472–76; D. Fleming, *Legacy of Israel*, 72–90.

[48] Albert de Pury, "Situer le cycle de Jacob: Quelques réflexions, vingt-cinq ans plus tard," in *Studies in the Book of Genesis: Literature, Redaction and History*, ed. A. Wénin, BETL 155 (Leuven: Leuven University Press, 2001), 213–41; Erhard Blum, "The Jacob Tradition," in *The Book of Genesis: Composition, Reception, and Interpretation*, ed. Craig A. Evans, Joel N. Lohr, and David L. Petersen, VTSup 152 (Leiden: Brill, 2012), 181–211; Israel Finkelstein and Thomas Römer, "Comments on the Historical Background of the Jacob Narrative in Genesis," *ZAW* 126 (2014): 317–38. Contra Nadav Na'aman, "The Jacob Story and the Formation of Biblical Israel," *TA* 41 (2014): 95–125.

prophetic material, the name "Jacob" is consistently associated with the kingdom of Israel (see Isa 8:17, Jer 2:4, Ezek 20:5, Hos 12:3, Amos 3:13, Mic 3:8).

Although the name Jacob is common in biblical materials, expressions associated with Jacob and God—the "God of Jacob" (אלהי יעקב) and the "Mighty One of Jacob" (אביר יעקב)—are unusual. Moreover, these divine titles often, though not always, reflect a Judahite perspective. The MT attests to the "Mighty One" of Jacob five times (Gen 49:24; Isa 49:26; 60:16; and Ps 132:2, 5)[49] and to the God of Jacob seventeen times, eleven times in the Psalms alone (Pss 20:2; 46:8, 12; 75:10; 76:7; 81:2, 5; 84:9; 94:7; 114:7; and 146:5 [אל יעקב]). The Greek contains two further attestations to the "God of Jacob" in psalms that may contain quite old traditions: Ps 132:2, 5 (= LXX 131:2, 5) in place of the MT's "Mighty One" of Jacob; and Ps 24:6 (= LXX 23:6) over the MT's "Jacob." In Ps 24, the "God of Jacob" is also preserved in Syriac witnesses.[50] Altogether, seven of these psalms link the God of Jacob explicitly with Zion and the temple (Pss 20, 24, 46, 76, 84, 132, and 146).

Outside the Psalms, we see the God of Jacob in the formulaic expression "God of Abraham, God of Isaac, God of Jacob" (Exod 3:6, 15; 4:5) and, more notably, in Isa 2:3 (= Mic 4:2), which is also connected with Zion.[51] Finally, 2 Sam 23:1 refers to David as the "anointed of the God of Jacob." In the case of 2 Sam 23:1–7, Judah is nowhere in view, and YHWH is called the "God of Israel" (v. 3) and the "Rock of Israel" (v. 4), in addition to the "God of Jacob" (v. 1).

Meanwhile, the "God of Jacob" is unattested in Amos or Hosea, prophets to the northern kingdom. It is similarly unattested in books that arguably have the greatest likelihood of reflecting northern traditions, including Genesis and Judges. Indeed, the "God of Jacob" is most consistent in the Zion psalms, which demonstrates that the God of Jacob is essential to the religious institution of Judah. Some of these psalms, including Pss 24, 46, 114, and 132, exhibit archaic features and shared motifs with other, arguably early biblical material, including Judg 5 and Ps 29.[52] In the "psalms of Asaph" (Pss 50, 73–83), Ps 81 describes Israel, the God of

---

[49] Note also the single reference to the "Holy One of Jacob," קדוש יעקב, in Isa 29:23.

[50] Priority is often given to the Greek and Syriac witnesses of Pss 132 and 24; see, e.g., Kraus, *Psalms 1–59*, 311; and Craigie and Tate, *Psalms 1–50*, 210.

[51] H. G. M. Williamson explores the notion of the God of Jacob in Isaiah and Micah, two prophets associated with Judah ("Judah as Israel in Eighth-Century Prophecy," in *A God of Faithfulness: Essays in Honour of J. Gordon McConville on His 60th Birthday*, ed. Jamie A. Grant, Alison Lo, and Gordon J. Wenham, LHBOTS 538 [London: T&T Clark, 2011], 81–95).

[52] Cross incorporated these psalms into his treatment of the divine warrior motif. According to Cross, Pss 24 (esp. vv. 7–10) and 132 preserve "very old traditions" of the divine warrior coming to take up his abode in Jerusalem (*Canaanite Myth*, 90–99). See also Craigie and Tate, *Psalms 1–50*, 211–12; Kraus, *Psalms 1–59*, 312; and Kraus, Psalms 60–150: *A Commentary*, trans. Hilton C. Oswald (Minneapolis: Augsburg, 1989), 475–83; Frank Lothar Hossfeld and Erich Zenger, *Psalm 1–50*, vol. 1 of *Die Psalmen*, NEchtB 29 (Würzburg: Echter, 1993), 156–58; Beat Weber, *Die Psalmen 1 bis 72*, vol. 1 of *Werkbuch Psalmen* (Stuttgart: Kohlhammer, 2001), 130. Hossfeld and Zenger subscribe to a postexilic dating of Ps 132, even while they review arguments

Jacob, and Joseph coming out of Egypt, and scholars agree that this psalm (and possibly other Asaph psalms) may have originated in the northern kingdom.[53]

Some scholars might argue that the term "God of Jacob" as linked with the Jerusalem temple in the Psalms and with David is a late preexilic development at best. This view proposes the following: Judah was never part of Israel; the early monarchy (i.e., David) never ruled over Israel; and Judah would claim the identity of Israel only after the fall of the northern monarchy.[54] Therefore, any biblical references that incorporate Judah into Israel or refer to Judah as Israel would be anachronistic, for Judahites would have no memory of ever having been part of the larger and more dominant kingdom of Israel. Based on this view, one could extend this argument to propose that the God-of-Jacob terminology in relation to Zion or Jerusalem would represent a Judahite adoption of the identity of Israel, perhaps based on a desire to be remembered as Israel, perhaps as an attempt to have the Davidic monarchy accepted by northern refugees, or perhaps even to create a common identity with these refugees.

Yet this perception of a clean dating line in which Judah would adopt the name Israel only after 722 BCE is unsatisfying. It raises the question of why Judahites would have understood themselves to be inheritors of Israel or wished to assume the name Israel, if they had no traditional basis for this identification at any level prior to the fall of Israel. These arguments also fail to take seriously the religious

---

for dating that extend "from the time of Solomon to the Maccabean period" (*Psalms 3: A Commentary on Psalms 101–150*, trans Linda M. Maloney, Hermeneia [Minneapolis: Fortress, 2011], 458–60). Cross also proposes that Ps 46 (esp. vv. 7–11) includes ancient material (*Canaanite Myth*, 174; see also Craigie and Tate, *Psalms 1–50*, 343–44; Kraus, *Psalms 1–59*, 460–61), and he notes that the hymn of Ps 114 utilizes the old mythic pattern of the "pairing of River and Sea" that is shared with Judg 5:4–5 and Ps 29 (*Canaanite Myth*, 138–39; see also Kraus, *Psalms 60–150*, 371–75; contra Hossfeld and Zenger, *Psalms 3*, 193).

[53] See Beat Weber, *Die Psalmen 73 bis 150*, vol. 2 of *Werkbuch Psalmen* (Stuttgart: Kohlhammer, 2003), 70; also Hossfeld and Zenger, *Psalms 2: A Commentary on Psalms 51–100*, trans. Linda M. Maloney, Hermeneia (Minneapolis: Fortress, 2005), 321–22; Marvin E. Tate, *Psalms 51–100*, WBC 20 (Dallas: Word, 1990), 322; Kraus, *Psalms 60–150*, 148–49.

[54] This current argument among various (mainly Continental) scholars pertains to the question of whether and when Israel would be a shared identity for the two kingdoms specifically in the David material and in the book of Isaiah: see Alexander A. Fischer, *Von Hebron nach Jerusalem: Eine redaktionsgeschichtliche Studie zur Erzählung von König David in II Sam 1–5*, BZAW 335 (Berlin: de Gruyter, 2004); Fischer, "Flucht und Heimkehr Davids als integraler Rahmen der Abschalomerzählung," in *Ideales Königtum: Studien zu David und Salomo*, ed. Rüdiger Lux, ABIG 16 (Leipzig: Evangelische Verlagsanstalt, 2005), 42–69; Reinhard G. Kratz, *The Composition of the Narrative Books of the Old Testament*, trans. John Bowden (London: T&T Clark, 2005); Kratz, "Israel in the Book of Isaiah," *JSOT* 31 (2006): 103–28; Nadav Na'aman, "The Israelite–Judahite Struggle for the Patrimony of Ancient Israel," *Bib* 91 (2010): 1–23; and Jacob L. Wright, *David, King of Israel, and Caleb in Biblical Memory* (New York: Cambridge University Press, 2014). Campbell comments briefly on 2 Sam 23:1–7 in light of these arguments ("2 Samuel 21–24," 357).

nature of such an identity, which likely has deeper roots.⁵⁵ Indeed, H. G. M. Williamson has proposed that the term *Israel* was used to describe both kingdoms prior to the fall of the northern kingdom, based on such texts as Isa 8:14 and its reference to the "two houses of Israel."⁵⁶ In the case of the God of Jacob in the Zion psalms, Williamson argues persuasively that the Jerusalem religious institution was "notoriously conservative" and unlikely to incorporate new language easily, particularly if there was no previous engagement with or meaningful connection to such language.⁵⁷ In the temple liturgy, then, we are more likely to find vestiges of once-meaningful language that had passed out of common usage rather than examples of new and unexpected language.

The prevalence of the God-of-Jacob terminology in the Psalms, combined with the complete absence of this terminology in Joshua–Kings and Chronicles, is further evidence that the original context of 2 Sam 23:1–7 may have been the Psalms. Elsewhere in the Psalms, David is connected to the "Mighty One of Jacob" (אביר יעקב) in Ps 132 in relation to Zion and the covenant (ברית) with the Davidic line. Resonance with the Balaam poetry in the pairing of Jacob and Israel is also noteworthy; the Balaam poetry contains seven examples of this pairing (Num 23:7, 10, 21, 23; 24:5, 17, 19), yet there is only one reference to "Jacob" elsewhere in Numbers (in the stock oath to Abraham, Isaac, and Jacob in 32:11). According to some, the poetic parallelism between Israel and Jacob does not occur in preexilic texts, but there are many examples of this pairing in Second Isaiah, for example.⁵⁸

---

⁵⁵ Philip R. Davies has posited a shared religious, rather than political, connection to Israel's God, stating, "*this common divine title forms the basis for the idea of an Israelite nation descended from the same ancestor, rather than the other way around*" (italics his own). Relying on such texts as 2 Kgs 17 and Jer 3, Davies proposes that the key position of the tribe of Benjamin and its Bethel sanctuary become the channels through which the God of Israel gradually comes to be identified with Jerusalem, and through which Israel and Judah are gradually joined under a single religious identity after 720 BCE (*The Origins of Biblical Israel*, LHBOTS 485 [London: T&T Clark, 2007], 76–77, 116–26, 159–73). For critiques of Davies's proposal, see Nadav Na'aman, "Saul, Benjamin and the Emergence of 'Biblical Israel,'" *ZAW* 121 (2009): 211–24 (part 1) and 335–49 (part 2); also Williamson, "Judah as Israel," esp. 84–90.

⁵⁶ Williamson, "Judah as Israel," 81–95; also D. Fleming, *Legacy of Israel*, 47–51; and Mahri Leonard-Fleckman, *The House of David: Between Political Formation and Literary Revision* (Minneapolis: Fortress, 2016); contra Davies, *Origins of Biblical Israel*, 146 n. 44.

⁵⁷ Williamson, "Judah as Israel," 87.

⁵⁸ See, e.g., Stefan Timm, *Moab zwischen den Mächten: Studien zu historischen Denkmälern und Texten*, ÄAT 17 (Wiesbaden: Harrassowitz, 1989), 97–157. In relation to the Psalms, Hermann Spieckermann has argued that all explicit references to Israel and Jacob are postexilic (*Heilsgegenwart: Eine Theologie der Psalmen*, FRLANT 148 [Göttingen: Vandenhoeck & Ruprecht, 1989], 156–64). On the pairing of Jacob and Israel in Second Isaiah, see Kratz, "Israel in the Book of Isaiah," 103–28. Kratz notes that, aside from a few individual references to "Israel" and "Judah" in Second Isaiah, the "Jacob–Israel" pair occurs exclusively in Isa 40–48 and 49:1–6, while "Zion–Jerusalem" is in the forefront of the passages that follow. Kratz argues that "Israel" and "Jacob" in First and Second Isaiah, as well as the divine title "Holy One of Israel," represent a theological

Yet the pairing occurs also in such material as Gen 49:2, 7, 24; Deut 33:10, 28; and Pss 78:5, 21, 71; 81:2, 5; and it is difficult to make a sweeping statement that all such references are postexilic.[59]

While 2 Sam 23:1–7 reflects a later conceptual framework for David, the God-of-Jacob terminology may be deeply rooted in the political and religious history of Judah as tied with Israel, ideas that were current when there were two kingdoms. In the case of 2 Sam 23:1–7, the poetry envisions David linked with the "God of Jacob" and "Israel," with no mention of Judah or Jerusalem. As with other features in 2 Sam 23:1–7, the poetry is therefore quite distinctive in its application of the God of Jacob and gives one pause. The poem draws from old terminology of Jacob that reflects the northern tradition, and at some point God of Jacob became a divine title within the religious institution of Judah, as demonstrated in the Psalms. Whether the Bible contains evidence that this divine title initially developed in the northern kingdom is a question that warrants further investigation. Yet 2 Sam 23:1–7 is unique in associating the God of Jacob with Israel and David, without reference to Jerusalem or the temple tradition.

## IV. Conclusion

Second Samuel 23:1–7 is remarkable poetry. It applies older biblical terminology and imagery to David in a way that is unmatched elsewhere in biblical writing. Although the prophetic image of David is likely rooted in 2 Sam 23:1–7, the poetry draws from arguably old material associated with Balaam. The God-of-Jacob terminology similarly draws from prophetic imagery and traditions associated with Jacob, while applying this terminology in a unique and creative way to David. The core imagery and instructions regarding the just ruler versus the wicked resonate with texts in Proverbs, the Prophets, and Psalms, while the reference to the "perpetual covenant" is the only biblical example in which the term ברית עולם is applied to David.

Chronicles' lack of awareness of 2 Sam 23:1–7 suggests that the poetry was written after, or simultaneously with, the composition of Chronicles.[60] Or perhaps 2 Sam 23:1–7 had a long textual life circulating independently of other material in a context that is lost to us. At some point, the end of 2 Samuel may have become the natural place to deposit all final David traditions, even if many of these texts lay "outside the sweep" of other known traditions.[61] There is evidence both within the poem and at Qumran to suggest that the poetry was originally more at home

---

evolution in Isaiah that postdates the union (post-720 BCE) of the "two houses of Israel" in Isa 8:14.

[59] See the argument in Russell, *Images of Egypt*, 88.
[60] Edenburg, "II Sam 21,1–14 and II Sam 23,1–7," 180.
[61] Campbell, "2 Samuel 21–24: The Enigma Factor," 347.

in the Psalms than at the end of 2 Samuel, where its lofty imagery about David and its anachronistic reference to "David's last words" hardly fit the arc of the story line in Samuel–Kings. The placement of 2 Sam 23:1–7 next to 2 Sam 22, with its parallel poetry in Ps 18, is further evidence of an association between this material and the Psalms. Perhaps the two poems were eventually placed side by side, in the heart of the appendix of 2 Samuel, to compare David with Moses and Joshua, both of whom have back-to-back speeches prior to their deaths.[62] Whatever the transmission history of 2 Sam 23:1–7, the poetry is indeed enigmatic, both in its unique use of language and in its current placement at the end of 2 Samuel.

[62] Noll, *Many Faces of David*, 154–55.

*"**The Paulist Biblical Commentary** represents the fruit of the past half century and more of the modern Catholic biblical renewal."* — from the introduction

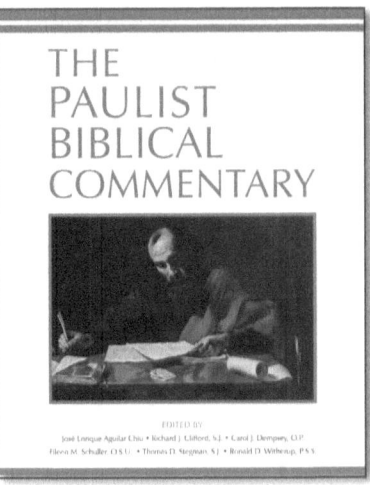

edited by José Enrique Aguilar Chiu, Richard J. Clifford, SJ, Carol J. Dempsey, OP, Eileen M. Schuller, OSU, Thomas D. Stegman, SJ, Ronald D. Witherup, PSS, INTRODUCTION BY DONALD SENIOR, CP

A one-volume commentary on the books of the Bible designed for a wide variety of Bible readers, especially those engaged in pastoral ministry. The volume consists of a commentary on each of the seventy-three books of the Catholic canon of the Bible along with twelve general articles.

- Brings together more the collaboration of more than seventy international biblical scholars
- Contains solid exegesis of the biblical text
- Pays close heed to the Church's teaching and practice on Scripture
- Is international and ecumenical in scope
- Features a distinguished editorial board and outstanding contributors
- Offers in one volume information that would otherwise be widely scattered in many books

978-0-8091-0613-4   8 X 10   1686 pp.   $149.95   Hardcover with jacket   Slipcase   Ribbons

**Available at bookstores or from PAULIST PRESS**
1-800-218-1903 • fax: 1-800-836-3161 • www.paulistpress.com

# "Your Torah Is My Delight": Repetition and the Poetics of Immanence in Psalm 119

SEAN BURT
sean.burt@ndsu.edu
North Dakota State University, Fargo, ND 58108

Psalm 119's massive length and curious constraints—its rigorous acrostic structure and use of one of eight torah terms in nearly every couplet—have long puzzled interpreters. Though the poem dwells on pedagogy, the reader who seeks to learn from the text finds not a structured explication of torah but rather a string of seemingly interchangeable terms (עדות, משפט, מצות, חוק, דבר, אמרה, פקודים, and תורה). Scholars have made several attempts to delineate the boundaries of Ps 119's concept of torah. However, this search for a substantive definition of torah is misguided because what this text envisions is not sober-minded instruction but delight (שעשועים), to use a term characteristic of the poem. Psalm 119's repetitions provide a field for playfulness and newness and show that a definition of torah is less important than an account of what torah does. The repetition of the eight terms is to be understood not as a platonic repetition of real and copy but as a repetition of simulacra, in which each individual term is fully an instantiation of torah in its own right. This psalm, in other words, produces a torah that is immanent to the poem. Psalm 119 is a poem of torah whose torah is the poem itself.

---

Scholars of Ps 119, the great acrostic poem of torah, have long delighted in rejecting the wisdom of their elders, much like the psalm itself.[1] In his 1938 commentary on Psalms, for example, Moses Buttenwieser, then professor of biblical exegesis at Hebrew Union College, observed,

> Biased by the high regard in which Psalm 119 was held in the past by church and synagogue alike, some interpreters still consider it a great, profound psalm. Yet it is anything but this, being void of the essential qualities of literary creation —spontaneity and originality. There could not be either in anything as artificial

I would like to thank Blake Couey, Davis Hankins, Elaine James, and the members of Twin Cities Hebrew Bible Colloquium for their helpful comments and feedback on this essay.

[1] "I understand more than the elders / because I pursue your precepts" (Ps 119:100). Unless otherwise indicated, all translations are my own.

as this psalm—an eightfold acrostic, each letter of the alphabet being repeated eight times in succession. It is by this external bond that the lines are held together, not by logical connection or progress of thought.[2]

Buttenwieser's harsh remarks are characteristic of late nineteenth- and early twentieth-century critical scholarship on Ps 119.[3] Yet, beginning at least with Mitchell Dahood's 1970 Anchor Bible commentary, contemporary scholars have in turn rejected the claim that this poem is a derivative and forgettable text.[4] While one can still find the stray negative evaluation of Ps 119 in current work—as recently as 2011 Philip Davies called it "doggerel"—recent interpreters have argued strenuously for the value of the psalm as a living, dynamic exposition of the delight in torah.[5]

I find much to agree with in these recent positive evaluations, but in the present essay I too wish to continue the tradition of rejecting the teaching of my elders (or, at the least, my very recent predecessors) by calling into question the stark difference between those who delight in this poem and the supposed זדים (usually translated "arrogant"; see 119:21, 51, 69, 78, 85, 122) who critique it. Let us begin by examining the most notorious scholarly rejection of Ps 119, Bernhard Duhm's scurrilous exclamation that the psalm is "the most contentless product that ever blackened paper."[6] One can hardly find a recent work on Ps 119 that does not portray Duhm as a villain. I too recoil at the venom in these words and—perhaps more importantly—at the implicit permission they give for ignoring this powerful text.[7]

---

[2] Moses Buttenwieser, *The Psalms Chronologically Treated with a New Translation*, with introduction by Nahum M. Sarna (Jersey City, NJ: Ktav, 1969), 871. On Buttenwieser, see Sarna's introduction; also Bernard J. Bamberber, "Buttenwieser, Moses," *EncJud* 4:319.

[3] For other examples of what William Soll calls Ps 119's "legacy of disdain," see *Psalm 119: Matrix, Form, and Setting*, CBQMS 23 (Washington, DC: Catholic Biblical Association of America, 1991), 5–6.

[4] Dahood notes that reading Ps 119 in Hebrew "revealed, in verse after verse, a freshness of thought and a felicity of expression unnoticed and consequently unappreciated" (*Psalms: Introduction, Translation, and Notes*, 3 vols., AB 16–17A (Garden City, NY: 1966–1970), 3:172.

[5] Philip R. Davies, "Reading the Bible Intelligently," *Relegere* 1 (2011): 145–64, here 152. David Noel Freedman, however, calls it "endlessly inventive" (*Psalm 119: The Exaltation of Torah*, BJSUCSD 6 [Winona Lake, IN: Eisenbrauns, 1999], 87). For recent positive evaluations, see Soll, *Psalm 119*; Walter Brueggemann and W. H. Bellinger, *Psalms*, NCBiC (New York: Cambridge University Press, 2014); John Goldingay, *Psalms*, 3 vols., BCOTWP (Grand Rapids: Baker Academic, 2006–2008); Gordon J. Wenham, *Psalms as Torah: Reading Biblical Song Ethically*, STI (Grand Rapids: Baker Academic, 2012).

[6] Bernhard Duhm, *Die Psalmen*, KHC 14 (Freiburg im Breisgau: Mohr, 1899), 268: "Jedenfalls ist dieser 'Psalm' das inhaltloseste Produkt, das jemals Papier schwarz gemacht hat."

[7] See, e.g., Artur Weiser, *The Psalms: A Commentary*, trans. Herbert Hartwell, OTL (Louisville: Westminster John Knox, 1959), 740: "The simple form of the diction makes it unnecessary to expound the psalm in detail." True to his words, Weiser includes no verse-by-verse commentary for Ps 119. (In the entire volume only eight other psalms receive no commentary, and those—53,

Nevertheless, attention to the larger context of his remarks shows that Duhm follows his infamous statement with the interjection, "If only the author had imparted just something of the great achievements of his studies [of *torah*]!," which may make his words as much a cry of exasperation as they are an insult.[8] From Duhm's perspective, Ps 119 clearly and ostentatiously invites careful study and promises learned reflection—but then it reveals no additional exegetical treasures. Further, compare Duhm's charges with the comments of another reader who takes what seems to be an opposing view of the psalm—Augustine of Hippo:

> The plainer Psalm 118 [MT Ps 119] seems, the more profound does it appear to me, so much so that I cannot even demonstrate how profound it is. When in other psalms some passage presents difficulty, at least the obscurity itself is obvious, even though the meaning is hidden; but in [this] psalm not even the obscurity is evident, for on the surface the psalm is so simple that it might be thought to require a reader or listener only, not an expositor. (*Enarrat. Ps.* 118)[9]

On one level, juxtaposing Duhm's words with Augustine's presents us with a neat contrast between a skeptical higher critic dismissing the psalm and a theologian praising it. Yet, if one sets aside the tone of each quotation, *are they not but two sides of the same coin?* Duhm and Augustine each encounter a poem that conspicuously displays its profundity but also blocks readers precisely at the point where they seek to penetrate below its surface. Psalm 119 unambiguously shows its delight in torah as that which gives life and creates desire. Nonetheless, as the thread common to Duhm and Augustine presumes, it does not yield "meaning"; it seems to hide no exegetical secrets. In other words, perhaps the psalm is contentless—but not because it lacks anything—and is no less complete, joyful, and productive for being so.

It is no surprise, however, that the charge that Ps 119 is contentless has made recent readers recoil, since, in a sense, it is a text defined by completeness, even excess. Extensively and rigorously structured, Ps 119 is a uniform acrostic poem with twenty-two stanzas, one for each letter of the Hebrew alphabet. Each stanza

---

70, 88, 108, 117, 136, 140, and 150—are very brief or otherwise treated in discussion of parallel psalms).

[8] Duhm, *Die Psalmen*, 268–69: "Wenn doch der Verf. auch nur etwas von den gerühmten Errungenschaften seines Studiums mitgeteilt hätte!" While I do believe that one can mine Duhm's words for insight, I fully concur that his and similar comments belong to an outdated, indeed darker, chapter in scholarship on the Psalms. (See, e.g., Weiser's gratuitously vicious backhanded compliment of Ps 119: "[it] does not yet exhibit that degeneration and hardening into a legalistic form of religion to which it succumbed in late Judaism and which provoked Jesus' rebuke" [*Psalms*, 740]).

[9] Augustine, *Expositions of the Psalms: 99–120*, trans. Maria Boulding, ed. Boniface Ramsey, vol. 3.19 in *The Works of Saint Augustine: A Translation for the 21st Century* (Hyde Park, NY: New City Press, 2003), 342.

includes eight couplets,[10] the first letter of each couplet beginning with the appropriate letter of the alphabet. In addition to the acrostic structure, nearly every single line includes one of eight interrelated nouns, each of which indicates some kind of utterance or declaration: פקודים, עדות, משפט, מצות, חק/הקים, דבר, אמרה, and תורה.[11] In other words, the most obvious elements of the poem's form clearly, perhaps ostentatiously, display its overflowing nature.

In this essay I wish to explore Ps 119 as the site of a paradoxical simultaneity of fullness and emptiness, or of completeness and incompleteness. The poem dwells on pedagogical matters yet in fact teaches very little. Rather than sober-minded instruction, this poem approaches the topic with playfulness and spontaneity—or, in the text's own terms, with "delight" (שעשועים). As numerous frustrated interpreters have observed, the overwhelming repetition of the eight torah terms hints at order, but no clear configuration can be found. Additionally, the structure of the entire poem cannot be outlined according to an overarching logic (apart from the alphabetic acrostic structure), yet the individual stanzas are the sites of inventive poetic wordplay. This "delight" offers the reader what I call a poetics of immanence, wherein wonder and joy and mystery can be present even—and perhaps especially—if the poem refuses to allow concepts external to the poem to determine its shape and value. Psalm 119 offers a nonmimetic poetics in which torah is the source of delight precisely insofar as torah remains immanent to the text. Psalm 119 is a poem of torah whose torah is the poem itself.

## I. The Search for the Concept of Torah in Psalm 119

One of the most striking problems of Ps 119 is that it attends so deeply to torah without ever offering any clear definition of it. As evidenced by the numerous usages of the root למד ("to teach" or "to learn"; vv. 7, 12, 26, 64, 66, 68, 71, 73, 99, 108, 124, 135, 171), the psalm appears to be a text intimately concerned with teaching and learning. Yet with this clear emphasis on instruction, what does the

---

[10] With the exceptions of triplets in 119:48, 145, and 176. See J. P. Fokkelman, *The Remaining 65 Psalms*, vol. 3 of *Major Poems of the Hebrew Bible: At the Interface of Prosody and Structural Analysis*, SSN 43 (Assen: Van Gorcum, 2003), 235. The terminology for the constituent parts of a biblical Hebrew poem is a matter of debate. In this essay, I follow F. W. Dobbs-Allsopp's use of "line" to indicate the syntactic building block of poetry, rather than, as in other scholarship, the terms *colon* or *verset* (*On Biblical Poetry* [New York: Oxford University Press, 2015]).

[11] Some couplets include none of the terms (119:3, 37, 90, 122), while some contain two terms (119:16, 43, 48, 160, 168). Translators usually gloss the terms as follows: אמרה ("word"), דבר ("word"), חק/חקים ("statute/statutes"), מצות ("commandments"), משפט ("judgment"), עדות ("testimonies"), פקודים ("precepts"), תורה ("instruction/law/torah"). As I will argue, though, the precise meaning of each individual term is not important to the poem—in fact, detailed attention to the definitions of each individual term distracts from the primary thrust of the text. Accordingly, I leave these eight terms for the most part untranslated.

attentive reader of the psalm learn? As commentators such as Jon D. Levenson have noted, Ps 119 contains no references to the story of Israel, nor to any particular laws or religious/ethical covenant stipulations, nor to any Israelite ritual practices, nor to any notable torah terms, such as ברית ("covenant"), Moses, ככתוב ("as it was written"), or ספר ("book").[12] The absence of ספר is particularly suggestive. In a study of Ps 119 as "constrained writing," Scott N. Callaham argues that the *samek* stanza (vv. 113–120) is one of the three most constrained of the poem's twenty-two stanzas.[13] That is, this stanza uses a relatively low number of couplet-initial words that are found elsewhere in the poem.[14] Additionally, the *samek* stanza contains the rarest vocabulary in the poem (according to Callaham's counts, the words in *samek* appear 159 times in the remainder of the poem, in comparison to *ḥet*'s 214 and *pe*'s 216). In other words, the fact that the writer chooses to reach for relatively rare *samek* words to achieve the acrostic's demands, rather than using ספר, suggests a strategy of active avoidance.

The idea that Ps 119 rejects traditions is not merely an argument from the absence of certain terms or ideas. Psalm 119 resists assimilation to Israel's literary and intellectual heritage in other, more explicit ways. The *lamed* stanza (vv. 89–96) explicitly states that the psalmist's search is not limited to traditional venues, including the stunning statements that "I have more insight than all my teachers," and "I understand more than the elders" (vv. 99–100). These proclamations, striking even without context, become even more telling when one notes, as Nancy deClaissé-Walford observes, that this stanza contains a number of terms elsewhere related to wisdom literature (חכם ["wisdom"] in v. 98, שכל ["insight"] in v. 99, and בין ["understanding"] in vv. 100 and 104).[15] Psalm 119 points the seeker of torah neither to an external text nor to an intellectual tradition but to the authority of the poem itself.

Accordingly, the reader who turns to the poem discovers its fundamental orientation from the very first line: "Happy are those who are perfect in their ways,

---

[12] Jon D. Levenson, "The Sources of Torah: Psalm 119 and the Modes of Revelation in Second Temple Judaism," in *Ancient Israelite Religion: Essays in Honor of Frank Moore Cross*, ed. Patrick D. Miller Jr., Paul D. Hanson, and S. Dean McBride (Philadelphia: Fortress, 1987), 559–74. Most recently, see Kent Aaron Reynolds, *Torah as Teacher: The Exemplary Torah Student in Psalm 119*, VTSup 137 (Leiden: Brill, 2010).

[13] The other two stanzas are *ḥet* and *pe*. See Scott N. Callaham, "An Evaluation of Psalm 119 as Constrained Writing," *HS* 50 (2009): 121–34. "Constrained writing" is a literary practice in which a writer executes a project within a predefined constraint, such as the absence of one or more letters (a "lipogram") or, well, an acrostic. On the phenomenon of constrained writing more broadly, see Daniel Levin Becker's book on the French "Oulipo" group, *Many Subtle Channels: In Praise of Potential Literature* (Cambridge: Harvard University Press, 2012).

[14] The verb סור ("to turn aside") is the only couplet-initial term in this stanza (v. 115) that appears elsewhere in the poem (vv. 29, 102).

[15] Nancy L. deClaissé-Walford, Rolf A. Jacobson, and Beth LaNeel Tanner, *The Book of Psalms*, NICOT (Grand Rapids: Eerdmans, 2014), 883.

who walk in the torah of YHWH" (v. 1). Psalm 119 is a text that seeks to unfold and celebrate the powers of torah. Though often grouped with the other "Torah Psalms" (Pss 1, 19), Ps 119 differs markedly from each of them. Psalm 1 explicates torah by means of metaphor (more properly simile), likening life under torah to the plant fed by the sustaining stream, while Ps 19 links torah metonymically with the order of creation. In contrast to both, Ps 119 continually defers a definition of torah by leading readers not to illustrative metaphors or other dominant concepts but, instead, through a stream of interchangeable *synonyms*.

The eight torah terms, in the context of Ps 119, show little semantic variation. Scholars have expended much effort to tease out the precise meaning of each term, but the burden of finding shades of meaning among the eight terms falls solely on the lexicon. That is, the reader may be able to discern subtle differences between clusters of terms,[16] but the psalm itself does not support such nuances. To illustrate the interchangeability of the synonyms, we can note, with Kent Aaron Reynolds, that several important verbs in the poem (שמר ["observe"], נצר ["guard"], שכח ["forget"], אהב ["love"], שיח ["meditate upon"]) take any number of the eight terms as objects—for example, the psalmist "observes" (שמר) all eight of them.[17] The only verb that could possibly be considered to adhere to one particular torah term is למד, which appears with חקים in eight of its thirteen occurrences (vv. 12, 26, 64, 68, 71, 124, 135, 171),[18] though it also is seen alongside משפטים and מצות.[19] Additionally, no commentator has been able to discern any order for the use of terms across stanzas, in contrast to a poetic form like the English sestina.[20] Not every

---

[16] See, e.g., Wenham, *Psalms as Torah*, 86–88. Wenham's attempt at a brief lexicon of the eight terms implies the limitations of this approach. For example, he notes that פקודים occurs outside of Ps 119 only in Pss 19:8; 103:18; 111:7. To broaden the scope, he then draws attention to the verbal form of פקד as "visit, intervene," and then finally notes that the word פקודים is paired with "covenant" in Ps 103:18 and "the works of his hands" in Ps 111:7, leading to the less-than-grand conclusion that פקודים "may refer to wide variety of divine words and deeds" (88).

[17] Reynolds also notes that נצר occurs with five; לא שכח with five; אהב with five; שיח with three (*Torah as Teacher*, 116–17). Additionally, I observe that דרש occurs with פקודים (vv. 45, 94), and חקים (v. 155); שעשוע occurs with חקות (v. 16), עדות (v. 24), מצות (vv. 47, 143), and תורה (vv. 70, 77, 92, 174); *piel* חיה occurs with דבר (vv. 25, 107), אמרה (vv. 50, 116, 154), פקודים (v. 93), and משפטים (vv. 149, 156).

[18] Reynolds, *Torah as Teacher*, 127 n. 54.

[19] Ibid. Reynolds also points out that the poem reveals "no discernable difference in meaning" between the masculine and feminine forms of חק (*Torah as Teacher*, 110 n. 14).

[20] See Freedman, *Psalm 119*, 77–80. J. P. Fokkelman argues that some of the eight terms reveal tendencies based on where they appear in a stanza. For example, דבר appears in the first two couplets of a stanza sixteen times; in the second two, five times; in the third two, once; and in the final two couplets zero times (in other words, a distribution of 16, 5, 1, 0). This leads Fokkelman to conclude only that this term "like[s] to be in front." See his *Remaining 65 Psalms*, 269. The impact of Fokkelman's observations is unclear, however. The term דבר that I cite as an example in fact displays the starkest discrepancy in distribution among all the terms (מצות, on the other hand, has a distribution of 4, 6, 4, 8, while אמרה, which he groups with דבר as a term

couplet contains a torah term, and no stanza uses all eight. Nor is each term used an equal number of times. The most frequent is, unsurprisingly, תורה (twenty-five times) and the least common is אמרה (nineteen times). Neither the semantic ranges of the terms nor their placement in the poem reveals substantial differentiation among them.

The strongest argument for some distinction among the terms comes from Reynolds, who argues for a twofold, not eightfold, division: "instantiations" of torah and "abstract" torah terms.[21] The instantiations include all uses of חקים, עדות, and פקודים (the terms that occur only in plural form), which he defines as references to "specific commandments" and "directives that can be enumerated and should be obeyed, observed or performed." The abstract terms, in comparison, include the words תורה and אמרה, always in the singular. The remaining terms (דבר, משפט, and מצות) are more difficult, because they occur in both singular and plural forms. The relationship between instantiations and abstract terms is hierarchical—"hyponymy" is the linguistic term Reynolds uses to express a "unilateral" semantic relationship, in which one term (such as an instantiation like עדות) implies the other (abstract term like תורה) but not necessarily vice versa. Reynolds acknowledges some difficulties with this division, noting that this scheme has "inconsistencies, since some of the eight terms are used for both instantiations and for the abstract conception." Part of the problem boils down to the poem's refusal to make a hard-and-fast distinction between singular and plural terms (משפט, דבר, and מצות are all inconsistent in their grammatical number).[22] Indeed, Reynolds concedes that grammatical number is not sufficient on its own to make a differentiation and does not "consistently correspond with the two different levels of meaning, but it does generally correspond."[23] Ultimately, though, the text itself gives no justification *beyond grammatical number* for making a two-tiered division. If, as we have seen above, each of the terms functions much like any other (if any number of terms can be the "observed," "guarded," "loved," "delighted in," and so on), the text itself makes no distinction among the functions of each of them. The relationship among the eight terms is best defined as coequal and interchangeable.

Neither is Reynolds explicit about what makes for an "abstract" concept. A solid case can perhaps be made for the primacy of one of the terms, תורה. It is the most frequently used (25x); it appears in the first verse; and it never occurs in the

---

that has a preference for the front of the stanza, has a distribution of 7, 8, 3, 1). Fokkelman makes no claim about the behavior of the terms as a set but only about some of the terms individually. Even further, it is not clear to what extent these numbers are large enough to be significant. Accordingly, I still concur with Freedman's judgment that the precise distribution of the terms does not reveal any discernible order.

[21] For the discussion in this paragraph and the quoted material, see Reynolds, *Torah as Teacher*, 112–20.

[22] See Freedman, *Psalm 119*, 445–47.

[23] Reynolds, *Torah as Teacher*, 114.

plural.²⁴ Yet what would justify including other "abstract" terms alongside it? Granted, תורה is the most frequent term, but אמרה, which Reynolds unambiguously categorizes as an "abstract" term, is the least frequent (19x). Reynolds's position is intriguing, and it indeed emerges out of a curious feature of the text, the hint of a macrostructural plan with the eight terms (see the discussion of David Noel Freedman's work below), but it cannot fully capture the function of the terms in the poem. It falls short, in other words, not just because the categories of "instantiation" and "abstract" concept cannot be maintained with any consistency but because it proceeds from the presumption—mistaken in my estimation—that Ps 119 includes anything that can defensibly be labeled as an abstract concept.

At its core, Reynolds's distinction between instantiation and abstract concept is useful for his definition of torah in Ps 119. The idea that abstract terms are elucidated with a variety of instantiations presents us with what he calls an "expansive" concept of torah, in which no individual instantiation can capture the entirety of torah.²⁵ He thus defines torah as a concept that is "greater than the sum of its parts."²⁶ Reynolds's claim here resonates with that of other commentators who work under the assumption that the eight terms *must* refer to some given extratextual concept. For example, Jerome Creach writes that Ps 119's torah "assumes normative written texts, but it is not limited to them."²⁷ This view portrays torah as something that includes the nuances of the eight terms but which is not encapsulated by any of them, not even the term תורה itself. This argument creates an entity, a transcendent Torah-beyond-torah (or Torah-beyond-תורה).²⁸ This assumption is simply not warranted, I submit, by the poem itself. The repetition that characterizes Ps 119 is not a "platonic" repetition, in which every instantiation must be considered a partial, incomplete version of the real thing.²⁹ At most, we can posit that the term תורה,

---

²⁴ Reynolds, *Torah as Teacher*, 112. Reynolds cites Erich Zenger, "Torafrömmigkeit: Beobachtungen zum poetischen und theologischen Profil von Psalm 119," in *Freiheit und Recht: Festschrift für Frank Crüsemann zum 65. Geburtstag*, ed. Christof Hardmeier, Rainer Kessler, and Andreas Ruwe (Gütersloh: Kaiser, 2003), 380–96, here 387.

²⁵ Reynolds further writes, "The repetition of the eight Torah terms is therefore essential to the author's goal of describing and promoting an expansive conception of Torah" and that this repetition "contributes to a network of interrelated ideas and enables the author to expand the conceptual sphere further" (*Torah as Teacher*, 107.)

²⁶ Ibid., 136–46.

²⁷ Jerome F. D. Creach, *The Destiny of the Righteous in the Psalms* (St. Louis: Chalice, 2008), 139. Creach makes this point in even stronger terms when he notes that Ps 119 "encourage[s] meditation on written texts, of course. It recalls many other biblical texts, thereby implicitly recognizing their authority and encouraging attention to their truths" (138). See also Wenham's claim that "in this psalm the law *is not limited to* the laws in the Pentateuch, or wisdom teaching or the book of Deuteronomy" (*Psalms as Torah*, 84; emphasis added).

²⁸ I use this somewhat awkward formulation to show that Reynolds (and many others) presumes a stable, translatable concept ("torah" in English) that lies beyond the poem's term (תורה in Hebrew).

²⁹ See Krystyna Mazur, "Repetition," in *The Princeton Encyclopedia of Poetry and Poetics*, 4th ed., ed. Roland Greene et al. (Princeton: Princeton University Press, 2012), 1168–71.

as the initial and slightly more frequent term, hints at a primary position, but, because it behaves indistinguishably from the rest, remains a first among equals, so to speak. Psalm 119 perhaps evokes a hierarchy of terms but steadfastly refuses to explicate any such hierarchy. Rather, I propose that Ps 119's repetition of terms frustrates the division between abstract and instantiation, or between real and copy. These terms relate to one another in virtually identical ways, and, because they do not appear in predictable places in the stanzas (as would be the case in a poetic form like the sestina), surprise and newness emerge out of sameness. The repetitions in this poem, then, are repetitions of continual becoming, of undefined difference. As we have seen, the reader who comes to this text looking for the meaning of torah, for the "real" torah behind the copies (or synonyms or instantiations) will either turn away from the poem toward extratextual solutions or, like Duhm, simply throw their hands up in frustration.

The eight terms in Ps 119 relate to one another on the level of nearly pure synonymy. This, however, does not imply that the arrangement of terms is random or "thoughtless."[30] As Freedman has shown in his thorough research on the psalm, an analysis of the uses of the terms throughout the poem indicates several suggestive near-symmetries. Even though not every verse uses precisely one term per verse, the first half of the poem (stanzas *aleph* through *kaph*) uses eighty-eight terms, while the second half (*lamed* through *tav*) uses eighty-nine. Additionally, the poem uses equal numbers of feminine terms (אמרה, מצות, עדות, תורה) and masculine terms (דבר,[31] חקים, משפט, פקודים) (88 and 89) and, within each of those groups, uses half plural and half singular (44 and 44/45).[32] These remarkable properties suggest great care for the purposeful use of the eight terms—a purpose that, I submit, *is* playful synonymy.

While the distribution of the synonyms as a whole evokes a sense of balance and completeness, the progression of the individual terms as the text unfolds highlights a surprising absence of order and balance. Freedman argues that, given the tight control of other parts of the poem, this lack of order cannot be coincidental.

---

[30] Reynolds uses rhetorical questions to express his objection to the idea that the terms have a synonymous relationship: "Is it possible that the author thoughtlessly interchanges the eight Torah terms? Does he simply follow the poetic constraints of using one of the terms in each verse?" (*Torah as Teacher*, 115). The second question seems to conflate the issue of poetic constraint (that the distribution of terms is determined by a certain sequence) with that of synonymity. Nevertheless, even a precisely constrained order of the eight terms (which, again, is not present in this poem—see Freedman, *Psalm 119*) would not necessarily imply that the terms are synonymous.

[31] Freedman's scheme is weakened by the fact that חק appears in both masculine and feminine forms.

[32] The case of masculine nouns is more complicated, since two appear in either singular or plural—at any rate, the masculine nouns appear in two clusters of forty-four each: דבר and חק/חקים, and פקודים and משפט/משפטים. See Freedman, *Psalm 119*, 35–36; Frank Lothar Hossfeld and Erich Zenger, *Psalms 3: A Commentary on Psalms 101–150*, Hermeneia (Minneapolis: Fortress, 2011), 259.

He posits that the psalmist uses the unpredictability of the individual terms to create a fascinating tension between order and "chaos" that reflects the poem's simultaneous concern for the totality of torah and the tumultuousness of life under torah.[33] I agree that the lack of order in the distribution of the individual terms is purposeful (and I would go beyond Freedman to insist that the synonymity too is purposeful). I stop short of characterizing this as "chaos," however, because I understand the unpredictability of the psalm to represent not simply disordered tumult but a drive to push readers through the poem ever onward to the next line, to make the reader into a seeker and student of torah. In Reynolds's interpretation, Ps 119 becomes a portrayal of the ideal student of torah.[34] Despite its emphasis on pedagogical matters, however, the psalm does not instruct *about* torah. If a reader seeks to learn torah, the psalm's only instruction is: read on. The sheer length of this text provides the occasion for the ineluctable push forward.[35] The forward-moving dynamism in Ps 119 is made evident by the repetition of the eight synonyms and is enabled by the massive scope of the text. The reader who does read on finds not substantive content but rather a string of interchangeable terms. The use of these eight terms creates a fascinating and productive tension between completeness and incompleteness, which manifests itself here as a simultaneity of stasis and dynamism.

The poles of this tension between stasis and dynamism are simultaneously expressed through repetition in this text. On the side of stasis and completeness, the rigorous *aleph*-to-*tav* acrostic and the meditative (or, depending on one's view, numbing!) repetition of synonyms shows this poem to be complete, exhaustive, and self-containing. Yet, on the other side, the dance of desire satisfied and unsatisfied encoded in the repetitions creates a vision of torah in which contentment is always over the next horizon, in the additional explication. This productive tension is a both-and that creates some fascinating, perhaps even radical, implications. My argument here resembles a conclusion by Klaus Seybold: "There is no definition [of torah] in 119, because it is about the experience of a reality that can be described only obliquely in conceptual terms."[36] The question "what *is* torah in Ps 119?" is, in my estimation, the wrong question—and, most importantly, a question that the poem itself chooses not to answer. Rather, one should ask what does torah *do* in this poem? The "concept" of torah, in other words, functions something like a "MacGuffin" in Ps 119. The term *MacGuffin*, as coined (or perhaps popularized) by filmmaker Alfred Hitchcock, is an object in a film that provides the impetus for the plot but whose precise identity is itself beside the point.[37] Examples would include

---

[33] Freedman, *Psalm 119*, 92–93.

[34] Reynolds, *Torah as Teacher*, chapter 3.

[35] I thank Elaine James for this observation.

[36] Klaus Seybold, *Die Psalmen*, HAT 1/15 (Tübingen: Mohr Siebeck, 1996), as quoted in Hossfeld and Zenger, *Psalms 3*, 259.

[37] Slavoj Žižek describes the MacGuffin as follows: "the Hitchcockian object, the pure pretext whose sole role is to set the story in motion but which is in itself 'nothing at all'—the only significance of the MacGuffin lies in the fact that it has some significance for the characters—that

the titular statue in *The Maltese Falcon*, the "government secrets" in Hitchcock's *North by Northwest*, or the briefcase with mysterious contents in *Pulp Fiction*.[38] Like these MacGuffins in their respective films, torah is something that is absolutely essential to the poem. Yet pressing the question of the definition of torah, of the "semantic field" of the term, is, I suggest, akin to a misguided focus on what's *really* in the briefcase. Psalm 119 has not yet yielded to its readers a stable, identifiable concept of Torah-beyond-תורה underneath the shifting and slippery words of the poem. Psalm 119 directs the reader to torah, but then in turn keeps the seeker of torah within the unfolding lines of the poem itself.

## II. Delight in Torah, Delight in Poetry

I employ the analogy of a MacGuffin not to diminish or denigrate torah in this poem but to highlight the idea that, even though the content of torah is not revealed to us, such content is ultimately unimportant to the poem. Psalm 119 is not "about" torah, in the sense of delineating any concept, program of study, or progression of argument. Rather, torah is central for its effects.[39] In other words, while the exploration of Ps 119 does not reveal to the reader a definition of what torah is, it is abundantly clear on what torah does. Torah gives life;[40] it is the source and object of desire; it distinguishes the pious from the זדים ("arrogant").[41] Most important for the purposes of this essay, however, torah provides the occasion for delight.

"Delight," שעשוע, or שעשע in verb form, is the term most distinctive to Ps 119. Its eight occurrences (three verbs, five nouns; see table 1 below) do not make it the most frequently used term in the poem, but, given that it appears only eight

---

it must seem to be of vital importance to them.... Needless to add, the MacGuffin is the purest case of what Lacan calls *objet petit a*: a pure void which functions as the object-cause of desire" (*The Sublime Object of Ideology*, Phronesis [London: Verso, 2008], 183–84). The suggestion that a MacGuffin is simultaneously object and cause of desire (the "*objet petit a*") provides another intriguing suggestion about the function of torah in Ps 119, but one that is beyond the scope of this essay.

[38] In *Pulp Fiction*, the audience is shown *that* its contents are important when the opened briefcase illuminates Vincent's face, but the audience never sees what is inside.

[39] Compare Zenger's declaration that "this is not a psalm about the Torah; it is the meditative prayer of a human being to YHWH as the giver and teacher of Torah" (Hossfeld and Zenger, *Psalms 3*, 267).

[40] For example, Ps 119:116: "Support me, according to your word [אמרה], so I may live"; 119:93: "For all eternity I will not forget your precepts because in them you give me life."

[41] A curious feature of the זדים is that their behavior at times strongly resembles that of the psalmist. He accuses them of "sitting" and "chatting" (נדברו) where he, in the next line, "meditates" (שיח; v. 23). Most strikingly, the זדים "smear me with lies" (טפל עלי שקר; v. 69), to which the psalmist immediately responds, "their heart is dull like fat" (טפש כחלב לבם; v. 70). Finally, the common translation of זדים, "the arrogant," points up uncomfortable parallels with the persona of the psalmist, which, as mentioned, boasts that he "understand[s] more than my elders" (v. 100).

times in the Hebrew Bible outside of Ps 119 (four as a verb and four as a noun),[42] it is a characteristic term. Even more, I suggest not just that "delight" functions as one of the many effects of torah in the poem but that it describes the text's poetics more broadly. The reader does not discover the meaning of torah, but the reader does delight in it. The primary orientation of Ps 119 is, in other words, playful rather than pedagogical, ludic rather than lucid.

Table 1. Occurrences of שעשע/שעשוע in Psalm 119[43]

| v. 16 | In your statutes I delight [אשתעשע] / I will not forget your word |
| --- | --- |
| v. 24 | Indeed, your testimonies are my delights [שעשעי], / my men of counsel |
| v. 47 | I will delight [ואשתעשע] in your commandments / which I love |
| v. 70 | Their heart is dull like fat / but I will delight [שעשעתי] in your torah |
| v. 77 | Your mercies come to me that I may live / your torah is my delight [שעשעי] |
| v. 92 | Were your torah not my delight [שעשעי], / I would have perished in my straits |
| v. 143 | Distress and hardship fill me, / your commandments are my delights [שעשעי] |
| v. 174 | I long for your deliverance, O YHWH, / your torah is my delight [שעשעי] |

That Ps 119, notorious in some quarters for being repetitive and even boring, would be defined by playfulness may strike one as implausible. Yet precursors to this idea are already present in scholarship on Ps 119. J. P. Fokkelman calls the psalm "a multicolored pyrotechnic of variations and other formal devices glittering against the background of a baffling synonymy."[44] Two aspects of this quotation are worth highlighting. On the one hand, the work of Fokkelman (and others) has drawn out the extent to which Ps 119's "multicolored pyrotechnics" show it to be a poem that is playful and tightly constructed, though constructed so as to display a sense of spontaneity. The following section provides an indication of my sense of the text's "pyrotechnics." On the other hand, the poetic pyrotechnics "glitter," in Fokkelman's words, "against the background of a baffling synonymy." One of the aspects of the psalm that has frustrated interpreters is its practice of illuminating its central concept, torah, by means of a seemingly unenlightening array of synonyms. In contrast to Fokkelman, though, I would insist that this "baffling synonymy" is not the background of the poem but its foreground. In a sense, bafflement—which may be but the flip side of wonder or delight—is the fundamental orientation of this poem.

---

[42] As a verb (from שעע) in Isa 11:8; 29:9; 66:12; Ps 94:19; as a noun in Isa 5:7; Jer 31:20; Prov 8:30, 31.

[43] All instances of the noun שעשוע in Ps 119 are plural.

[44] Fokkelman, *Reading Biblical Poetry: An Introductory Guide*, trans. Ineke Smit (Louisville: Westminster John Knox, 2001), 45.

As a brief example of these so-called "pyrotechnics," consider the *qoph* stanza (vv. 145–52; see table 2). One of the most striking aspects of this stanza is the overwhelming use of anaphora, or the repetition of words in the successive couplets/triplets (קרוב + קרבו + קדם + קדמו + קדמתי ;קראתי + קראתיך + קראתי).[45] Additionally, this stanza reveals a number of interconnections via the device of consonance. So, ואשמרה in verse 146 is clearly consonant with אשמרות in verse 148, but it also resonates with אצרה in verse 145 and ואשועה in verse 147, which itself bears similarities with הושיעני in verse 146. A pun between ענני in verse 145 and עיני in verse 148 is also possible (especially when one considers that both couplets contain a reference to parts of the body), while verse 152 also suggests wordplay with the phrase ידעתי מעדתיך ("I have learned from your decrees").

TABLE 2. PSALM 119:145–152 (THE ק STANZA)

| I call out in my heart: | קראתי בכל־לב |
| "Answer me YHWH, | ענני יהוה |
| I will observe your statutes!" | חקיך אצרה |
| I call out to you: "Save me, | קראתיך הושיעני |
| So I may keep your testimonies!" | ואשמרה עדתיך |
| I wake at dawn and I cry for help; | קדמתי בנשף ואשועה |
| For your words I wait. | לדבריך יחלתי |
| My eyes wake in the middle of the night | קדמו עיני אשמרות |
| To meditate on your word. | לשיח באמרתך |
| Hear my voice according to your *ḥesed*; | קולי שמעה כחסדך |
| Make me live by your judgments, YHWH! | יהוה כמשפטך חיני |
| Schemers draw near; | קרבו רדפי זמה |
| But they are far from your torah. | מתורתך רחקו |
| You are near, YHWH, | קרוב אתה יהוה |
| And all your commandments are true. | וכל־מצותיך אמת |
| I have always known of your testimonies, | קדם ידעתי מעדתיך |
| Indeed you founded them eternally. | כי לעולם יסדתם |

---

[45] I am drawing on the observation of Fokkelman, *Remaining 65 Psalms*, 257. On anaphora, see J. Weare, "Anaphora," in Green et al., *Princeton Encyclopedia of Poetry*, 50. Even more, it is possible that the anaphora is extended with a visual pun by the use of two consecutive lines beginning with קד after two lines beginning with קר. The ר/ד affinity, present even in the Herodian script of Ps 119 in 11QPs[a] (which, unlike the other compositions in 11QPs[a] is laid out in poetic lines; see J. A. Sanders, *The Psalms Scroll of Qumrân Cave 11 (11QPs*[a]*)*, DJD IV [Oxford: Clarendon, 1965]), may be further evidence of wordplay in this stanza. If it is plausible to see playfulness in the graphic representation of letters here, I would also suggest that שוש/ששון ("rejoice/delight") in 119:14, 111, 162 might also be playing on the visual resemblance to the term שעשוע). The first occurrence of שעשוע in verse 16a, אשתעשע, parallels ששתי two verses prior in verse 14a (an observation made by Amos Ḥakham in *Psalms with the Jerusalem Commentary*, 3 vols., Bible with the Jerusalem Commentary [Jerusalem: Mosad Harav Kook, 2003], 215), perhaps indicating that the graphic and semantic "slant consonance" is purposeful in this poem.

To return to the larger issue of how Ps 119 interacts with torah, I contend that "delight" functions as a controlling concept not just in terms of the small-scale poetic devices but also in terms of the usage of the eight synonyms. This poem displays a sense of spontaneous experimentation in the distribution of the terms in interchangeably semantic situations. The surprising, even confounding, use of the terms becomes, then, a way to use the rigorous structural constraints as a site of playfulness and spontaneity. To be sure, a reader may find this situation highly dissatisfying. One could ask rhetorically, Are we to understand the poem's delight in torah as merely a superficial composition technique? Indeed, I wonder if Duhm's critique of Ps 119 fundamentally boils down to a charge that the poem is "pretentious": it pretends to be the site of deep insight but ultimately leaves the reader only with glittering formal devices and playful artifice.[46] This charge is, in a sense, correct; yet is not the only proper response simply to point the critic back to the opening verse of the poem: "And happy are those who walk in the torah of YHWH"? Psalm 119 is artificial and repetitive, but these very formal features of the text make the case that poetry can—through constraint and repetition—give life and create desire.

Even more, we should not rush to understand delight in poetry as "mere" delight. As Goldingay recognizes, "delight" in Ps 119 "suggests a child's uninhibited, carefree playfulness."[47] Nonetheless, he is also correct to puzzle that this playfulness is "paradoxical"[48] because it would seem to be at odds with the resolute *commitment* to torah that is expressed in a number of ways, whether by the frequent imagery of paths (דרך and ארח) or the numerous uses of the term אהב ("love").[49] The paradox for Goldingay is, implicitly, that the poem can be playful, even superficial, and still be purposeful. This paradox is at the heart of some critiques of the text: Duhm's wish that the "author [impart] just something of the great achievements of his studies!" is a demand that the poetic torah in which the poet delights conform to a discernible abstract concept of torah. Without some kind of clearer elucidation of the central argument, the central *concept*, Ps 119 becomes in this view merely an imitation of the real thing and therefore worthy of dismissal. Yet Ps 119 frustrates the division between "real" and "copy." Each mention of one of the eight terms is

---

[46] Compare Jonathan Culler's observation about reader response of repetition; he writes that, when confronted with repetition, "the interpreter's temptation … is to master the effects of repetition by casting them into a story, determining origins and causes, and giving it dramatic, significant coloring" (*On Deconstruction: Theory and Criticism after Structuralism* [Ithaca, NY: Cornell University Press, 1982], 260–68; quoted in Krystyna Mazur, *Poetry and Repetition: Walt Whitman, Wallace Stevens, John Ashbery*, Literary Criticism and Cultural Theory (London: Routledge, 2005), xii.

[47] Goldingay, *Psalms*, 3:754.

[48] Ibid.

[49] The term דרך occurs thirteen times (vv. 1, 3, 5, 14, 26, 27, 29, 30, 32, 33, 37, 59, 168); ארח occurs five times (vv. 9, 15, 101, 104, 128); אהב occurs twelve times (vv. 47, 48, 97, 113, 119, 127, 132, 140, 159, 163, 165, 167). Notably, Goldingay translates אהב as "be dedicated" (*Psalms*, 3:754).

just as much fully torah as any other. The entirety of torah—including both its presence and potentiality—is realized in the poem itself. Torah is not, in Reynolds's words, "more than the sum of its parts" in the sense of being an entity that transcends the text and can thus be abstracted from it. Neither, however, is it just its parts alone. Rather, torah in Ps 119 emerges as an immanent presence in the poem, unfolding as the series of its parts, the stream of synonymous terms that flows through the poem. This stream is the causal force that drives the reader to try to add it up, and it is also the intrinsic limit that keeps the reader from ever calculating a sum.[50] In other words, Ps 119's torah is to be discovered by relating it not to something outside the poem but solely by locating it among the overwhelming, delighting words of the poem itself. Psalm 119's use of repetition to push the reader ever onward within the poem, to frustrate attempts to go beyond its bounds, embodies a poetics of immanence.

### III. THINKING IMMANENCE WITH PSALM 119

Readers often approach Ps 119 with the expectation that the poem will open up a window onto some deeper meaning, only to find their expectations thwarted. Yes, this poem is a celebration of the torah of YHWH, but it is a celebration that startles readers because it resists explicating the meaning of torah. Psalm 119 delights in the proliferation of terms, poetic techniques, and play. Further, the poem does not unfold in a structure that reveals any kind of plot progression or central argument. Numerous readers have understood these features to be an indication that the text is, if not contentless, then at least without substance. Psalm 119's innovation is that the presence of torah can be found within the text itself. The poem rejects the demand that poetry be mimetic—the variations on the eight terms need not be in a relationship of "instantiations" of a singular abstract reality. Rather, and to draw out a term mentioned above, the repetition of the eight terms is not a "platonic" repetition of real and copy but a variety of repetition akin to what Gilles Deleuze terms the "simulacrum."[51] By way of defining *simulacrum*, I simply point to what we have seen so far in Ps 119: each individual appearance of each of the eight terms is to be affirmed and understood on its own, not merely insofar as it corresponds to a supposed pure (or abstract) original that is said to undergird it. As Zainab Bahrani writes regarding the ancient Mesopotamian iconic image, "Simulacra are images without dependence; they are not based on a pre-existing original

---

[50] I thank Davis Hankins for this observation.
[51] See Gilles Deleuze, *The Logic of Sense*, trans. Mark Lester with Charles Stivale, ed. Constantin V. Boundas, European Perspectives (New York: Columbia University Press, 1990), esp. 253–79. For a helpful guide to Deleuze's writings on simulacra, see Daniel W. Smith, "The Concept of the Simulacrum: Deleuze and the Overturning of Platonism," in *Essays on Deleuze* (Edinburgh: Edinburgh University Press, 2012), 3–26.

that they set out to imitate, like the mimetic copy, but exist as creations in their own right."⁵² We do not need to presume that the eight synonyms earn their meaning only if and when they participate in and refer to a larger concept, whether that be a text (the canonical Torah) or a broader abstract concept (Torah-beyond-תורה) that is outside of and beyond it.⁵³ Psalm 119 rejects the privileging of the "authentic" over the "artificial."

This poem, in other words, shows itself to be a rigorously structured and self-consciously complete text that nonetheless presses the seeker of torah continually onward, not to a unifying concept behind the poem but always back to the poem itself, to the next synonym. These features of the text suggest a connection with the philosophical notion of immanence in its refusal to posit a meaning-giving entity outside of the world that is necessary for understanding in and of the world.⁵⁴ In the case of Ps 119, the world described is the world of the poem; the subject of the psalm is poetry itself. The psalm points to torah, and torah returns the favor. In that way, perhaps this psalm fulfills a promise suggested by the very form of biblical Hebrew poetry. The Hebrew poets worked with a literary tradition that prizes balance but also always moves forward, a tradition in which received forms could be exploited to surprising effect.⁵⁵ This poem employs traditional theological language⁵⁶ but turns it inside out to place its power on the surface of the poem. Psalm 119 suggests that poetry's task lies not only in signifying worlds but also in creating them.

---

⁵²Zainab Bahrani, *The Infinite Image: Art, Time and the Aesthetic Dimension in Antiquity* (London: Reaktion Books, 2014), 70.

⁵³For "participation," see Smith, "Concept of the Simulacrum," 8.

⁵⁴For a concise discussion of the concept of immanence and some of its broader implications, see James Williams, "Immanence," in *The Deleuze Dictionary*, ed. Adrian Parr, rev. ed. (Edinburgh: Edinburgh University Press, 2010), 128–30.

⁵⁵See Robert Alter, *The Art of Biblical Poetry* (New York: Basic Books, 1985).

⁵⁶On the use of language from Israelite traditions, see Reynolds, *Torah as Teacher*, chapter 2.

# Gabriel's Entrance and Biblical Violence in Luke's Annunciation Narrative

## MICHAEL POPE
mike_pope@byu.edu
Brigham Young University, Provo, UT 84602

In this critical note I examine sexually violent biblical language and motifs that Luke includes in his annunciation narrative. Specifically, I show that Luke's introduction of Mary and his depiction of Gabriel's entrance make Mary an object of sexual advance and also sexual violence in a manner common in the LXX. Moreover, I argue that Gabriel's greeting to Mary and Mary's self-nomination as a slave further reinforce this violence. Sexually violent biblical language and tableaux are, I conclude, one manifestation of Luke's sustained biblical allusiveness early in his gospel.

---

In a series of narratives rich with themes of fecundity, reproduction, and parturition (Luke 1:1–2:40), Luke's annunciation scene is especially sexually fraught. Lineage, virginity, the threat of transgressed betrothal, paternity, an assertion of conception, the denial of sex, and some manner of impregnation are all in play from Luke 1:27 to 1:35.[1] In this context, it would probably be impossible for Luke not to employ *some* potentially sexually evocative language when describing Gabriel's dialogue with Mary. But Luke goes further and includes septuagintal diction and motifs that, at least to a modern audience, discomfit. Quite apart from sex and birth, at multiple points Luke appears to graft sexual coercion and violence into the scene. Although I address several instances of language suggesting sexual violence, each will center on Luke's depiction of Gabriel's initial approach to Mary.

Sexual encounters in the Hebrew Bible normally involve men as subjective actors, women as objects.[2] One could substantiate this rather uncontroversial claim in various ways, but I wish to look narrowly at verbs of motion relative to

---

[1] Pace Andrew T. Lincoln, who sees in Luke 1:26–38 "no hint of scandal or sexual irregularity" (*Born of a Virgin? Reconceiving Jesus in the Bible, Tradition, and Theology* [Grand Rapids: Eerdmans, 2013], 101).

[2] For another illustration of grammatical subjectivity and objectivity mirroring the sexual, see Eve Levavi Feinstein, *Sexual Pollution in the Hebrew Bible* (Oxford: Oxford University Press, 2014), 68.

male–female sexual situations.³ Of the numerous sex and sexual assault scenes in the Hebrew Bible, many communicate the sex itself, whether consensual or forcible, through a construction like בוא אל ("go/come to/into") indicating approach/entrance. In Luke's Bible, the LXX, two common verbs, εἰσπορεύεσθαι ("go into") and εἰσέρχεσθαι ("come into") combined with the preposition πρός ("to"), replicate בוא אל and related constructions and frequently denote sexual approach and entrance.⁴ The notion of sexual entrance can raise eyebrows, and modern readers may find difficulty giving full, literal significance to these locutions. Yet, as Christine Mitchell has recently argued regarding the Hebrew construction קרב/בוא אל ("approach"), it is squeamishness on the part of translators that produces euphemistic renderings implying spatial approach rather than orificial penetration.⁵ In the LXX most instances of εἰσπορεύεσθαι/εἰσέρχεσθαι + πρός in a sexual context depict a man penetrating a woman, though there are exceptions to this gendered schema (e.g., Esther approaching the king in 2:12–16).⁶ Examples abound: Jacob enters Leah (εἰσῆλθεν πρὸς αὐτήν) in Gen 29:23 and Rachel (εἰσῆλθεν πρὸς Ραχηλ) in Gen 29:30; metaphorical sexual congress with prostitutes (εἰσεπορεύοντο πρὸς αὐτήν, ὃν τρόπον εἰσπορεύονται πρὸς γυναῖκα πόρνην, "For they have gone in to her, as one goes in to a whore" [NRSV]) in Ezek 23:44; legal strictures prohibiting males from penetrating their aunts by marriage in Lev 18:14 (πρὸς τὴν γυναῖκα αὐτοῦ οὐκ εἰσελεύσῃ, "you shall not approach his [your father's brother] wife" [NRSV]) or any female during her menses in Lev 18:19 (πρὸς γυναῖκα ἐν χωρισμῷ ἀκαθαρσίας αὐτῆς οὐ προσελεύσῃ, "You shall not approach a woman … while she is in her menstrual uncleanness" [NRSV]); wisdom dictating against entering another man's wife (ὁ εἰσελθὼν πρὸς γυναῖκα ὕπανδρον, "one who goes into another man's wife") in Prov 6:29; and in Amos 2:7 the transgression of a son and his father penetrating the same female slave (υἱὸς καὶ πατὴρ αὐτοῦ εἰσεπορεύοντο πρὸς τὴν αὐτὴν παιδίσκην).

---

³ On male subjective actors and female or feminized male objects in the Hebrew Bible, see, e.g., Ken Stone, *Sex, Honor and Power in the Deuteronomistic History*, JSOTSup 234 (Sheffield: JSOT Press, 1996), 75–79.

⁴ The verbs εἰσπορεύεσθαι and εἰσέρχεσθαι can appear interchangeably in the same pericope, as in Esth 2:12–16.

⁵ Christine Mitchell, "Coming, Going, and Knowing: Reading Sex and Embodiment in Hebrew Narrative," *HBAI* 5 (2016): 1–18. Sometimes, however, spatiality is the issue. For recent discussion on norms and destabilization of female space and entrance/intrusion in the Hebrew Bible, see Amy Kalmanofsky, *Gender-Play in the Hebrew Bible: The Ways the Bible Challenges Its Gender Norms*, Routledge Interdisciplinary Perspectives on Biblical Criticism 2 (London: Routledge, 2017), 55–67. For gendered space, see also Harold Washington, "Violence and the Construction of Gender in the Hebrew Bible: A New Historicist Approach," *BibInt* 5 (1997): 324–63, here 337.

⁶ Perhaps the most famous scene of a woman approaching a man in a sexual encounter (Lot and his daughters), Gen 19:31–35 lacks the usual preposition πρός with the various forms of εἰσέρχεσθαι.

As with many other Septuagintalisms, Luke is also fond of the εἰσπορεύεσθαι/ εἰσέρχεσθαι + πρός construction, utilizing it several times in Luke-Acts.[7] Almost uniformly, these are approach and visit scenes without any sexual connotation.[8] Paul, for instance, entertains visitors during his confinement in Acts 28:30 (ἀπεδέχετο πάντας τοὺς εἰσπορευομένους πρὸς αὐτόν, "he welcomed all who came to him") and enters the presence of synagogue members in Acts 17:2 (εἰσῆλθεν πρὸς αὐτούς). As a comparandum for Gabriel's entrance in Luke 1:27–35, an angel from God approaches Cornelius in Acts 10:3 (ἄγγελον τοῦ θεοῦ εἰσελθόντα πρὸς αὐτόν), though Luke differentiates this visitation by noting that it occurs in a vision (ἐν ὁράματι). Paul can even enter Lydia's home in Acts 16:40 (εἰσῆλθον πρὸς τὴν Λυδίαν), and, although this ingress has the potential to be sexually charged, context prompts no such reading.

In view of these instances of benign entry, when Gabriel intrudes upon Mary in Luke 1:28 (εἰσελθὼν πρὸς αὐτήν), we may be justified if we opt in the first instance for a routine spatial interpretation. Indeed, I am aware of no critic who sees any significance to this entrance's wording.[9] Problematizing a straightforward reading of 1:28, however, is the fact that, unlike the aforementioned visitation narratives in Luke-Acts, Luke's description of Gabriel's entry immediately pings with biblical sex language in a scene that is sexually fraught. Luke has already thrice sexualized Mary in the preceding verse by mentioning her virginity twice (παρθένον, τῆς παρθένου) and her betrothed status once (ἐμνηστευμένην).[10] That Luke has potentially crafted the scene to suggest that the male Gabriel enters unbidden a betrothed virgin is sufficiently shocking. What is more, the language of verse 27 raises the possibility for again reading sex and sexual violence in the passage. The phrase "virgin betrothed to a man" (παρθένον ἐμνηστευμένην ἀνδρί), commentators regularly note, is, with two minor shifts in case, identical to the locution in Deut 22:23 (παρθένος μεμνηστευμένη ἀνδρί).[11] The context of the phrase in Deut 22:23–24 is capital

---

[7] For Luke's Septuagintalisms (but not including this one), see Joseph A. Fitzmyer, *The Gospel according to Luke (I-IX): Introduction, Translation, and Notes*, AB 28 (Garden City, NY: Doubleday, 1981), 113–16.

[8] Mitchell also recognizes that not every instance of approach in the Hebrew Bible is sexual penetration ("Coming, Going, and Knowing," 13).

[9] For example, John Nolland merely notes that εἰσελθὼν πρός "is Lukan idiom," which is not fully accurate since it was a standard LXX construction before Luke appropriated it (*Luke 1–9:20*, WBC 35A [Dallas: Word, 1989], 49). Although I agree with J.-P. Audet's biblical reading of Gabriel's visitation and message to Mary (i.e., that it follows biblical prophetic scenes with supramundane figures) ("L'Annonce à Marie," *RB* 63 [1956]: 346–74), I think that with Gabriel's entrance, Luke's scene already evokes other biblical tableaux before the angel ever speaks.

[10] Quite apart from discussion of what comprises technical virginity, to refer to a woman or girl with a term denoting her general age and marriageability is to sexualize her. See Gordon J. Wenham, "Betûlāh: 'A Girl of Marriageable Age,'" *VT* 22 (1972): 326–48.

[11] See, e.g., Fitzmyer, *Gospel according to Luke (I-IX)*, 343; see also Jane Schaberg, who asserts that Luke's allusion to the legal question of Deut 22:23–24 is purposeful (*The Illegitimacy*

punishment for a betrothed young woman or virgin[12] whom a man other than her husband-to-be has raped or with whom the man has engaged in something like consensual sex.[13] Whatever level of consent is granted a woman in the assault/act, her consent is presumed since she does not scream out in a location where people would hear.[14] In 1:26–38, Luke has constructed Gabriel's entrance in such a way as to suggest Mary's immediate aloneness since the angel's message of conception is apparently to her only. On the other hand, Luke also specifies her non-aloneness since he states that Gabriel enters her in a city (εἰς πόλις, 1:26), a venue in which, in Deut 22:24, a sexually accosted woman must be consenting if she does not scream out (οὐκ ἐβόησεν ἐν τῇ πόλει).[15] Alone with Gabriel but surrounded by others, the very contingency addressed by Deut 22:23–24, Mary's consent to impregnation appears to be a salient point of tension in the passage. Indeed, Mary protests that in no way can she be pregnant since she has not and is not granting subjective sexual consent by actively knowing a man (ἄνδρα οὐ γινώσκω, 1:34).[16] Even though

---

of Jesus: A Feminist Theological Interpretation of the Infancy Narrative, Expanded Twentieth Anniversary ed. [Sheffield: Sheffield Phoenix, 2006], 88–89).

[12] For the in/accuracy of the term *virgin* in regard to this pericope, see Hilary B. Lipka, *Sexual Transgression in the Hebrew Bible*, HBM 7 (Sheffield: Sheffield Phoenix, 2006), 77–80.

[13] I use the term *rape* here in a modern sense granting that no such term or discourse of a woman's agency over consent and her body existed in the Hebrew Bible. On the term *rape* as it pertains to modern usage, see Feinstein, *Sexual Pollution*, 69. Harold Washington notes, "For rape to be recognized as a crime of force, there must be an acknowledgment of a woman's capacity to consent to sexual relations. This means, of course, that she must also be assumed to be capable of refusing consent. Deuteronomic law ostensibly applies a standard of consent in the stipulation that a betrothed young woman who is assaulted in the open country is not culpable, as she presumably cried for help but was not heard (22.27). This standard of consent founders, however, in the treatment of sexual assault within a town" ("'Lest He Die in the Battle and Another Man Take Her': Violence and the Construction of Gender in the Laws of Deuteronomy 20–22," in *Gender and Law in the Hebrew Bible and the Ancient Near East*, ed. Tikva Frymer-Kensky, Bernard M. Levinson, and Victor H. Matthews, JSOTSup 262 [Sheffield: Sheffield Academic, 1998], 201–10).

[14] The matter at hand in these laws is property rights. Carolyn Pressler states, "In the two Deuteronomic cases [Deut 22:23–29], the woman's lack of consent is irrelevant to the nature and the gravity of the offense" ("Sexual Violence and Deuteronomic Law," in *Feminist Companion to Exodus to Deuteronomy*, ed. Athalya Brenner, FCB 6 [1994; repr., Sheffield: Sheffield Academic, 2001], 103). For many modern critics, the more pressing interpretive issue is sexual violence and consent. See, e.g., Jeffrey H. Tigay, *Deuteronomy* דברים: *The Traditional Hebrew Text with the New JPS Translation*, JPSTC (Philadelphia: Jewish Publication Society, 1996), 207; and Frank M. Yamada, *Configurations of Rape in the Hebrew Bible: A Literary Analysis of Three Rape Narratives*, StBibLit 109 (Bern: Lang, 2008), 44–45.

[15] In her close reading of Luke's sustained engagement with Deut 22:23–24, Schaberg does not register this additional verbal parallel, a parallel that may be notable since it is a detail not found in Matthew (*Illegitimacy of Jesus*, 88–96).

[16] One can even read Mary's statement as an initial refusal of consent, as in, "How will this be since I am *not* having sex with a man" (Πῶς ἔσται τοῦτο, ἐπεὶ ἄνδρα οὐ γινώσκω, 1:34). For

Mary may ultimately consent a few verses later ("let it happen to me according to your message," γένοιτό μοι κατὰ τὸ ῥῆμά σου, 1:38), by alluding to Deut 22:23–24 Luke has introduced the tableau of forcible sex and capital violence (death by stoning) even as he uses biblical language that literally communicates sexual penetration of a female object by a male subject. We must concede that the underlying assumptions at work in Deut 22:23–24 might not have been chilling to Luke's intended audience or that Luke and his audience may not have readily considered the greater source material along with the phrase. Still, importing this language and risking contamination from its context seem an uncomfortable choice given the scene's sexual focus and Gabriel's uninvited entrance.

But Luke seems to insist on making his scene distressing. The construction Luke uses to portray Gabriel's entrance is also famously used to describe the single instance in the LXX of divine or angelic beings transgressively consorting with or raping mortal women. In Gen 6:1–4 we find the strange narratological incursion of the "sons of god" (οἱ υἱοὶ τοῦ θεοῦ) who "approached the daughters of humans and sired children for themselves" (εἰσεπορεύοντο ... πρὸς τὰς θυγατέρας τῶν ἀνθρώπων καὶ ἐγεννῶσαν ἑαυτοῖς). Forcible sex, though not explicit,[17] can be readily inferred, and the action of these supramundane figures became the subject of varying interpretive trajectories that assume sexual coercion. Among these the Enochic tradition—a tradition especially influential on early Christian interpreters—developed the transgressive rape reading. By the second and early third centuries, these figures were widely understood to be fallen angels by early Christian writers like Justin Martyr, Athenagoras, Irenaeus, Clement of Alexandria, and Tertullian.[18] Much earlier, Paul likely gestures toward this interpretive vein in his cryptic pronouncement on women, their hair, and the angels in 1 Cor 11:10.[19] If

---

retaining the present tense of γινώσκω in translation rather than importing the perfect tense, see Jean Carmignac, "The Meaning of Parthenos in Luke 1.27: A Reply to C. H. Dodd," *BT* 28 (1977): 327–30.

[17] At face value, the language itself indicates a legal taking of wives, though this hardly eliminates the potential for implied sexual violence. For legal marriage language, see Umberto Cassuto, *A Commentary on the Book of Genesis*, 2 vols., trans. Israel Abrahams (Jerusalem: Magnes, 1961), 1:294–95.

[18] For early Christian interpretations of Gen 6:1–4 and the Watcher traditions, see Annette Yoshiko Reed, *Fallen Angels and the History of Judaism and Christianity: The Reception of Enochic Literature* (Cambridge: Cambridge University Press, 2005), 160–205. See also Reed, "The Trickery of the Fallen Angels and the Demonic Mimesis of the Divine: Aetiology, Demonology, and Polemics in the Writings of Justin Martyr," *JECS* 12 (2004): 141–71; and Jeffrey Burton Russell, *Satan: The Early Christian Tradition* (Ithaca, NY: Cornell University Press, 1981), 81–82.

[19] For Paul's plausible knowledge of the tradition, see L. J. Lietaert Peerbolte, "Man, Woman, and the Angels in 1 Cor 11:2–16," in *The Creation of Man and Woman: Interpretations of the Biblical Narratives in Jewish and Christian Traditions*, ed. Gerard P. Luttikhuizen, TBN 3 (Leiden: Brill, 2000), 87–92. For recent review of scholarship and interpretations, see Scott M. Lewis, "'Because of the Angels': Paul and the Enochic Traditions," in *The Watchers in Jewish and Christian*

Paul engages the tradition for his own rhetorical ends, might Luke also? With the confluence of sexual entrance language and the tableau of angelic visitation resulting in offspring, offspring which is to be "great" or "large" (μέγας, 1:32), the possibility is tantalizing.[20] Without additional evidence, we probably cannot know whether Luke, like other late first-century Christian writers, was aware of this tradition.[21] Still, Gen 6:1–4 remains the only instance in the LXX of divine or angelic entities sexually penetrating human women with children resulting.[22] It seems at least reasonable that Luke could have known this and co-opted the scene in some way.[23] Coincidentally perhaps, in 1 En. 10:9 it is the angel Gabriel who is given responsibility to destroy the fallen angels' gigantic progeny.[24] Strange and intriguing stuff indeed.

Returning to our scene, the angel Gabriel's visit to Mary hinges on his announcement that she will conceive and bear a son (συλλήμψῃ ἐν γαστρὶ καὶ τέξῃ υἱόν, 1:31). Critics point out the similarity of this phrase to language in Gen 16:11.[25] I will say more about this below, but for the moment I additionally note that the pregnancy in Gen 16:11 results from a man formulaically entering a woman (εἰσῆλθεν πρός, Gen 16:4). It is also noteworthy that this impregnation and birth prediction is preceded immediately by Gabriel's pronouncement that Mary has found favor with God (εὗρες γὰρ χάριν παρὰ τῷ θεῷ, 1:30). Commentators regularly

---

*Traditions*, ed. Angela Kim Harkins, Kelley Coblentz Bautch, and John C. Endres (Minneapolis: Fortress, 2014), 81–90.

[20] Note also that Gabriel says that Jesus "will be called a/the son of god" (κληθήσεται υἱὸς θεοῦ, 1:35), the very title of the divine figures in Gen 6:1–4.

[21] Arguments have been put forward that Matthew knew of the tradition. See David C. Sim, "Matthew 22.13a and 1 Enoch 10.4a: A Case of Literary Dependence?" *JSNT* 47 (1992): 3–19. Other sections of 1 Enoch have been examined as potential literary sources drawn upon by Luke. For a cautious assessment of parallel material, see George W. E. Nickelsburg, "Riches, the Rich, and God's Judgment in 1 Enoch 92–105 and the Gospel according to Luke," *NTS* 25 (1978): 324–44. The authors of Jude, 1 Peter, and 2 Peter, all texts from the late first or early second century, were also aware of the Watchers traditions. See Eric F. Mason, "Watchers Traditions in the Catholic Epistles," in Harkins, Bautch, and Endres, *Watchers in Jewish and Christian Traditions*, 69–79.

[22] There is, however, a strong case to be made that the annunciation and conception narrative of Samson (Judg 13:1–7) suggests that an angel penetrates (including the locution ἦλθεν πρός, v. 6) and impregnates a mortal woman. See Adele Reinhartz, "Samson's Mother: An Unnamed Protagonist," *JSOT* 55 (1992): 25–37, here 33–35.

[23] Although he does not comment on Luke and Gen 6:1–4, for Luke-Acts and the Enochic Son of Man tradition, see George W. E. Nickelsburg, *1 Enoch 1: A Commentary on the Book of 1 Enoch, Chapters 1–36; 81–108*, Hermeneia (Minneapolis: Fortress, 2001), 84.

[24] George W. E. Nickelsburg and James C. VanderKam, *1 Enoch: The Hermeneia Translation* (Minneapolis: Fortress, 2012), 29. See Kevin Sullivan, "The Watchers Tradition in 1 Enoch 6–16: The Fall of Angels and the Rise of Demons," in Harkins, Bautch, and Endres, *Watchers in Jewish and Christian Traditions*, 91–103, here 94.

[25] See, e.g., Alfred Plummer, *A Critical and Exegetical Commentary on the Gospel according to S. Luke*, 5th ed., ICC (Edinburgh: T&T Clark, 1922), 23.

acknowledge this phrase's verbal proximity to Gen 6:8, where Noah is said to have found favor before the Lord God (Νωε δὲ εὗρεν χάριν ἐναντίον κυρίου τοῦ θεοῦ).[26] The adversative force of δέ here is strong, since Noah's favor with God is going to save him from the coming deluge that God designs in order to eliminate all the evil deeds of humankind noted in Gen 6:5 (αἱ κακίαι τῶν ἀνθρώπων), including, it seems from the arrangement of the successive verses, the sons of God/angels' (forcible?) sex with mortal women and siring of the giants in verses 2 and 4. It is as though in a mash-up of the already confused biblical narrative, Mary's divine favor has secured for her not salvation from the evil consequences of coercive fallen angels but rather sexual advance from an angel sent from God (ἀπεστάλη ὁ ἄγγελος ... ἀπὸ τοῦ θεοῦ, 1:26), which ultimately brings her salvation (cf. 1:47–48). It does not necessarily follow that, if Luke repurposes language about Noah's divine favor from Gen 6:8, he is also intending to smuggle in the foregoing narrative unit concerning the heavenly sires and their sexual approach to mortal women in Gen 6:1–4. The inclusion of an angel and the εἰσπορεύεσθαι/εἰσέρχεσθαι + πρός construction does, however, offer a potential link. At any rate, beyond this puzzle, there is another, more concrete use of language suggesting sexual violence.

Mary's penultimate statement to Gabriel, "Look, the master's slave" (Ἰδοὺ ἡ δούλη κυρίου, 1:38), brackets and endorses the angel's initial greeting, "Your master is with you," (ὁ κύριος μετὰ σοῦ, 1:28).[27] It also regulates the ensuing dialogue according to gender and status.[28] In view of Gabriel's subsequent announcement of impending conception, Mary's acquiescence is both servile and sexual.[29] This

---

[26] See, e.g., I. Howard Marshall, *The Gospel of Luke: A Commentary on the Greek Text*, NIGTC 3 (Grand Rapids: Eerdmans, 1978), 66; and François Bovon, *Luke 1: A Commentary on the Gospel of Luke 1:1–9:50*, trans. Christine M. Thomas, Hermeneia (Minneapolis: Fortress, 2002), 50 n. 71.

[27] Mary's consternation over Gabriel's greeting (1:29) may perhaps be better explained by this immediate master–slave discursive framing than by the word of greeting (Χαῖρε) itself, *pace* August Strobel, "Der Gruss an Maria (Lc 1,28): Eine philologische Betrachtung zu seinem Sinngehalt," ZNW 53 (1962): 86–110.

[28] For the vocabulary and relationship of master (κύριος) and female slave (δούλη), see Exod 21:7–8. For finding favor with one's master ("May I find favor in your eyes, master," Εὕροιμι χάριν ἐν ὀφθαλμοῖς σου, κύριε), master–female slave dynamic (τῆς δούλης σου) with sexual undertones, and entering in to sire a son (εἰσῆλθεν πρὸς αὐτήν), see Ruth 2:13, 4:13. Nominating oneself a slave could also be polite abasement, as Raymond Westbrook points out ("The Female Slave," in Frymer-Kensky, Levinson, and Matthews, *Gender and Law in the Hebrew Bible*, 214–38, here 230). So, for example, 1 Sam 25:41 (Ἰδοὺ ἡ δούλη σου). Given the sexualized circumstances, however, it is difficult to see Mary's self-nomination as mere courtesy.

[29] The sexual abjectness of the status of the female slave was embedded in Luke's biblical sources and in his contemporary Greco-Roman world. Although it is largely inappropriate to map laws and customs of the ancient Near East onto Greco-Roman laws and customs, as it pertains to the basic personhood and sexual availability of female slaves there is agreement. Regarding the former, Westbrook states, "Since a female slave was property, her owner could exploit or dispose of her sexuality like any other beneficial aspect of property" ("Female Slave," 215).

connection, slave status and sex, brings us back to Luke's biblical formulation for Gabriel's entrance. The sexual objectification of a penetrated female, instantiated by the grammar itself, is manifest in the brute equation of male master and female slave.³⁰ We see this exact scheme in some of the Bible's foundational origin narratives. Jacob penetrates (εἰσῆλθεν δὲ πρὸς αὐτήν) the slaves Bilhah and Zilpah (παιδίσκη), who then conceive and bear sons (συνέλαβεν, Gen 30:4–5, 9–10). As the grammatical and sexual object of Abraham's penetration (εἰσῆλθεν πρός), Hagar the slave (παιδίσκη) conceives in her belly (συνέλαβεν, ἐν γαστρί, Gen 16:3, 4). Abused by Sarai, Hagar turns runaway slave until an angel of the Lord finds her, bids her return to her owner, informs her of her conception, and gives her instruction on how to name the son-to-be (Gen 16:8–11). Given similarities both lexical (e.g., συλλήμψῃ ἐν γαστρί) and thematic (e.g., angelic announcement of conception and naming instructions in Gen 16:11), the narrative of Abraham and Hagar is rightly noted for its proximity to Luke 1:31.³¹ Yet the fact that Hagar is a slave who is penetrated and that Mary nominates herself a slave after being entered/entered upon by an agent declaring her impending impregnation deserves more attention.³² The sexual violence of the biblical allusion is too easily neglected.³³

---

For Greco-Roman attitudes, two terse digests suffice. Serena S. Witzke observes that "female slaves were always available for their masters' pleasure" ("Violence against Women in Ancient Rome: Ideology versus Reality," in *The Topography of Violence in the Greco-Roman World*, ed. Werner Riess and Garrett G. Fagan [Ann Arbor: University of Michigan Press, 2016], 248–74, here 262). David Fredrick notes that "slaves ... are necessarily, forcefully penetrable" ("Mapping Penetrability in Late Republican and Early Imperial Rome," in *The Roman Gaze: Vision, Power, and the Body*, ed. David Fredrick and Arethusa Books [Baltimore: Johns Hopkins University Press, 2002], 236–64, here 243). Reading Mary's status as abject in terms of biblical motif is contrary to Bruce J. Malina and Jerome H. Neyrey's argument that her status was highly privileged because of priestly blood ties ("Honor and Shame in Luke-Acts: Pivotal Values of the Mediterranean World," in *The Social World of Luke-Acts: Models for Interpretation*, ed. Jerome H. Neyrey and Burce J. Malina [Peabody, MA: Hendrickson, 1991], 25–65, esp. 47).

[30] Elisabeth Schüssler Fiorenza's summation remains accurate and devastating: "Mary ... perfectly represents the feminine qualities of receptivity, subordination, humility, malleability, obedience, and passivity" (*Jesus: Miriam's Child, Sophia's Prophet; Critical Issues in Feminist Christology*, 2nd ed., Cornerstones [London: Bloomsbury T&T Clark, 2015], 188).

[31] For thematic and linguistic parallels to Gen 16:3–12 and other biblical annunciations, see Raymond E. Brown, *The Birth of the Messiah: A Commentary on the Infancy Narratives in Matthew and Luke*, rev. ed., ABRL (New York: Doubleday, 1993), 155–57.

[32] In counterpoint, Schaberg would have us consider Mary's self-appointment as slave to be a bestowal of an honorific in view of "a few outstanding men of Israelite history [e.g., Moses, Joshua, David] ... and one woman, Hannah" who were also described as slaves of God (*Illegitimacy of Jesus*, 124; bracketed material added).

[33] Similarly, interpretations of Luke 1:38 dependent on rendering δούλη as "servant" too readily mask the gendered power differential between male master and female slave and the constant opportunity for sexual violence of the former against the latter. See, e.g., D. M. Smith's use of the NEB ("Luke 1:26–38," *Int* 29 [1975]: 411–17). Acknowledgment of this dynamic would certainly complicate but also bolster Joel B. Green's argument that Luke first portrays Mary as

Finally, Gabriel makes only two narratological incursions in Luke-Acts (and in the New Testament in full). Before his entrance in 1:28, Gabriel appears to Zechariah as he is performing one of his priestly duties. The venue, mode, and message of the two encounters differ starkly. Zechariah is within the distinctly privileged male space of the sanctuary when Gabriel appears to him (ὤφθη δὲ αὐτῷ, 1:11; Gabriel identifies himself later in 1:19), and the announcement Gabriel delivers to Zechariah is that his wife Elizabeth will conceive.[34] As far as Zechariah is concerned, Gabriel's apparition raises no legal questions about a man and woman alone, no biblical language of sexual penetration, no biblical allusions to sex or rape, no assessment of Zechariah's orificial integrity (in contrast to Mary being twice called παρθένος), and no concerns over consent and servile agency. Zechariah's interview with Gabriel recapitulates the sexual security of maleness while, in manifold ways, Gabriel's unsolicited intrusion upon Mary highlights the real threat of sexual violence faced by women in both biblical narrative and lived experience.[35]

What are we to make of this constellation of suggestive language in Luke 1:27–35 taken from contexts rife with sexual objectification and violence? I offer two simple observations: (1) Luke has fashioned the scene to be thoroughly biblical in language and motif, substrates that encode and promulgate sexual objectification and violence against women, whatever our discomfort may be with his material and method.[36] (2) To an audience steeped in the Bible (to say nothing of

---

someone "who seemed to measure low on any status scale—age, family heritage, gender, and so on" ("The Social Status of Mary in Luke 1,5–2,52: A Plea for Methodological Integration," *Bib* 73 (1992): 457–71, here 468.

[34] Sometimes critics conflate the appearance of Gabriel to Zechariah (ὤφθη δὲ αὐτῷ) with Gabriel's approach to Mary (εἰσελθὼν πρὸς αὐτήν). See, e.g., Theodor Zahn, *Das Evangelium des Lucas*, KNT 3 (Leipzig: Deichert, 1920), 75.

[35] Over against Gabriel's unsolicited intrusion upon Mary, note that Luke 1:13 specifies that Gabriel's appearance and message to Zechariah are in answer to Zechariah's petition that Elizabeth would conceive (εἰσηκούσθη ἡ δέησίς σου). Luke 24:4, 23 also include a private interaction between two figures identified as male angels and a group of women (24:10). This is not a sexual tableau, and Luke does not employ sexual approach language. Instead, the two figures identified as angels "stood beside" (ἐπέστησαν αὐταῖς, 24:4) the women in a manner that produces the common biblical motif of terror ("since they were terrified," ἐμφόβων δὲ γενομένων αὐτῶν; 24:5). In no way is this a sexually suggestive or threatening posture. The verb ἐφιστάναι does occur once in the LXX in a sexual context, but the sexual sense of the passage is dependent on the presence of a slave girl and her bed rather than the verb itself (Sir 41:24).

[36] In regard to literary encoding of gendered violence, Washington states, "These imbrications of violence and gender in the Hebrew Bible are more than just reflections of the social conditions of biblical antiquity. In this literature, gender becomes a crucial articulator of the experience of violence, and thus gendered discourse becomes a means of *producing* relations of violence and domination, authenticating a violent male prerogative that remains culturally potent in the present. These texts supplied the discursive means by which both people legitimated and endured violence in biblical antiquity, and still do today" ("Violence and the Construction of Gender," 331–32; author's emphasis).

Greco-Roman literary traditions[37]), Luke's annunciation narrative is therefore eminently familiar and legible. Moreover, this conscious effort at biblical allusiveness is altogether consonant with the entirety of Luke's intensely biblical casting of Jesus's genesis and infancy.[38] Unnerving as it may be to us, if biblical authors could imagine God as a metaphorical rapist or facilitator of sexual violence against a feminized Jerusalem, a God who later rehabilitates his sexually violated object (e.g., Ezek 16:37–39, 61–63), Luke may not be abusing biblical themes if he makes Gabriel an agent of figural divine sexual violence against Mary.[39] Indeed, a few verses past our scene, Mary acknowledges her own rehabilitation before God by reiterating her previous servile and violent sexual submission (τὴν ταπείνωσιν τῆς δούλης, 1:48).[40] As a related addendum, I note finally that the theme of violence against Mary surfaces again when Simeon prophesies that a presumably metaphorical sword is going to run through Mary's soul (τὴν ψυχὴν διελεύσεται ῥομφαία, 2:35), another figure potentially suggestive of the master's design for his favored slave girl (1:28).[41] As for what this all might mean, I cautiously wonder whether there might be significance in Luke opening his gospel with the mother of an ultimately crucified Jesus suffering the distinctive violence faced by women in antiquity—the plight of both mother and son being, at one level, grossly mundane.[42] But I leave that question to others.

---

[37] For a recent review of primary and secondary sources on Greco-Roman literary milieus, though not on divine rape motifs, see Lincoln, *Born of a Virgin?*, 57–67, 108–12.

[38] For Luke's sustained employment of biblical themes and language in Luke 1:5–2:52, see Joel B. Green, *The Gospel of Luke*, NICNT (Grand Rapids: Eerdmans, 1997), 52–58.

[39] For God's violence against and rehabilitation of feminized Israel, see also Hos 1–2, though the metaphorical sexual violence is somewhat less pronounced (esp. 2:9–10). See Gale A. Yee, *Poor Banished Children of Eve: Women as Evil in the Hebrew Bible* (Minneapolis: Fortress, 2003), 81–109. See also Renita J. Weems, *Battered Love: Marriage, Sex, and Violence in the Hebrew Bible*, OBT (Minneapolis: Fortress, 1995), 78–80.

[40] To be sure, in reference to language and theme (conception), the most immediate intertexts for Luke 1:48 are 1 Sam 1:11 and Gen 29:32. In neither of the respective narratives, however, is there the sustained tableau of violence found in Luke 1:27–35. Ragnar Leivestad, in his survey of the LXX and New Testament, neither considers Deut 22 nor registers that ταπείνωσις also means sexual subjection ("ταπεινός–ταπεινόφρων," *NovT* 8 [1966]: 36–47). We should observe that ταπείνωσις, clearly meaning violation or rape in Deut 22:29, is also the very issue broached in Deut 22:23–24 (ἐταπείνωσεν τὴν γυναῖκα τοῦ πλησίον, 22:24), contextual material to which Luke seems to allude by borrowing the phrase παρθένον ἐμνηστευμένην ἀνδρί from Deut 22:23 to describe Gabriel's initial approach to Mary.

[41] Gabriel's salutation, "Greetings, favored one, your master is with you" (Χαῖρε, κεχαριτωμένη, ὁ κύριος μετὰ σοῦ), read with an eye to the ever-present threat of sexual violence in a master–slave relationship colors the scene more ominously.

[42] Similar theological ground—that Mary has a share in the suffering of her son—has been trod before, though without focus on the sexual violence suffered by Mary. See, e.g., A. Feuillet, "L'epreuve prédite à Marie par le vieillard Siméon (Luc 2,35a)," in *À la rencontre de Dieu: Mémorial Albert Gelin*, ed. André Barucq, BFCLL 8 (Le Puy: Mappus, 1961), 249.

*JBL* 137, no. 3 (2018): 711–732
doi: http://dx.doi.org/10.15699/jbl.1373.2018.409291

# Mixed Metaphors: Resolving the "Eschatological Headache" of John 5

**HUGO MÉNDEZ**
hmendez@email.unc.edu
University of North Carolina at Chapel Hill, Chapel Hill, NC 27599

Exegetes have long puzzled over the purported clash of eschatologies in John 5:19–30—one framed by an apparent shift between figurative and literal speech in the passage. In this article I argue that the evidence for such a shift—most of it rooted in inconsistencies in the imagery and language of verses 24–25 and 28–29—is weak. Literary-oriented studies of the Fourth Gospel have called attention to the dynamism and fluidity of its imagery. Metaphorical vehicles, once introduced into a given discourse, are often further developed, modified, or altogether reimagined in successive lines—a technique known as "metaphor shifting." I identify this technique as the best explanation for the discrepancies observed between verses 24–25 and 28–29. When the entire passage is read as a continuous stream of shifting and interpenetrating metaphors, it contains no sudden clash of eschatologies and no tensions for the interpreter to resolve. Rather, the passage reads as a coherent and more complete exposition of the gospel's realized eschatology.

## I. Realized and Future Eschatologies in John 5

In his landmark essay "The Elusive Christ," Mark W. G. Stibbe remarks that the Jesus of the Fourth Gospel speaks "a language worthy of deity," "a reflection in speech of the mystery of his nature."[1] This cryptic tongue is none other than "the heavenly language of metaphor."[2] Only within the past three decades have scholars made a concerted effort to document this language. Following the dramatic advances in the linguistic theorization of metaphor during the 1980s, the field of Johannine studies "moved the imagery of John into central focus."[3] Scholars have

---

[1] Mark W. G. Stibbe, "The Elusive Christ: A New Reading of the Fourth Gospel," *JSNT* 44 (1991): 19–38, here 26, 29.
[2] Ibid., 27.
[3] Ruben Zimmermann, "Imagery in John: Opening up Paths in the Tangled Thicket of John's

711

fruitfully applied the new theoretical frameworks to various examples of figurative speech in the gospel, illuminating its literary artistry and sophistication.

To the extent that these studies have focused on questions of style, they have often bypassed traditional exegetical and theological concerns. In a text in which metaphor is pervasive, however, their insights touch on the very sentences and words at stake in interpretive debates. In this essay, I will consider how these literary-linguistic approaches can be brought to bear on an old problem in the gospel—what Jörg Frey identifies as "the core problem of Johannine eschatology"—that is, "the hard, abrupt juxtaposition of present and future statements, most sharply in John 5:24–29."[4]

Contemporary studies of that passage generally work from two premises. The first is that the passage unites two distinct outlooks: a realized eschatology concentrated in verses 24–25, and a future eschatology concentrated in verses 28–29.[5] The former verses take up apocalyptic images of a divine voice calling "the dead" to life, but in a figurative sense:[6]

*Present*
5:24–25    "Truly, truly, I say to you, the one who hears my word and believes in the one who sent me has eternal life; that one does not come into judgment, but has passed from death to life. Truly, truly, I say to you, the hour is coming, and is now, when the dead will hear the voice of the Son of God, and those who hear will live."

---

Figurative World," in *Imagery in the Gospel of John: Terms, Forms, Themes, and Theology of Johannine Figurative Language*, ed. Jörg Frey, Jan G. van der Watt, and Ruben Zimmermann, WUNT 200 (Tübingen: Mohr-Siebeck, 2006), 1–43, here 6. Linguistic advances include Cognitive Metaphor Theory (George Lakoff and Mark Johnson), Conceptual Blending Theory (Gilles Fauconnier and Mark Turner), and empirical studies on metaphor in discourse. Periodizations and surveys of Johannine metaphor studies appear in Zimmermann, "Imagery," 2–9; and Jan G. van der Watt, *Family of the King: Dynamics of Metaphor in the Gospel according to John*, BibInt 47 (Leiden: Brill, 2000), xvii–xviii.

[4] Jörg Frey, *Die johanneische Eschatologie*, 3 vols., WUNT 96, 110, 117 (Tübingen: Mohr Siebeck, 1997–2000), 1:418.

[5] "Realized eschatology" encompasses events and states realized through the coming and departure of Jesus and present from the perspective of the Johannine circle. "Future eschatology," by contrast, encompasses events in the still-unrealized, apocalyptic future.

[6] Literal and figurative language occurs along a continuum (Andrew Goatly, *The Language of Metaphors*, 2nd ed. [New York: Routledge, 2011], 14). In a rough sense, literal language is language whose meaning is not extended from another meaning by metaphor or metonymy, unlike figurative speech (Barbara Dancygier and Eve Sweetser, *Figurative Language*, Cambridge Textbooks in Linguistics [Cambridge: Cambridge University Press, 2014], 4). In metaphor, "a unit of discourse is used to refer to" a word or concept "to which it does not conventionally refer … on the basis of similarity or analogy" (Goatly, *Language of Metaphors*, 109). Translations of biblical passages are mine, adapted from the RSV.

In these verses, "the dead" are not the physically deceased, since corpses are not in a position to "believe." Instead, "the dead" here are the figurative dead: individuals who have no spiritual life in them (6:53) but who receive eternal life as they embrace Jesus's words (3:15, 6:47). In 5:28–29, by contrast, scholars detect a reference to the literal dead within a conventional image of a future, bodily resurrection:

Future
5:28–29 "Do not be astonished at this; for the hour is coming when all who are in the tombs will hear his voice and come forth: those who have done good to the resurrection of life, and those who have done evil to the resurrection of judgment."

The second premise, in turn, recognizes this shift from figurative to literal speech and from realized to future eschatology as nothing less than the "eschatological headache" of the gospel—a *crux interpretum* for which a consistent interpretation remains elusive.[7] The problem, it should be noted, is not a theological one. Realized and future perspectives can, and often do, coexist in Jewish and Christian texts. Instead, the problem is a literary one. The two eschatologies are juxtaposed in a highly peculiar way in the compressed space of 5:24–29, confronting interpreters with several puzzling questions. Where in the intertwined imagery of the passage should one locate the transition between these views? (Writers alternately place it at either v. 26, v. 27a, v. 27b, or v. 28, with no consensus in sight.[8]) Why is that transition so murky and difficult to isolate? Why does the passage shift so abruptly from one eschatology to the other, never expressly relating the two?[9] And how does each view function within the passage's argumentation?

---

[7] Jan G. van der Watt, "A New Look at John 5:25–9 in the Light of the Use of the Term 'Eternal Life' in the Gospel according to John," *Neot* 19 (1985): 71–86, here 71.

[8] These views are distributed across four prominent twentieth-century commentaries on John: verse 26 (Raymond E. Brown, *The Gospel according to John: Introduction, Translation, and Notes*, 2 vols., AB 29–29A [Garden City, NY: Doubleday, 1966–1970], 1:220); verse 27a (Rudolf Bultmann, *The Gospel of John: A Commentary* [Philadelphia: Westminster, 1971], 260–61); verse 27b (Rudolf Schnackenburg, *The Gospel according to St. John*, 3 vols., HTC [New York: Crossroad, 1987–1990], 2:113, also entertained in Bultmann, *Gospel of John*, 261); verse 28 (C. K. Barrett, *The Gospel according to St. John: An Introduction with Commentary and Notes on the Greek Text*, 2nd ed. [Philadelphia: Westminster, 1978], 263). Some have argued for a transition as early as verse 25, though the phrase "and is now" undermines this view (e.g., Julius Wellhausen, *Das Evangelium Johannis* [Berlin: Reimer, 1908], 26).

[9] Craig S. Keener denies that there is a "problem" in the passage, arguing that ancient audiences would not have seen a dissonance between realized and future outlooks (*The Gospel of John: A Commentary*, 2 vols. [Peabody, MA: Hendricksen, 2003], 1:321–23, 652–55). This overlooks the literary dimensions of the problem. The two eschatologies are distinct enough to be encoded in different modes of speech (figurative vs. nonfigurative), leaving open the questions of why the passage shifts so abruptly between these speech modes, where the transition between them lies, and how each supports the passage's argumentation.

As Jan van der Watt writes, "The expression 'so many men, so many minds' can justly be applied to the efforts made by various scholars over several decades to solve this problem"—words no less true a quarter century later.[10] Before the 1970s, most attempts to explain the clash of eschatologies in the passage relied on one of several theories of the gospel's composition under the rubrics of tradition, source, or redaction criticism.[11] Bultmann, for one, famously credited the abrupt insertion of a future perspective in the passage to a later redactor who sought "to reconcile the dangerous statements of vv. 24f. with traditional eschatology."[12] But if the redactor sought to "reconcile" these views, why did he juxtapose them so nakedly, taking no further steps to relate and integrate them?

In more recent decades, these approaches have been displaced by a newer consensus insisting on the literary unity of 5:19–30—one built on the recognition that the passage, despite its tensive features, is extensively structured by parallelism.[13] If a redactor meant to correct the realized eschatology of the text, van der Watt asks, "why did he so crudely leave the 'obvious' eschatological tension unsolved, while he took the trouble to harmonize the passage structurally by means of parallelism?" These harmonizations hardly suggest "that [vv. 28–29] were simply forced in here by a later redactor without thinking any further."[14] This appeal to the tightly woven artistry of 5:19–30 is, nevertheless, a two-edged sword. If it is true the gospel writer has woven two perspectives into the passage with care and deliberation, it is still more difficult to understand why he has left glaring literary tensions in the text at all.

More recently, studies building on this newer consensus argue that the parallelism itself may eliminate these tensions, precisely as it implies some relationship between these eschatologies. But what is that relationship? Here the scholarship diverges yet again. In the extensive secondary literature devoted to the passage, that parallelism is purported either: (1) to affirm the complementarity of the two eschatologies,[15] (2) to configure the two into a single inaugurated, two-stage, or progressive framework,[16] (3) to support an *a minore ad maius* argument, whereby

---

[10] Van der Watt, "New Look at John 5:25–9," 73.

[11] A tradition-critical treatment of the passage appears in Brown, *Gospel according to John*, 1:220–21. M. E. Boismard's analysis depends on a reconstruction of various sources integrated into the Gospel ("L'évolution du thème eschatologique dans les traditions johanniques," *RB* 68 [1961]: 507–24, here 514–18). An extensive bibliography of redaction-critical solutions appears in Hans Christian Kammler, *Christologie und Eschatologie: Joh 5, 17–30 als Schlüsseltext johanneischer Theologie*, WUNT 126 (Tübingen: Mohr Siebeck, 2000), 188–90.

[12] Bultmann, *Gospel of John*, 261.

[13] Van der Watt, "New Look at John 5:25–9," 76.

[14] Ibid., 75–76.

[15] Tim O'Donnell, "Complementary Eschatologies in John 5:19–30," *CBQ* 70 (2008): 750–65.

[16] E.g., Josef Blank, *Krisis: Untersuchungen zur johanneischen Christologie und Eschatologie* (Freiburg im Breisgau: Lambertus, 1964), 172–82; Albert Vanhoye, "La composition de Jean 5,19–30," in *Mélanges bibliques en hommage au R. P. Béda Rigaux*, ed. Albert Descamps and André

Jesus defends his ability to give eternal life now by citing his ability to resurrect physical bodies in the future,[17] (4) to extend Jesus's interest beyond the fate of his hearers to those dead before his earthly ministry,[18] or (5) to indicate that the realized judgment requires a future "public and open demonstration,"[19] among other options.

The sheer number of these proposals betrays their common weaknesses. None is so obvious that it can command a consensus, and, though each suggests plausible relationships between realized and future eschatologies—some reflecting syntheses found in other early Christian texts—none can cite an express word of the passage in its favor. Indeed, "the gospel does not explain how the relationship between the two eschatologies works" in any passage, leaving all these views on the shakiest possible ground.[20]

## Aims

I have no intention of supplementing these attempts to reconcile the realized and future eschatologies in this passage—now numbering in the dozens—with yet another. Instead, I believe it is best simply to cut the Gordian knot they all seek to untie. Over the past half-century, no English-language contribution has critically examined the bases on which interpreters identify a shift from present to future eschatology in 5:19–30.[21] Those bases are surprisingly weak, a fact that accounts for the problems encountered by exegetes building on them. The problem is, at its core, a literary-linguistic one. Exegetes have read the imagery of 5:28–29 literally when it is, in fact, figurative.

---

de Halleux (Gembloux: Duculot, 1970), 259–74, here 272–74; John T. Carroll, "Present and Future in Fourth Gospel Eschatology," *BTB* 19 (1989): 63–69.

[17] E.g., Frey, *Die johanneische Eschatologie*, 3:389.

[18] Van der Watt, "New Look at John 5:25–9," 71–86; D. Moody Smith, *John*, ANTC (Nashville: Abingdon, 1999), 138.

[19] Andrew T. Lincoln, *The Gospel according to Saint John*, BNTC (London: Continuum, 2005), 205.

[20] Harold W. Attridge, "From Discord Rises Meaning: Resurrection Motifs in the Fourth Gospel," in *The Resurrection of Jesus in the Gospel of John*, ed. Craig R. Koester and Reimund Bieringer, WUNT 222 (Tübingen: Mohr Siebeck, 2008), 1–19, here 6.

[21] In the same period, two German-language studies have defended a realized-eschatological interpretation of the passage: Alois Stimpfle, *Blinde sehen: Die Eschatologie im traditionsgeschichtlichen Prozeß des Johannesevangeliums*, BZNW 57 (Berlin: de Gruyter: 1990), 188–225; and Kammler, *Christologie und Eschatologie*. This essay incorporates and refines arguments from these texts, subsuming them under the robustly literary-linguistic approach preferred here—one informed by research subsequent to the "linguistic turn" in Johannine studies and "rediscovery of Johannine imagery" (Zimmermann, "Imagery in John," 6). One English-language study has also suggested a realized-eschatological reading of the passage, but only in passing: Jeffrey A. Trumbower, *Born from Above: The Anthropology of the Gospel of John*, HUT 29 (Tübingen: Mohr Siebeck, 1992), 64–65, 136 n. 6.

The conventional reading of the passage identifies several inconsistencies in the imagery and language of 5:24–25 and 5:28–29 and interprets these as evidence of a shift from figurative to literal speech. I believe that these inconsistencies are better explained as shifts within figurative speech. Recent studies of metaphor in John highlight the fluidity with which the Johannine Jesus adjusts his imagery from line to line within larger patterns of "repetition," "variation," and "amplification" in his discourses.[22] The evangelist, van der Watt writes, "does not feel himself bound to the formal structure of an image" but often "violates" and "moves beyond the logical boundaries of the imagery" in consecutive lines of speech.[23] "As soon as an image has served its purpose, it is abandoned, changed, or adapted" at the service of developing discourse aims.[24] The inconsistencies across 5:24–25 and 5:28–29 fit within this pattern of use.

In 5:24–25, the Johannine Jesus uses resurrection imagery to communicate the idea that the one who receives his word receives eternal life. In 5:28–29, in turn, Jesus creatively develops, reworks, and redeploys the same metaphorical vehicle to capture a more expansive idea: the same word that gives eternal life to some ("resurrection of life") can bring condemnation to others ("resurrection of judgment"). In this reading, there is no clash of eschatologies in the passage and, thus, no problem for the exegete to resolve. The entire passage represents a single, continuous exposition of the gospel's realized eschatology.[25]

## II. The Case against Figurative Speech in 5:28–29

I begin by revisiting the arguments in favor of reading a break in figurative speech at or before 5:28–29. Those arguments can be consolidated under five headings:[26]

---

[22] Major works on "repetition," "variation," and "amplification" in John include Thomas Popp, *Grammatik des Geistes: Literarische Kunst und theologische Konzeption in Johannes 3 und 6*, ABIG 3 (Berlin: Evangelische Verlagsanstalt, 2001); and Gilbert van Belle, Michael Labahn, and Petrus J. Maritz, eds., *Repetitions and Variations in the Fourth Gospel: Style, Text, Interpretation*, BETL 223 (Leuven: Peeters, 2009).

[23] Van der Watt, *Family of the King*, 146.

[24] Ibid., 144–46.

[25] This thesis holds even if future eschatology is present elsewhere in John, as it certainly is in the appendix (21:22). Further, this thesis does not eliminate other apparent clashes of eschatology in the gospel. Up to five more appear in the "last day" sayings of 6:39, 40, 44, 54; 12:48—texts that must remain outside this discussion for reasons of space and the unique challenges they present. Nevertheless, Jaime Clark-Soles has recently argued in favor of a figurative and realized-eschatological reading of these sayings as well ("'I Will Raise [Whom?] Up on the Last Day': Anthropology as a Feature of Johannine Eschatology," in *New Currents through John: A Global Perspective*, ed. Francisco Lozada Jr. and Tom Thatcher, RBS 54 [Atlanta: Society of Biblical Literature, 2006], 29–53, here 47, 51 n. 8).

[26] This list compresses five of six arguments presented by Schnackenburg to support the

1. Different conceptions of resurrection
2. Image of "tombs"
3. Intertextualities with Daniel
4. Excision of καὶ νῦν ἐστιν
5. Emphasis on works

As we will see, most of these features reflect some misunderstanding of the nature of metaphor or of the Fourth Gospel's use of metaphor in particular.

## Different Conceptions of Resurrection

The first argument brings the inconsistent imagery of the passage into central focus. Although 5:24–25 and 28–29 share numerous figures in common (hearing, voice, life, death, judgment), they present these in slightly different configurations. In 5:25, only some of the dead "hear" the voice of Jesus, and those who do share the same destiny: "those who hear will live" (v. 25). This text depicts a selective or single resurrection of the righteous alone. In 5:28–29, by contrast, "all" the dead "hear his voice, and come forth," but whereas some enter "life," others enter "judgment." This text depicts a general or double resurrection. Since "[vv.] 28f. do not agree with what has gone before," Bultmann argues, "it is quite wrong to give a spiritualizing interpretation of vv. 28f. in terms of vv. 24f."[27]

On the one hand, this argument highlights a crucial difference between 5:25 and 5:28–29. Although these texts share numerous expressions, one cannot (or cannot easily) coalesce them into a single, consistent image. But does the end of a particular image necessarily indicate the end of figurative speech altogether? Over the past three decades, studies of the use of metaphor in spoken and written discourse have called attention to the fact that speakers "seldom produce a neatly constructed figure in a single utterance."[28] Metaphors, after all, are selective, highlighting only one aspect of a given topic at a time. In order to capture the complexity of a topic and highlight more than one of its aspects, it is often necessary to introduce more than one metaphor into discourse.[29] Thus, metaphors in talk or

---

claim that "27b–29 introduces an alien element" (*Gospel according to St. John*, 2:114–15). It includes an additional argument (c) introduced by Schnackenburg (113).

[27] Bultmann, *Gospel of John*, 261 n. 8.

[28] Lynne Cameron, "Metaphor Shifting in the Dynamics of Talk," in *Confronting Metaphor in Use: An Applied Linguistic Approach*, ed. Maria Sophia Zanotto, Lynne Cameron, and Marilda C. Cavalcanti, Pragmatics and Beyond NS 173 (Philadelphia: John Benjamins, 2008), 45–62, here 60. Although Cameron's work focuses on spoken discourse, she connects her data to similar formations in written discourse (45–46). See also Lynne J. Cameron and Juurd H. Stelma, "Metaphor Clusters in Discourse," *Journal of Applied Linguistics* 1 (2004): 107–36, here 108.

[29] George Lakoff and Mark Johnson, *Metaphors We Live By* (Chicago: University of Chicago Press, 1980), 95–96.

text tend to occur in "clusters" or "bursts," generally consisting of "explanations of a single topic."[30]

In turn, the complementary metaphors united in these clusters are often developed from earlier metaphors through a dynamic process called "metaphor shifting."[31] Speakers frequently adjust or adapt images already introduced into talk or text to clarify their meaning or to elucidate difficult or abstract concepts.[32] They may elaborate a particular metaphor ("vehicle explication"), alter its imagery and language ("vehicle relexicalization"), introduce points of contrast and antonyms ("vehicle contrast"), or recycle earlier images used to describe different topics ("vehicle redeployment"). What results from this process of reuse and adaptation are strings of closely related and interconnected metaphors.[33]

Metaphors in these clusters are not often "consistent"; that is, they cannot always coalesce into a single image.[34] After all, if a single image could capture a topic in its entirety, there would be no need to introduce further metaphors into the discourse. Nevertheless, these metaphors do meet George Lakoff and Mark Johnson's criteria of "coherent" metaphors for the subtle ways in which they "fit together" in vehicle and/or topic.[35]

In light of this research, it should come as little surprise that the Fourth Gospel boasts numerous examples of inconsistent but coherent metaphor clusters, all stemming from the forms of "metaphor shifting" outlined above. As Ruben Zimmermann notes, "The connection and superimposition of various images within a small number of verses"—including "contradictory representations"—is a regular feature of Johannine figurative speech.[36] In the Fourth Gospel,

---

[30] Cameron and Stelma, "Metaphor Clusters," 107–36. On metaphor "clusters" or "bursts," see Daniel P. Corts and Howard R. Pollio, "Spontaneous Production of Figurative Language and Gesture in College Lectures," *Metaphor and Symbol* 14 (1999): 81–100; Daniel P. Corts and Kristina Meyers, "Conceptual Clusters in Figurative Language Production," *Journal of Psycholinguistic Research* 31 (2002): 391–408; Lynne J. Cameron, *Metaphor in Educational Discourse*, Advances in Applied Linguistics (London: Continuum, 2003), 106, 120–23.

[31] See Cameron, "Metaphor Shifting," 45–62. Cameron connects metaphor shifting to the creation of metaphor clusters (46). Goatly, who illustrates the same process in literary works, prefers the expression "metaphor interplay" (*Language of Metaphors*, 271–303).

[32] Cameron and Stelma, "Metaphor Clusters," 134–35.

[33] Cameron, "Metaphor Shifting," 48–61.

[34] The distinction between "consistent" and "coherent" metaphors is developed in Lakoff and Johnson, *Metaphors We Live By*, 41–45.

[35] Ibid., 44, 95–96. As an example of inconsistent metaphors that are, nonetheless, coherent metaphors occurring in the same running discourse, consider: "We're at a crossroads"; "We can't turn back now"; "We're stuck"; "We've gotten off track" (44–45).

[36] Zimmermann, "Imagery in John," 30–32. This pattern suits the gospel's broader technique of redundancy, in which a concept is communicated "as many times as possible, in *different ways*" (Wayne A. Meeks, "The Man from Heaven in Johannine Sectarianism," *JBL* 91 [1972]: 44–72, here 48, https://doi.org/10.2307/3262920).

however, this technique of figurative speech is generalized and elaborated well beyond conventional discourse aims. Metaphor clustering is, instead, a "conscious principle of design" in the gospel, carried to extremes to imbue Jesus's speech with an elusive, paradoxical character.[37]

Examples of this practice appear in nearly every discourse in John. In the Bread of Life discourse (6:32–59), Jesus relexicalizes an opening claim that the Father "gives … the true bread from heaven" into the claim that Jesus himself "will give" his own "flesh" as "bread" (6:32, 51). In the final discourse, Jesus tells his disciples that he will travel on the "way" to the Father's house (14:3–4), before redeploying the same imagery to cast himself as that "way" (14:6):

> "And you know the way where I am going." Thomas said to him, "Lord, we do not know where you are going; how can we know the way?" Jesus said to him, "I am the way, and the truth, and the life; no one comes to the Father but by me." (John 14:3–6)

Most startling of all is the Good Shepherd discourse (10:1–18), in which Jesus is both "the door of the sheep" (v. 7) and, quite jarringly, "the shepherd" "who enters by the door" (vv. 2, 11). As the discourse continues, Jesus moves sharply back and forth between these dissonant images:[38]

> [Shepherd:] "Truly, truly, I say to you … the one who enters by the gate is the shepherd of the sheep…. [Gate:] Truly, truly, I say to you, I am the gate of the sheep. [Shepherd:] All who came before me are thieves and robbers, but the sheep did not heed them. [Gate:] I am the gate; if anyone enters by me, he will be saved…. [Shepherd:] I am the good shepherd. The good shepherd lays down his life for the sheep. (10:2, 7b–9, 11)

This "paradoxical … mixture of metaphors" grows still more complex as Jesus extends the imagery in various directions to incorporate figures for his opponents. The end result weaves no fewer than "five" clashing but "interrelated images, flowing one after the other with abruptness and unexpectedness."[39] In these "interlocking, overloaded, multi-faceted, yet curiously focused images," Harold Attridge

---

[37] Zimmermann, "Imagery in John, 32; Stibbe, "Elusive Christ," 19–38; Robert Kysar, "Johannine Metaphor—Meaning and Function: A Literary Case Study of John 10:1–8," *Semeia* 53 (1991): 81–111, here 99–101.

[38] Unsurprisingly, these sharp transitions have attracted redaction-critical explanations like those proposed for 5:24–29. See, e.g., Bultmann, *Gospel of John*, 359–60; John Painter, "Tradition, History, and Interpretation in John 10," in *The Shepherd Discourse of John 10 and Its Context: Studies by Members of the Johannine Writings Seminar*, ed. Johannes Beutler and Robert T. Fortna, SNTSMS 67 (Cambridge: Cambridge University Press, 1991), 53–74, here 57; Urban C. von Wahlde, *The Gospel and Letters of John*, 3 vols., ECC (Grand Rapids: Eerdmans, 2010), 2:451–69.

[39] Kysar, "Johannine Metaphor," 99, 101.

recognizes a "'cubist' aesthetic," which represents ideas from multiple viewpoints "like the facets of a gem."[40]

In light of these examples, we have no reason to assume that a strictly realized-eschatological 5:19–30 would have uniform and consistent imagery from line to line. On the contrary, we should be ready to see the passage make several adjustments to its resurrection imagery, representing its realized eschatology from multiple viewpoints. In fact, I would argue that the imagery of the earlier verses in the passage is already dynamic and tensive in ways not appreciated by the conventional reading of the text. Consider the imagery of 5:24 more carefully:

> Truly, truly, I say to you, the one who hears my word and believes the one who sent me has eternal life; that one does not come into judgment, but has passed from death to life.

At first glance, the language of the verse is close to another Johannine text, 1 John 3:14, that certainly envisions a single resurrection of the righteous alone:

> We know that we have passed out of death into life.... The one who does not love remains in death.

The claim in 5:24 that "the one who hears my word ... does not come into judgment" sits uneasily in a single-resurrection image, however. If some of the dead are excused from judgment, how will the rest enter into it? No solution within a single-resurrection framework is entirely adequate. The reason for this is that the image of the dead coming into judgment is derived from double-resurrection schemes inspired by LXX Dan 12:2–3.

On the one hand, it is possible that the conventional reading has misinterpreted the imagery of 5:24, which should instead be analyzed as a double-resurrection image parallel to 5:28–29. In this reading, the passage "from death to life" in verse 24 would correspond not so much to resurrection in general as to "the resurrection of life" in particular, by which those who believe avoid "judgment." Alternatively, one could read verse 24 as a blend of single- and double-resurrection imagery. In either case, the interpreter has all the more reason to be sensitive to the shifting and intertwined imagery in the discourse, including at least one strand built on the idea of a double resurrection. More importantly, the interpreter should recognize double-resurrection imagery as a possible vehicle for communicating the gospel's realized eschatology.

### *Image of "Tombs"*

At its core, this second argument claims that the language of 5:28–29 is simply too concrete to support a metaphorical reading. Whereas 5:24–25 speaks of "the

---

[40] Harold W. Attridge, "The Cubist Principle in Johannine Imagery: John and the Reading of Images in Contemporary Platonism," in Frey, van der Watt, and Zimmermann, *Imagery in the Gospel of John*, 47–60, here 49–50.

one" in "death" (θανάτου [v. 24]) or "the dead" (οἱ νεκροί [v. 25]), 5:28–29 speaks of "all who are in the tombs" (πάντες οἱ ἐν τοῖς μνημείοις). This mention of "tombs" is said to resist a metaphorical interpretation, so that the text focuses on the "physically dead," that is, those who "in every human way ... should be regarded as being dead."[41]

If a shift between metaphorical and literal planes of meaning occurs in the passage, it can hardly be derived from a shift from "the dead" to "all who are in the tombs." Indeed, if contemporary studies of metaphor can shed any light on our discussion, it is the insight that there is simply no such thing as a language too concrete or vivid to be used in a figurative sense. On the contrary, any word, phrase, or image "can be a metaphor if its context makes it such and if its speaker intends it as such."[42] This is because "metaphor is a feature of language use or 'discourse.'"[43] It is not a function of individual words but emerges as speakers bring these words into relation with other words.[44]

In this instance, the context points to a metaphorical sense for "all who are in the tombs" since the phrase is synonymous with two phrases used figuratively only a few lines before—"the dead" in 5:25 and "the one" in "death" in 5:24. Variants of the same expressions are set in parallel in LXX Isa 26:19, a possible intertext for this passage: "The dead will rise, and those in the tombs will be raised."[45] More importantly, they are also juxtaposed in the account of the resurrection of Lazarus —a miracle Jesus presents as a "sign" of his realized-eschatological power to give life (cf. 11:25–27): "he called Lazarus out of the tomb and raised him from the dead" (12:17).[46]

The substitution of one phrase for another, then, reflects a strategy we have already discussed: vehicle relexicalization. Examples of this practice appear earlier in the same discourse. In 5:24–25, a reference to "the word" of the Son is exchanged for the metonymic "voice" of the Son, and a reference to "the one" in "death" is exchanged for a reference to "the dead":

> Truly, truly, I say to you, the one who hears my word and believes in the one who sent me has eternal life; that one does not come into judgment, but has passed from death to life. (5:24)

> Truly, truly, I say to you, the hour is coming, and is now, when the dead will hear the voice of the Son of God, and those who hear will live. (5:25)

---

[41] Van der Watt, "New Look at John 5:25–9," 72.

[42] Jonathan Charteris-Black, *Corpus Approaches to Critical Metaphor Analysis* (New York: Palgrave Macmillian, 2004), 35.

[43] Jonathan Charteris-Black, *Politicians and Rhetoric: The Persuasive Power of Metaphor* (New York: Palgrave Macmillan, 2005), 31.

[44] Ibid.

[45] Stimpfle, *Blinde Sehen*, 89–90; Kammler, *Christologie und Eschatologie*, 212. On the relationship between 5:28–29 and LXX Isa 26:19, see Frey, *Die johanneische Eschatologie*, 3:382.

[46] The raising of Lazarus is, in effect, a performed metaphor of the realized-eschatological resurrection (cf. Bultmann, *Gospel of John*, 405–9).

Nothing about the shift from "the dead" to "all those in the tombs" is out of character with these earlier shifts.

To the extent that the relexicalization of "the dead" to "all who are in the tombs" makes Jesus's speech more vivid, it reflects another documented discourse pattern in the gospel—namely, the Johannine Jesus's tendency to intensify the vividness of his metaphors as his discourses continue. The best illustration of this pattern appears in the Bread of Life discourse (6:22–59). In that passage, Jesus responds to mounting opposition to his message by intensifying the provocative character of his figurative speech (6:41, 43, 52, 66).[47] At the outset of the discourse, Jesus describes himself as "the bread of life," foregrounding the idea that one must "believe" in him to receive eternal life. As the Jews increasingly "murmur" against him, however (6:41, 43), he relexicalizes this earlier metaphor, converting it into the more vivid, literalizing, and opaque assertion that one must "chew" his "flesh" and "drink" his "blood" to receive "eternal life":

| 6:35, 40 | I am the bread of life. The one who comes to me will never be hungry, and the one who believes in me will never be thirsty.... For this is the will of my Father, that everyone who sees the Son and believes in him should have eternal life.... |
| --- | --- |
| 6:51 | If anyone eats of this bread, he/she will live forever. |
| 6:54 | The one who chews[48] my flesh and drinks my blood has eternal life, and I will raise that one up on the last day. |

By imbuing his figurative speech with a more concrete and crude quality, Jesus not only provokes and alienates his skeptical audience further; he also compounds their incomprehension. The progression from less opaque to more opaque statements embodies the claim that, as individuals persist in unbelief, their understanding of spiritual truths is increasingly darkened (9:39).

A similar dynamic may be in play in the present passage, culminating in the especially vivid and opaque language of 5:28–29. It is perhaps no coincidence that these verses begin with a clear sign of mounting opposition to Jesus in the injunction: "do not be astonished at this [μὴ θαυμάζετε τοῦτο]." In the Fourth Gospel, θαυμάζειν is never "used of the attitude of believers, of disciples, or of the community" (3:7; 7:15, 21).[49] Rather, it connotes "not merely some kind of surprise but rather the reaction of unbelief."[50]

---

[47] As G. R. Beasley-Murray writes, "the development perceptible in vv. 35, 40, 50, 51" is "the image of eating the bread of life increasing in intensity" (*John*, WBC 36 [Dallas: Word, 2002], 95). Obviously, this analysis reflects a nonsacramental interpretation of John 6, which I share.

[48] This translation captures the lexical and, arguably, semantic contrast of φάγῃ and τρώγων. A semantic contrast would represent another example of intensification.

[49] Georg Bertram, "θαῦμα κτλ.," *TDNT* 3:27–42, here 40.

[50] Jörg Frey, "Eschatology in the Johannine Circle," in *Theology and Christology in the Fourth*

In context, Jesus's admonition alerts the reader to the negative reception of his discourse up to that point by "the Jews." It is against this emerging opposition that we can best understand the discourse's next turn. Reacting to the astonishment of his hearers, Jesus relexicalizes the metaphorical vehicle he introduced earlier along a similar arc as John 6, adopting more concrete language ("all who are in the tombs") and decreasing the transparency of his speech (e.g., dropping references to "belief").

*Intertextualities with Daniel*

A related argument cites intertextualities with Daniel after 5:27—especially the reference to the "Son of Man" (5:27b; cf. Dan 7:13) and the image of a twofold resurrection (5:28–29; cf. LXX Dan 12:1–3)—as evidence that the Fourth Evangelist intends to import the future eschatology of Daniel into these verses.[51] The problem with this view is that the entirety of the gospel's realized eschatology emerges from a reuse and reinterpretation of stock apocalyptic images from various texts, especially Daniel.[52] Points of contact with these images are to be expected and are hardly evidence that Jesus is speaking literally in the text (a claim that falls once again into the fallacy that individual images can be too literal to be extended in a metaphorical direction).

Ironically, the very intertextualities cited in this argument demonstrate this point. In John, the phrase "Son of Man" does not always correlate with future eschatology but is also encountered in realized-eschatological passages, where it is used interchangeably with "Son" and "Son of God" (3:13–21).[53] Similarly, we have already seen 5:24 partially transpose the double-resurrection imagery of LXX Dan 12:2–3 onto the realized-eschatological plane.

---

*Gospel: Essays by the Members of the SNTS Johannine Writings Seminar*, ed. Gilbert van Belle, Jan G. van der Watt, and Petrus J. Maritz, BETL 184 (Leuven: Leuven University Press, 2005), 47–82, here 77. Jesus issues a similar admonition to Nicodemus, who ultimately falls short of belief (μὴ θαυμάσῃς, 3:7).

[51] E.g., Schnackenburg, *Gospel according to St. John*, 2:113–15.

[52] The passage reinterprets the Danielic images of the Son of Man receiving divine authority (5:21–23, 26–27; cf. LXX Dan 7:13–14), and the "hour" of resurrection (5:25; cf. LXX Dan 1:2–3), along realized-eschatological lines (Stefanos Mihalios, *The Danielic Eschatological Hour in the Johannine Literature*, LNTS 436 [New York: T&T Clark, 2011] 4 n. 11, 106–15).

[53] J. Ramsey Michaels, *The Gospel of John*, NICNT (Grand Rapids, MI: Eerdmans, 2010), 319. Some writers try to distinguish this instance of "Son of Man" (5:27) from others by noting that the phrase is anarthrous here, as in LXX Dan 7:13 (e.g., Schnackenburg, *Gospel according to St. John*, 2:113). In LXX Dan 7:13, however, "son of man" is anarthrous as an indefinite phrase ("a son of man"). In 5:27, the phrase is anarthrous again but clearly definite. In this case, the lack of the article is best explained by Colwell's rule (so Michaels, *Gospel of John*, 320).

*Excision of* καὶ νῦν ἐστιν

The fourth argument—perhaps the most frequently cited—draws a contrast between the expressions, "the hour is coming and is now" (ἔρχεται ὥρα καὶ νῦν ἐστιν) in 5:25 and the shorter "the hour is coming" (ἔρχεται ὥρα) in 5:28–29. The longer formula unites two propositions in a tensive syntax: "the hour is coming" | "[the hour] is now." Although interpretations of this formula differ, it is generally agreed that the incorporation of καὶ νῦν ἐστιν emphasizes the immediacy or imminence of the "hour" on at least some plane of fulfillment.[54] By contrast, the same phrase's omission in 5:28–29 is thought to eliminate any hint of the hour's proximity. Where "the words *for a time* (lit. 'hour', *hōra*) *is coming* are no longer qualified by 'and now is,'" D. A. Carson writes, "the future, final apocalyptic resurrection is in view."[55]

The problem with this argument is that the two expressions are not contrastive in the only other passage in John to use both in close proximity, 4:21–23, but interchangeable. There, both refer to the same realized-eschatological "hour":[56]

> Jesus said to her, "Woman, believe me, the hour is coming [ἔρχεται ὥρα] when you will worship the Father neither on this mountain nor in Jerusalem. You worship what you do not know; we worship what we know, for salvation is from the Jews. But the hour is coming, and is now [ἔρχεται ὥρα καὶ νῦν ἐστιν], when the true worshipers will worship the Father in spirit and in truth, for such the Father seeks to worship him. (4:21–23)

That the same "hour" is in view in both verses is clear, first, from the fact that the two verses form a single, coherent idea when read together: a time is materializing when worship "in/on" (ἐν) Mount Gerizim and "in" (ἐν) Jerusalem will be supplanted by worship "in" (ἐν) spirit and truth.[57] It is also indicated in the recurrence

---

[54] Bultmann collapses the formula into the present (*Gospel of John*, 190; also Kammler, *Christologie und Eschatologie*, 176). Brown sees "an inchoative or anticipated effect" in it (*Gospel according to John*, 1:518). Beasley-Murray, by contrast, claims that it "brackets future and present without eliminating either" (*John*, 62). Frey defends this view on strictly syntactic grounds (*Die johanneische Eschatologie*, 2:144–46), failing to recognize that the meaning of a paradox is not transparent in its syntax. Instead, paradoxes generally resolve themselves "into a consistent proposition at some higher level," that is, at a pragmatic level (Neal R. Novick, "How Paradox Means," *Poetics Today* 10 [1989]: 551–62, here 551).

[55] D. A. Carson, *The Gospel according to John*, PilNTC (Grand Rapids: Eerdmans, 1991), 258.

[56] Kammler, *Christologie und Eschatologie*, 175–76.

[57] Michaels, *Gospel of John*, 851. Ernst Haenchen's suggestion that the "hour" of 4:21 is fulfilled not in the coming of the Spirit but in the future destruction of the Jerusalem temple is unconvincing (*John: A Commentary on the Gospel of John*, trans. Robert W. Funk, 2 vols., Hermeneia [Philadelphia: Fortress, 1984], 1:222). First, this reading disrupts the unity of the Johannine "hour," an unnecessary consequence of all future-eschatological interpretations of 5:28–29. Second, the text speaks of ongoing worship on Mount Gerizim despite the destruction of the Samaritan temple in the Hasmonean period. In this case, one must explain (1) why the destruction of the Jerusalem temple, and not the destruction of the Samaritan temple, should represent the

of ἔρχεται ὥρα at the beginning of 4:23. Elsewhere in the gospel, Jesus uses repetition anaphorically, to resume a discussion from a previous line (cf. 3:3, 5).

The "hour" Jesus references is, of course, none other than the "hour" par excellence in the gospel, that is, the hour of his departure and glorification, when the Spirit comes. It is, after all, impossible to "worship in spirit and in truth" before the coming of "the Spirit," who guides believers "into all truth" (16:13).[58] In this case, then, the progression of phrases leads the reader from an anticipation of the future hour (ἔρχεται ὥρα) to a recognition of its immediacy (ἔρχεται ὥρα καὶ νῦν ἐστιν)—similar to Brown's claim that the longer phrase has "an inchoative or anticipated effect."[59] Jesus clarifies that the hour of judgment he previously described as "coming" is, in fact, "now" taking shape. It is not fully realized in the period when "the Spirit had not been given" (7:30, 39), but it is taking root in the preaching of Jesus and human responses to that preaching. In a similar vein, Jesus speaks of the imminent moment when the disciples will abandon him through the related phrase in 16:32: "the hour is coming, and indeed it has come" (ἔρχεται ὥρα καὶ ἐλήλυθεν).

If the two expressions are not contrastive in chapter 4, there is every reason to believe that neither are they in chapter 5. In 5:25, Jesus begins by speaking of the coming hour in the future tense but stresses its immediacy ("the hour is coming, and is now"). In 5:28–29, Jesus simply resumes his earlier discussion of the "hour." Here, the free alternation of the longer and shorter formulae may reflect an attempt to (1) evoke their alternation in 4:21–23, (2) avoid repetition for stylistic reasons, or (3) avoid repeating the more cumbersome phrase. All three options fall under the rubric of vehicle relexicalizations.

The obvious comparisons between 4:21–23 and 5:25–29 are so damaging to the conventional reading that some writers feel the need to distance the texts. J. Ramsey Michaels, for one, concedes that the longer and shorter expressions are "used interchangeably" in 4:21, 23 but insists that they are "differentiated" in 5:19–30 since they are presented in a different order in the latter passage.[60] This solution, meant to salvage the original appeal to καὶ νῦν ἐστιν, actually empties it of its force. If the two expressions are contrastive only when they are placed in a certain relative order, they are not intrinsically contrastive. In short, Michaels concedes that the mere presence or absence of καὶ νῦν ἐστιν is insufficient to distinguish between the hours cited in the texts.

---

end of worship on a given site, and (2) when the evangelist imagines worship will cease on Mount Gerizim. A better approach recognizes that the transition from localized to spiritual worship is dependent not on the presence or absence of holy sites but on the establishment of the Spirit-filled community, which "displaces the Temple as the locus of the divine dwelling" (Mary L. Coloe, *God Dwells with Us: Temple Symbolism in the Fourth Gospel* [Collegeville, MN: Liturgical Press, 2001], 14).

[58] Clark-Soles, "'I Will Raise [Whom?] Up,'" 35.
[59] Brown, *Gospel according to John*, 1:518.
[60] Michaels, *Gospel of John*, 321 n. 71, 851; Frey, *Die johanneische Eschatologie*, 2:146.

## Emphasis on Works

The final argument continues many of the concerns of the first. In 5:24, Jesus claims that one must "believe" to receive "life." In 5:28–29, however, his emphasis falls on deeds: "those who have done good" enter "the resurrection of life," while "those who have done evil" enter the "resurrection of judgment." Citing this difference, some interpreters claim that the passage must have two judgments in view: one based on belief (realized), and one based on works (future).[61]

This dichotomization of belief and works is completely foreign to the gospel, however. In other discourses, both belief and works are linked to realized-eschatological judgment since, in Johannine thought, good works precede and predispose one to belief, just as evil works precede and predispose one to unbelief (3:20–21, 7:17).[62] Thus, in 3:18–21, Jesus shifts abruptly between references to belief and references to works when describing the judgment taking shape through his coming into the world:

> The one who believes in him is not judged; the one who does not believe is judged already.... And this is the judgment: that the light has come into the world, and human beings loved darkness rather than light because their deeds were evil.... But the one who does what is true comes to the light, that it may be clearly seen that his or her deeds have been wrought in God. (3:18–21)

Far from distinguishing 5:19–29 from other realized-eschatological passages, then, the introduction of "good deeds" and "evil deeds" in verses 28–29 conforms the passage more closely to them. In this final instance of vehicle relexicalization, we can appreciate one of the primary advantages of the gospel's multifaceted imagery—its ability to facilitate "connections with several other important images and themes within the Gospel."[63]

## III. Reading 5:28–29 as Figurative Speech

Up to this point, I have argued that there is no reason why 5:28–29 cannot be read figuratively, that is, as realized eschatology. But what would such a reading look like? How would we interpret its individual elements? To answer this question,

---

[61] Von Wahlde, *Gospel and Letters of John*, 1:286; van der Watt, "New Look at John 5:25–9," 80–84.

[62] J. Ramsey Michaels, "Baptism and Conversion in John: A Particular Baptist Reading," in *Baptism, the New Testament and the Church: Historical and Contemporary Studies in Honour in R. E. O. White*, ed. Stanley E. Porter and Anthony R. Cross, JSNTSup 171 (Sheffield: Sheffield Academic, 1999), 136–56, here 145. This explanation is superior to Kammler's argument that works appear in 5:28–29 as the products of belief or unbelief (*Christologie und Eschatologie*, 213–14).

[63] Attridge, "Cubist Principle," 3.

we must consider how other realized-eschatological texts correlate the destinies of "life" and "judgment" with human responses to the word of Jesus.[64]

As first developed in the dialogue with Nicodemus (3:1–21), the gospel's realized eschatology centers on the claim that the judgment of the world and the distribution of eschatological rewards occur as individuals respond to Jesus's message (3:19, 12:31).[65] The one who receives the words of Jesus and "believes ... is not judged" (3:18, 21), that is, condemned (cf. 3:19, 5:29, 16:11). Instead, by embracing these words of "life" (cf. 6:68, 12:49–50), that individual receives the Spirit, who imparts "eternal life" (6:63; 3:15–16, 36). By contrast, the one who hears Jesus's sayings and does not keep them has the "word" of Jesus as "judge" (3:36, 12:47–48). That one, "who does not obey the Son," does "not see life" (3:36) but "is judged already, because he or she has not believed" (3:18–19).

The Johannine Jesus adjusts earlier metaphors of resurrection in the passage to encode all these ideas in 5:28–29. The image of the Son speaking to the dead and raising them to alternate fates of "life" and "judgment" symbolizes the effects of Jesus's preaching. Depending on how humans receive the word Jesus speaks, they either receive eternal life or stand condemned.

| 5:28–29 | Paraphrase |
| --- | --- |
| Do not be astonished at this | Do not react in unbelief to what I have just said, |
| for the hour is coming | for the climactic "hour" of my departure is coming |
| when all who are in the tombs | when all the spiritually dead |
| will hear his voice and come forth | will enter their realized-eschatological reward through the word I preach. |
| those who have done good to the resurrection of life | The righteous will receive eternal life through that word, |
| and those who have done evil to the resurrection of judgment. | but the wicked will be condemned because of it. |

---

[64] This reading is mostly consistent with other realized-eschatological interpretations of the text (cf. Stimpfle, *Blinde Sehen*, 75–93; Kammler, *Christologie und Eschatologie*, 188–225; Trumbower, *Born from Above*, 64–65). The consistency of these readings stands in stark contrast to the many solutions to the "eschatological headache" summarized earlier.

[65] R. Alan Culpepper, "Realized Eschatology in the Experience of the Johannine Community," in Koester and Bieringer, *Resurrection of Jesus in the Gospel of John*, 253–76, here 265.

*"Do not be astonished at this ..."* At the outset, Jesus admonishes his readers against unbelief. This admonishment marks a shift in tone in the passage. Jesus moves from earlier, optimistic images of his word giving life (5:24–25) to the idea that his word can also bring condemnation (5:28–29).

*"... for the hour is coming when ..."* Through the expression ἔρχεται ὥρα, Jesus resumes his discussion of the "hour" from 5:25. As in 4:21–23, this "hour" is precisely the "hour" of the departure of Jesus, culminating in the coming of the Spirit (12:23, 13:1, 16:7). This "hour," which at this point in the narrative "has not yet come" (2:4), is the climactic time of judgment when eschatological rewards are distributed. It is, on the one hand, the time when Jesus definitively "draws all people to" himself (12:32), so that those who receive his word may "come" and have life through the Spirit (5:40, 6:35). One cannot possess life before receiving the Spirit, since it is "the Spirit who gives life" (6:44, 63). "The hour" is also the time when the world is definitively condemned (12:31), precisely as the Spirit prosecutes and convicts the world (16:8–11; cf. 8:46).[66]

*"... all who are in the tombs ..."* The adjective "all" (πάντες) affirms the universal impact of this "hour" (cf. "when I am lifted up, I will draw all people to myself"; 12:23).

*"... will hear his voice ..."* The idea that the preaching of Jesus produces divergent eschatological outcomes is aptly captured in the image of the dead hearing the "voice" of the Son with two different results. In this instance, the writer uses the verb "to hear" (ἀκούω) in a subtly different way than in 5:25, aligned with a different use of the verb in John. In certain texts, hearing is an active response to Jesus's summons, with the sense "to heed" or "to embrace." Only the righteous "hear" in this sense: "The one who is of God hears the words of God; the reason why you do not hear them is that you are not of God" (8:47; cf. 10:27). This usage is the one represented in 5:25: "those who hear [the Son] will live." In other texts, however, hearing refers only to the simple exposure to Jesus's words. Both the righteous and unrighteous "hear" the word of Jesus in this sense, albeit with different results. The former embrace the word and the latter reject it: "If anyone hears my sayings and does not keep them ... the word that I have spoken will be that one's judge" (12:47–48). This second use of "to hear" resonates with the image of 5:28, in which the dead "hear, and come forth" with two different results: life or judgment. This subtle redeployment of the verb "to hear," then, suits the writer's pattern of exploiting polysemy in other texts, through the rhetorical device of antanaclasis.[67]

*"... and come forth ... to the resurrection of life, and ... judgment"* The realized destinies of life and judgment are consciously taken up in images of a "resurrection

---

[66] Hugo Méndez, "'Night' and 'Day' in John 9:4–5," *NTS* 61 (2015): 468–81.
[67] Cf., e.g., πνεῦμα in 3:8.

to life" and a "resurrection of judgment." Jesus's word provokes a response in all human beings, resulting in life for some (8:51–52, 3:21) and condemnation for others (3:20). The image of a "resurrection of judgment," in which the dead rise at the word only to fall again, finds an interesting parallel in the gospel's light–darkness metaphorical complex. There, the world, previously in darkness, enjoys a fleeting experience of "light" in the presence of Jesus before descending again into darkness (3:19, 9:5, 12:35).[68]

### IV. The Case for Figurative Speech in 5:28–29

As I see it, the above reading is not only plausible; it is, in fact, the intended one. In place of the earlier arguments against a figurative reading of 5:28–29, I offer five positive reasons why this reading should be preferred:

1. Continuity with 5:19–27
2. Seamless integration into 5:19–27
3. Illustration of the realized judgment
4. Continuity with 5:30
5. Conformity to other realized-eschatological sayings

#### *Continuity with 5:19–27*

As noted earlier, a particular image can become a metaphor "if its context makes it such."[69] The context of 5:28–29 points directly toward a metaphorical reading of these verses, which (1) border clustering metaphors, (2) share the basic imagery of all constituent metaphors within that cluster, (3) make no more drastic adjustments to that imagery than other metaphors in the cluster, and (4) share the incipit of one metaphor in the cluster ("for the hour is coming," 5:25). Even the central image of the verses—a twofold resurrection—is transposed to the figurative plane in the preceding verses (5:24). There is every reason, then, to interpret these verses within the matrix of figurative speech in which they are embedded.

#### *Seamless Integration into 5:19–27*

Interpreters have struggled to isolate the point of transition between the eschatologies in the passage, placing it at either 5:26a, 27a, 27b, or 28. The

---

[68] Méndez, "'Night' and 'Day,'" 478–81. Alternatively, the depiction of this judgment as a "resurrection" may have no symbolic value, since metaphors do not highlight all features of a particular vehicle (Lakoff and Johnson, *Metaphors We Live By*, 10). In either case, the phrase "resurrection of judgment" is not a "cynical euphemism," as Stimpfle claims (*Blinde Sehen*, 89).

[69] Charteris-Black, *Corpus Approaches*, 35.

challenges of finding a clear seam between these presentations might as well be evidence that none exists at all. If the language of verses 26–27 collocates well with either the preceding verses or the following verses, then the differences between verses 24–25 and 28–29 should be seen as negligible.[70] The entire passage is better read as a continuous stream of intertwined and interpenetrating realized-eschatological images.

*Illustration of the Realized Judgment*

A key clue that 5:28–29 forms part of the realized-eschatological discourse in which it is embedded is the way it completes what would otherwise be an underdeveloped discourse. Precisely when read as realized eschatology, 5:28–29 supplies an image missing in the preceding verses—namely, the Son exercising his realized-eschatological power of judgment. The broader passage contains two parallel units of discourse (5:21–25 and 5:26–30), in which "the sequence of the main ideas is roughly the same."[71] Jesus pivots from claims that the Father has granted the Son eschatological authority to individual images of the Son wielding that authority:[72]

Structure of 5:21–29
I. Unit 1
   A  Bestowal of authority (vv. 21–23)
   B  Exercise of authority (vv. 24–25)
II. Unit 2
   A´  Bestowal of authority (vv. 26–27)
   B´  Exercise of authority (vv. 28–29)

Both "bestowal" subunits are realized-eschatological in orientation. They insist that Jesus has already received the authority to give life and judge (perfect or aorist tense)—a power he is now beginning to exercise in the "word" he preaches (cf. v. 21: "so also the Son gives life"). In the first "exercise" subunit, however, Jesus depicts only his realized-eschatological power to give life, and not his power to judge (vv. 24–25)—a puzzling omission given the prominence of the theme of judgment in the verses preceding. In the reading defended here, that missing image appears in verses 28–29:

---

[70] "The collocation of verse 26 is problematic" (Harold W. Attridge, "Argumentation in John 5," in *Rhetorical Argumentation in Biblical Texts: Essays from the Lund 2000 Conference*, ed. Anders Eriksson, Thomas H. Olbricht, and Walter Übelacker, ESEC 8 [Harrisburg, PA: Trinity Press International, 2002], 188–99, here 193.

[71] Brown, *Gospel according to John*, 1:219.

[72] The "bestowal" subunits share three features: (1) the formulaic incipit ὥσπερ γὰρ ὁ πατήρ, (2) the implicit or explicit claim that the Father has given the Son authority to give life, and (3) the claim that the Father has given the Son authority to judge.

Structure of 5:21–29, Expanded
I. Unit 1
   A  Prior bestowal of authority to give life and judge (vv. 21–23)
   B  Present exercise of authority to give life (vv. 24–25)
II. Unit 2
   A′  Prior bestowal of authority to give life and judge (vv. 26–27)
   B′  Present exercise of authority to give life and judge (vv. 28–29)

Analyzed in this way, the two units are not doublets in a strict sense. Rather, they are complementary units, illustrating the realized-eschatological activity of the Son in two passes. In the first pass, Jesus depicts himself giving life through his word. In the second pass, Jesus expands the image, portraying himself as the one who not only gives life but also judges through his word. Far from introducing a different line of thought, then, the imagery of 5:28–29 completes the realized-eschatological discussion already in progress and gives it coherence.

## *Continuity with 5:30*

If a figurative and realized-eschatological reading 5:28–29 configures it better to the material preceding it, it also allows the text to be read continuously with the verse immediately following it: "I can do nothing on my own authority; as I hear, I judge; and my judgment is just, because I seek not my own will but the will of the one who sent me" (5:30). When Jesus speaks of his work of judgment in this text, he maintains the strict use of the present tense in keeping with the idea that this judgment is now taking root in his preaching: "I judge" (κρίνω); "my judgment is just" (ἡ κρίσις ἡ ἐμὴ δικαία ἐστίν).

To accommodate this text, the conventional reading must identify a second, abrupt shift in eschatologies immediately after 5:28–29. This move isolates 5:30 from the affirmations of a realized-eschatological judgment on which it supposedly comments some three to seven verses earlier and breaks the continuity between the references to "judgment" in 5:29, 30. In my reading, by contrast, 5:30 extends the discussion of the verses adjacent to it.

The text is, in fact, a very suitable commentary on 5:28–29 when those verses are read as realized eschatology. Following the image of Jesus's word leading to the judgment of the unrighteous—an image developed only in 5:28–29—Jesus insists that the words that condemn his hearers come from the Father: "as I hear, I judge." In turn, he illustrates this realized-eschatological work of judgment in the end of the second half of the discourse (5:33–47). As if handing down a judicial sentence, Jesus berates his hearers for rejecting his words, declaring that they stand accused (5:38, 40). The entire discourse, then, develops a single idea: "the equality of Jesus' activity with God's activity is to be seen in that Jesus is the eschatological Judge," within a judgment that "takes place in his present activity as the Revealer ... in accordance with 3.19."[73]

### Conformity to Other Realized-Eschatological Sayings

Not only does a realized-eschatological reading of 5:28–29 give the passage greater coherence; it also strengthens its links to other presentations of realized eschatology in the gospel. In fact, this reading is necessary to draw together all the major threads of that outlook in 5:19–30, especially: the coming "hour" as a time of judgment (12:27–31), the role of works in the judgment, and the words of Jesus as the catalyst for condemnation—elements otherwise missing in the broader passage.

## V. Conclusion

I have argued that 5:19–30 is a perfect site for a synthesis of exegetical methods with newer, literary-linguistic approaches to the Fourth Gospel. The interpretive problems associated with this passage rest precisely on a linguistic claim—specifically, that verses 28–29 represent an example of nonfigurative speech. The arguments marshaled for that claim, however, are largely rooted in misunderstandings of what metaphor is and how it is used in the gospel.

In the end, there is no definitive evidence that Jesus has ceased to speak figuratively at or before 5:28–29. On the contrary, these verses are tightly integrated into a cluster of metaphors and contain a constellation of images already transposed onto the figurative plane. When the verses themselves are placed on the same plane—the "divine" and "heavenly" plane on which Jesus characteristically speaks in the gospel—their meaning resolves easily. After using resurrection imagery to depict the life-giving power of his word, Jesus turns to a modified form of the same image to depict the two-edged effect of the same word—a pivot that completes the argument in process and gives the passage greater coherence.

Read in this way, 5:28–29 communicates the ideas Bultmann placed at the core of the larger passage but failed to see in a text he too quickly dismissed as the work of a second hand: "Everyone who hears the word of Jesus ... stands before the decision between life and death ... as the question of faith is put to all who hear the word."[74] The puzzles of the passage, in turn, are finally seen for what they are. They are effects of the elusive language of Jesus, a language "opaque to the earthly mind because of its extravagant use of metaphor."[75]

---

[73] Bultmann, *Gospel of John*, 256–57.
[74] Ibid., 257.
[75] Stibbe, "Elusive Christ," 26.

# Romans 5:12, Once Again: Is It a Grammatical Comparison?

## JAMES W. HARING
jharing@nd.edu
University of Notre Dame, Notre Dame, IN 46556

Commentators have long noted and discussed the several difficulties of Rom 5:12. Among them is that, while the verse appears to open with a comparison (Διὰ τοῦτο ὥσπερ δι' ἑνὸς ἀνθρώπου ἡ ἁμαρτία εἰς τὸν κόσμον εἰσῆλθεν ..., "Therefore, just as through one man sin came into the world ..."), the second part of that comparison is never clearly formulated. Instead, the verse seems to trail off with no obvious conclusion to the comparison (καὶ οὕτως εἰς πάντας ἀνθρώπους ὁ θάνατος διῆλθεν ..., "and so death came to all men ..."). Many have suggested that Paul simply lost track of his thought, and modern translations and commentaries typically accept the incoherence, translating "and so" and often concluding the sentence with a dash. However, this is not the only syntactic possibility. This article aims to supplement John Kirby's discussion of the adverbial meaning of καὶ οὕτως ("even so") in Rom 5:12, a translation that understands the verse to be a complete and cogent comparison. I will survey a broader range of linguistic evidence, taking note of the textual history of Rom 5:12 and will reconsider the contextual objections to this translation. I will show that syntactically and conceptually "even so" or "in the same way" is the best translation of καὶ οὕτως in Rom 5:12.

---

Commentators have long noted and discussed the several difficulties of Rom 5:12. Among them is that, while the verse appears to open with a comparison (Διὰ τοῦτο ὥσπερ δι' ἑνὸς ἀνθρώπου ἡ ἁμαρτία εἰς τὸν κόσμον εἰσῆλθεν ..., "Therefore, just as through one man sin came into the world ..."), the second part of that comparison is never clearly formulated. Instead, the verse seems to trail off with no obvious conclusion to the comparison (καὶ οὕτως εἰς πάντας ἀνθρώπους ὁ θάνατος διῆλθεν ..., "and so death came to all men ...").[1] Some modern translations have

---

[1] Biblical translations are my own unless otherwise noted. In order to reflect the parallelism in Paul's language between the sin of "one man," Adam (ἑνὸς ἀνθρώπου), and the subsequent sin of "all men" (πάντας ἀνθρώπους), I have used the noninclusive "men" in my translation, even while recognizing the inherent limitations of this language. Since the focus here is especially on the

taken note of this and conclude the sentence with a dash, signifying that the thought is indeed incomplete (e.g., NRSV, ESV).

Among the first to note the difficulty, Origen suggests that Paul's apparent anacoluthon was an intentional ellipsis. The idea that death came to all through the sin of one might seem to imply that through the righteousness of one, life would come to all. Thus, Origen suggests, "on account of certain negligent people who perhaps could become slack, should they hear that just as death passed through to all men through sin, so also life will pass through to all men through Christ, [Paul] took care that these matters ought not be spoken of openly and publicly" (*Com. Rom.* 5.4).[2] Paul, on Origen's interpretation, refrained from making explicit the universalism implicit in his argument for fear that it would be misused. Modern scholars have likewise noted that Paul's sentence appears to trail off, observing, for example, "The structure of the paragraph introduced by this word [ὥσπερ] (to the end of ver. 14) is broken in a manner very characteristic of St. Paul.... It is a want of finish in style due to eagerness and intensity of thought; but the meaning is quite clear."[3] Others suggest that Paul became "sidetracked," went "off at a word," or was simply composing his letter on the fly as an amanuensis wrote down his thoughts, some of which were incoherent.[4]

Perpetuating the need for such explanations, modern translations and commentaries typically translate καὶ οὕτως as "and so." A few, however, use the rendering "so too" or "so also," which in effect reverses the order of the words from καὶ οὕτως to οὕτως καί.[5] The former ("and so") is certainly the most obvious translation,

---

literary structure of the verse, it seemed appropriate to highlight Paul's repetition of key words throughout the verse in this manner.

[2] Origen, *Commentary on the Epistle to the Romans*, trans. Thomas P. Scheck, 2 vols., FC 103, 104 (Washington, DC: Catholic University of America Press, 2001), 1:305.

[3] William Sanday and Arthur C. Headlam, *A Critical and Exegetical Commentary on the Epistle to the Romans*, 2nd ed., ICC (New York: Scribner's Sons, 1896), 132.

[4] Douglas J. Moo, *The Epistle to the Romans*, NICNT (Grand Rapids: Eerdmans, 1996), 318; Richard N. Longenecker, *The Epistle to the Romans: A Commentary on the Greek Text*, NIGTC (Grand Rapids: Eerdmans, 2016), 586; Ben Witherington III, with Darlene Hyatt, *Paul's Letter to the Romans: A Socio-rhetorical Commentary* (Grand Rapids: Eerdmans, 2004), 145. The third hypothesis makes sense only if one presupposes the others. There is no reason to assume that Paul could not compose a coherent sentence merely because he dictated his letter. Thomas Aquinas, for example, dictated some of the most complex argumentation in the history of Western theology (see Paul J. Griffiths, *Religious Reading: The Place of Reading in the Practice of Religion* [Oxford: Oxford University Press, 1999], 56).

[5] For "and so," see C. E. B. Cranfield, *A Critical and Exegetical Commentary on the Epistle to the Romans*, 2 vols., ICC (Edinburgh: T&T Clark, 1975), 1:269; Moo, *Epistle to the Romans*, 318; Simon Légasse, *L'épître de Paul aux Romans*, LD 10 (Paris: Cerf, 2002), 358; Romano Penna, *Lettera ai Romani*, 3 vols., SOCr 6 (Bologna: EDB, 2004), 1:441; Robert Jewett, *Romans: A Commentary*, Hermeneia (Minneapolis: Fortress, 2007), 373; Alain Gignac, *L'épître aux Romains*, Commentaire biblique: Nouveau Testament 6 (Paris: Cerf, 2014), 234; Michael Wolter, *Der Brief an die Römer*, EKKNT 6 (Neukirchen-Vluyn: Neukirchener Theologie, 2014), 1:340; Longenecker,

the latter alternatives being somewhat imprecise. John Kirby is perhaps the only commentator on Rom 5:12 to discuss in any detail the more precise adverbial meaning of καὶ οὕτως, "even so."[6] As will be seen below, Kirby offers the most plausible translation of the verse, but his evidence is weak at three points: First, it is limited to the New Testament and to the authority of Herbert Weir Smyth's grammar. Second, Kirby does not discuss whether καὶ οὕτως ever occurs in combination with ὥσπερ as part of a comparison. Third, he does not consider the textual history of Rom 5:12. The following discussion, then, will supplement these three points of Kirby's argument before briefly reconsidering how the translations "even so" or "in this way" make better sense of the verse's meaning.

Although it is not discussed in BDAG, the phrase καὶ οὕτως is recognized by LSJ (s.v. "καί") and Smyth (§§1246, 2882), who translate it "even so," "even on this supposition," or "likewise." In some cases, καὶ οὕτως is open to multiple translations and might be rendered "and so" just as easily as "even so." Such examples, while initially suggestive, are somewhat inconclusive for our purposes. Thus, one finds the following in Athenaeus's *The Learned Banqueters*:

καὶ ἡ πίννη διαστήσασα τὸ ὄστρακον ἡσυχάζει τηροῦσα τὰ ἐπεισιόντα ἰχθύδια, ὁ δὲ πιννοτήρης παρεστὼς ὅταν εἰσέλθῃ τι δάκνει αὐτὴν ὥσπερ σημαίνων, ἡ δὲ δηχθεῖσα συμμύει. καὶ οὕτως τὸ ἀποληφθὲν ἔνδον κατεσθίουσι κοινῇ.

The pinna opens its shell and remains still, waiting for small fish to approach; the pinna-guard stands by and nips it, as if giving it a signal, when something goes in; and after the pinna is nipped, it closes. In this way [καὶ οὕτως] they consume whatever is caught inside together. (*Deipn.* 3.38e [Olson, LCL])

Similarly, Paul writes, "But as the Lord distributed to each, as God called each, so let each live. In this way [καὶ οὕτως] I commanded in all the churches" (1 Cor 7:17). While both examples may be translated "in this way" or "even so," in both cases one might also translate "and so." Hence, "and so they consume" or "and so I commanded."[7]

Other examples are less ambiguous. Philo writes, Ἔτι καὶ οὕτως ἴδωμεν τὸ προκείμενον, "Now let us go on to look at our subject in this way" (*Leg.* 1.23 [Colson and Whitaker, LCL]). The Epistle to the Hebrews reads, "We are confident about you, beloved, with respect to better things and to the possessions of salvation, if we speak in this way [εἰ καὶ οὕτως λαλοῦμεν]" (Heb 6:9). In both cases, the rendering

---

*Epistle to the Romans*, 375. For "so too," "even so," and "so also," see John Kirby, "The Syntax of Romans 5.12: A Rhetorical Approach," *NTS* 33 (1987): 283–86; Arland J. Hultgren, *Paul's Letter to the Romans: A Commentary* (Grand Rapids: Eerdmans, 2011), 223–24. Michael Cosby suggests "in the same way/likewise" ("Paul's Persuasive Language in Romans 5," in *Persuasive Artistry: Studies in New Testament Rhetoric in Honor of George A. Kennedy*, ed. Duane F. Watson, JSNTSup 50 (Sheffield: Sheffield Academic, 1991), 209–26, here 220.

[6] Kirby, "Syntax of Romans 5.12," 283–86.
[7] See also Acts 7:8, 27:44, Heb 6:15, Rev 9:17.

"and so" simply does not work, and the translation "even so" or "in this way" is demanded. In the Septuagint, one finds similar cases: "The water of Nemrim will be desolate, and her grass will fail, for there will be no green grass. Even so [καὶ οὕτως], will she be saved?" (Isa 15:6–7 NETS). And again,

ἐὰν δὲ γενομένη γένηται ἀνδρὶ καὶ αἱ εὐχαὶ αὐτῆς ἐπ᾽ αὐτῇ κατὰ τὴν διαστολὴν τῶν χειλέων αὐτῆς, οὓς ὡρίσατο κατὰ τῆς ψυχῆς αὐτῆς, καὶ ἀκούσῃ ὁ ἀνὴρ αὐτῆς καὶ παρασιωπήσῃ αὐτῇ, ᾗ ἂν ἡμέρᾳ ἀκούσῃ, καὶ οὕτως στήσονται πᾶσαι αἱ εὐχαὶ αὐτῆς, καὶ οἱ ὁρισμοὶ αὐτῆς, οὓς ὡρίσατο κατὰ τῆς ψυχῆς αὐτῆς, στήσονται.

But if, when she grows up, she becomes a man's and her vows are upon her according to the parting of her lips, as many things as she determined for herself against her soul and if her husband hears and says nothing to her on the day when he hears, then thereby [καὶ οὕτως] all her vows shall stand, and her determinations that she determined for herself against her soul—they shall stand. (Num 30:7–8 NETS)[8]

The last example is particularly interesting for our purposes in that it demonstrates the use of καὶ οὕτως to introduce a subordinate clause with the meaning "even so" or "in this way."

Despite the prima facie plausibility that these examples grant to the translation "even so" or "in this way" in Rom 5:12, the latter verse possesses a key characteristic that they lack. None of these initial cases of καὶ οὕτως involves a comparison using the word ὥσπερ. As far as I can tell, such comparisons are not mentioned in any of the grammars or lexica—but they do occur, albeit rarely. Most clearly, Aristotle writes,

οἱ δὲ μελαγχολικοὶ διὰ τὸ σφόδρα, ὥσπερ βάλλοντες πόρρωθεν, εὔστοχοί εἰσιν. καὶ διὰ τὸ μεταβλητικὸν ταχὺ τὸ ἐχόμενον φαντάζεται αὐτοῖς· ὥσπερ γὰρ τὰ Φιλαινίδος ποιήματα καὶ οἱ ἐμμανεῖς ἐχόμενα τοῦ ὁμοίου λέγουσι καὶ διανοοῦνται, οἷον Ἀφροδίτην φροδίτην, καὶ οὕτω συνείρουσιν εἰς τὸ πρόσω.

Choleric people, because of their impetuosity, are (to use a metaphor) good marksmen when shooting from a distance; and because of their liability to change, the next image in the series comes rapidly before them; for just as [ὥσπερ] the insane recite and con over the poems of Philaegides, such as the Aphrodite, in which the ideas are all associated; so [καὶ οὕτω] the choleric pursue the series of impulses. (*Spir.* 464a32–464b5 [Hett, LCL])[9]

A second example comes from John Chrysostom, who writes,

---

[8] Cf. Num 13:34, 30:8, Sir 16:10, 1 Macc 2:61.
[9] For discussion of the authorship of *De spiritu*, see Abraham P. Bos and Rein Ferwerda, *Aristotle, On the Life-Bearing Spirit (*De Spiritu*): A Discussion with Plato and His Predecessors on* Pneuma *as the Instrumental Body of the Soul; Introduction, Translation, and Commentary* (Leiden: Brill, 2008).

γὰρ μόνον στεῖρα ἦν ἡ Ἐκκλησία, ὥσπερ ἡ Σάρρα, οὐδὲ μόνον πολύπαις ἐγένετο, ὥσπερ ἐκείνη, ἀλλὰ καὶ οὕτως ἐγέννησεν, ὥσπερ ἡ Σάρρα. (*Hom. Gal.* 4.28 [PG 61:663])

It is not merely that the Church was barren like [ὥσπερ] Sarah, or became a mother of many children like [ὥσπερ] her, but she bore them in the same way [καὶ οὕτως], just as [ὥσπερ] Sarah did. (*NPNF*[1] 13:35 modified)

Although the sequence of ὥσπερ and καὶ οὕτως in the final clause of this sentence is the reverse of that in Rom 5:12, it nonetheless demonstrates that ὥσπερ and καὶ οὕτως may be used together in a comparison. Indeed, without changing his meaning, Chrysostom could equally have written, ὥσπερ ἡ Σάρρα ἐγέννησεν, καὶ οὕτως ἡ Ἐκκλησία (and this possibility is reinforced by the implied comparison between καὶ οὕτως and the initial ὥσπερ ἡ Σάρρα with which Chrysostom opens his statement).

Finally, Plotinus writes,

εἰ δὲ τὸ ζῷον τὸ συναμφότερον οὕτως, ὡς ἕτερον ἐξ ἀμφοῖν εἶναι, πρῶτον μὲν ἄτοπον μήτε σῶμα μήτε ψυχὴν τὸ ζῷον λέγειν· οὐ γὰρ δὴ μεταβαλόντων ἀμφοτέρων ἕτερόν τι ἔσται τὸ ζῷον οὐδ' αὖ κραθέντων, ὡς δυνάμει τὴν ψυχὴν ἐν τῷ ζῴῳ εἶναι· ἔπειτα καὶ οὕτως οὐδὲν ἧττον τῆς ψυχῆς τὸ μνημονεύειν ἔσται, ὥσπερ ἐν οἰνομέλιτος κράσει εἴ τι γλυκάζει, παρὰ τοῦ μέλιτος τοῦτο ἔσται.

But if the composite living thing is something of such a sort as to be different from both its components, first of all it is absurd to say that the living thing is neither body nor soul: for the living thing will not be something different as the result of both of them having changed, nor again as the result of their having been mixed, so that the soul is in the living thing potentially. And then even so [ἔπειτα καὶ οὕτως] remembering would belong just as much to the soul, as [ὥσπερ] in a mixture of wine and honey any sweetness there is will be due to the honey. (*Enn.* 4.3 [Armstrong, LCL])

As in the example from Chrysostom, the order here is the opposite of Paul's, but the use of καὶ οὕτως to signify similarity with another item marked by ὥσπερ is nonetheless present. Comparisons involving ὥσπερ and καὶ οὕτως, then, although rare, were in use as early as the fourth century BCE and as late as the fourth century CE. There is no necessary reason, therefore, to imagine that Paul could not have used such a construction, even if it is highly unusual and perhaps awkward.

As for its textual history, most of the versions shed little new light on Rom 5:12. For ὥσπερ ... καὶ οὕτως, Jerome follows the reading of Origen, with *sicut ... et ita*, "just as ... and so." Several Old Latin manuscripts, however, simply read *ita* ("so," with no *et*), which suggests either that the translator felt the need to smooth over the text, or that Rom 5:12 was in fact understood in some cases as a proper comparison.[10] It is also noteworthy that Rom 5:12 is understood as a grammatical

---

[10] These texts were accessed through the Brepolis *Vetus Latina Database* (http://www.brepolis.net/).

comparison by some English translations of the Peshitta. Daniel King translates, "For just as sin entered the world through a single man, and death through sin, so [ܘܗܟܢܐ] death has come upon everyone, since everyone has sinned."[11] Although by no means conclusive, the textual history of Rom 5:12 suggests nonetheless that there have been those in the history of its interpretation who regarded it as a true comparison. That John Chrysostom and Theodoret of Cyrus simply pass over this aspect of the passage in silence suggests the possibility that neither of them found its syntax unintelligible.[12]

The strength of the interpretation advocated here is reinforced by the structure of the two parts of Rom 5:12, outlined as follows:

a. ὥσπερ
b. δι' ἑνὸς ἀνθρώπου
c. ἡ ἁμαρτία εἰς τὸν κόσμον εἰσῆλθεν
d. καὶ διὰ τῆς ἁμαρτίας ὁ θάνατος,

$a^1$. καὶ οὕτως
$b^1$. εἰς πάντας ἀνθρώπους
$c^1$. ὁ θάνατος διῆλθεν
$d^1$. ἐφ' ᾧ πάντες ἥμαρτον

Each side of the comparison repeats the prepositions διά ($b/c^1$ [διῆλθεν]) and εἰς ($c/b^1$), but in reverse order. Each repeats the ideas of sin ($c/d/d^1$) and death ($d/c^1$), again in reverse order. The ideas of the cosmos and of "all men" are analogous ($c/b^1/d^1$), as is the connection between sin and death in each half of the verse. The comparative logic of the verse is in fact so evident that it leads Douglas Moo nearly to contradict himself. For after having denied that verse 12 is a grammatically complete comparison, he writes,

> With the majority of commentators, then, we think that "in this way" draws a comparison between the manner in which death came into the world—through sin—and the manner in which death spread to everyone—also through sin. Verse 12 then is a neatly balanced chiasm:

---

[11] George A. Kiraz, ed., *The Syriac Peshiṭta Bible with English Translation: Romans-Corinthians*, trans. Daniel King (Piscataway, NJ: Gorgias, 2013). Also see the earlier translations of George M. Lamsa, *The Holy Bible from Ancient Eastern Manuscripts: Containing the Old and New Testaments* (Philadelphia: A. J. Holman, 1957); John Wesley Etheridge, trans., *The Apostolical Acts and Epistles, from the Peschito, or Ancient Syriac: To Which Are Added, the Remaining Epistles, and the Book of Revelation, after a Later Syrian Text* (London: Longman, Brown, Green & Longmans, 1849), http://archive.org/details/apostolicalactse00ethe.

[12] John Chrysostom, *Hom. Rom.* 10 (PG 60:473–74; *NPNF*[1] 11:401); Theodoret of Cyrrhus, *Com. Rom.* 5:12 (PG 82:98–100). See Theodoret of Cyrrhus, *Commentary on the Letters of St. Paul*, trans. Robert Charles Hill, 2 vols. (Brookline, MA: Holy Cross Orthodox Press, 2001), 1:72. Unfortunately, the Syriac author Ishoʻdad of Merv does not discuss this verse in his commentary on the epistle to the Romans. See *The Commentaries of Ishoʻdad of Merv, Bishop of Hadatha (c. 850 A.D.) in Syriac and English*, ed. and trans. Margaret Dunlop Gibson, 5 vols., Horae Semiticae 5–7. 10–11 (Cambridge: University Press, 1911–1916), 5.2:7. Aphrahat cites a rather garbled version of Rom 5:12–14 in his twenty-second "demonstration," which is equally unhelpful regarding the matter under consideration here. See Aphrahat, *The Demonstrations of Aphrahat, the Persian Sage*, trans. Adam Lehto, Gorgias Eastern Christian Studies 27 (Piscataway, NJ: Gorgias, 2010).

A   sin (12a) produces
B   death (12b);
B   all die (12c)
A   because all sin (12d).[13]

As Moo aptly demonstrates, there is no reason to think of this sentence as sloppy or rushed. The parts reflect each other quite nicely, which suggests that Paul was neither distracted nor rushed when he composed it.[14] The undeniable comparative meaning of the verse suggests that one should recognize the syntax as comparative as well, especially given the occurrence of this particular type of grammatical comparison in other contexts.

Further, how one interprets the controverted last clause of the verse, ἐφ' ᾧ πάντες ἥμαρτον, is inconsequential to the comparison. Whether it means (1) "because all sinned," or (2) "in whom all sinned" (referring to Adam), or (3) "with the result that all sinned," the meaning is clarified if one follows the translation "even so."[15] Thus, in the first case, one would translate, "Therefore, just as through one man sin came into the world, and death through sin, even so death came to all men, because all sinned." Here, the sin of "all men" parallels the "original" sin of Adam. Sin by its very nature brings death.[16] In the second case, one would translate, "Therefore, just as through one man sin came into the world, and death through sin, even so death came to all men, in whom all sinned." Here, death comes to all in just the same way that it came to the first man: viz., through participation of some sort in the sin of that first man. In the third case, one would translate, "Therefore, just as through one man sin came into the world, and death through sin, even so death came to all men, with the result that all sinned." Here, the meaning would be something to the

---

[13] Moo, *Epistle to the Romans*, 320; cf. Joseph A. Fitzmyer, *Romans: A New Translation with Introduction and Commentary*, AB 33 (New York: Doubleday, 1993), 413, 416.

[14] Brian Vickers argues similarly that the force of Paul's argument in Rom 5:12 implies that "the verse comes close to being a comparative construction—the very thing that is widely denied on the basis of the syntax. If it [ἐφ' ᾧ] means, 'because all sinned,' then this makes καὶ οὕτως essentially mean 'so also' since the same course of events follow for 'all' just as for Adam" ("Grammar and Theology in the Interpretation of Rom 5:12," *TJ* 27 [2006]: 271–88, here 282).

[15] It seems to me that Witherington is right to reduce the many possible interpretations of ἐφ' ᾧ πάντες ἥμαρτον to these three, at least as the most commonly suggested interpretations (*Paul's Letter to the Romans*, 146). For a more detailed analysis, see Joseph A. Fitzmyer, "The Consecutive Meaning of ἐφ' ᾧ in Romans 5.12," *NTS* 39 (1993): 321–39. One might also add Jewett's idea that ἐφ' ᾧ means "on which [world]" (*Romans*, 369), but I find it difficult to see how this interpretation makes sense of the verse.

[16] This interpretation may seem to support Pelagianism, but some have argued that it may be understood without Pelagian implications. See Hultgren, *Paul's Letter to the Romans*, 223; C. E. B. Cranfield, "On Some of the Problems in the Interpretation of Romans 5.12," *SJT* 22 (1969): 324–41. Nonetheless, given Augustine's liberal use of this verse and his reading "in whom all sinned" in his anti-Pelagian writings, one has to suspect that the interpretation proposed here may have been overlooked in the history of Western Christianity for theological reasons.

effect that through the sin of the one man, death entered the world and thus spread to all, and the result of death entering the world was the spread of sin in all humans. In each case, the meaning is prima facie intelligible and need not be understood to conflict necessarily with Paul's thought more broadly. The basic idea in all three readings is that, just as sin entered the world through one man, and death entered the world through sin (whether with specific reference to *Adam*'s sin, or simply with reference to the fact that sin was now in the world), in just the same way, death came to all people (whether *because* all sinned, or *in whom* all sinned, or *with the result that* all sinned). It is not my purpose to evaluate the theological coherence of these interpretations but simply to show that, however one reads the last clause, Rom 5:12 is more coherent when καὶ οὕτως is translated "even so" than when it is not.

Finally, while it is correct to note, as many have, that this passage as a whole compares Christ and Adam, not every part of the passage need be forced to deal with this particular theme. Verse 15 suggests, in fact, that the preceding verses (vv. 12–14) explicate the nature of Adam's characteristic activity (Ἀλλ' οὐχ ὡς τὸ παράπτωμα, οὕτως καὶ τὸ χάρισμα, "But the free gift is not like the trespass" [NRSV]), while the subsequent verses discuss the nature of the "free gift." Indeed, verses 13–14 are focused primarily on the nature of sin and death with reference to Adam and *Moses* (i.e., the law of Moses), not Adam and *Christ*. Thus, it appears that the comparison between Adam and Christ is under explicit consideration only after the transition of verse 15a. There is no reason, then, not to see all of verse 12 as the introductory statement of the theme that is expanded in the following two verses, namely, the theme of the relationship between sin and death and—following in some way the pattern of the sin of Adam—the spread of sin and death to all.

This means that verse 18 does not pick up the forgotten comparison begun in verse 12. Rather, it contrasts with that comparison, not only conceptually but grammatically. In the case of the trespass (παράπτωμα, v. 15) of Adam, just as sin and death entered the world through one man, even so (καὶ οὕτως) sin and death came to all (v. 12). But in the case of the free gift (τὸ χάρισμα, v. 15), as one trespass led to condemnation, so also (οὕτως καί) one righteous act leads to life (v. 18). This "so also"—the inverse of the "even so" (καὶ οὕτως) of verse 12—occurs in verses 15, 18, 19, and 21, and these verses emphatically contrast with verse 12. The situation that was the case before Christ has been altered fundamentally, and it is as if Paul's very syntax reflects the significance of that change. In fact, given the above examples of καὶ οὕτως (and assuming that this analysis of the argument of Rom 5:12–21 is correct), it is quite possible that Paul intentionally chose καὶ οὕτως in verse 12. For καὶ οὕτως may carry the nuance of "in just the same way," as is shown in particular by the text above from John Chrysostom. The ὥσπερ … καὶ οὕτως sort of comparison is appropriate when the sin of Adam is put alongside the sin of humanity as a whole. There is a proper analogy in this case, whatever the differences may be. On the one hand, when the righteousness of Christ is being compared to the sin of Adam, οὕτως καί is more appropriate, since this locution sometimes carries the nuance of, "in a similar manner [οὕτως], but what's more [καί]," as Paul's usage in Rom 5:15–21 indicates (cf. Rom 6:4, 1 Cor 11:12, 15:22, Jas 2:26). In the latter case, in other words, Paul signifies not "in just the same way" but a commonality alongside a much more substantial difference.

One might object, following James D. G. Dunn, that this interpretation does not flow naturally into verse 13: "sin was indeed in the world before the law, but sin is not reckoned when there is no law" (NRSV).[17] Given all that has already been said, however, verse 13 is easily understood as a more precise explanation of how it was that sin and death had come to all before the giving of the law. My interpretation of verse 13 is not particularly innovative, except that, on my reading of verse 12, Paul does not interrupt himself to make his point in verse 13. Dunn's explanation of verse 13, for example, works just as well on my reading of verse 12:

> v 13 functions as an explanation of v 12c; and v 14 makes it clear that v 13 is to be regarded as raising a possible objection to the claim that death's sway has been unbroken from the beginning. The objection centers ... on the nexus between sin and law.... It must be tied up with Paul's evident concern here to emphasize the role and power of sin and death as ultimately independent of the law (vv 13–14).[18]

Indeed, Dunn's reading makes *more sense*, not less, when verse 12 is understood as a grammatical comparison. The comparison in verse 12 heightens the fact that sin and death spread to all in just the same way that they came to Adam, which, as Dunn rightly points out, requires clarification given what Paul says in verse 13 about sin not being "reckoned" apart from the law (cf. 4:15, "where there is no law, there is no transgression").

Thus, although dense and difficult on one level, Rom 5:12–21 is not carelessly constructed, nor was it necessarily written on the fly by an amanuensis too harried to write a complete sentence. It possesses an internal logic and a natural progression from the situation before Christ (vv. 12–14) to the situation after Christ (vv. 15–21), with verse 15a serving as the transition. Romans 5:12 is a coherent verse in a coherent passage, and there are syntactic and conceptual reasons to leave behind the strained attempts to argue that Paul was distracted to the point of incoherence.[19]

---

[17] See James D. G. Dunn, *Romans 1–8*, WBC 38A (Dallas: Word, 1988), 273.

[18] Ibid., 275.

[19] Pieter W. van der Horst makes a formally similar argument ("'Only Then Will All Israel Be Saved': A Short Note on the Meaning of καὶ οὕτως in Romans 11:26," *JBL* [2000]: 521–25, https://doi.org/10.2307/3268412). His analysis supports mine in the sense that he seeks to challenge a common and perhaps myopic view of the meaning of οὕτως, but the specific content of his argument, and the syntax of καὶ οὕτως in Rom 11:26, are somewhat different than the matters under consideration here. Significantly, καί is not used adverbially in Rom 11:26, a difference that affects the meaning of οὕτως in Rom 5:12. One might say, however, that there is an analogous nuance in the use of οὕτως in Rom 5:12 and 11:26. For the nuance "only then" (11:26) could be regarded as a temporal application of the nuance "in just this way" (5:12).

# WISDOM COMMENTARY

## SIGN UP FOR A STANDING ORDER & SAVE

Volumes are **30% off** the cover price and **shipped to you for FREE*** as they are published.

### OR

Pre-pay for the entire series for <u>additional savings!</u>

*Free standard shipping to US addresses only.
Liturgical Press plans to publish six volumes per year,
available in both print and eBook format.

Learn more at
**WisdomCommentary.org/StandingOrder**

# "Wretch I Am!" Eve's Tragic Speech-in-Character in Romans 7:7–25

NICHOLAS ELDER
nick.elder@marquette.edu
Marquette University, Milwaukee, WI 53233

Despite the myriad approaches to the identity of the "I" in Rom 7:7–25, there is one aspect of the passage that has not been considered: its similarity to the tragic Greek laments. I offer a new perspective on the identity of the "wretched man"—rather, the "wretched woman"—in Rom 7:7–25, contending, based on generic and intertraditional arguments, that Eve, not Adam, is the individual identified in Paul's speech-in-character in this chapter. Paul has recast Eve in the role of the female lamenter who bemoans her tragic condition. In this way, he has uniquely fused Second Temple Jewish traditions about Eve with tragic traditions that were prevalent in his Greco-Roman context. I argue that Paul evokes Gen 3 in Rom 7 but that the intertextual themes and lexemes concern Eve, not Adam. A comparison of Rom 7 with portrayals of Eve from Paul's Second Temple Jewish context shows that Paul is evoking an established tradition about Eve. Finally, I argue that Paul has recast Eve in the role of the tragic, lamenting woman to serve a pedagogical function in the unfolding argument of Rom 5–8. The constituent aspects of her character fit the Aristotelian model of the ideal tragic figure who provokes fear and pity in the audience's mind and ultimately effects a cathartic release of these emotions.

---

*Ah me, what unhappiness is mine! What shall I utter, what sound, what cry of lamentation, since I am wretched with wretched old age and slavery unbearable, unendurable? Ah me! Who is my protector? What family, what city? Gone is my aged husband, gone are my children. What road shall I walk, this one or that?*

---

I am grateful to the many readers and hearers who offered feedback on various iterations of this article, including Michael Cover; Tyler Stewart; Courtney Friesen; two anonymous *JBL* reviewers; students in the spring 2015 Romans doctoral seminar at Marquette University; and the panel, chair, and audience of the Pauline Literature section of the 2016 Midwest Regional Meeting of the Society of Biblical Literature.

*Where shall I reach safety? Where is there god or power to help me?* (Euripides, *Hec.* 154–165 [Kovacs, LCL])[1]

Despite the myriad approaches to the identity of the ἐγώ ("I") in Rom 7:7–25, there is one aspect of the passage that has not been considered: its similarity to the tragic Greek laments. In view of this lacuna, I offer a new perspective on the identity of the "wretched man"—or, rather, the "wretched *woman*"—in Rom 7:7–25. I contend on the basis of generic and intertraditional arguments that Eve, not Adam, is the subject of Paul's speech-in-character (προσωποποιΐα) in Rom 7. Paul has cast Eve in the role of the lamenter who bemoans her tragic condition. By doing so he has uniquely fused Second Temple Jewish traditions about Eve with tragic traditions that were prevalent in his Greco-Roman context. Thus, the ἐγώ in Rom 7 is Eve lamenting herself on account of the conditions of sin and death that she has brought into the cosmos.

The article proceeds in four sections. First, I review the evidence for a speech-in-character in Rom 7:7–25. Second, I reformulate the arguments often made for an Adamic speech to argue that Eve is the speaking subject in the pericope. Third, I demonstrate that there is an active tradition in Second Temple Judaism concerned with Eve's role in the primeval history and that in Rom 7 Paul recalls many of the themes and tropes that were integral to this tradition. Finally, I argue that Paul recasts Eve in a tragic, lamenting mode and that this accounts for a number of the text's syntactical and verbal features, particularly the numerous first-person verbal and nominal forms.

## I. Romans 7:7–25 as a Speech-in-Character

That Paul has indeed constructed a speech-in-character in Rom 7:7–25 is foundational to the argument here. The work of Stanley K. Stowers is seminal for this theory, and at present this is also the consensus position on the text.[2] Stowers

---

[1] οἴ 'γὼ μελέα, τί ποτ' ἀπύσω; / ποίαν ἀχώ, ποῖον ὀδυρμόν, / δειλαία δειλαίου γήρως / <καὶ> δουλείας τᾶς οὐ τλατᾶς, / τᾶς οὐ φερτᾶς; ὤμοι μοι. / τίς ἀμύνει μοι; ποία γενεά, / ποία δὲ πόλις; φροῦδος πρέσβυς, / φροῦδοι παῖδες. / ποίαν ἢ ταύταν ἢ κείναν / στείχω; ποῖ δὴ σωθῶ; ποῦ τις / θεῶν ἢ δαίμων ἐπαρωγός;

[2] Stanley K. Stowers, "Romans 7.7–25 as a Speech-in-Character (προσωποποιΐα)," in *Paul in His Hellenistic Context*, ed. Troels Engberg-Pedersen, SNTW (Edinburgh: T&T Clark, 1994), 180–202. His argument was slightly revised and then incorporated into Stowers, *A Rereading of Romans: Justice, Jews, and Gentiles* (New Haven: Yale University Press, 1994), 264–84. Before contesting Stowers's theory about Paul's speech-in-character in Rom 7, Will Timmins ("Romans 7 and Speech-In-Character: A Critical Evaluation of Stowers' Hypothesis," ZNW 107 [2016]: 94–115, here 95 n. 6) produces a litany of over twenty scholars who have accepted Stowers's προσωποποιΐα thesis, indicating that this is now the majority position. Timmins's critique of the theory will be addressed below.

defines speech-in-character as "a rhetorical and literary technique in which the speaker or writer produces speech that represents not himself or herself but another person or type of character."[3] His argument for this kind of speech in Rom 7:7–25 is threefold. First, there is an abrupt change in voice following the rhetorical question "What then should we say?" (τί οὖν ἐροῦμεν;) in 7:7. According to Stowers, this abrupt change, which the grammarians call ἐναλλαγή or μεταβολή, will have prompted an ancient reader or hearer to look or listen for διαφωνία, "a difference in characterization from the authorial voice," in what followed.[4] This is precisely what the reader finds in 7:7–25. It appears that Paul is no longer speaking in his own voice since whoever this subject is lived happily before they became aware of "the law." This is not consistent with autobiographical details that Paul offers about himself in his other letters.[5] Second, Origen's fragmentary commentary on Rom 7 indicates that there is ancient precedent for reading this pericope as a speech-in-character.[6] Third, the theory solves a textual problem in Rom 8:2,[7] in which σε ("you") was altered to με ("me") in several manuscripts. Codexes Alexandrinus and Claromontanus and the majority text support με, yet σε is surely the better reading, and the scribal confusion is obvious: the text was emended to με in order either (a) to continue the speech-in-character into 8:1–2, or, more likely, (b) to have the speech in 7:7–25 be in Paul's own voice, making it no speech-in-character at all. As Stowers notes, apart from recognizing the speech-in-character in 7:7–25, the reading σε makes little sense, and so some scribes augmented it to με.[8] Acknowledging the rhetorical device, however, renders σε perfectly fitting. Paul resumes his authorial voice in 8:2 and addresses the fictive speaking subject of 7:7–25. Moreover, as the *lectio difficilior*, σε is the better reading.[9]

Collectively, these three arguments create a compelling case for reading Rom 7:7–25 as a speech-in-character. While there are divergent opinions on the specific identity of the "I" in Rom 7, most interpreters find the general theory persuasive. Yet not all have been convinced. Stowers has been criticized by R. Dean Anderson and, more recently, by Will Timmins.[10] Both claim that evidence from classical sources suggests that a προσωποποιΐα was usually introduced formally by its author.

---

[3] Stowers, *Rereading of Romans*, 16–17.
[4] Ibid., 269.
[5] Ibid., 270. For example, in Phil 3:6 Paul states that he was blameless (ἄμεμπτος) with respect to the law's righteousness.
[6] Ibid., 266–69.
[7] Ibid., 282.
[8] Ibid.
[9] To this end, Bruce M. Metzger writes, "The latter [σε], as the more difficult reading, is more likely to have been replaced by the former [με] (which harmonizes better with the argument in chap. 7) than vice-versa" (*A Textual Commentary on the Greek New Testament*, 2nd ed. [New York: United Bible Societies, 1994], 456).
[10] R. Dean Anderson, *Ancient Rhetorical Theory and Paul*, CBET 18 (Kampen: Kok Pharos, 1996), 178–83; Timmins, "Romans 7," 94–115.

There are no formal introductions to any of the purported speeches-in-character in Romans.[11] Stowers's response is that a speech-in-character need not be signaled by the author explicitly stating something like "now I am going to shift into προσωποιΐα."[12] The device can be indicated simply by "speaking words that imitate a particular person or a recognized character type."[13] Stowers reaches back to Rom 2:1–16 for this character type in Rom 7. He suggests that the mention of ἐπιθυμία ("sexual desire" or "lust") in the context of a question ("What then shall we say?") in 7:7–25 will have easily recalled to the mind of an ancient reader or hearer the akratic gentile that Paul introduced in 2:1–16.[14]

Toward the end of this article, I will part ways with Stowers in this respect. I agree that Paul enters into a speech-in-character in Rom 7:7–25. And, with Stowers, I contend Paul has recalled a recognized character type and indeed a particular person in this text. I will argue, however, that Rom 7:1–6, not 2:1–16, introduces the speech-in-character in 7:7–25. This explanation not only answers the critiques of Anderson and Timmins but also provides a more proximate literary context for the introduction of the speaking subject than 2:1–16 does. Before addressing this introduction, however, I will look to the particular person and the character type that Paul is recalling in the pericope: Eve.

## II. Eve in Genesis 2–3 and Romans 7

In an innovative article, Austin Busch proposed that Eve is the subject of Paul's speech-in-character in Rom 7.[15] Busch advances his argument on both ideological and intertextual grounds. Ideologically, he employs a deconstructionist method and suggests that Paul frequently destabilizes the binary categories of social and psychological identity that were inherent in the Hellenistic world. He shows that, in antiquity, female and male categories were simultaneously psychosocial and intellectual distinctions marked by a dichotomous configuration.[16] One of the prominent gendered oppositions was that of male activity and female passivity.

---

[11] According to Stowers's theory, Rom 7:7–25 is not the only προσωποιΐα in the letter. The device appears also in 2:1–5, 17–29; 3:1–9; and 3:27–4:2 (Stowers, *Rereading of Romans*, 20).

[12] Stanley K. Stowers, "Apostrophe, Προσωποιΐα and Paul's Rhetorical Education," in *Early Christianity and Classical Culture: Comparative Studies in Honor of Abraham J. Malherbe*, ed. John T. Fitzgerald, Thomas H. Olbricht, and L. Michael White, NovTSup 110 (Leiden: Brill, 2003), 351–69, here 353.

[13] Ibid., 355.

[14] Ibid., 367.

[15] Austin Busch, "The Figure of Eve in Romans 7:5–25," *BibInt* 12 (2004): 1–36. Busch's proposal about Eve has not been significantly advanced elsewhere. In contrast to the position argued here, Busch specifically rejects the notion that Paul is evoking a tragic ethos, seeing that as incommensurate with Eve's προσωποιΐα (14 n. 28).

[16] Ibid., 2.

Busch purports that Eve's speech in Rom 7 deconstructs this dichotomy. Eve is simultaneously and paradoxically a figure of passivity and activity, and this tension helps explain the self-conflict that is inherent in every human.[17]

Busch then offers intertextual arguments from Gen 2–3 for Eve's speech-in-character in Rom 7. These are particularly relevant for the present argument. He states that "the association of the law with 'fruit for death' (καρποφορῆσαι τῷ θανάτῳ, [Rom] 7:5) and mention of a commandment unto life that proved to be death ([Rom] 7:10) suggest that Paul is evoking the scene of the primeval transgression."[18] James D. G. Dunn, Ernst Käsemann, and Stanislas Lyonnet similarly contend that the Genesis narrative is the prominent interpretive intertext at work in Rom 7:7–25. They, however, argue that Adam is the ἐγώ in the pericope.[19] Many of the themes in Rom 7:7–25 will have recalled the Genesis narrative for Paul's audience, but the primeval history is most clearly evoked by the arresting verbal parallel between Rom 7:11 and Gen 3:13:[20]

Rom 7:11: ἡ γὰρ ἁμαρτία ... ἐξηπάτησέν με καὶ ... ἀπέκτεινεν ("for sin deceived me and I died").

Gen 3:13: ὁ ὄφις ἠπάτησέν με καὶ ἔφαγον ("the serpent deceived me and I ate").

While this allusion is sometimes noted by those arguing for an Adamic speech-in-character, there are two aspects of it that indicate that Paul is speaking as Eve here.

---

[17] Ibid., 12.
[18] Ibid., 13.
[19] James D. G. Dunn, *Romans*, 2 vols., WBC 38A–38B (Dallas: Word, 1988), 1:377–411; Ernst Käsemann, *Commentary on Romans*, ed. and trans. Geoffrey W. Bromiley (Grand Rapids: Eerdmans, 1980), 196–212; Stanislas Lyonnet, "L'histoire du salut selon le chapitre 7 de L'épître aux Romains," *Bib* 43 (1962): 117–51. Their proposals are based primarily on three arguments: (1) Adam was the only human who both experienced life apart from the law and the entrance of the commandment that brought death (Dunn, *Romans*, 1:401; Werner Georg Kümmel, *Römer 7 und das Bild des Menschen im Neuen Testament: Zwei Studien*, TB 53 [Munich: Kaiser, 1974], 196). For an overview of ancient Jewish and rabbinic texts that posit that Adam possessed the law in paradise, see Hermann Lichtenberger, *Das Ich Adams und das Ich der Menschheit: Studien zum Menschenbild in Römer 7*, WUNT 164 (Tübingen: Mohr Siebeck, 2004), 205–41. Examples include Philo, *Decal.* 142, 150, 153, *Opif.* 152, James 1:15, and LAE 19:3. (2) There are significant shared themes between Rom 7:7–25 and Gen 2–3: the personification of sin, the reality of death because of sin, and a similar sequence of events (Dunn, *Romans*, 1:384). And (3) there is a strong verbal parallel between Rom 7:11 and Gen 3:13 in its septuagintal form (ibid).

[20] Dunn, *Romans*, 1:384; Busch, "Figure of Eve," 13–14. There is, of course, a slight difference in the verbal forms here, as Gen 3:13 in the LXX does not use the prefix ἐξ-. The form of the verb ἀπατάω, with the prepositional prefix ἐξ- is used by Paul also in 2 Cor 11:3 and 1 Tim 2:14 with respect to Gen 2–3. It could be that the prefix is an attempt to express the *hiphil* form of the verb in Gen 3:13. It could also be the case that this is simply the Greek form of the verb Paul knows for Gen 3:13.

First, the reference in 7:11 is to Eve's words in the Genesis narrative, not Adam's.[21] Second, when the verbs ἐξαπατάω and ἀπατάω ("deceived") appear in the Pauline and deutero-Pauline corpora echoing Gen 2–3, they are always appended to Eve's action, never Adam's.[22] This is the case in 2 Cor 11:3, where Paul parenthetically states ὡς ὁ ὄφις ἐξηπάτησεν Εὖαν ἐν τῇ πανουργίᾳ αὐτοῦ ("just as the serpent deceived Eve in his craftiness"). Even more decisive is a text from the deutero-Pauline tradition. First Timothy 2:13–14 explains why women, according to this author, must learn in silence and may not teach: Ἀδὰμ γὰρ πρῶτος ἐπλάσθη, εἶτα Εὖα. καὶ Ἀδὰμ οὐκ ἠπατήθη, ἡ δὲ γυνὴ ἐξαπατηθεῖσα ἐν παραβάσει γέγονεν ("for Adam was formed first, then Eve. And Adam was not deceived, but the woman, being deceived, became a transgressor"). Here, the author not only explicit asserts that Eve was the one deceived, but he unambiguously denies that Adam was misled. As will be evidenced below, Adam is commonly and consistently distanced from accusations of deception in Second Temple traditions about the primeval history.

On the basis of the intertextual parallels between Rom 7 and Gen 2–3, I contend, following Dunn, Käsemann, and Lyonnet, that Paul is indeed constructing a speech-in-character of a specific character from the primeval history in Rom 7:7–25. This need not imply, however, that Rom 7:7–25 is an Adamic discourse. Eve fits the bill better than Adam. Käsemann's dictum "there is nothing in the passage which does not fit Adam, and everything fits Adam alone,"[23] might be revised to read "there is nothing in the passage which does not fit *Eve*, and everything fits *Eve* alone." Paul, however, does not evoke Eve to engage a single septuagintal textual tradition or, contra Busch, to deconstruct a social-psychological binary. Rather, he offers his own contribution to an existing Second Temple Jewish tradition that ruminated on Eve and her role as the originator of sin and death in the cosmos. Because Eve had been commonly cast in this role, Paul evokes the tragic mode and recasts Eve in the part of a popular tragic subject: the lamenting, morally torn woman.

### III. Jewish Traditions concerning Eve

Paul's literary predecessors, contemporaries, and successors all had traditions of their own about Eve that have often been overlooked because of a scholarly

---

[21] Busch ("Figure of Eve," 15–17), following the feminist literary critic Judith Fetterly, believes that the assumption that Adam must be speaking if Gen 2–3 is intertextually recalled results from an androcentric bias in the academy (Fetterley, *The Resisting Reader: A Feminist Approach to American Fiction* [Bloomington: Indiana University Press, 1978], xi–xii).

[22] Forms of ἀπατάω occur three times in the New Testament: Eph 5:6, 1 Tim 2:14, and Jas 1:26. Forms of ἐξαπατάω occur six times: Rom 7:11, 16:18, 1 Cor 3:18, 2 Cor 11:3, 2 Thess 2:3, and 2 Tim 2:14.

[23] Käsemann, *Commentary on Romans*, 196.

predilection for Second Temple Adamic traditions. Remarking on these traditions, Dunn writes, "Paul was entering into an already well-developed debate and his own views were not uninfluenced by its earlier participants."[24] Dunn's statement is just as true of traditions about Eve as it is of traditions about Adam. There are three consistent features of the tradition about Eve from this context that relate to Rom 7:7–25: (1) she is connected with pleasure and desire; (2) she is presented as a transgressor of the law or the primeval commandment; and (3) her transgression ushers sin and death into the world.

### Sirach 25:24 and 2 Baruch 48:42–43

One of the most unambiguous statements in Second Temple Jewish literature that sin originates from Eve is Sir 25:24: ἀπὸ γυναικὸς ἀρχὴ ἁμαρτίας, καὶ δι' αὐτὴν ἀποθνῄσκομεν πάντες ("the beginning of sin came from the woman, and through her we all die").[25] Not only does the text ascribe the beginning of sin to Eve, but she is also the conduit of death to all humanity. The passage is reminiscent of the themes of sin and death in Rom 7, and particularly 7:11: ἡ γὰρ ἁμαρτία ἀφορμὴν λαβοῦσα διὰ τῆς ἐντολῆς ἐξηπάτησέν με καὶ δι' αὐτῆς ἀπέκτεινεν ("for sin, taking an opportunity through the law, deceived me and through it killed me"). Moreover, in 7:11 sin is the conduit of death (δι' αὐτῆς [ἁμαρτία] ἀπέκτεινεν), and in Sir 25:24 Eve serves as a similar channel (δι' αὐτὴν [γυνή] ἀποθνῄσκομεν πάντες).[26] An analogous idea appears in 2 Bar 48:42–43. Here, sin is not explicitly attributed to Eve alone but is the collective result of the two protoplasts' actions: "And I [Baruch] answered and said, 'O Adam, what have you done to all those who are born from you? And what will be said to the first Eve who heeded the serpent? For all this multitude are going to corruption. Nor is there any numbering those whom the fire devours."[27] Similar to Rom 7, this utterance occurs within a nomistic discourse.[28] Also

---

[24] James D. G. Dunn, *The Theology of Paul the Apostle* (Grand Rapids: Eerdmans, 1998), 90.

[25] Eve is not explicitly mentioned here, but, as Felipe de Jesús Legarreta-Castillo notes, the context strongly suggests that she is in mind (*The Figure of Adam in Romans 5 and 1 Corinthians 15: The New Creation and Its Ethical and Social Reconfigurations*, Emerging Scholars [Minneapolis: Fortress, 2014], 45).

[26] The antecedent of the feminine personal pronoun αὐτῆς could be ἁμαρτίας. However, given the focus on the wiles of women in this passage, γυναικός is preferred as the antecedent. This is reflected in the NETS translation, "From a woman is the beginning of sin, and because of *her* we all die" (italics added). If ἁμαρτίας is the antecedent, however, this would more closely connect Sir 25 and Rom 7 both thematically and verbally. The movement in both would be from Eve to sin to death.

[27] Daniel M. Gurtner, ed. and trans., *Second Baruch: A Critical Edition of the Syriac Text; With Greek and Latin Fragments, English Translation, Introduction, and Concordances*, Jewish and Christian Texts in Contexts and Related Studies 6 (New York: T&T Clark, 2009), 87.

[28] On this passage's occurrence in the nomistic discourse, see Legarreta-Castillo, *Figure of Adam*, 108–9.

reminiscent of Rom 7, 2 Bar 48:42–43 explores the broader consequences of transgressing the law with reference to Gen 2–3. As in the Pauline corpus, deception is more closely associated with Eve than with Adam.

## *Philo's* De Opificio Mundi

Philo presents the idea that Eve is the originator of sin in his allegorical interpretation of Gen 2–3 in *De opificio mundi*. Beginning in *Opif.* 151, after extensively relaying the excellence of the first created human (§§136–150),[29] Philo narrates the first man's fall from well-being (εὐδαιμονία) into misfortune (κακοδαιμονία) (§§144, 150, 156). The relevant sections particularly focus on the latter. The root cause of this fall, for Philo, is the first woman. Philo explains that "the first human being too had to enjoy some ill fortune. The starting point [ἀρχή] of a blameworthy life [τῆς ὑπαιτίου ζωῆς] becomes for him woman [γυνή]" (§150).[30] Not only does this section introduce Eve into Philo's allegory, but, as David T. Runia notes, it "focus[es] attention on the chief cause of human decline into misery."[31] When the two progenitors meet, pleasure (ἡδονή) is birthed out of their desire (πόθος) for one another. For Philo, this pleasure is the beginning (ἀρχή) of all iniquities (ἀδικμάτων) and transgressions (παρανομημάτων) and is closely connected with ἐπιθυμία (cf. Rom 7:7–8).[32]

Philo interprets Gen 2–3 allegorically in §§157–170 (see also *Leg.* 2). In his interpretation, the snake represents pleasure (ἡδονή),[33] Adam represents the rational mind (νοῦς), and Eve represents sense perception (αἴσθησις).[34] It is only through

---

[29] David T. Runia notes that the bodily excellence of the first created man is, for Philo, rooted in Greek, rather than Jewish, tradition (*Philo of Alexandria: On the Creation of the Cosmos according to Moses*, PACS 1 [Leiden: Brill, 2001], 333). This has led John R. Levison to write, "Most details and general tendencies in Philo's portrait of the first man are his own and should not be amalgamated with other early Jewish interpretations into a hypothetical 'Adam tradition'" (*Portraits of Adam in Early Judaism: From Sirach to 2 Baruch*, JSPSup 1 [Sheffield: JSOT Press, 1988], 88). Given the allegorical interpretation of Gen 2–3 that is to follow, however, it is judicious to interpret Philo, against Levison, as a representative of the Jewish Adam tradition, even if the parameters of this tradition are quite wide and its representatives diverse.

[30] Trans. Runia, *Philo of Alexandria*, 87.

[31] Ibid., 354.

[32] In Rom 7:7–8, desire (ἐπιθυμία) and the commandment against it serve as synecdoche for the entire law. While the terms *pleasure* and *desire* are not identical, the concepts are similar. Moreover, for Philo, ἡδονή is the foundational passion on which ἐπιθυμία and the other passions operate; ἐπιθυμία is only one step removed from ἡδονή in Philo's hierarchy of passions (*Leg.* 1.86; 2.8, 18, 72; 3.113, 148, 250).

[33] Philo goes to great lengths to demonstrate this, using a variety of proofs in §§157–164. He makes the same allegorical interpretation of the snake and Gen 2–3 as a whole in *Leg.* 2.72: ἡδονῆς, ἣν συμβολικῶς ὄφιν ὠνόμασε ("pleasure, which is symbolically called the snake").

[34] This is especially evident in *Opif.* 165: ἐν ἡμῖν γὰρ ἀνδρὸς μὲν ἔχει λόγον ὁ νοῦς, γυναικὸς δ' αἴσθησις· ἡδονὴ δὲ προτέραις ἐντυγχάνει καὶ ἐνομιλεῖ ταῖς αἰσθήσεσι, δι' ὧν καὶ τὸν ἡγεμόνα νοῦν

sense perception that pleasure can get a foothold on the dominant reasoning faculty and enslave it.³⁵ Not only is Eve the beginning of humanity's fall into misery, but she is allegorically the cause—the beginning (ἀρχή)—of all sin. She is also affiliated with deception and pleasure in a manner that Adam is not. According to Philo, the serpent would never dare to offer its trickeries (γοητείας) and deceit (ἀπάτας) to Adam but can only produce his downfall through Eve (*Opif.* 165). This coheres well with the Pauline corpus, which does not predicate deception of Adam but only of Eve, making it even more likely that she utters the phrase ἡ γὰρ ἁμαρτία ... ἐξηπάτησέν με ("for sin deceived me") in Rom 7:11.

The consequences of Eve's actions as interpreted in *De opificio mundi* also have two significant connections with the women's lament genre and with Rom 7. First, echoing and expounding the injunction of Eve's grievances and groaning in Gen 3:16, Philo divulges that, because of her actions, Eve received excessive sorrows (ἀνίας) and, more importantly for the lament genre, grievances (λύπας) "that occurred successively during the rest of her life" (*Opif.* 167).³⁶ Thus, Philo associates Eve with a life of sorrow and grief. This is an element of the tradition that is taken up in both the Life of Adam and Eve, which will be explored below, and Rom 7. Second, in *Opif.* 167 Philo explicitly writes that Eve is in a state of captivity and lacks freedom (εἶτ᾽ ἀφαίρεσιν ἐλευθερίας καὶ τὴν ἀπὸ τοῦ συνόντος ἀνδρὸς δεσποτείαν).³⁷ This is significant on two counts. First, it correlates well with Rom 7:1–6, which purports that, by law, a woman is not free from her man as long as he is alive and which introduces Paul's Eve, as will be argued below. Second, a consignment

---

φενακίζει ("For in us the mind has the rank of man, and sensations the rank of woman. And pleasure appeals and associates with the sensations first, through which it tricks the governing mind"). See also *Leg.* 2.24.

³⁵ In *Leg.* 2.38, Philo explains that this is because men and the mind are active, while women and sense perceptions are passive. This interpretation has been the object of feminist critiques of Philo. See Daniel Boyarin, *Carnal Israel: Reading Sex in Talmudic Culture*, New Historicism 25 (Berkeley: University of California Press, 1993), 77–83; and the response by David Winston, "Philo and the Rabbis on Sex and the Body," *Poetics Today* 19 (1998): 41–62. For a collection of the texts related to Philo's view of women, see Richard Arthur Baer, *Philo's Use of the Categories Male and Female*, ALGHJ 3 (Leiden: Brill, 1970). For a neutral to optimistic interpretation of Philo's view of women, see Dorothy Sly, *Philo's Perception of Women*, BJS 209 (Atlanta: Scholars Press, 1990), 58; and Judith Romney Wegner, "Philo's Portrayal of Women—Hebraic or Hellenic?," in *"Women like This": New Perspectives on Jewish Women in the Greco-Roman World*, ed. Amy Jill Levine, EJL 1 (Atlanta: Scholars Press, 1991), 41–66, here 50–51. For a general overview of the issues involved and the history of scholarship, see William Loader, *Philo, Josephus, and the Testaments on Sexuality: Attitudes Towards Sexuality in the Writings of Philo and Josephus and in the Testaments of the Twelve Patriarchs*, Attitudes towards Sexuality in Judaism and Christianity in the Hellenistic Greco-Roman Era (Grand Rapids: Eerdmans, 2011), 2–251.

³⁶ Runia, *Philo of Alexandria*, 91.

³⁷ In the preceding sentence, Philo writes that those who find the recompense of pleasure become slaves of harsh and incurable sufferings. Eve is his representative example. Runia (*Philo of Alexandria*, 387) notes that the idea here is related to 1 Tim 2:11–15.

to slavery, in one form or another, is a recurring characteristic of the tragic lamenting woman. But before turning to Eve's introduction and the lament genre, there is one more textual tradition about Eve from the Second Temple period that ought to be explored.

### *The Life of Adam and Eve*

The Life of Adam and Eve is the strongest testimony to a vibrant textual tradition about Eve in ancient Judaism.[38] In this narrative, Eve is the lead actor, who is, more often than not, standing center-stage. All the themes concerning Eve that were investigated above are amplified and clearly presented in the Greek Life of Adam and Eve.[39]

Just as Philo purported that pleasure (ἡδονή) is the root of sin, so also does

---

[38] The textual tradition of the LAE is complicated. At best, we can infer that "a single copy of the Greek *Life of Adam and Eve* is at the fountainhead of the entire manuscript tradition" (Johannes Tromp, *The Life of Adam and Eve in Greek: A Critical Edition*, PVTG 6 [Leiden: Brill, 2005], 71; see 17–111 for an overview of the manuscript tradition). Marinus de Jonge makes a similar contention in "The Literary Development of the Life of Adam and Eve," in *Literature on Adam and Eve: Collected Essays*, ed. Gary A. Anderson, Michael E. Stone, and Johannes Tromp, SVTP 15 (Leiden: Brill, 2000), 239–49, here 239. There are, however, other approaches to the textual tradition that do not posit a single textual archetype. For an overview of these, see Michael E. Stone, *A History of the Literature of Adam and Eve*, EJL 3 (Atlanta: Scholars Press, 1992), 68–69. John R. Levison suggests that LAE 15–30 was originally transmitted independently of the rest of the narrative in what might be called a "Testament of Eve" ("The Exoneration of Eve in the Apocalypse of Moses 15–30," *JSJ* 20 [1989]: 135–50).

It is possible that Life of Adam and Eve actually belongs to a Christian provenance. For this position, see Marinus de Jonge, "The Christian Origin of the *Greek Life of Adam and Eve*," in Anderson, Stone, and Tromp, *Literature on Adam and Eve*, 347–63; Stone, *History of the Literature*, 58–61. Evidence for a Christian provenance is also presented in Marinus de Jonge, "The Greek Life of Adam and Eve and the Writings of the New Testament," in *Religionsgeschichte des Neuen Testaments: Festschrift für Klaus Berger zum 60. Geburtstag*, ed. Axel von Dobbeler, Kurt Erlemann, and Roman Heiligenthal (Tübingen: Francke, 2000), 149–60, here 154–55; de Jonge, however, ultimately takes an agnostic approach about the text's provenance (esp. 156). A Christian provenance for the text would be no less relevant for the present argument. In fact, if the narrative is of Christian provenance, the strong thematic and lexical parallels between Rom 7 and Life of Adam and Eve presented below might suggest that the tradition about Eve was vibrant among early Christian circles and developed out of Rom 7:7–25.

[39] Most have been skeptical about the possibility that Life of Adam and Eve exerted influence on Paul. See esp. de Jonge, "Greek Life," 157–60. John R. Levison, however, makes the case that Life of Adam and Eve is indispensable to the interpretation of Rom 1:18–25 in particular and of the Pauline corpus at large ("Adam and Eve in Romans 1:18–25 and the Greek Life of Adam and Eve," *NTS* 50 [2004]: 519–34). It is not impossible that an *Ur*-form or oral tradition that later came to be represented by the extant textual witnesses of Life of Adam and Eve influenced Paul and Rom 7. However, the relationship between Paul and Life of Adam and Eve need not be intertextual, but only intertraditional for the present argument.

LAE 19:3 employ this root for desire: ἐπιθυμία γάρ ἐστι [κεφαλὴ]⁴⁰ πάσης ἁμαρτίας ("desire is the head of every sin"). Earlier in this verse the snake places this desire on the fruit as poison. Desire appears three times in Rom 7:7-8 and is connected to sin in a manner similar to that in LAE 19:3: ἡ ἁμαρτία ... κατειργάσατο ἐν ἐμοὶ πᾶσαν ἐπιθυμίαν ("sin works up every desire in me").

Others have previously recognized this supposed intertextual connection between LAE 19:3 and Rom 7:7-12,⁴¹ but they typically make little of it. John Levison has critiqued this minimalist approach, arguing that it does not offer anything constructive to Paul's theology nor to the interpretation of the Life of Adam and Eve.⁴² He wants interpreters to place more weight on the intertextual echoes. There is danger, however, in heeding Levison's advice and relying too heavily on the parallel for an interpretation of either text. By making too much of the relationship between LAE 19:3 and Rom 7:7-12, interpreters run the risk of drawing connections that are historically dubious or anachronistic, since the dating of Life of Adam and Eve is highly uncertain. Determining which way the textual influence runs, or if there is textual influence at all, is no straightforward task. In my estimation, however, this does not bring interpreters to an impasse. Rather, by considering the connection between the texts from an intertraditional—rather than a strictly intertextual—perspective, we can walk the narrow path and avoid the pitfalls of making dubious textual inferences, on the one side, and of minimizing the connection between the texts, on the other. My contention is that LAE 19:3 and Rom 7:7-12 interweave the themes of sin, desire, commandment, and Eve because these were traditional tropes about Eve in Second Temple Judaism. By comparing how Eve is constructed and the ends for which she is utilized in each text, interpreters can draw significant conclusions about both Paul's theology and the Life of Adam and Eve.

One of the consistent tropes throughout the Life of Adam and Eve is that Eve's sin is the root cause of human transgression and death.⁴³ Adam first presents this idea in LAE 7:1, where he relates to Seth how disease (νόσον) and infirmities (πόνους) came upon him.⁴⁴ Introducing Eve into his discourse about the garden, Adam

---

⁴⁰ See the discussion of this variant in de Jonge, "Greek Life," 158; and the apparatus in Tromp, *Life of Adam and Eve*, 144-45.

⁴¹ Dunn and M. D. Johnson both make this connection (Dunn, *Theology of Paul*, 88; M. D. Johnson, "Life of Adam and Eve," OTP 2:249-96, here 255). The idea that pleasure or desire is the root of all evil was not uncommon in Second Temple Judaism. See Jas 1:14-15, 1 Cor 10:6, 4 Macc 2:6; Philo, *Spec.* 4.84-85 and *Decal.* 142, 173.

⁴² Levison, "Adam and Eve in Romans," 521.

⁴³ On this, de Jonge writes, "the sin of Adam and Eve is seen as basically a transgression of God's commandment (LAE 8:2; 10:2; 14:3; 23:3; 24:1, 4; 25:1). Eve in particular is to blame and she realizes that (LAE 9:2; 10:2; 14:3; 25:1, 3). It is the central point in Eve's description of what happened in the Garden" ("Greek Life," 154).

⁴⁴ The importance of these terms in Life of Adam and Eve is noted by John R. Levison, "The Primacy of Pain and Disease in the Greek Life of Adam and Eve," *ZNW* 94 (2003): 1-16.

states that it is "through her [that] even I die" (δι' ἧς καὶ ἀποθνήσκω).[45] Adam repeats Eve's culpability in a stronger form in LAE 14:2. This happens after Eve, Seth, and Adam learn from the archangel Michael that Adam will indeed die. He then asks Eve: τί κατηργάσω [cf. Rom 7:13, 15, 17, 18, 20] ἐν ἡμῖν καὶ ἐπήνεγκας ἐφ' ἡμᾶς ὀργὴν μεγάλην, ἥτις ἐστὶν θάνατος [cf. Rom 7:10, 11, 13, 24] κατακυριεύων παντὸς τοῦ γένους ἡμῶν; ("what have you done to us, bringing great wrath on us, which is death that rules over all our generations?").[46] Other characters in Life of Adam and Eve also make Eve liable for death and transgression entering into the world.[47] Significantly, Eve herself reinforces this trope throughout the narrative, often recognizing that she is primarily to blame for what happened in the garden.[48] This occurs in LAE 10:2, where Eve laments how her actions have caused enmity between the human and animal worlds: ἔκλαυσεν δὲ Εὔα λέγουσα· οἴμοι οἴμοι, ὅτι ἐὰν ἔλθω εἰς τὴν ἡμέραν τῆς ἀναστάσεως, πάντες οἱ ἁμαρτήσαντες καταράσονταί με, λέγοντες ὅτι οὐκ ἐφύλαξεν ἡ Εὔα τὴν ἐντολὴν τοῦ θεοῦ ("Eve wept, saying, 'Woe is me! Woe is me! Because when I come to the day of resurrection all the sinners will accuse me, saying, "Eve didn't guard God's commandment!"'"). There are two consequential connections with Rom 7 here. First, Eve is clearly lamenting. The contrast between past and future time, the verb ἔκλαυσεν, the use of the phrase οἴμοι οἴμοι, and the presence of a hypothetical situation differentiated from reality are all features of the lament genre that will be outlined below. Second, the text implies that sin and death are a result of Eve's transgression of the commandment (τὴν ἐντολήν), as is also the case in Rom 7:9–11.

Eve's confession in LAE 32 is a fitting text to conclude our discussion of Eve in this narrative and Eve traditions in the Second Temple period. Lying on his deathbed, Adam reports to Eve that she too will die, and he suggests that she pray to God, because neither of them knows "how they will meet [their] maker—whether he will be wrathful or will turn and pity [them]" (LAE 31:4). In her subsequent confession, there is a striking constellation, as in Rom 7, of sin, death, repentance, and rescue. Eve repeats the verb ἥμαρτον nine times, each time with a different object that she has sinned against. Her last confession of sin is particularly significant, as it is another representation of the idea that sin enters the cosmos on Eve's account: ἥμαρτον ἐναντίον σοῦ, καὶ πᾶσα ἁμαρτία δι' ἐμὲ γέγονεν ἐν τῇ κτίσει ("I have sinned against you and every sin in creation comes through me").

---

[45] For the Greek text, I use Tromp, *Life of Adam and Eve*. All English translations are my own.

[46] Significantly, Rom 7:13 also directly links a participial form of κατεργάζομαι with θάνατος.

[47] This is the case with devil's instructions to the snake in LAE 16:3 and the talking beast in LAE 11:1.

[48] In LAE 9:2, for example, Eve requests that Adam give her half of his disease, because she knows it is on her account that Adam is experiencing death.

## IV. Lament Genre

### Laments as Women's Speech Acts and Moral Psychology

Thus far I have argued that certain thematic and lexical elements of Rom 7:7–25 evoke Gen 3 and corresponding Second Temple traditions about Eve. I have yet to address the reason that Paul formulates these themes in first-person form. In this section, I will argue that Paul has recast Eve in the role of the tragic, lamenting woman. Because Paul is evoking Eve in this pericope, utilizing a speech-in-character to do so is a natural choice for two reasons. First, Gen 3:16 indicates the female protoplast's grievances and groaning (τὰς λύπας σου καὶ τὸν στεναγμόν σου) would be multiplied. This is a theme that both Philo and the Life of Adam and Eve expound, characterizing Eve as a lamentable and lamenting figure. Second, tragic laments were predominantly feminine speeches in Paul's Hellenistic literary context, making it an obvious role in which to recast a woman who was characteristically lamentable.

That laments were characteristically feminine speeches is nearly axiomatic in the relevant secondary literature, and laments as women's speech acts are particularly pronounced in the tragedies.[49] Casey Dué notes that "one thing that female characters do in tragedy above all else is lament."[50] The objects of laments in the tragedies are of varying sorts. Particularly relevant is the personal lament. Dué offers the following list: "Cassandra, the suppliant women of Aeschylus, Jocasta, Antigone, Deianeira, Alcestis, Hecuba, Polyxena, Medea, Phaedra, Andromache, and Iphigeneia all perform laments for themselves in anticipation of death or disaster."[51] Pauline scholarship on Rom 7:7–25 has focused on one of these female figures in particular: Medea in her eponymous Euripidean tragedy.

Gerd Theissen and Stowers both argue that Rom 7 is a part of the Greek moral psychologizing tradition that has its roots in the figure Medea.[52] They do so with specific reference to the proverbial expressions in verses 15b and 19. Theissen

---

[49] The argument that the tragic lament is characteristically a women's speech act is made by Laura McClure, *Spoken like a Woman: Speech and Gender in Athenian Drama* (Princeton: Princeton University Press, 1999), 40–47; Margaret Alexiou, *The Ritual Lament in Greek Tradition*, 2nd ed., Greek Studies (Lanham, MD: Rowman & Littlefield, 2002); Casey Dué, *The Captive Woman's Lament in Greek Tragedy* (Austin: University of Texas Press, 2006), 30–56; Helene P. Foley, *Female Acts in Greek Tragedy*, Martin Classical Lectures (Princeton: Princeton University Press, 2009), 19–55. This is not to suggest that male characters do not lament in the tragedies or comedies. It is simply to claim that there are a disproportionate number of female laments as compared to male laments.

[50] Dué, *Captive Woman's Lament*, 46.

[51] Ibid., 20. Here Dué has distilled Alexiou, *Ritual Lament*, 113.

[52] Gerd Theissen, *Psychological Aspects of Pauline Theology*, trans. John P. Calvin (Philadelphia:

demonstrates that there is a long-standing trope in Greek moral psychology regarding desire's power over reason that originates in Medea.[53] Stowers further contends that this battle between desire and reason is a battle for self-mastery.[54] Following the precedent set by Medea, women came to represent the epitome of ἀκρασία in Greek moral psychology. Lines 1077–1080 of Euripides's tragic play *Medea* represent this tradition and are echoed in Rom 7:7–25.[55]

Stowers and Theissen both suggest that the intertextual resonances between Rom 7 and *Medea* are the result of Paul's evocation of moral psychology.[56] Neither makes anything of this connection with respect to the speaker's gender in Rom 7:7–25, much less to the women's lament tradition as a whole. Instead, Theissen concludes that, with the ἐγώ in Rom 7, Paul is speaking not fictively but autobiographically.[57] Stowers contends that Paul follows the Medean tradition and that this is what causes him to employ first-person forms in his speech-in-character. But the referent of these forms is, according to Stowers, a constructed gentile interlocutor first introduced in Rom 2, presumably male, who is finding it difficult to live according to Torah.[58]

In contrast to Stowers and Theissen, I suggest that the intertextual resonances with Medea are a result of Paul's recasting Eve in the tragic, lamenting mode. I have already argued that Eve is portrayed as a lamentable and lamenting figure in Philo and the Life of Adam and Eve and that many features of the Second Temple Eve tradition are recalled in Rom 7:7–25. I have also shown that the lament genre was characterized by tragic feminine speech acts in antiquity. This makes it likely that Paul is evoking the tragic, lamenting woman.

## *Paul and Tragedy*

A recent swell of studies claims that Paul's rhetoric is influenced by the theater.[59] Courtney J. P. Friesen and Michael B. Cover each find dramatic logic at work

---

Fortress, 1987), 211–19; Stowers, *Rereading of Romans*, 270–72; Stowers, "Romans 7:7–25," 180–202.

[53] Theissen, *Psychological Aspects*, 212.

[54] Stowers, *Rereading of Romans*, 262–84.

[55] Stowers, "Romans 7:7–25," 199.

[56] This is clear in Theissen's contention that the underlying notion of the Medean text—and the tradition that follows it—is that "in everyone, not only in Medea, passion is the cause of evil" (*Psychological Aspects*, 212).

[57] Ibid., 201.

[58] Stowers, *Rereading of Romans*, 277–79. Stowers refers to Paul's interlocutor with masculine personal pronouns in this section.

[59] Courtney J. P. Friesen, "*Paulus Tragicus*: Staging Apostolic Adversity in First Corinthians," *JBL* 134 (2015): 813–32, https://doi.org/10.15699/jbl.1344.2015.3088; Michael B. Cover, "The Death of Tragedy: The Form of God in Euripides's *Bacchae* and Paul's *Carmen Christi*," *HTR* 111 (2018): 66–89, here 67–68; Cover, "The Divine Comedy at Corinth: Paul, Menander, and the

in Pauline letters.[60] The former dubs the apostle *Paulus tragicus*, suggesting that Euripides's *Bacchae* and Sophocles's Oedipus cycle were intended to be heard in 1 Corinthians.[61] The latter has added that the apostle is simultaneously *Paulus comicus*. Cover argues that there are echoes of the *Bacchae* in Phil 2:6–8 that transgress tragic logic and that 1 Cor 5–15 is rife with type scenes and motifs from New Comedy.[62] Both claim that these evocations of tragedies and comedies are not simply window dressing for Paul's purposes but are vital to his rhetorical strategies in these texts. This also appears to be the case with Rom 7, wherein Paul evokes a popular Jewish tradition about Eve's lamentable action and brings her on stage to speak in her tragic voice.

While Eve is not yet speaking in Rom 7:1–6, it appears that she is being ushered onto the stage. These verses serve as an introduction to her speech that follows in Rom 7:7–25. There are ideological and verbal resonances with both Gen 2–3 and the captive woman's lament tradition in this introduction. Resonances with Gen 2–3 can be detected in the themes of life and death, marital union between man and woman, transgression of a commandment, the term flesh (σάρξ), and the verb καρποφορέω ("bear fruit"). By evoking these themes in Rom 7:1–6 Paul recalls Gen 2–3, and he begins to move toward his speech-in-character in Rom 7:5. Here he speaks of a time when "*we* were in the flesh" (ὅτε γὰρ ἦμεν ἐν τῇ σαρκί) and how at that time the desires of sin worked "in *our* members" (ἐν τοῖς μέλεσιν ἡμῶν). By speaking in the first-person plural, Paul evokes humanity's shared experience with

---

Rhetoric of Resurrection," *NTS* 64 (forthcoming 2018; Michael Cover kindly provided me with the final prepublication form of his article, but page numbers of the *NTS* issue were not available at the time of this publication). That Paul and his audience will have been familiar with the tragedies and Euripides in particular can be argued on the basis of the ubiquity of performances of classical tragedies in the first century, manuscript evidence, and educational practices. Friesen notes that Philo witnessed a performance of Euripides (Friesen, "*Paulus Tragicus*," 816 and n. 12; Philo, *Prob.* 141; *Ebr.* 177) and that the presence of theaters in Caesarea, Jerusalem, and Jericho suggests that Greek drama will have been known in both the diaspora and Palestine (Friesen, "*Paulus Tragicus*," 817 n. 14). As to manuscript evidence, Euripides is the best-attested tragedian (William H. Willis, "A Census of the Literary Papyri from Egypt," *GRBS* 9 [1968]: 205–41, here 212–15; Cover, "Death of Tragedy"). Finally, the tragedies were employed in basic writing exercises and grammatical education (Raffaella Cribiore, *Gymnastics of the Mind: Greek Education in Hellenistic and Roman Egypt* [Princeton: Princeton University Press, 2001], 198–99; Friesen, "*Paulus Tragicus*," 817).

[60] Friesen, "*Paulus Tragicus*," 827–31; Cover, "Death of Tragedy," 72–76; Cover, "Divine Comedy at Corinth."

[61] Friesen, "*Paulus Tragicus*," 828–31.

[62] Cover argues for Bacchic intertexts in "Death of Tragedy," 72–76. There he suggests that Paul's Christ in Phil 2 appropriates and subverts features of Euripides's Dionysius. In "Divine Comedy at Corinth," he finds a literary resemblance between the topoi of 1 Cor 5–15 and New Comedy, using Menander's *The Woman from Samos* as a test case. He does not argue for a "genetic relationship" between the two texts. Rather, the similarities between 1 Corinthians and the comedy indicate that Paul is familiar with New Comedy and imbues its rhetoric in the letter.

the protoplasts Adam and Eve. This is further confirmed by the purpose clause that follows, "to bear fruit for death" (εἰς τὸ καρποφορῆσαι τῷ θανάτῳ), which echoes Gen 2–3. While assuring his Roman audience that they are not in the same state as the protoplasts in Rom 7:6, Paul evokes the categories of captivity and slavery with the passive imperfect κατειχόμεθα ("we were captive") and the complementary infinitive δουλεύειν ("we are slaves"). I propose that it is precisely the constellation of captivity, slavery, sin, and death that sends Paul into Eve's speech-in-character in the following verses. He speaks as the female protoplast who laments that she is held captive by the law.

This introduction prepares the reader for the themes and echoes from traditions about Eve that are found in Rom 7:7–25. But it also provides a cogent answer to Anderson's and Timmins's critique of Stowers's theory. Anderson writes, "The absence of any other markers in context suggesting that Paul means anyone other than himself by his use of the first person, must weigh heavily against this [Stowers's] interpretation."[63] Stowers's response is that this context is provided by Rom 2:1–16, where Paul's akratic gentile interlocutor was first introduced.[64] Yet this rebuttal has difficulty contending with the time gap between Rom 2 and 7 and with the fact that the interlocutor in Rom 2:1–16 does not seem to share the same personality as the individual in Rom 7:7–25.[65] The former does not grasp the gravity of his or her sin as the latter does.[66] If Paul begins to introduce a new interlocutor in Rom 7:1–7, however, both the time gap and the differing personalities pose no problem to reading Rom 7:7–25 as a tragic speech-in-character.

To demonstrate that Eve speaks in this tragic mode, it is crucial to understand the features of the lament speeches. As we shall see, these elements from the lament genre help explain Paul's syntax in Rom 7:7–25:[67]

    a. A hesitant beginning with an initial question
    b. Questions, sporadic or successive, that carry the lament along
    c. A series of hypotheses, differentiated from reality, that are proposed and rejected
    d. A contrast between past, present, and future time, resulting in a variety of verbal tenses
    e. A prominence of the invocational *now* (νῦν)
    f. An abundance of first-person pronouns and verbal forms

---

[63] Anderson, *Ancient Rhetorical Theory*, 182.

[64] Stowers, "Apostrophe, Προσωποποιία and Paul's Rhetorical Education," 366–67.

[65] These are two critiques that Timmins offers ("Romans 7," 105–7). He ultimately concludes that Paul must not be employing a speech-in-character at all in this chapter.

[66] Ibid., 107.

[67] I have synthesized these elements of the lament from Alexiou, *Ritual Lament*, 161–68; Dué, *Captive Woman's Lament*, 12–15, 53–55; and R. L. Fowler, "The Rhetoric of Desperation," *HSCP* 91 (1987): 5–38, here 6. On questions in laments, see Edgar Wright Smith, "Form and Religious Background of Romans 7:24–25a," *NovT* 13 (1971): 127–35, here 130–31.

g. Self-deprecation on behalf of the lamenter (often expressed by words such as δύστηνος, ταλαίπωρος, or τάλας)

h. Lament ending with the speaker in a desperate situation, often feeling utterly abandoned to slavery or death

i. Standard words of woe, such as οἴμοι or ἰώ

Many of these features were present in Eve's brief lament in LAE 10:2 that was considered above. Before examining the aspects of Eve's lament in Rom 7, it will be instructive to see how a different Hellenistic text from a vastly different genre than Paul's epistles similarly evokes the woman's lament genre, employing many of these features. This will give us a second point of reference for interpreting Rom 7 as a tragic lament.

### Aseneth's Lament

Joseph and Aseneth is a narrative that recounts the circumstances surrounding the marriage of Pharaoh's right-hand man, Joseph, to Aseneth, the daughter of the Egyptian priest Pentephres.[68] When Pentephres initially proposes that Aseneth be betrothed to Joseph, she ridicules the idea. Upon seeing Joseph for the first time in all his stateliness, however, she realizes that she has made a huge mistake. This sends her into a personal lament that encompasses Jos. Asen. 6:2–8:

| | |
|---|---|
| τί νῦν ἐγὼ ποιήσω ἡ ταλαίπωρος; | What now will I, the wretched one, do? |
| οὐχὶ λελάληκα λέγουσα ὅτι Ἰωσὴφ ἔρχεται ὁ υἱὸς τοῦ ποιμένος ἐκ γῆς Χαναάν; | Didn't I speak saying that Joseph the son of the shepherd of Canaan is coming? |
| καὶ νῦν ἰδοὺ ὁ ἥλιος ἐκ τοῦ οὐρανοῦ ἥκει πρὸς ἡμᾶς ἐν τῷ ἅρματι αὐτοῦ | And now, behold, the sun from heaven comes to us on his chariot. |
| καὶ εἰσῆλθεν εἰς τὴν οἰκίαν ἡμῶν σήμερον | And he came into our home today |
| καὶ λάμπει εἰς αὐτὴν ὡς φῶς ἐπὶ τῆς γῆς | And he lights it up like a light on the earth. |
| ἐγὼ δὲ ἄφρων καὶ θρασεῖα ἐξουδένωσα αὐτὸν | But I foolishly and arrogantly despised him. |
| καὶ ἐλάλησα ῥήματα πονηρὰ περὶ αὐτοῦ | And I spoke evil words to him. |
| καὶ οὐκ ᾔδειν ὅτι Ἰωσὴφ υἱὸς τοῦ θεοῦ ἐστιν. | And I hadn't known that Joseph is a son of God. |

---

[68] The scholarship on the date and provenance of Joseph and Aseneth is notoriously divided. For the most recent overview of these issues, see Angela Standhartinger, "Recent Scholarship on Joseph and Aseneth (1988–2013)," *CurBR* 12 (2014): 353–406. My intention here is only to demonstrate that the lament in Jos. Asen. 6 is an example of the women's lament genre that is roughly contemporaneous with Paul and that Rom 7:7–25 exhibits generic parallels to this text. The text and verse enumeration of Joseph and Aseneth used here are from Christoph Burchard, ed., *Joseph und Aseneth*, PVTG 5 (Leiden: Brill, 2003). English translations are my own.

| | |
|---|---|
| τίς γὰρ ἀνθρώπων ἐπὶ γῆς γεννήσει τοιοῦτον κάλλος | For who from earth's humanity will beget such beauty? |
| καὶ ποία κοιλία γυναικὸς τέξεται τοιοῦτον φῶς; | And what kind of womb of woman can bear this kind of light? |
| ταλαίπωρος ἐγὼ καὶ ἄφρων ὅτι λελάληκα τῷ πατρί μου περὶ αὐτοῦ ῥήματα πονηρά. | I am wretched and foolish because I have spoken evil words about him to my father. |
| καὶ νῦν ποῦ ἀπεπλεύσομαι καὶ ἀποκρυβήσομαι ἀπὸ προσώπου αὐτοῦ | And now, where will I go and hide from his face |
| ὅπως μὴ ὄψηταί με Ἰωσὴφ ὁ υἱὸς τοῦ θεοῦ; | so that Joseph, the son of God, will not see me, |
| διότι λελάληκα πονηρὰ περὶ αὐτοῦ; | since I have spoken evil words about him. |
| καὶ ποῦ ἀπελεύσομαι καὶ κρυβήσομαι | And where will I go and hide, |
| ὅτι πᾶσαν ἀποκρυβὴν αὐτὸς ὁρᾷ | because he sees every hiding place |
| καὶ οὐδὲν κρυπτὸν λέληθεν αὐτὸν | and nothing hidden escapes him |
| διὰ τὸ φῶς τὸ μέγα τὸ ὂν ἐν αὐτῷ; | because of the great light that is in him? |
| καὶ νῦν ἵλεώς μοι κύριε ὁ θεὸς τοῦ Ἰωσὴφ | And now, have mercy on me, Lord, the God of Joseph, |
| διότι λελάληκα ἐγὼ κατ'αὐτοῦ ῥήματα πονηρὰ ἐν ἀγνοίᾳ. | since I've spoken evil words about him in ignorance. |
| καὶ νῦν δότω με ὁ πατήρ μου τῷ Ἰωσὴφ εἰς παιδίσκην καὶ εἰς δούλην. | And now, let my father give me to Joseph as a maidservant and as a slave. |
| καὶ δουλεύσω εἰς τὸν αἰῶνα χρόνον. | And I will serve him forever. |

Aseneth's speech in this chapter is replete with elements from the Greek lament genre. The lament contains at least five questions (criterion a). Two of these questions begin the lament, and the remaining questions are peppered throughout to flavor her speech (criteria b, c). The contrast between time and tense is prominent in Aseneth's lament. In the indicative mood alone, five present-tense verbs occur alongside nine futures, six perfects, and three aorists (criterion d). Four invocational νῦνs are present (criterion e). Aseneth's speech ends in utter desperation. She expresses her desire to be given to Joseph as a maidservant or slave (criterion h). Finally, and important for our purposes, Aseneth uses the first-person personal pronoun (ἐγώ) seven times, along with another fifteen first-person singular verbal forms (criterion f).

In these ways, Aseneth's speech is a significant testimony to the Hellenistic form of the lament. Moreover, Aseneth's lament has strong parallels to Rom 7:7–25, and especially verses 14–25. None of these parallels, however, is more significant than the shared lexeme, ταλαίπωρος. Aseneth applies the self-deprecating term twice, once in 6:2 and again in 6:4. The word also appears in Rom 7:24: ταλαίπωρος ἐγὼ ἄνθρωπος ("Wretch I am!"). Joseph and Aseneth 6:4 is the closest contemporary parallel with the strongest verbal resonance to Paul's phrase here. In fact, it appears to be the only other occasion in Hellenistic literature where ταλαίπωρος ("wretch") is immediately followed or preceded by the nominative ἐγώ.[69] This is not because the two are in some kind of direct intertextual relationship. Rather, both are the product of the women's lament genre.

## Eve's Lament

Romans 7:7–25 contains most of the features of the lament genre listed above. Eve's speech begins with two initial questions (v. 7). Although there are not sporadic questions throughout the lament, there is a third question posed toward the end of the lament in verse 24 (criteria a, b). There is a series of eight hypotheticals, conditionals, and contrasts that runs from verse 14 to verse 24. In each case, there is a differentiation between what might be and what actually is (criterion c). For example, in verse 20 Eve offers the conditional statement with the protasis, "if I do the thing that I don't want to" (εἰ δὲ ὃ οὐ θέλω ἐγὼ τοῦτο ποιῶ) and completes it with the apodosis, "it's no longer I who do it, but the sin dwelling in me" (οὐκέτι ἐγὼ κατεργάζομαι αὐτὸ ἀλλὰ ἡ οἰκοῦσα ἐν ἐμοὶ ἁμαρτία). Similar conditionals and hypotheticals that are differentiated from reality carry these verses along. There are a variety of tenses in the speech: Eve uses ten aorists, two imperfects, twenty-seven presents, three futures, two perfects, and one imperfect (criterion d). There is an invocational νῦν in 7:17 and 8:1 (criterion e). First-person pronouns and verbal forms abound: there are twenty-three instances of the first-person personal pronoun in 7:7–25, along with another twenty-nine first-person verbal forms (criterion f).[70] Eve applies a self-deprecating term, ταλαίπωρος, typical of laments in verse 24 (criterion g). Finally, Eve's speech ends in a desperate situation, as she declares her wretchedness, asks who will rescue her from her body of death, and consigns herself to service to the law of God in her mind, but the law of death in her body (criterion h).

The conclusion of Eve's speech in Rom 7:25 is not atypical. Greek tragic laments and desperation speeches often end with the speaker in a state of utter helplessness. At the end of the lament, the lamenter often bemoans her wretchedness and expresses her desire for a hasty death. This is the case with Medea's petition in *Med.* 143–147.[71] It is also the situation in Polyxena's lament and subsequent

---

[69] It is significant, however, that ταλαίπωρος and closely related words do occur elsewhere on the lips of the lamenter. See, e.g., Euripides, *Suppl.* 1094: τί δὴ χρὴ τὸν ταλαίπωρον με δρᾶν. Medea also uses a similar phrase, ἡ τάλαιν᾽ ἐγώ, in *Med.* 1016, and another, ὦ τάλαν, in *Med.* 1057.

[70] Or perhaps twenty-four, depending on the variant reading in Rom 7:20 wherein several manuscripts omit ἐγώ.

[71] In the end, Medea does not commit suicide or die. She is, in fact, the only tragic offender who is not brought to justice in some way (Edith Hall, *Greek Tragedy: Suffering under the Sun* [Oxford: Oxford University Press, 2010], 242).

heroic sacrifice in *Hecuba*, where she expresses her desire for death (213–215, 346–348, 369–378).[72] Another option was for the lamenter to consign herself to slavery. Aseneth, at the end of her lament in Jos. Asen. 6:8, states, "And now may my father give me to Joseph as a servant and slave, and I will serve him forever." The lamenting woman may also seek rescue by means of a savior or the gods. Hecuba asks if she might receive divine aid at the conclusion of her lament (Euripides, *Hec.* 96–97). She does this again in interrogative form in 164–165: πῶς τις θεῶν ἢ δαίμων ἐπαρωγός; ("what god or intercessor is my helper?"). Eve's question near the end of her lament in Rom 7:25 resembles this tradition, as she asks who will save her from her body of death. Dissimilar from the tragic lament tradition, however, Eve *does* receive intercessory aid. Following the lament's conclusion, Eve obtains a positive response to her lament in Rom 8:2.

In tragic literature, the lamenter was frequently addressed by the chorus or another character in the tragedy at the conclusion of the lament. This occurs, for example, in *Med.* 148–159 and 357–363. Just as the chorus is concerned with who Medea's advocate and protector might be in the latter case, so also does Paul assure Eve that she has her own advocate "in Christ Jesus" (ἐν Χριστῷ Ἰησοῦ). Directly opposing Eve's own lamentable conclusion that she is consigned to slavery in both her mind and her flesh, Paul assures her that the law of the spirit of life has freed (ἐλευθέρωσεν) her from the law of sin and death. This is Paul's own creative twist on Eve's tragic lament in Rom 7.

## V. Conclusion

According to Aristotle, the function of the tragic character is to provoke fear, pity, or a mixture of the two in the audience's mind (*Poet.* 1452b1; 1452b30–1453a6). He argues that the character who most successfully evokes fear or pity is the one who falls into adversity (εἰς τὴν δυστυχίαν) not through evil or depravity (διὰ κακίαν καὶ μοχθηρίαν) but by some error (δι' ἁμαρτίαν τινά) (*Poet.* 1453a7–13). It is in this sense that Paul's literary contemporary, the Stoic Epictetus, can evoke Medea as a tragic figure who is to be pitied (*Diatr.* 28.5–9).[73] According to Epictetus, it is

---

[72] On the heroism of the lamenter's consignment to death, see Fowler, "Rhetoric of Desperation," 6. Dué specifically argues that Polyxena's self-consignment to death follows a traditional heroization pattern (*Captive Woman's Lament*, 131).

[73] Aristotle (*Poet.* 1453a29–30) also indicates that Euripides is the most tragic of the poets. This could be why Medea continued to exert literary influence in Paul's own context. Stowers and Theissen emphasize that Medea's words were retold and reinterpreted in several women's speech contexts and that rewritten *Medea* eventually became its own genre. This genre was incredibly popular in first-century Rome (Stowers, *Rereading of Romans*, 260–72; Stowers, "Romans 7:7–25," 188–99; Theissen, *Psychological Aspects*, 211–19; Hildebrecht Hommel, "Das 7. Kapitel des Römerbriefs im Licht Antiker Überlieferung," *ThViat* 8 [1961–1962]: 90–116). Some significant

because Medea is deceived (ἐξηπάτηται) by her passions, not because she is evil or depraved, that she commits her tragic actions. Epictetus then tells his interlocutor that he ought not to be angry with the wretch (ἡ ταλαίπωρος), who has become a viper rather than a human (ἔχις ἀντὶ ἀνθρώπου γέγονεν), but rather ought to pity her (ἐλεεῖς).

Eve's tragic speech-in-character in Rom 7:7–25 ultimately has a pedagogical function. Eve is the perfect pitiable and lamenting figure that fits Paul's unfolding argument in chapters 5–8 for three reasons. First, she falls into adversity not because of her inherent evil of depravity. On the contrary, and perfectly in line with Aristotle's conception of the ideal tragic figure, sin (ἁμαρτία) was the cause of her fall into misfortune. Second, Gen 3:16 indicates that Eve's grievances and groaning will be excessively multiplied, and this characteristic of Eve was a consistent trope about her in various Second Temple traditions. She was an ideal candidate to be presented as lamenting in Rom 7 because grieving was an indelible mark of her character in Paul's context. Third, she was a perfect counterpart to the Adamic argument that Paul expounded in Rom 5:12–21. As a result, Paul presents the two protoplasts as jointly culpable in humanity's downfall: Adam in Rom 5 and Eve in Rom 7.

The protoplasts' joint culpability, however, is not the end of the story for Paul. He addresses Eve in Rom 8:1–2, indicating that the consequences of her error are apocalyptically undone.[74] If, as Aristotle suggests, the purpose of tragic lament is to provoke pity or fear, the purpose of this provocation is for the cathartic release of these emotions in the audience itself (*Poet.* 1449b26–27). By addressing Eve and assuring her that she now has no condemnation, Paul provokes a cathartic release of the pity the audience felt for Eve and for themselves. This release makes it possible for the audience to choose a new path. By addressing Eve in such a rhetorical form, Paul can more effectively address and provoke a response in his Roman audience as his discourse moves forward in Rom 8.

---

examples of references to or retellings of *Medea* include Euripides, *Hipp.* 377–383; Galen, *Hippoc. et Plat.* 4.244.2–9; 4.274.15–22; Seneca, *Med.*; Plutarch, *Virt. mor.* 6 (446a); Plautus, *Trin.* 657–658; Albinus, *Ep.* 243; Aelius Aristides, *Or.* 50; and Lucian, *Apol.* 10.

[74] On Paul's conception of the two apocalyptic powers that characterize the cosmos, see John M. G. Barclay, "Under Grace: The Christ-Gift and the Construction of Christian *Habitus*," in *Apocalyptic Paul: Cosmos and Anthropos in Romans 5–8*, ed. Beverly Roberts Gaventa (Waco, TX: Baylor University Press, 2013), 59–76, here 59–69.

# SBL PRESS

## New and Recent Titles

### BIBLICAL ANIMALITY AFTER JACQUES DERRIDA
Hannah M. Strømmen
Paperback $32.95, 978-1-62837-212-0   196 pages, 2018   Code: 060692
Hardcover $47.95, 978-0-88414-297-3   E-book $32.95, 978-0-88414-298-0
Semeia Studies 91

### A NEW APPROACH TO TEXTUAL CRITICISM
An Introduction to the Coherence-Based Genealogical Method
Tommy Wasserman and Peter J. Gurry
Paperback $19.95, 978-1-62837-199-4   162 pages, 2017   Code: 060399
Hardcover $34.95, 978-0-88414-267-6   E-book $19.95, 978-0-88414-266-9
Resources for Biblical Study 80

### INVENTION OF THE FIRST-CENTURY SYNAGOGUE
Lidia D. Matassa
Paperback $39.95, 978-1-62837-218-2   288 pages, 2018   Code: 062826
Hardcover $54.95, 978-0-88414-319-2   E-book $39.95, 978-0-88414-320-8
Ancient Near East Monographs 20

### THE AGGADA OF THE BAVLI AND ITS CULTURAL WORLD
Geoffrey Herman and Jeffrey L. Rubenstein, editors
Paperback $56.95, 978-1-946527-08-0   430 pages, 2018   Code: 140362
Hardcover $76.95, 978-1-946527-09-7   E-book $56.95, 978-1-946527-10-3
Brown Judaic Studies 362

### SENNACHERIB, KING OF ASSYRIA
Josette Elayi
Paperback $34.95, 978-1-62837-217-5   236 pages, 2018   Code: 061730
Hardcover $49.95, 978-0-88414-317-8   E-book $34.95, 978-0-88414-318-5
Archaeology and Biblical Studies 24

### HOW AMERICA MET THE JEWS
Hasia R. Diner
Paperback $31.95, 978-1-946527-02-8   152 pages, 2018   Code: 140360
Hardcover $46.95, 978-1-946527-04-2   E-book $31.95, 978-1-946527-03-5
Brown Judaic Studies 360

SBL Press • P.O. Box 2243 • Williston, VT 05495-2243
Phone: 877-725-3334 (toll-free) or 802-864-6185 • Fax: 802-864-7626
Order online at www.sbl-site.org/publications

# The Blood of Goats and Calves ... and Bulls? An Allusion to Isaiah 1:11 LXX in Hebrews 10:4

## JUSTIN HARRISON DUFF
jd221@st-andrews.ac.uk
University of St Andrews, St Andrews KY16 9JU, Scotland, United Kingdom

Hebrews 9:12–10:4 characterizes the blood of the first covenant in four ways: as the blood of goats and calves (9:12), as the blood of goats and bulls (9:13), as the blood of calves and goats (9:19), and finally as the blood of bulls and goats (10:4). Despite the noun transpositions and shifts from μόσχος ("calf") to ταῦρος ("bull") in 9:13 and 10:4, the changes usually elicit little comment from interpreters. When the changes are noted, the differences are often attributed to the author's imprecision or dwindling concern for the actual practice of Yom Kippur, which in Rahlfs's LXX depicts χίμαρος ("he-goat") and μόσχος, not ταῦρος and τράγος ("he-goat"), as the sacrificial animals used in Lev 16. The argument, however, is rarely brought into conversation with the greater LXX tradition and other Second Temple Jewish sources. I argue that these four phrases betray a continued interest in the practice of Yom Kippur and reveal a carefully crafted pattern that builds into a scriptural allusion to Isa 1:11 LXX. The allusion evokes Isaiah's criticism of injustice and hypocrisy, tempering Hebrews' denunciation in 10:4 of the Levitical cult.

---

Hebrews 10:4 has been described as a radical,[1] brutal,[2] and uncompromising[3] critique of the Jewish cult. Through the declaration "It is impossible for the blood of bulls and goats to take away sins," the author of Hebrews seems to extract all of the purifying power from the principal "ritual detergent"[4] used by ancient Levitical

---

[1] Hans Windisch, *Der Hebräerbrief*, HNT 14 (Tübingen: Mohr Siebeck, 1931), 89.
[2] Ceslas Spicq, *L'Épître aux Hébreux*, 2 vols., EBib (Paris: Gabalda, 1952–1953), 2:303.
[3] Erich Grässer, *An die Hebräer*, 3 vols. EKKNT 17 (Zurich: Benziger, 1990–1997), 2:212. See also Cynthia Long Westfall, *A Discourse Analysis of the Letter to the Hebrews: The Relationship between Form and Meaning*, LNTS 297 (London: T&T Clark, 2005), 220–21.
[4] In order to emphasize its purgative function, Jacob Milgrom regularly refers to the blood from a Levitical purification offering as a "ritual detergent" (*Leviticus 1–16: A New Translation with Introduction and Commentary*, AB 3 [New York: Doubleday, 1991], 239, 254–56, 311).

765

priests.⁵ The enervation of the Jewish cult not only disputes Torah, where the Lord graciously institutes the sacrificial system so that Israel may remove its ritual and moral impurity,⁶ but also disrupts the author of Hebrews' own a fortiori rhetorical strategy developed earlier in the address. As Christian A. Eberhart succinctly states, "The total denial of the validity of the Judean sacrificial cult in Heb 10:4 is inconsistent with Hebrews' own argument in Heb 9:13. There the effectiveness of this cult is the foundation of the metaphor of Christ's sacrifice."⁷

An Isaianic allusion appears to have a tempering effect on the author's otherwise sharp denunciation. On the heels of an allusion to Isa 53:12 in Heb 9:28,⁸ the phrase αἷμα ταύρων καὶ τράγων⁹ ("blood of bulls and goats") evokes Isa 1:11. The Old Greek (OG) text of the verse, which reverberates throughout the greater Greek

---

⁵ See Gareth Lee Cockerill's analysis in *The Epistle to the Hebrews*, NICNT (Grand Rapids: Eerdmans, 2012), 432: "The pastor categorically condemns the saving efficacy of all Old Covenant animal sacrifices *in toto*. Spicq rightly describes the sharpness of this statement as 'almost brutal.'" See Spicq, *L'Epître aux Hébreux*, 2:303. James Moffatt describes the statement as a "ringing assertion" that reveals the "inherent defectiveness of animal sacrifices," which "necessitated a new sacrifice altogether, the self-sacrifice of Jesus" (*A Critical and Exegetical Commentary on the Epistle to the Hebrews*, ICC [Edinburgh: T&T Clark, 1924], 137). See also F. F. Bruce, *The Epistle to the Hebrews*, NICNT (Grand Rapids: Eerdmans, 1972), 238; B. F. Westcott, *The Epistle to the Hebrews: The Greek Text with Notes and Essays*, 3rd ed. (London: Macmillan, 1903), 307; Harold W. Attridge, *The Epistle to the Hebrews: A Commentary on the Epistle to the Hebrews*, Hermeneia (Philadelphia: Fortress, 1989), 250; James W. Thompson, "Hebrews 9 and Hellenistic Concepts of Sacrifice," *JBL* 98 (1979): 567–78, here 571, https://doi.org/10.2307/3265669.

⁶ Jonathan Klawans describes ritual impurity as a contagious, more or less unavoidable, impermanent impurity that arises from naturally occurring phenomena (e.g., the birth of a baby, sexual relations, and death; cf. Lev 11–15 and Num 19) (*Impurity and Sin in Ancient Judaism* [Oxford: Oxford University Press, 2000], 21–91). Conversely, moral impurity is a noncontagious, avoidable, more permanent impurity that results from disobeying God's commands (cf. Lev 18:24–30, 20:1–3, Num 25:33–34). For the use of Jewish sacrifices to remove these impurities, see Milgrom, *Leviticus 1–16*, 45–47, 1039–58. Luke Timothy Johnson concludes that the author of Hebrews' "understanding of the cult's goal" is "not one shared by Torah" (*Hebrews: A Commentary*, NTL [Louisville: Westminster John Knox, 2006], 249–50).

⁷ See Christian A. Eberhart, "Characteristics of Sacrificial Metaphors in Hebrews," in *Hebrews: Contemporary Methods, New Insights*, ed. Gabriella Gelardini, BibInt 75 (Leiden: Brill, 2005), 37–64, here 60. See also Susan Haber, "From Priestly Torah to Christ Cultus: The Re-Vision of Covenant and Cult in Hebrews," in *"They Shall Purify Themselves": Essays on Purity in Early Judaism*, ed. Adele Reinhartz, EJL 24 (Atlanta: Society of Biblical Literature, 2008), 143–58, here 143–44.

⁸ For this and other uses of Isaiah in Hebrews, see J. Cecil McCullough, "Isaiah in Hebrews," in *Isaiah in the New Testament*, ed. Steve Moyise and Maarten J. J. Menken, NTSI (London: T&T Clark, 2005), 159–73.

⁹ The transposed variant τράγων καὶ ταύρων in ℵ and P46 probably represents assimilation to 9:12 and/or 9:13. See Paul Ellingworth, *The Epistle to the Hebrews: A Commentary on the Greek Text*, NIGTC (Grand Rapids: Eerdmans, 1993), 498; Grässer, *An die Hebräer*, 2:212.

Isaianic tradition,[10] can be translated as "'What to me is the multitude of your sacrifices?,' says the Lord. 'I am full of whole burnt offerings of rams and the fat of lambs and I do not desire the blood of bulls and goats [αἷμα ταύρων καὶ τράγων], not even if you come to appear before me.'"

In the Greek canon, the precise alliterative phrase αἷμα ταύρων καὶ τράγων appears only in Isa 1:11, Heb 10:4, and other early Christian evocations of both verses, prompting commentators as far back as Jerome[11] to list Isa 1:11 as an alluded text[12] for this verse. Two scholars have also begun intertextual analyses of the allu-

---

[10] By "Old Greek" I refer to the hypothetical reconstruction of the original Greek text presented in the Göttingen LXX. For OG Isa 1:11, see Joseph Ziegler's *Isaias*, 3rd ed., SVTG 14 (Göttingen: Vandenhoeck & Ruprecht, 1983), 124. Ziegler notes that one witness to the Aquila text family (minuscule 710) presents καὶ ἀμνῶν ["lambs"] καὶ καίριμων ("seasonal offerings") instead of καὶ τράγων for Isa 1:11. See also J. Ross Wagner's representation of the OG text for Isa 1:11 in *Reading the Sealed Book: Old Greek Isaiah and the Problem of Septuagint Hermeneutics*, FAT 88 (Tübingen: Mohr Siebeck, 2013), 107.

[11] See Jerome, *Commentary on Isaiah: Including St. Jerome's Translation of Origen's Homilies 1–9 on Isaiah*, trans. Thomas P. Scheck, ACW 68 (New York: Newman, 2015), 84. See also Westcott, *Epistle to the Hebrews*, 258; Attridge, *Epistle to the Hebrews*, 248 n. 52; Hans-Friedrich Weiss, *Der Brief an die Hebräer*, 15th ed., KEK 13 (Göttingen: Vandenhoeck & Ruprecht, 1991), 505 n. 32; Moffatt, *Epistle to the Hebrews*, 122; Ellingworth, *Epistle to the Hebrews*, 454; Grässer, *An die Hebräer*, 2:212 n. 96; Albert Vanhoye, *A Different Priest: The Epistle to the Hebrews*, trans. Leo Arnold, Rhetorica Semitica (Miami, FL: Convivium, 2011), 310. Most commentators note that comparable language is also contained in Ps 49:13 LXX (μὴ φάγομαι κρέα ταύρων ἢ αἷμα τράγων πίομαι, "I will not eat the flesh of bulls, nor will I drink the blood of goats"). Hebrews 10:4 may contain a double allusion, but the precise phrase αἷμα ταύρων καὶ τράγων is only found in Isa 1:11 LXX.

[12] For the difference between a quotation and an allusion, I draw from William A. Tooman's *Gog of Magog: Reuse of Scripture and Compositional Technique in Ezekiel 38–39*, FAT 2/52 (Tübingen: Mohr Siebeck, 2011). Tooman describes a quotation as an intentional reproduction that requires both *literalness* (verbal repetition) and *discreteness* (observable division in the alluding text). Conversely, an allusion lacks discreteness and does not *require* literalness: it is any intentional and semantically enriching activation of an independent text. Lacking discreteness, Heb 10:4 *alludes* to Isa 1:11. It must be noted that an allusion is not necessarily less significant or evocative than a quotation. As Tooman notes, the dynamic power of an allusion is its ability to evoke "anything from a single clause to an entire independent text" (8). One could argue that the verbal parallel between Heb 10:4 and Isa 1:11 is neither intentional nor semantically enriching, representing either the "influence" of Isa 1:11 or a semantically insignificant "echo" of the text (8–10). Either judgment, however, largely depends on whether the allusion instigates interpretively valuable intertextual dialogue, dialogue that will be explored in this study. For some other initial points in defense of an allusion, see the criteria outlined by Richard B. Hays, *Echoes of Scripture in the Letters of Paul* (New Haven: Yale University Press, 1989), 29–32. Since Isaiah is elsewhere used in Hebrews, since other interpreters have identified the allusion in Heb 10:4 and explored its effects, since the phrase αἷμα ταύρων καὶ τράγων appears at the end of a long list of references to the blood of calves/bulls and goats in Heb 9:12–10:4, and since Isa 1 presents points of thematic correspondence with Heb 10, there seems to be initial warrant for undergoing an intertextual investigation.

sion by mapping the effects created by the author of Hebrews' recontextualization of the phrase.[13] J. Cecil McCullough and David A. deSilva both note that Isaiah does not criticize αἷμα ταύρων καὶ τράγων due to an inherent flaw in the Levitical system but because Israel is acting like the wicked nations (1:10).[14] The people have ignored the orphan and the widow (Isa 1:17) and have covered their hands with innocent blood (Isa 1:15), rendering the blood of their own atonement offerings useless (Isa 1:11–16). But neither McCullough nor deSilva concludes that the Isaianic allusion changes the perspective of Hebrews' critique. DeSilva argues, "What was in the prophetic texts an attempt to safeguard the integrity of the sacrificial system becomes in Hebrews a declaration of the inefficacy of the system itself."[15]

DeSilva perceives a distance between the two critiques, with the criticism of hypocritical animal offerers[16] in Isaiah being stretched into a rejection of animal offerings[17] in Hebrews. Part of the reason the allusion seems to demand this particular

---

[13] Susan Graham notes that studies in biblical allusions usually "indicate connections between texts and suggest nuances of meaning when various connotations are possible" but are not "typically concerned with the effects of recontextualization," which remain the domain of intertextual inquiry ("A Strange Salvation: Intertextual Allusion in Mt 27,39–44," in *The Scriptures in the Gospels*, ed. C. M. Tuckett, BETL 131 [Leuven: Leuven University Press, 1997], 501–11, here 501). Cf. also David M. Moffitt's use of Graham's work in "Righteous Bloodshed, Matthew's Passion Narrative, and the Temple's Destruction: Lamentations as a Matthean Intertext," *JBL* 125 (2006): 299–320, esp. 300, https://doi.org/10.2307/27638362. Graham's use of the term *intertextuality* echoes what Steve Moyise calls "dialogical intertextuality" or a two-way "interaction between text and subtext" (see Moyise, "Intertextuality and the Study of the Old Testament in the New Testament," in *The Old Testament in the New Testament: Essays in Honour of J. L. North*, ed. Steve Moyise, JSNTSup 189 [Sheffield: Sheffield Academic, 2000], 14–41, here 17). Graham's use of the term *intertextuality* thus represents one of a number of possible uses, as the term can also refer to a study of an author's sources or the broader dialogicality of signs. See Stefan Alkier, "Intertextuality and the Semiotics of Biblical Texts," in *Reading the Bible Intertextually*, ed. Richard B. Hays, Stefan Alkier, Leroy A. Huizenga (Waco, TX: Baylor University Press, 2009), 3–21, here 4–9.

[14] See McCullough, "Isaiah in Hebrews," 172 (cf. Vanhoye, *Different Priest*, 310); David A. deSilva, *Perseverance in Gratitude: A Socio-rhetorical Commentary on the Epistle "to the Hebrews"* (Grand Rapids: Eerdmans, 2000), 319–20. DeSilva's analysis is echoed by Lloyd Kim, *Polemic in the Book of Hebrews: Anti-Semitism, Anti-Judaism, Supersessionism?* PTMS 64 (Eugene, OR: Pickwick, 2006), 178–80.

[15] DeSilva, *Perseverance in Gratitude*, 320. Confusingly, McCullough ("Isaiah in Hebrews," 172) concludes that "Hebrews uses the phrase in the same way as Isaiah" even though Isaiah and Hebrews criticize the Jewish cult for different reasons.

[16] It is not simply *sacrifices* that the Lord criticizes in Isa 1:11 but *Israel's* sacrifices (τί μοι πλῆθος τῶν θυσιῶν ὑμῶν). Isaiah's solution, moreover, is not to offer cleaner sacrifices but for the offerers themselves to become clean through repentance and just practices. See Wagner, *Reading the Sealed Book*, 106–7. See also Amos 4:4–6, Hos 8:11–14, Jer 6:19–21, Ezek 23:36–39.

[17] See also Spicq, *L'Épître aux Hébreux*, 304: "C'est le troisième ἀδύνατον de l'épître (VI, 4, 18; cf. p. 168), et la condamnation la plus radicale de l'ancienne Loi et de son culte, en vertu de leur nature même."

intertextual effect can be traced to the disparaging or imprecise attitude Hebrews is perceived to display toward the Jewish cult.[18] The author's use of τράγος and ταῦρος in Heb 10:4 and elsewhere to describe the blood used for sacrifice has drawn particular ire. For instance, Susan Haber, who identifies a "forceful and deliberate" polemic against the Jewish cult in Hebrews, writes that these nouns are "generalized but inaccurate references to the sacrificial offerings of the Yom Kippur ritual in which a bull, two goats, and a calf were used. The imprecision with which the author of Hebrews refers to these sacrificial animals is an obvious expression of his disdain for what he considers antiquated offerings."[19]

Haber's assessment is echoed by Harold W. Attridge, Paul Ellingworth, Gareth Cockerill, and others,[20] who identify a blasé or imprecise reference to Yom Kippur through the author's use of ταύρων and τράγων.[21] As a result, the use of these nouns

---

[18] On 9:19 deSilva writes, "As in 9:13, so here, the author conflates rites from different places in Torah prescribed for different occasions and purposes to stress both the exterior nature of these acts and, by virtue of having included many different rites in his comparison, the supersession of the whole cultic system in the rite of the new covenant" (*Perserverance in Gratitude*, 310),

[19] Haber, "From Priestly Torah," 154. In n. 53, she states, "In the LXX the following sacrificial animals are mentioned: μόσχος (Lev 16:6, 11), χίμαρος (Lev 16:15), and κριός (Lev 16:5)."

[20] Attridge writes that the appearance of τράγος, μόσχος, and ταῦρος are "inexact reminiscences of the atonement ritual where one bull, two rams, and one he-goat were involved. The deprecatory generalizing of the sacrifices has biblical precedents and is a way to express disdain for what may be considered antiquated and superficial offerings" (*Epistle to the Hebrews*, 248). Attridge and Haber's analyses are, ironically, both inaccurate recollections of Yom Kippur. Haber writes that Yom Kippur involved a bull, two goats, and a calf, and Attridge a bull, two rams, and one he-goat. But according to Lev 16, Yom Kippur involved one bull, two rams, and two he-goats. Numbers 29:7–11 also instructs that a bull, a ram, and seven lambs be offered as a burnt offering along with a goat as a sin offering, mirroring the additional sacrifices offered on other holy days.

Ellingworth states: "The author did not specify in vv. 1–10 which animals were used in OT sacrifices, and neither here nor later is he concerned with precise verbal consistency.... What mattered was their blood; that is, the fact that they were killed in sacrifice" (*Epistle to the Hebrews*, 452). See also Cockerill, *Epistle to the Hebrews*, 396; Moffatt, *Epistle to the Hebrews*, 121–22; Westcott, *Epistle to the Hebrews*, 258; Bruce, *Epistle to the Hebrews*, 213–14; David L. Allen, *Hebrews: An Exegetical and Theological Exposition of Holy Scripture*, NAC 35 (Nashville: Broadman & Holman, 2010), 471; Spicq, *L'Épître aux Hébreux*, 257; Westfall, *Discourse Analysis*, 199. For scholars who see a specific Yom Kippur reference, see Weiss, *Der Brief an die Hebräer*, 467–69, 505–6; and Craig R. Koester, *Hebrews: A New Translation with Introduction and Commentary*, AB 36 (New York: Doubleday, 2001), 410, 415, 432. Gabriella Gelardini notes that all four references to the blood of goats and calves/bulls in 9:12–10:4 recall the sin offerings of Yom Kippur ("The Inauguration of Yom Kippur according to the LXX and Its Cessation or Perpetuation according to the Book of Hebrews: A Systematic Comparison," in *The Day of Atonement: Its Interpretations in Early Jewish and Christian Traditions*, ed. Thomas Hieke and Tobias Nicklas, TBN 15 [Leiden: Brill, 2012], 225–56, here 241).

[21] A common argument is that the use of the plural nouns for the animals generalizes the sacrifices (see, e.g., Allen, *Hebrews*, 471, following Bruce, *Epistle to the Hebrews*, 213). The plural nouns, however, may not encompass *all* the sacrifices but *every* Yom Kippur sacrifice. The scope

in Heb 10:4 seems to pollute the verse's intertextual air with the author's deprecating tone. It is difficult to imagine the author carefully excising an Isaianic text for a specific purpose if the author has blindly hacked a way through Leviticus.

Since the appearance of ταύρων and τράγων seems to condition the effect of Isa 1:11 in Heb 10:4, I begin this production-oriented study[22] of the Isaianic intertext by comparing Hebrews' use of ταῦρος and τράγος to the extant textual remnants of the constructed author's cultural encyclopedia.[23] I identify a logic to Hebrews' use of these nouns, namely, that the author has read Lev 16 together with Isa 1. A two-way intertextual conversation thus proceeds: Hebrews identifies threads of Yom Kippur lurking in Isa 1; Isaiah draws Hebrews' attention to the problem of hypocritical worship; and Hebrews responds by celebrating a better, more obedient high priest.

## I. Τράγος and Yom Kippur

In the case of Hebrews' use of τράγος, an engagement with John William Wevers's critical edition of Greek Leviticus reveals the strong possibility that the author of Hebrews used a Greek text of Leviticus that read τράγος, not χίμαρος, throughout Lev 16.[24] Although χίμαρος, as Wevers notes, represents the Old Greek

---

of the author's argument includes all previous Yom Kippur sacrifices since none of them provided the level of cleansing that was generated by Jesus's once-for-all sacrifice.

[22] Production-oriented intertextual studies are described by Alkier in "Intertextuality and the Semiotics of Biblical Texts," 12. A production-oriented study inquires "about effects of meaning that result from the processing of identifiable texts within the text to be interpreted. Under the stipulations of the respective encyclopedia to which the text owes its existence, this perspective observes not only which texts are cited or referred to in some way but also the ways in which that occurs." Methodologically, I therefore seek to juxtapose texts the author might have known with the text the author produced. Granted, determining texts the author knew is difficult, particularly for an anonymous ancient text like Hebrews. There are, however, verbal signals in Hebrews that pressure modern readers toward a specific range of textual interlocutors. This is particularly true in the case of Heb 10:4, as it activates a specific text located in the LXX tradition, a tradition recalled throughout Hebrews. As is the case with any recitation of LXX texts in Hebrews, the allusion to the independent textual world of Isaiah LXX produces effects of meaning regardless of what the original author consciously intended, but a production-oriented study nevertheless seeks to identify effects that *could* have been intended by the author. Therefore, this study verifies contended effects of meaning against the remnants of the constructed author's cultural encyclopedia as well as the text of Hebrews itself.

[23] With the term *encyclopedia* I recall Umberto Eco's description of a given culture's "encyclopedia," or its code of meaning in which signs have been recorded in a unique configuration with other signs, creating a particularly netted "labyrinth" of semiosis (see *Semiotics and the Philosophy of Language*, Advances in Semiotics [Bloomington: Indiana University Press, 1986], 46–86).

[24] Lev 16:5, 7, 8, 9, 10, 15, 18, 20, 21 (2x), 22 (2x), 26, 27. John William Wevers, *Leviticus*,

translation of שעיר,[25] the author of Hebrews did not necessarily know the form of the text represented by Wevers's OG eclectic text, as Haber and other commentators imply.[26] For all fourteen occurrences of χίμαρος in the OG of Lev 16, τράγος appears as a well-represented variant in the LXX manuscript tradition, albeit particularly dominant in the later Hexaplaric and Byzantine text traditions. For example, in the margins of the seventh-century Codex Coislinianus, one will find τράγος for verses 5, 7, 8, 10, and 20.[27] Wevers's secondary apparatus further reveals that Coislinianus's reading in verse 8 corresponds with other witnesses to Symmachus as preserved, for example, in the Syro-Hexapla,[28] and the codex's marginal reading for verse 10 is echoed by other witnesses in the Symmachus and Aquila text families.[29]

Every appearance of χίμαρος in the OG of Lev 16, moreover, is contested with τράγος in a number of different minuscule families, including the Hexaplaric *oII* family, the text and marginal readings of the *s* family, the Byzantine *n* family, and all members of the Hexaplarically influenced catena text form.[30] Τράγος also appears

---

SVTG 2.2 (Göttingen: Vandenhoeck & Ruprecht, 1986), 183–95. The third-century papyrus Schøyen MS 2649 (Göttingen #830) was found after Wevers's edition was published, but it contains no discernible text from Lev 16.

[25] See John William Wevers, *Notes on the Greek Text of Leviticus*, SCS 44 (Atlanta: Scholars Press, 1997), 242–50. Wevers also notes that τράγος never translates שעיר elsewhere in the Hebrew Bible.

[26] Wevers acknowledges that later users of the LXX had access to different forms of the Greek text (*Notes on the Greek Text*, xxviii). This statement should not imply that two or more Hebrew "editions" of Leviticus were available in the first century. The LXX and targumic manuscript data suggest that Leviticus had achieved a high degree of textual uniformity by the Second Temple period, especially when compared to Exodus and Numbers. See Sarianna Metso and Eugene Ulrich, "The Old Greek Translation of Leviticus," in *The Book of Leviticus: Composition and Reception*, ed. Rolf Rendtorff and Robert A. Kugler, VTSup 93 (Leiden: Brill, 2003), 247–68, esp. 267–68.

[27] For a description of this codex, see Henry Barclay Swete, *An Introduction to the Old Testament in Greek*, 2nd ed. (Cambridge: Cambridge University Press, 1914), 140. A sixth-century date for the codex is also possible.

[28] The OG ἕνα τῷ ἀποπομπαίῳ appears as εἰς τράγον ἀπερχόμενον. This reading is also preserved in Procopius of Gaza's *Catena on the Octateuch* and some minuscules.

[29] The OG ὁ κλῆρος τοῦ ἀποπομπαίου appears as εἰς τράγον ἀφιέμενον in witnesses to both recensions (though Aquila only in minuscule 344), εἰς τράγον ἀπερχόμενον in other Symmachus text types (e.g., Theodoret's *Quaestiones*), and εἰς τράγον ἀπολελυμένον in other texts from the Aquila family. See also *Origenis Hexaplorum quae supersunt sive veterum interpretum graecorum in totum Vetus Testamentum fragmenta*, ed. Frederick Field, 2 vols. (Oxford: Oxford University Press, 1875), 1:194–95. Westcott (*Epistle to the Hebrews*, 258), Moffatt (*Epistle to the Hebrews*, 121), Attridge (*Epistle to the Hebrews*, 248 n. 50), Otto Michel (*Der Brief an die Hebräer*, 12th ed., KEK 13 [Göttingen: Vandenhoeck & Ruprecht, 1966], 312), and Spicq (*L'Épître aux Hébreux*, 257) note that Aquila and Symmachus both employ τράγος, but none of these scholars considers whether the noun might have appeared in the Greek text of Leviticus used by the author of Hebrews.

[30] For a description of the catena tradition, see Wevers's *Text History of the Greek Genesis*, MSU 11 (Göttingen: Vandenhoeck & Ruprecht, 1974), 228–29.

in every member of what Wevers calls the *b* family starting in 16:9[31] and in members of the Alexandrian *y* and *z* text families starting in 16:15.[32]

Given these relatively late LXX manuscript data, however, more interesting for Hebrews is the use of τράγος in early citations of Lev 16. For example, τράγος appears in Barn. 7.6–7: "Pay attention to what he commands: 'Take two fine goats [δύο τράγους] who are alike and offer them as a sacrifice; and let the priest take one of them as a whole burnt offering for sins.' But what will they do with the other? 'The other,' he says, 'is cursed'" (Ehrman, LCL). Other early Christian allusions to Lev 16 also contain τράγος, for example, Justin Martyr's *Dialogue with Trypho* (40.15–30) and Origen of Alexandria's *Homilies on Leviticus* (8.9).[33] But since these Christian texts may have been influenced by Hebrews itself, the best data come from a Second Temple Jewish author, Philo of Alexandria.[34]

When Philo mentions goats, he uses αἴξ[35] for a female goat, χίμαρος (see *Mut.* 159) for a male goat, ἔριφος[36] for a goat kid, and αἰπόλια[37] for a herd of goats. When describing a sin offering, Philo agrees with the OG of Lev 4–5 and Lev 10:16 by using χίμαρος.[38] But when interpreting Lev 16, Philo mentions only a τράγος, a male goat.[39] For example, in the second book of his *Legum allegoriae* (2.52), he writes:

> Passion becomes the portion of the lover of passion, but the portion of Levi the lover of God is God. Do you not see again that he prescribes that on the tenth day of the seventh month they should bring two goats [δύο τράγους], "one portion for the Lord and one for the averter of evil?"

Again, in *Plant.* 61, Philo states, "An illustration of what has been said is afforded by that which is done year by year on the day called the 'Day of Atonement.' It is enjoined on that day 'to assign by lot two goats [δύο τράγους], one for the Lord, and one for separation,' a twofold description, one for God and one for created things."[40]

---

[31] See 16:9–10, 20–21, 22b, and 26.

[32] See 16:18, 20–22, 26–27. One member of Wevers's *x* family (minuscule 527) presents τράγους in the margin of Lev 16:5. Several mixed codices (e.g., 55, 319, 426, 416) also present forms of τράγος across Lev 16.

[33] Cf. also Cyril of Alexandria, *Against Julian* 9.960.

[34] I take Philo's Greek text from Cohn-Wendland's critical edition: *Philonis Alexandrini opera qua supersunt*, ed. Leopold Cohn and Paul Wendland, 7 vols. (Berlin: Reimer, 1896–1930). English translations of Philo are from Colson and Whitaker, LCL.

[35] See *Spec.* 1.135; *Virt.* 95. Some witnesses to *Spec.* 1.228 present χίμαιρα. Hebrews also employs a form of αἴξ in 11:37 (αἰγείοις δέρμασιν, "goat skins").

[36] See *Fug.* 149; *Ios.* 14; cf. Matt 25:32–33 and Luke 15:29.

[37] See *Virt.* 126; *Ios.* 257.

[38] See *Spec.* 1.226–233; *Fug.* 157. Philo occasionally uses αἴξ when referring to other sacrificed goats, e.g., Abraham's offering in *Her.* 106.

[39] For other uses of τράγος in Philo's writings, see *Spec.* 3.36, 46, 113. For more of Philo's engagement with Leviticus, see Paul Harlé and Didier Pralon, *Le Lévitique: Traduction du texte grec de la Septante*, Bible d'Alexandrie 3 (Paris: Cerf, 1988).

[40] See also *Post.* 70.

Philo elsewhere specifies that a τράγος, which he defines as a male leader of goats, purifies the soul:

> "He lifted up his eyes and saw the he-goats [τοὺς τράγους] and the rams mounting upon the sheep and the goats [τὰς αἶγας]." A he-goat [τράγος] is leader of a herd of goats [αἰπολίου], a ram of a flock of sheep; and these animals are figures of two perfect ways of thinking, of which the one cleanses and purges a soul from sin, and the other nourishes it and renders it full of high achievements. (*Somn.* 1.197–198)

Granted, it is possible that Philo's citations of Leviticus 16 were later emended to match a Hexaplaric recension of the LXX. But Peter Katz's study of Philo's Bible, in which Philo's citations are compared with other LXX manuscript families and recensions, concludes that Philo worked from a recension of the LXX that is no longer extant.[41] In the case of τράγος, this conclusion seems substantiated by the unlikelihood that a later scribe not only changed Philo's citations of Lev 16 but also changed the above passage from *De somniis* as well as *Her.* 179, where Philo again refers to the Yom Kippur goats with τράγος without directly citing Lev 16.

It must be noted that Philo does, at one point, use χίμαρος for the Yom Kippur goats. But this peculiar use in *De specialibus legibus* (1.188) is an interpretation not of Lev 16 but of Num 29:7–11. There a χίμαρος in the OG and greater LXX tradition is offered as an additional sin offering for Yom Kippur along with other burnt offerings (cf. Num 29:11). Instead of distinguishing between the goats from Lev 16 and this additional sin offering, it seems Philo regarded the χίμαρος here as representative of the two Lev 16 goats, as he does not explore an additional sin-offering goat at all. Philo's account of Yom Kippur thus diverges from other Second Temple documents like the Temple Scroll, which differentiates between the additional sin-offering goat from Numbers and the other two goats from Lev 16.[42]

Philo's writings thus suggest that his text of Lev 16 read τράγος. Interestingly, the peculiarity of τράγος to Yom Kippur in Philo's writings is later echoed throughout the LXX manuscript tradition: except for a minor variant reading in Lev 4:23 and 23:19,[43] nowhere else in Wevers's Göttingen volume are the nouns χίμαρος or

---

[41] Peter Katz, *Philo's Bible: The Aberrant Text of Bible Quotations in Some Philonic Writings and Its Place in the Textual History of the Greek Bible* (Cambridge: Cambridge University Press, 1950), esp. 96.

[42] There was some disagreement in the Second Temple period about whether the sacrifices outlined in Num 29:7–11 constituted additional sacrifices or overlapped with the sacrifices described in Lev 16. See Lawrence H. Schiffman, "The Case of the Day of Atonement Ritual," in *Biblical Perspectives: Early Use and Interpretation of the Bible in Light of the Dead Sea Scrolls; Proceedings of the First International Symposium of the Orion Center for the Study of the Dead Sea Scrolls and Associated Literature, 12–14 May 1996*, ed. Michael E. Stone and Esther G. Chazon, STDJ 28 (Leiden: Brill, 1998), 181–88, here 184–85.

[43] Cf. the marginal reading in minuscule 58 (*O* family) for Lev 4:23 and the addition in minuscule 767 (*n* family) for Lev 23:19.

αἴξ replaced by τράγος.⁴⁴ Philo and the LXX manuscript tradition thus suggest that sacrificing a τράγος became specific to Yom Kippur.

When read against Philo and the LXX manuscript tradition, Hebrews' use of τράγος also becomes a particular remembrance of Yom Kippur.⁴⁵ This possibility becomes even more likely when one compares other portions of Hebrews with Philo's writings. As Gert J. Steyn recently observed, the form of nearly all of the Greek Pentateuch quotations in Hebrews is paralleled in Philo's works, often agreeing together against the LXX tradition and the MT. The strong affinity confirms for Steyn that, if Hebrews did not use Philo, they knew the same literary and/or oral pentateuchal tradition.⁴⁶ It therefore becomes all the more probable that τράγος appeared in the Greek text of Lev 16 used by the author of Hebrews. Indeed, given the current horizon in LXX studies, Hebrews itself remains an early, important, and independent textual witness to a recension of the LXX available in the first century.⁴⁷ In addition, since Hebrews, as Susan Docherty has recently concluded, seems to remain generally faithful to the Greek text known to the author,⁴⁸ Hebrews' use of τράγος may even be read as further evidence that this particular variant existed in the first century.

## II. Μόσχος, ταῦρος, AND YOM KIPPUR

Hebrews' use of μόσχος in 9:12 and 9:19 indicates strong agreement with the Lev 16 LXX tradition.⁴⁹ Μόσχος remains, with the exception of spelling variations,

---

[44] See Wevers's notes on Lev 3:12; 4:23, 24, 28, 29; 5:6; 7:13; 9:3, 15; 10:16; 17:3; 22:19, 27; 23:19 (Wevers, *Leviticus*).

[45] Contra Richard M. Davidson, "Christ's Entry 'Within the Veil' in Hebrews 6:19–20: The Old Testament Background," *AUSS* 39 (2001): 175–90, esp. 182–90. Since τράγος does not appear in "the Pentateuch," Davidson argues that Hebrews' use of τράγος activates the covenant inauguration sacrifices in Num 7 LXX. Davidson does not, however, consider whether the Greek text of Leviticus known to Hebrews diverged from the OG Leviticus text. Norman H. Young, in a rebuttal article, highlights the appearance of τράγος in Philo and the Epistle of Barnabas ("The Day of Dedication or the Day of Atonement? The Old Testament Background to Hebrews 6:19–20 Revisited," *AUSS* 40 [2002]: 61–68, here 65–66), but Young also overlooks whether τράγος appeared in the Greek text of Leviticus used by the author of Hebrews.

[46] See Gert J. Steyn, *A Quest for the Assumed LXX Vorlage of the Explicit Quotations in Hebrews*, FRLANT 235 (Göttingen: Vandenhoeck & Ruprecht, 2011), esp. 383. Since Steyn analyzes biblical quotations in Hebrews, not allusions, Steyn does not directly address the appearance of τράγος in Hebrews.

[47] See the discussion of the New Testament as a source for textual criticism of the LXX tradition in Karen H. Jobes and Moisés Silva, *Invitation to the Septuagint*, 2nd ed. (Grand Rapids: Baker Academic, 2015), 206–8. See also Tooman, *Gog of Magog*, 15–17.

[48] See Susan E. Docherty, *The Use of the Old Testament in Hebrews: A Case Study in Early Jewish Bible Interpretation*, WUNT 2/260 (Tübingen: Mohr Siebeck, 2009), 121–42, esp. 140–42. Docherty also does not discuss the appearance of τράγος in Hebrews.

[49] See Wevers's notes for μόσχος in Lev 16:3, 6, 11 (2x), 14, 15, 18, 27 (Wevers, *Leviticus*).

virtually uncontested in the manuscript tradition. Philo also uses μόσχος when he describes Yom Kippur. There is little reason to doubt, therefore, that the version of the LXX used by the author of Hebrews read μόσχος throughout Lev 16.

Puzzling, then, is the author's switch from μόσχος to ταῦρος in 9:13 and 10:4. What could have prompted this change? James Moffatt suggests literary variety, and F. F. Bruce notes that ταῦρος is semantically close enough to μόσχος to make little difference.[50] Yet, while μόσχος and ταῦρος both appear in sacrificial contexts across the LXX tradition[51] and translate comparable Hebrew words,[52] μόσχος is not the same as ταῦρος. The former usually designates a smaller, less-developed male.[53] Moreover, the ears of a cultically sensitive culture, like the ones we glimpse in the Dead Sea Scrolls and the Mishnah, would certainly be pricked at the switch.

There is some reason to believe that the author's use of ταῦρος reflected a growing movement toward the sacrifice of a larger bull on Yom Kippur. Josephus, for instance, uses both μόσχος[54] and ταῦρος[55] when he describes sacrificial bovines and prefers ταῦρος for sin offerings,[56] including Yom Kippur.[57] Josephus does not, however, actually cite Lev 16 in his description of Yom Kippur, nor is he the most reliable source for Second Temple sacrificial practice or forms of the LXX.[58] His use of ταῦρος may simply reflect the Greek tendency to describe the sacrifice of a ταῦρος over a μόσχος, a tendency that can be traced back to Homer, whose sacrifices to Poseidon, Zeus, and other gods of the pantheon comprised either a ταῦρος or a βοῦς.[59] The trend can also be traced through to the later Hellenistic period. Philo, for instance, notes that Augustus offered two lambs and a ταῦρος as a burnt offering at the temple even though Philo's preferred word for a sacrificial bovine is μόσχος

---

[50] Moffatt, *Epistle to the Hebrews*, 121; Bruce, *Epistle to the Hebrews*, 213.

[51] For burnt offerings of a ταῦρος, see 1 Esd 6:28; 7:7; 8:14, 63; and Dan 3:40. In OG Dan 3:40, Azariah compares a broken life and humbled spirit to a whole burnt offering of κριῶν καὶ ταύρων in the hope that his offering will propitiate (ἐξίλασαι) God. A sacrifice of a ταῦρος appears also in Ps 49:13 LXX and Isa 1:11 LXX.

[52] Both nouns translate שור, פר, and עגל in the LXX tradition. Μόσχος also translates בקר and ταῦρος translates אבר. See, e.g., Pss 21:13, 49:9–13.

[53] According to the LXX tradition and Aristotle, *Probl.* 11.24; *Physiogn.* 811a.

[54] See *A.J.* 3.221–222, 244–247, 253–254. Josephus also uses forms of βοῦς in *A.J.* 3.221–222, 238; 10.70–72. I take Josephus's Greek text from the Niese volumes.

[55] See *A.J.* 3.239; 9.268–271; 11.107, 137.

[56] See *A.J.* 3.204–206. In this passage, Moses purifies Aaron, his sons, and the tabernacle with αἵματι τῶν ταύρων καὶ κριῶν, "the blood of bulls and rams." See also *A.J.* 3.232, where rulers bring a bull (ταῦρον) and a kid (ἔριφον) for a sin offering.

[57] See *A.J.* 3.240–243. For the Yom Kippur goat, Josephus uses ἔριφος.

[58] For the differences between Josephus's account of Yom Kippur, Lev 16, and other Second Temple Jewish texts, see Christopher T. Begg, "Yom Kippur in Josephus," in Hieke and Nicklas, *Day of Atonement*, 97–120.

[59] For ταῦρος, see *Od.* 11.130; 23.278; *Il.* 2.728. For βοῦς, see *Il.* 2.773–776, 401–410; 7.314; 15.373; *Od.* 12.24. For other uses of ταῦρος, see Lycophron, *Alex.* 1192; Strabo, *Geogr.* 8.16; Lucian, *Sacr.* 2–3.

(*Legat.* 317). Books 3 (vv. 254–55, 624–27, 562–67), 5 (vv. 351–56), and 8 (vv. 485–93) of the Sibylline Oracles describe burnt offerings of a ταῦρος, never a μόσχος. In Acts 14:13, the priest of Zeus brings bulls (ταύρους) to sacrifice to Paul and Barnabas. Conversely, outside of Heb 9:12 and 9:19, a μόσχος is never offered as a sacrifice in the New Testament.[60]

Despite Josephus's reflection of Hellenistic sacrificial practice, his use of ταῦρος may have also been rooted in actual Jewish practice. 4Q156, the Leviticus Targum found at Qumran, also presents the high priest's sacrifice for himself on Yom Kippur as a תור instead of a פר.[61] The Aramaic noun תור, which also appears in Neophyti, Onqelos, and the Syriac targum,[62] appears to be the result of Semitic borrowing from the Greek ταῦρος.[63] The borrowing does not necessarily demand that the Leviticus targum's תור signaled a larger bull, like the Greek ταῦρος, but there is reason to consider it. The Cairo Genizah fragments of Aramaic Levi distinguish between a תור and a פר in a list of sacrifices.[64] The communicative intention of the targum may therefore be that a larger bull was to be sacrificed on Yom Kippur.

Although Josephus and the targum suggest that the sacrifice of a ταῦρος may not necessarily represent a spurious remembrance of Yom Kippur, the author of Hebrews still seems to draw particular attention to the use of the noun by juxtaposing ταῦρος with μόσχος. The switch results in an AB AC BA CA pattern:

| Heb 9:12: | τράγων | A | B | μόσχων |
| 9:13: | τράγων | A | C | ταύρων |
| 9:19: | μόσχων | B | A | [τράγων][65] |
| 10:4: | ταύρων | C | A | τράγων |

---

[60] For other appearances of μόσχος in the New Testament, see Luke 15:23–30, Acts 7:41, and Rev 4:7.

[61] פר is found in the MT, Mishnah, and the other Dead Sea Scroll accounts of Yom Kippur.

[62] See Józef T. Milik's comparison of the four targums with 4Q156 in Roland de Vaux and Józef T. Milik, *Qumrân grotte 4.II: I. Archéologie, II. Tefillin, Mezuzot et Targums (4Q128–4Q157)*, DJD VI (Oxford: Clarendon, 1977), 87–88. The Samaritan Targum parallels the MT with פר.

[63] See Alois Walde and Julius Pokorny, *Vergleichendes Wörterbuch der indogermanischen Sprachen* (Berlin: de Gruyter, 1930; repr., 1973), 711.

[64] See CTLevi ar Bodleian col. d. תור appears also in 11QNew Jerusalem as a burnt offering (frag. 13, line 1; cf. also frag. 28, line 5) and in the Animal Apocalypse as the bovine symbol for Noah and his sons (see 4Q206 5 I [1 En. 88:3–89:6]). Cf. also Ezra 6–8 LXX.

[65] This particular pattern depends on the contested presence of καὶ τράγων in 9:19. The text-critical arguments have resulted in a stalemate. See Bruce M. Metzger, *A Textual Commentary on the Greek New Testament*, 2nd ed. (New York: United Bible Societies, 1994), 598–99. The omission of καὶ τῶν τράγων in some important witnesses (e.g., ℵ² and P46) may represent accidental omission with Heb 9:12 (through homoioteleuton) or deliberate conformity to Exod 24:5 LXX. The phrase may have been added, however, through assimilation with Heb 9:12–13. The words are enclosed in square brackets in NA²⁸. Ellingworth argues that the author adds καὶ τῶν τράγων to reinforce a Yom Kippur typology (*Epistle to the Hebrews*, 468). This point is also argued by Westcott (*Epistle to the Hebrews*, 267), Spicq (*L'Épître aux Hébreux*, 262–63), Grässer (*An die Hebräer*, 2:166, 180), Michel (*Der Brief an die Hebräer*, 315), Weiss (*Der Brief an die Hebräer*, 474,

By recalling the calf from Lev 16 LXX in 9:12 and 9:19 and then switching to ταῦρος in 9:13 and 10:4, the author seems to do more than exploit terminological ambiguity. The presence of an identifiable pattern, moreover, particularly one that hints at an Isaianic allusion in 9:13 and then realizes one in 10:4, suggests that the context of Isa 1:11 itself might hold some clues as to why the author has incorporated ταῦρος into the address.

### III. Isaiah 1:11 LXX in Hebrews 10:4

A review of Isa 1:10–18 reveals that Hebrews' selection of ταῦρος may have been motivated by the Yom Kippur imagery that surfaces in the passage.[66] Commentators on OG Isaiah have long observed that Isaiah seems to draw particular attention to the Day of Atonement. In the list of Jewish holy days denounced in 1:13, the OG translator has curiously rendered קרא מקרא ("convocations") with ἡμέραν μεγάλην ("great day"). The Greek translation, which is traded in the Hexaplaric recensions for forms of κλητός ("called"),[67] appears to recall what Philo of Alexandria labeled the greatest (μεγίστη) of holy days and festivals: the Day of Atonement (Spec. 2.19).[68] J. Ross Wagner, in his recent study of OG Isaiah, further defends this possibility and identifies other threads of Yom Kippur lurking throughout Isa 1:10–18. Wagner first notes that Yom Kippur was identified as a "great day" in 4Q265 7 II, 4, the Book of Parables (1 En. 54:6), the second-century Kerygma Petri, and possibly 1 Enoch (10:6).[69] The immediate connection of the day to a fast

---

481), and Moffatt (Epistle to the Hebrews, 129). George Wesley Buchanan (To the Hebrews, AB 36 [New York: Doubleday, 1972], 152) also notes that "calves and goats" may echo Josephus's inaugural "bulls and rams" from A.J. 3.204–206. For the shorter reading, see Attridge (Epistle to the Hebrews, 253), William L. Lane (Hebrews 9–13, WBC 47B [Dallas: Word, 1991], 232), Bruce (Epistle to the Hebrews, 225), and Johnson (Hebrews, 233–34). Koester also prefers the shorting reading (Hebrews, 419), adding that "deliberate omission seems unlikely since Heb 9:19 differs at many other points from Exod 24:3–8 … and none of the other differences were altered to make Hebrews conform to the OT." Cockerill echoes this argument (Epistle to the Hebrews, 408). Koester's argument, however, is double-edged, since Hebrews' divergence from Exod 24 LXX may increase the likelihood that a scribe did not remove the phrase, but it also increases the likelihood that the author of Hebrews added the phrase.

For another argument in favor of καὶ τράγων, I point out the unlikelihood that καὶ τράγων should appear in the second position if it represents assimilation to 9:12 and 9:13. If scribes accidentally included καὶ τράγων through dittography, why did they not place τράγων in the first position, as it previously appears?

[66] As noted earlier, conflating different accounts of Yom Kippur is typical of Second Temple Jewish writers. Philo, Josephus, and 11QT XXV, 10–12 combine Num 29:7–11 with Lev 16, and Jub. 34:18–19 connects Gen 32 with Lev 16. Cf. also m. Yoma 7:1.

[67] Forms of κλητός appear in Aquila, Symmachus, and Theodotion.

[68] Isac Leo Seeligmann also identifies an evocation of Yom Kippur in Isa 1:13 (The Septuagint Version of Isaiah: A Discussion of Its Problems, MEOL 9 [Leiden: Brill, 1948], 103.

[69] Wagner, Reading the Sealed Book, 115–18. The relevant passage from the Kerygma Petri is preserved in Clement of Alexandria, Strom. 6.5.41.2–3.

(νεστείαν)⁷⁰ in Isa 1:13 further confirms for Wagner and Richard Ottley that Isa 1 would have recalled images of Yom Kippur,⁷¹ as the day was frequently designated "the fast" in Second Temple literature.⁷²

Wagner also notes that the Lord's refusal to forgive sins in Isa 1:14,⁷³ the injunction against petitions and prayers in 1:15,⁷⁴ and the command to cleanse the soul in 1:16⁷⁵ all evoke the Day of Atonement. Wagner concludes, "It is highly probable that, however one parses them individually, the whole cluster of images here—temple, holy days, 'great day,' fasting—would conjure up for a Jewish reader of the second or first centuries BCE the principal fast of the year and the sole fast day prescribed in the Law's sacred calendar: Yom Kippur."⁷⁶

One can identify other motifs in Isa 1:10–18 that correspond to the Day of Atonement. The mention of whole burnt offering of rams and fat of lambs in verse 11 echoes Num 29:7–11, where the additional burnt offerings required on Yom Kippur include rams and lambs. Wagner also notes that the appearance of σεμίδαλιν ("fine flour") in verse 13 evokes the flour mixed with animal sacrifices on holy days, including Yom Kippur (cf. Num 29:9–11).⁷⁷ The reference to incense in verse 13 may have called to mind the incense brought by the high priest into the adytum to protect himself from the glorious vision of the Lord (Lev 16:12–13). The designation of Yom Kippur as a "sabbath of sabbaths" (Lev 16:29–31)⁷⁸ also corresponds to the appearance of σάββατα in Isa 1:13. Even the appearance of ἑορτάς ("festival") in Isa 1:14 need not necessarily distract from Yom Kippur. Philo says that Yom Kippur is, paradoxically, both a joyous festival (ἑορτῆς) and a self-reflective fast (*Spec.* 1.186–187; 2.93–94). Finally, as Wagner notes, the emphasis in Isa 1 on the forgiveness of sins (v. 14), purification of the soul (v. 16), and removal of scarlet stains (v. 18) would have evoked Yom Kippur more than any other ritual would have.⁷⁹ Indeed, the Mishnah itself cites Isa 1:18 in m. Yoma 6:8: "R. Ishmael says,

---

⁷⁰ The OG's νεστείαν appears as ἀνωφελές in Aquila and ἀδικίαν in Symmachus/Theodotion.

⁷¹ Wagner, *Reading the Sealed Book*, 120–22; Richard R. Ottley, *Isaiah according to the Septuagint (Codex Alexandrinus)*, 2 vols. (Cambridge: Cambridge University Press, 1906), 2:107.

⁷² See Josephus, *A.J.* 3.240, *B.J.* 5.236; Philo, *Spec.*1.186–187; 1QpHab XI, 6–8; Acts 27:9.

⁷³ Wagner, *Reading the Sealed Book*, 132–33: "So dire is Israel's plight, the Greek version suggests, not even the Day of Atonement will avail any longer to reconcile the people to their God."

⁷⁴ Ibid., 136. Philo and the Dead Sea Scrolls also emphasize the importance of prayer on Yom Kippur.

⁷⁵ Ibid., 139 n. 323. The Israelites were commanded to humble their souls on Yom Kippur (see Lev 16:31; 23:27, 32). Wagner also points to Philo (*Spec.* 1.188), who describes the scapegoat as effective for those who cleanse themselves through inner repentance and faithfulness.

⁷⁶ Wagner, *Reading the Sealed Book*, 122.

⁷⁷ Ibid., 112. The OG's σεμίδαλιν appears as δῶρον in Aquila, προσφοράν in Symmachus, and μαναα in Theodotion.

⁷⁸ See Milgrom, *Leviticus 1–16*, 1057; cf. 1QpHab XI, 6–8; Philo, *Spec.* 2.196.

⁷⁹ Wagner, *Reading the Sealed Book*, 132–33, 139 n. 323.

'Now did they not have another sign? There was a crimson thread tied to the door of the sanctuary. When the goat had reached the wilderness, the thread would turn white, as it says, *Though your sins be as scarlet, they shall be as white as snow.*'"[80]

The vivid imagery of Isa 1:10–18 suggests that an author of a document like Hebrews could have seen the Lord's refusal to accept αἷμα ταύρων καὶ τράγων as a specific denunciation of Yom Kippur.[81] The phrase, which already brims with evocative potential, may have found new life in the author's comparison between the blood of the Yom Kippur animals and the blood of Jesus. As a result, the author of Hebrews may not have filled the argument with ritual conceits by including ταῦρος in the address but rather may have given attention to the reciprocally clarifying threads that seem to tie Lev 16 and Isa 1 together.

Granted, Hebrews does not evoke only Yom Kippur. Hebrews 9 also invites reflection on the Num 19 red heifer ritual (Heb 9:13, σποδὸς δαμάλεως) and the Exod 24 inauguration ceremony (Heb 9:18–20).[82] Yet mention of these other rituals does not necessarily preclude a Yom Kippur typology.[83] The very mention of blood in conjunction with bulls and goats and forgiveness begins to limit the range of sacrifices to those offered on Yom Kippur since not all Levitical sacrifices required blood, not even all sin offerings.[84] In 9:7–10:3, the author describes blood offered "yearly" by the high priest.[85] The red heifer ritual also contains several points of contact with Yom Kippur: both are labeled sin offerings[86] officiated by a high priest (or a pure priest according to the Dead Sea Scrolls),[87] involve the sprinkling of

---

[80] Jacob Neusner, *The Mishnah: A New Translation* (New Haven: Yale University Press, 1988), 276.

[81] Contra Davidson, "Christ's Entry," 184 n. 27. Davidson argues that Hebrews' inclusions of ταῦρος "broaden the reference from the inauguration to include the whole complex of sacrifices in the OT ritual service" *because* of the allusion to Isa 1:11, where there appears "a comprehensive list summarizing the whole sacrifice system." Young grants the point, concluding that the appearance of ταῦρος "indicates the author is choosing his terms for the sacrificial animals with less than a precise match with the LXX" ("Day of Dedication," 65).

[82] Burnt offerings, which were offered on Yom Kippur (see Num 29:7–10), appear also in Heb 10:6–8. The author also mentions daily sacrifices (καθ' ἡμέραν) designed to remove sin (10:11).

[83] Contra Felix H. Cortez, "From the Holy to the Most Holy Place: The Period of Hebrews 9:6–10 and the Day of Atonement as a Metaphor of Transition," *JBL* 125 (2006): 527–47, here 528, https://doi.org/10.2307/27638378.

[84] In Lev 5:11–13, a burnt cereal offering is permitted when an animal is unaffordable.

[85] See Heb 9:7: ἅπαξ τοῦ ἐνιαυτοῦ (cf. Exod 30:10 and Lev 16:34); 9:25, 10:1–3: κατ' ἐνιαυτόν (cf. 3 Macc 1:11).

[86] Cf. Num 19:9–17; 4Q394 3–7 I, 16–18.

[87] For a high priest, see Num 19:3; Josephus, *A.J.* 4.78; Philo, *Spec.* 1.268; m. Parah 3:5. For a pure priest, see 4Q277 frag. 1, line 6; 4Q394 3–7 I, 16–18.

blood toward the tabernacle,[88] and aim to remove impurity.[89] Mishnah tractate Parah also instructs a high priest to cleanse himself with the waters of the red heifer during his week-long separation before Yom Kippur,[90] an instruction that resonates with Philo's note that all worshipers, including the high priest, must be sprinkled with ashes and water prior to offering sacrifices (*Somn.* 1.211–218).

The Sinai sacrifice evoked in Heb 9:18–20 does not align as easily with Yom Kippur since it concerns the Mosaic covenant's inauguration and is labeled a well-being offering, not a sin offering (Exod 24:5). This particular well-being offering, however, involved dividing blood and casting blood directly onto people, a perplexing addition that seems to invite additional ritual interpretation. Targums Onqelos and Pseudo-Jonathan, for instance, interpret the Exod 24 ritual as an atoning rite.[91] Moreover, since Exod 24 confirms Israel's installation as a royal priesthood (cf. parallels with Exod 19:3–8), the ritual suggests dialogue with Lev 8, where Moses sprinkles Aaron and his sons with blood leftover from sin, burnt, and validation offerings (8:30). Interpreters of Hebrews have also missed the connection drawn by Philo between Exod 24 and Lev 16 (*Her.* 179–187). Philo uses the immolated goat of Yom Kippur and the scapegoat as types of the two bowls of blood offered by Moses on that day: one for God and one for the people.[92]

In any case, the author of Hebrews at least appears to interpret the Exod 24 ritual as a ritual of purification. The author stirs materials from the red heifer ritual—water, scarlet wool, and hyssop (Num 19:6–9)—into the blood sprinkled by Moses (9:19), shaping it into a substance that removes impurity from Israel and her holy objects.[93] The focus on Yom Kippur is then reinforced by other references to

---

[88] See Num 19:4 and 4Q276 frag. 1, lines 1–5. It is not clear, however, whether the red heifer's blood purifies the sanctuary. The blood also becomes part of the ashes used for purification (19:5). Milgrom argues that the inclusion of the blood in the ashes, as well as the crimson color of the heifer and the use of red wood and scarlet, signals the importance of blood to the ritual ("The Paradox of the Red Cow [Num xix]," *VT* 31 [1981]: 62–72).

[89] See Num 19:9–21; 4Q277 frag. 1, lines 6–10; m. Parah 3:9.

[90] Note Hananiah's comment in m. Parah 3:1. A seven-day period of separation is also required for priests during their inauguration (Lev 8), of the leper during purification (Lev 14), and of a corpse-contaminated person during purification (Num 19). Attridge (*Epistle to the Hebrews*, 249–50), Weiss (*Der Brief an die Hebräer*, 469), and Koester (*Hebrews*, 410) consider whether the linking of the red heifer ritual with Yom Kippur may have been based on a ritual logic and/or an exegetical tradition.

[91] See Steyn, *Quest for the Assumed LXX Vorlage*, 274, 281. See also Matt 26:26–29, where Jesus recalls the Exod 24 inauguration rite and states that his blood will be shed for the forgiveness of sins.

[92] The typology in *Her.* 179–187 does not, however, suggest that Philo believed goats were used during the Exod 24 ritual. He stresses in *QE* 2.32 that only calves were offered. But the typology does suggest that linking Yom Kippur with Exod 24 was a known exegetical move in the Second Temple period (cf. also Jub. 6:1–14).

[93] The addition of water, scarlet wool, and hyssop recalls Heb 9:13, where the author notes that the blood of goats and bulls and the ashes of a heifer purify the flesh.

the ritual in Hebrews (see 9:23–26) and the continued contrasts between repeated sacrifices and Jesus's one-time sacrifice. This contrast is rendered hollow if the dedication sacrifices are primarily in view since the tabernacle was only dedicated once.[94]

If Hebrews maintains a Yom Kippur typology, the author may have been attracted to a specific denunciation of Yom Kippur in Isaiah. If this be the case, and if the intertextual air of the Isaianic allusion in Heb 10:4 can be cleared of the immediate charge of cultic carelessness, how might the allusion change the perspective of Hebrews' criticism? Hebrews invites considerable reflection on this question by placing the Isaianic allusion at the end of a chain that hints at an allusion in 9:13 and then realizes one in 10:4. If the prophet breathes interpretive life into the intertextual dialogue, the reader seems to be reminded of what deSilva argues that Hebrews actively suppresses: Israel's disobedience.

As many Isaianic commentators have noted, chapter 1 does not criticize prayer, Sabbath observance, or the multiplicity of animal sacrifices per se but rather the Israelites who hypocritically observe these ordinances.[95] The Israelites were offering animal sacrifices while their hands were already stained red with the blood of innocents: the wronged, the orphan, and the widow.

Isaiah is joined by a chorus of voices in the Pentateuch and Second Temple tradition that condemn an *ex opere operato* approach to sacrifice. The high priest, for instance, must confess sins, transgressions, and iniquities during Yom Kippur (Lev 16:21). The Israelites are required to fast and humble their souls (Lev 16:29–31, 23:27, Num 29:7).[96] In 1QS III, 1–11, the unrighteous man cannot become clean by acts of atonement or ablutions, but the righteous man's sin is atoned when his compliant soul meets the sprinkled waters.[97] Sirach 34:23 plainly states, "The Most High is not pleased with the offerings of the ungodly, nor by many sacrifices does he atone for sins" (my translation). Jubilees and Philo also demand inner reflection and corresponding obedience while offering sacrifices.[98] Mishnah tractate Yoma 8:9 instructs, "He who says, 'I will sin and the Day of Atonement will atone,' the Day of Atonement does not atone."[99] Flicking blood on the sancta does not guarantee forgiveness. One cannot manipulate God by manipulating blood.

---

[94] Young, "Day of Dedication," 63.

[95] E.g., J. J. M. Roberts, *First Isaiah: A Commentary*, Hermeneia (Philadelphia: Fortress, 2015), 23; H. G. M. Williamson, *Isaiah 1–5: A Critical and Exegetical Commentary*, 2nd ed., ICC (London: Bloomsbury T&T Clark, 2006), 82.

[96] See Milgrom, *Leviticus 1–16*, 1054–55.

[97] The connection between cleansing the flesh and cleansing the soul in the Dead Sea Scrolls might prompt reexamination of Heb 9:13–14. The logic of Hebrews' a fortiori argument here seems to resonate with the assumption that cleansing the flesh affects the conscience. In other words, if Christ's blood cleanses the conscience *more than* the blood of animals and the heifer's ashes, purification of the flesh in 9:13 might entail a limited purification of the conscience.

[98] See Jub. 5:17–18; Philo *Spec.* 1.167, 202–204, 257, 269–271; *Deus* 7–9; *Plant.* 107–109.

[99] Neusner, *Mishnah*, 279.

The Isaianic allusion reminds Hebrews that unfaithful offerers changed the potency of Levitical blood. Thus, by declaring the impossibility that αἷμα ταύρων καὶ τράγων could remove sin, Hebrews may also intend to condemn blood offered without corresponding obedience. As a result, Hebrews may not eviscerate the entire Levitical system but rather criticize what Isaiah also criticized, namely, blood offered hypocritically.

This particular intertextual effect receives further corroboration from Hebrews' subsequent presentation of an obedient worshiper. After detailing the superior space, content, and durability of Jesus's offering in 9:1–10:3, Heb 10:5 pivots to celebrate Christ's obedience. The author places Ps 39:7–9 LXX on Jesus's lips, declaring the Lord's dissatisfaction with burnt and sin offerings and acknowledging that the Lord has prepared a body for sacrifice. Hebrews' use of the psalm does not demand that the Lord has rejected all sin offerings. Rather, the Lord desires a particular type: Jesus's body, whether a beaten body on earth or a resurrected life in the heavens.[100] By offering this body, Jesus fulfills God's will, giving his very self, his very life. As Moffitt has noted, the author emphasizes the point by ending the citation of Ps 39:8 LXX with θέλημά σου instead of ἐβουλήθην, shifting the psalmist's *desire* to do God's will into Jesus's *fulfillment* of God's will.[101] Priests in Isa 1 would have struggled to cleanse their guilty hands before flicking blood on the sancta. Jesus's hands were also covered with innocent blood, but not the blood of his victims. They were covered with his own blood, offered for the sake of his people.

The appearance of Ps 39 LXX thus seems to resonate with Isaiah's critique of disobedient worship. Together, they suggest that the Lord rejects all sin offerings save one: a sacrifice offered by a faithful high priest.[102] Sacrifices that *remove* sin (Heb 10:4: ἀφαιρεῖν) require a soul *removed* (Isa 1:16: ἀφέλετε) from sin. The intertextual effect echoes Hebrews' earlier discussion of priests' unfaithfulness to the first covenant (Heb 8:7–9) and bridges the critique with the rest of Hebrews' a fortiori rhetoric.[103] Hebrews does not reject the Levitical cult wholesale but rather compares hypocritically offered blood of bulls and goats with the blood of a better and more obedient high priest.

---

[100] See David M. Moffitt, *Atonement and the Logic of Resurrection in the Epistle to the Hebrews*, NovTSup 141 (Leiden: Brill, 2011), 230–56.

[101] See David M. Moffitt, "The Interpretation of Scripture in the Epistle to the Hebrews," in *Reading the Epistle to the Hebrews: A Resource for Students*, ed. Eric F. Mason and Kevin B. McCruden, RBS 66 (Atlanta: Society of Biblical Literature, 2011), 77–97, here 95–96.

[102] Cf. Heb 5:7–8, where Jesus learns obedience by offering up (προσενέγκας) prayers and supplications to God.

[103] See Heb 1:1–2, 4; 3:3–6; 5:1–10; 7:6–10, 23–26; 8:3–6; 9:13–14, 22–24; 10:1; 12:2, 24. In 8:1–9, the first covenant is not found "faultless" (8:7, ἄμεμπτος) because the Lord found fault *with them* (8:8, μεμφόμενος γὰρ αὐτούς/αὐτοῖς), the ministers of Israel (cf. 8:1–6). The recitation of Jer 31:31–34 further highlights Israel's unfaithfulness to the first covenant's commands (cf. Heb 8:9).

## IV. Conclusion

Haber, who characterized τράγος, μόσχος, and ταῦρος as inaccurate recollections of Yom Kippur, concludes that Hebrews misrepresents and suppresses Levitical conceptions of atonement in order to preserve the a priori uniqueness and efficacy of Christ's sacrifice. The reasoning of Hebrews, she contends, is purely theological. Unconcerned with Jewish temple practice, Hebrews employs "pervasive scriptural revisions" in order to distance the audience from Judaism, or the audience's "closest and most threatening ideology."[104]

Following the work of Docherty and Steyn, I have problematized such analyses by revealing that allusions to Scripture in Hebrews may accurately recall a Greek text of Leviticus different from the OG. Moreover, comparing Hebrews to other Second Temple Jewish texts reveals continuity with nonpolemical representations of the Levitical cult. Hebrews, therefore, does not necessarily suppress or misrepresent the cult to ground its case for Jesus's high priesthood and sacrifice. Hebrews rather seems to faithfully represent the Levitical cult while exploring limitations of the cult already known to the Second Temple Jewish world. Individual Levitical sin offerings—including the Yom Kippur offerings—were never intended to perfect the conscience once for all (Lev 16:29–34; cf. Heb 10:1–3). Philo also argued that Levitical sacrifices bring to God only a "reminder of sin" (ἀναμιμνήσκουσαν ἁμαρτίαν) when offered by sinful people (cf. Heb 10:3, ἀνάμνησις ἁμαρτιῶν).[105] Moreover, the Isaianic intertext in Heb 10:4 seems to recall God's refusal to receive sacrifices offered by unfaithful priests and worshipers (cf. also Lev 26:31, Amos 5:16–24, Mal 1:6–14).

Hebrews' careful appeals to Israel's scriptural tradition pushes the case beyond a priori theological commitments and begins to locate the argument within the broad spectrum of Second Temple intra-Jewish dialogue. The Jewish cultic law, a "shadow" of the coming good things (10:1, σκιάν), is not denounced but rather affirmed as a typological framework that continues to place constraints and demands on the operation of the new covenant's high priesthood (cf. 5:1–10, 8:3–4, 9:22–23). This framework, as Hebrews seems to spotlight, always resisted an *ex opere operato* approach to sacrifice through its demand for integrity and broader faithfulness to the Mosaic covenant.

---

[104] Haber, "From Priestly Torah," 156–58.
[105] See Philo, *Plant.* 107–109. As a result of Jesus's faithful sacrifice, God no longer "remembers" (οὐ μὴ μνησθήσομαι) the sins and lawlessness of the people (cf. Heb 10:5–18).

# Cambridge Scholars Publishing

## Proving Jesus' Authority in Mark and John
*Overlooked Evidence of a Synoptic Relationship*

### Gary Greenberg

"Greenberg offers a fresh and compelling study on the literary relationship between the Gospels of Mark and John. The study offers striking parallels between these two Gospels as well as a comprehensive and compelling explanatory theory for them. This careful and erudite comparison of Mark and John should be read by any engaged in the field of comparative gospel studies."
**Adam Winn**
*Professor of Christian Studies, University of Mary Hardin-Baylor*

"In an engaging new approach to these issues, Gary Greenberg explores ways that the Gospel of John may actually represent an augmentation of Mark, with a bit of corrective engagement along the way. And if so, such a thesis has profound implications for understanding more clearly the Jesus of history, not simply the Christ of faith."
**Paul N. Anderson**
*Professor of Biblical and Quaker Studies, George Fox University*

ISBN 978-1-5275-0790-6
Hardback 244pp
£61.99 UK
$99.95 US

20% Discount available
Order online at our website
www.cambridgescholars.com
Discount Code: JESUS20

Our books are also sold worldwide on Amazon, Blackwell and Ingram
www.cambridgescholars.com
orders@cambridgescholars.com

# How basic Hebrew can save Christianity from becoming a boring and meaningless religion.

Well, perhaps that overstates it a little! But learning a language is like learning a worldview. Those who learn Biblical Hebrew can better understand not only what biblical authors wrote, but also how they thought. Unfortunately, those insights come only after years of study. This book is about getting right to the important, exciting insights. It's an opportunity to be transformed by the renewing of our minds as we better understand how biblical authors used their language to express their experience of God and the world.

Matthew Richard Schlimm (Ph.D., Duke) is Professor of Old Testament at the University of Dubuque Theological Seminary in Iowa. He has published numerous books and articles and served as one of the editors for The CEB Study Bible. He is also an ordained elder in The United Methodist Church, having served churches in Michigan, Minnesota, and North Carolina.

AbingdonAcademic.com  **Abingdon ACADEMIC**

www.ingramcontent.com/pod-product-compliance
Lightning Source LLC
Chambersburg PA
CBHW021824300426
44114CB00009BA/311